Also by G. Scott Thomas

History
Counting the Votes
A New World to Be Won
Advice From the Presidents
The United States of Suburbia
The Pursuit of the White House

Demographics
Micropolitan America
The Rating Guide to Life in America's Fifty States
Where to Make Money
The Rating Guide to Life in America's Small Cities

Sports
The Best (and Worst) of Baseball's Modern Era
Leveling the Field

PRESIDENTIAL
ELECTION
RECORD BOOK
2020

PRESIDENTIAL ELECTION RECORD BOOK 2020

A COUNTING THE VOTES ALMANAC

G. SCOTT THOMAS

 NIAWANDA BOOKS

Niawanda Books
949 Delaware Road
Buffalo, NY 14223
www.countingthevotes.com

Printed in the United States of America

First Edition
10 9 8 7 6 5 4 3 2 1

"I have learned from bitter experience that Americans somehow regard a political campaign as a sporting event."

— Thomas Dewey

CONTENTS

PRESIDENTIAL
ELECTION
RECORD BOOK
2020

INTRODUCTION

Thomas Dewey was a highly successful politician, yet he is remembered primarily for his most spectacular failure.

The three-term governor of New York, the Republican nominee for the presidency in 1948, was the odds-on favorite to reach the White House that year. The Democratic incumbent, Harry Truman, was decidedly unpopular, and voters seemed anxious for an alternative. *Newsweek* polled 50 political experts a month before the election. All 50 said that Dewey would win.

Yet he lost.

Dewey affected a public attitude of nonchalance, but his upset defeat stunned and demoralized him. It instantly transformed him from the next leader of the planet's most powerful nation to a political has-been at the youthful age of 46. The presidency would never be his.

It took awhile, but he eventually accepted his fate. Dewey had never enjoyed the daily grind of political campaigns — the speeches, the handshaking, the fundraising, "being dragged from pillar to post, with no time to think," and the vague sense that he was merely a player in a quadrennial diversion for the masses. He declared that he would have "to be touched with madness" to ever run for president again.

"I have learned from bitter experience," Dewey concluded, "that Americans somehow regard a political campaign as a sporting event."

He was right, of course. I have written two histories of America's presidential elections — *The Pursuit of the White House* (1987) and *Counting the Votes* (2015) — and versions of this Dewey anecdote appear in both. I know of nothing that better dramatizes the compelling similarities between politics and sports. Both enterprises feature intense competition for extremely high stakes. Both also galvanize widespread national attention.

And both are driven by numbers. Presidential candidates obsess about vote counts, poll results, and fundraising totals. Sports fans, players, and team executives devour a myriad of individual and team statistics.

Yet there is a key difference. Every sport has its record book, a collection of statistical extremes, career rundowns, and year-by-year results. There is no counterpart in politics, no place to find the relevant numbers for all 58 national elections since 1789. Hence this volume, the *Presidential Election Record Book 2020*.

The following pages are divided into five sections, each of which has a counterpart in the sporting world:

1. Elections — Think of these statistical summaries as box scores for every presidential contest from George Washington's initial victory to Donald Trump's shocking upset.

2. Candidates — Baseball's record book offers career listings for Babe Ruth, Ted Williams, or any other player who might be of interest. The same here for 302 presidential candidates.

3. States — What are the 51 states (including the District of Columbia) but the arenas where candidates compete? A sports record book would contain stats for each stadium, just as this book offers state-by-state breakdowns.

4. Records — The most home runs, the most touchdown passes, the most electoral votes — the concept is the same. You'll find 179 listings of extreme accomplishments in presidential politics.

5. Election 2020 — Sports fans are always talking about players who seem to be prospects for future stardom. This book's concluding chapter fulfills the same function, offering statistical profiles of 2020's 31 presidential candidates.

My previous books on this subject were heavy on text, and why not? The political history of the United States has been brightened by hundreds of captivating characters and thousands of fascinating stories. But they aren't the focus here. The *Presidential Election Record Book 2020* deals with more than two centuries of competition, permanently captured in statistics.

Tom Dewey would not have appreciated such an emphasis — not in the least — but he certainly would have understood it.

G. Scott Thomas
Tonawanda, New York

1

ELECTIONS

The Founding Fathers wanted to make the process of electing a president as simple — and safe — as possible.

That's why they established the Electoral College, a small assembly of political and financial elites. Each of its members would cast two votes. The candidate receiving the most support would become president, while the runnerup would be vice president. The Founders didn't foresee the advent of political parties or multiyear campaigns, and they found it impossible to imagine the common man being allowed to vote. "It would be [as] unnatural to refer the choice of a proper character for chief magistrate to the people," Virginia's George Mason scoffed, "as it would to refer a trial of colors to a blind man."

The Electoral College worked to perfection when it debuted in 1789. All 69 electors voted for George Washington. John Adams, the new vice president, finished a distant second with 34 electoral votes. Nobody else received more than nine.

But the double-ballot system was inherently flawed, as became clear in 1800. The Democratic-Republican Party's nominees for president and vice president, Thomas Jefferson and Aaron Burr, received 73 electoral votes apiece, leaving it to the House of Representatives to break the tie. A week of legislative skirmishing ensued — 36 roll calls in all — before Jefferson was declared the winner. The new president pushed Congress to enact the 12th Amendment prior to the election of 1804, henceforth requiring members of the Electoral College to cast separate votes for president and vice president.

This was the only significant alteration during the first three decades of presidential politics, though its impact was not especially large. The 12th Amendment, rather than greatly changing the original process, merely streamlined it. The elites, acting through the Electoral College, still held total control. The common people were still barred from participation.

This monopoly, of course, was destined to fall. The everyday Americans who were helping to build the new country inevitably demanded more say in how it was run. Some states began allowing white men to vote for members of the Electoral College or even for presidential candidates themselves. This practice became sufficiently widespread by 1824 that meaningful national totals of popular votes could be tabulated for the first time.

A second innovation followed in less than a decade. The Anti-Masonic Party, a fringe movement energized by a rabid hatred of Freemasonry, decided to hold a national convention to choose its 1832 presidential nominee. The outcome should have raised doubts about the value of such gatherings. The Anti-Masons nominated William Wirt, a former Mason who fondly remembered his lodge as "a social and charitable club." Yet the major parties were impressed. They had previously relied on congressional caucuses and informal networks of state leaders to anoint their presidential candidates. They now decided to convene national meetings of their own.

The first conventions of the Democratic and National Republican parties were harmonious. The Democrats unanimously nominated Andrew Jackson for a second term in 1832, and 167 of 168 National Republican delegates endorsed Henry Clay. But subsequent conventions were often drenched in acrimony or indecision. The Whigs, for instance, required 53 ballots to select a nominee in 1852, the same year the Democrats called the roll 49 times.

The convention remained the sole vehicle for nominating presidential candidates into the 20th Century. That began to change with the advent of the primary election in 1912. Primaries were relatively insignificant at first — serving as simple barometers of public opinion — but they grew to be much more important over time. No candidate can be nominated these days without running successfully in the primaries, especially the initial midwinter contests. The summer conventions merely rubber-stamp the decisions made by primary voters months before. There hasn't been a multi-ballot convention since 1952, and it's unlikely we'll ever see one again.

The Electoral College, popular voting, conventions, and primaries can be considered the four building blocks of presidential politics. The statistics they've spawned can be found throughout this book.

Qualification Standards for Candidates

Registering as an official candidate for president is remarkably easy. Go to the Federal Election Commission's website, download FEC Form 2, answer the eight questions, and mail the completed document to Washington. That's all there is to it.

Hundreds of people file the necessary paperwork every four years, which creates a problem for anybody who studies presidential elections. Most official candidates are incapable of mounting effective campaigns. They simply clog up the works, making it impossible to effectively analyze the results.

That's why it's essential to separate the serious contenders from the mass of minor-party fanatics, publicity seekers, and occasional lunatics who clog the presidential ballot. This books stipulates five requirements — known as qualification levels — that address this need. If a candidate achieves any of these benchmarks in a given year, he or she is considered to be a qualified candidate:

1. Receive **at least 3.95 percent of all votes cast in a party's primary elections,** with an added requirement that the candidate be listed on the ballots of at least two states. The latter stipulation eliminates "favorite son" candidates who run only in their home states, a fairly common occurrence prior to 1972.

2. Receive **at least 3.95 percent of all votes cast on the first ballot or last ballot (if there is more than one) at a major-party convention.** A candidate doesn't need to reach both of these thresholds. Either one suffices.

3. Receive **at least 1.95 percent of all popular votes** cast nationwide in a general election.

4. Receive **one or more electoral votes.**

5. And a special level that applies only to candidates in the Modern Era (1960 to the present day): Receive **at least 3.95 percent of the votes cast within a given party in either the Iowa caucuses or the New Hampshire primary.** This rule acknowledges the inflated importance of those two states in the current nomination process.

To repeat: A presidential hopeful needs to reach just one of these levels in a given year to be designated as a qualified candidate, thereby warranting inclusion in this book. Anybody who falls short of all five levels is labeled as nonqualified and is essentially ignored. (You might be curious, by the way, about the precision in a few of the rules above. Why 1.95 or 3.95 percent? Because they round to 2 or 4 percent, that's all.)

A total of 302 men and women have met these statistical standards in the 58 presidential elections since 1789, mounting 459 qualified candidacies in all. (Henry Clay and James Blaine share the record with five apiece.) Most of these contenders belonged to the seven major parties recognized by this book, which are abbreviated this way:

D: Democratic (1832-present)
DR: Democratic-Republican (1789-1828)
F: Federalist (1789-1816)
NR: National Republican (1828-1832)
R: Republican (1856-present)
SD: Southern Democratic (1860)
W: Whig (1836-1852)

The only major party that might throw you for a loop is the Southern Democratic Party, which split off from the main Democratic organization in 1860, surely the most contentious year in American political history. The two factional nominees in that race — Democrat Stephen Douglas and Southern Democrat John Breckinridge — essentially battled to a tie. Douglas received more popular votes, Breckinridge more electoral votes. They went head to head in 29 states, with Breckinridge drawing more votes in 15, Douglas in 14. It seems only fair to treat both as major-party candidates.

It also should be explained why this book dates the Democratic-Republicans and Federalists back to 1789. No parties functioned as such during that first campaign, but not everything was sweetness and light. Opposing factions were already bickering, and much to George Washington's great displeasure, they soon blossomed into full-blown parties. "How unfortunate and how much it is to be regretted," he moaned. But this split was a fact of political life from the very beginning. Its existence has been acknowledged by the insertion of the subsequent political affiliations of 1789's qualified candidates.

The American political system has always had remarkable symmetry, starting with those early skirmishes between the Federalists and Democratic-Republicans. The former faded away after 1816, eventually replaced in turn by National Republicans, Whigs, and Republicans. The latter morphed into Democrats by 1832. This evolutionary process guaranteed that two major parties were (almost always) in the field at any given time, prepared to do battle.

This book recognizes 115 major-party nominees in the 58 presidential elections, an average of 1.98 per year. Nominations have been matters of official record since the convention made its debut in 1832, but a bit of subjectivity is needed to designate nominees for a few elections between 1789 and 1828 (and a couple that came later):

■ George Washington is considered to be the only major-party nominee in 1789 and 1792. Plenty of other candidates received electoral votes in those two elections — primarily for vice president under the double-ballot system — but Washington was the nation's obvious favorite.

■ John Adams (Federalist) and Thomas Jefferson (Democratic-Republican) are listed as nominees in the remaining two double-ballot elections, 1796 and 1800. Jefferson tied with his running mate, Aaron Burr, in the Electoral College in 1800, but he was clearly his party's choice for president.

■ James Monroe faced no competition in 1820, the last election to feature only one major-party nominee.

■ The election of 1824 was a real mess. The Democratic-Republican congressional caucus formally nominated William Crawford, essentially making him the party's designated candidate. But three-quarters of its members boycotted the caucus, opting to support other contenders. Andrew Jackson and John Quincy Adams emerged as the major players, and hence are considered by this book to be 1824's major-party nominees. Crawford suffered a stroke, which left him paralyzed and almost blind. He played no major role in the fall campaign.

■ The Whigs chose a confusing strategy in 1836. They decided not to hold a convention, but rather to run a team of regional candidates for president. Two of them — William Henry Harrison and Hugh White — received enough support to be considered official nominees.

■ We've already discussed the special case of 1860, the last election with more than two major-party nominees.

There are plenty of minor parties, too. You'll encounter 21 minor parties in the charts throughout this book. You'll even find a few cases where a single candidate is tied to a major party and minor party in the same election. If the two parties are linked by a hyphen, the candidate ran on both tickets at the same time. If they're separated by a slash, the candidate began in one party and switched in midstream to the second.

Here are the minor-party abbreviations:

AI: American Independent
AM: Anti-Masonic
AW: American-Whig
CU: Constitutional Union
FL: Farmer-Labor
FS: Free Soil
GBK: Greenback
GRN: Green
I: Independent
LIB: Libertarian
LR: Liberal Republican
LTY: Liberty
NU: National Unity
P: Progressive
POP: Populist
PRO: Prohibition
REF: Reform
SOC: Socialist
SRD: States' Rights Democratic
TC: Taxpayers and Constitution
U: Union

So much for the basics. Let's move on to a discussion of concepts of a more advanced nature.

New Statistics

This book features four untraditional statistics that were unveiled in my 2015 book, *Counting the Votes*. Each was explained in great detail at the time. If you want to go step by step through a particular formula, I recommend that you refer back to that book, since the following explanations are considerably (and blissfully) shorter:

Potential index

The dictionary defines potential as "a quality that something has that can be developed to make it better" or "an ability that someone has that can be developed to help that person become successful." The key phrase in both of those definitions — "can be developed" — makes it clear that potential, by itself, is no guarantee of victory. If a candidate doesn't aspire to success, doesn't work hard enough, and doesn't benefit from an occasional lucky break, his or her potential is unlikely to be fulfilled.

American history is replete with politicians who appeared formidable on paper, yet were unable to rendezvous with destiny. They failed to develop their qualities and abilities.

Counting the Votes assigned a potential index (PI) to each candidate, based on nine quantifiable factors that have an impact on a presidential hopeful's chances for success. It's impossible to measure spirit, intensity, and other intangible qualities, of course, but several aspects of a prospective candidacy can be measured. History tells us that the odds of reaching the White House are better for a senator or governor than a congressman or Cabinet member, better for a candidate in his 50s than somebody in his 30s or 70s, and better for a resident of California or New York than a person who hails from Utah or Wyoming.

The potential index is expressed on a 10-point scale, rounded to one decimal place. History shows a strong correlation between a candidate's PI and his or her likelihood of success. The odds are three times better for somebody with an index of 8.0 or higher than for a competitor in the range of 6.0 to 7.9.

Campaign score

The overall performance of each qualified candidate — we're no longer dealing with potential here, but with actual outcomes — has been reduced to a 100-point scale, rounded to two decimal places. This is known as a campaign score (CS).

A candidate's CS is based on votes received in primary elections, conventions, and general elections, with bonuses for securing a major-party nomination and winning in November. Different versions of the formula are applied to different eras, reflecting changes in conditions. The earliest candidates, for example, did not run in primaries, advance to conventions, or receive popular votes. The formula takes these disparities into account.

Campaign score is a remarkably good indicator of a candidate's performance in a given year. General-election winners typically land between 75 and 100 points, ranging from landslide victors in the 90s to nail-biters in the upper 70s. Major-party nominees who lost general elections are grouped from the 50s to the middle 70s. They're followed by significant minor-party candidates and strong (but ultimately unsuccessful) contenders for major-party nominations, who can be found in the 30s and 40s. The remaining qualified candidates — those who had little, if any, impact — are lumped between 10 and 29 on the scale.

Return on potential

Return on potential (ROP) determines whether a candidate fulfilled his or her promise in a given election. The underlying principle is the same one that is followed by portfolio managers when they calculate whether they're receiving a suitable return on their investments. It's a simple comparison of performance to potential.

The formula in this case is CS divided by PI. The result is converted to a 100-point scale and rounded to the nearest whole number.

If a candidate's ROP exceeds 100, he or she has done better than could have been expected. A two-digit score, on the other hand, is a sign of underperformance.

Equalized votes

It's useless to compare vote totals from different contests, especially when the separation in time is a lengthy one. William McKinley won the election of 1896 with roughly 7.1 million votes, while Barack Obama secured a second term in 2012 with almost 66 million. McKinley's accomplishment seems puny, doesn't it? But his share of the popular vote (51.10 percent) was actually a shade better than Obama's 51.06 percent.

The reason for the vast difference between these two victors, of course, is that the electorate continues to expand. Only 13.9 million votes were cast in 1896, dwarfed by 2012's total of slightly more than 129 million.

Equalized votes allow us to make sensible comparisons of the results of different elections or career totals for different candidates.

The same equalization process is employed for primaries, conventions, and general elections. The concept is simple. Each candidate's percentage of the total number of votes is applied to a standard base. The respective bases are 10 million votes for a party's primaries, 1,000 votes for its convention, and 100 million votes for a general election.

McKinley's share of the 1896 general-election total, for example, is 51.097767 percent when carried to six decimal places. Multiply that by a base of 100 million votes, and he received 51,097,767 equalized popular votes. That's slightly better than Obama's 2012 equalized sum of 51,063,710.

Reading the Charts

This chapter contains chronological breakdowns of all 58 presidential elections. The box scores for the early elections are fairly sparse, reflecting the electorate's limited participation and the correspondingly small yield of statistics. The process — and its numerical output — grew more complicated through the years, expanding the entries in this book.

Below is a guide to what you'll find. Let me preface it with an apology to anybody offended by the frequent use of masculine pronouns. All of America's presidents — and almost all of the presidential candidates meeting the qualification standards — have been men. The use of "he" instead of "he or she" is meant to be simpler, not discriminatory.

Basics

Incumbent: Sitting president as of election day, followed by his party affiliation at the time.

Prior streak: Party that won the most recent presidential election or string of elections, with the streak's length in parentheses.

Prior 5: Parties that won any of the five previous presidential elections.

Population: Official census population for any year ending in 0. Estimate by the author (through 1896) or the U.S. Census Bureau (since 1904) for any other year. The estimate for 1864 encompasses all of the United States, even those that were in revolt at the time.

States: Number of states that cast votes in the Electoral College. (The District of Columbia is counted as a state.)

Electoral votes: Number of electoral votes cast. (If one or more electors did not vote, this figure will not equal the total membership of the Electoral College.) The number for each double-ballot election (1789-1800) is the number of electors, not the number of electoral votes cast.

Popular votes: Number of popular votes cast.

Field

Candidate: Any candidate who posted a campaign score of 10.00 or higher, followed by his party abbreviation. Candidates are ranked in order of CS.

PI: Potential index.

Age: Age as of November 1 of the given year, rounded to two decimal places.

State: State in which the candidate maintained a voting address.

Position: Position by which the candidate was best known, usually his current or most recent position.

N: Major-party nominees are designated by an X.

W: General-election winner is designated by an X.

CS: Campaign score.

Nomination

Candidate: Any candidate in the field who received support for a given party's nomination. Candidates are ranked in order of ConLB, then ConFB, then PriV.

ConFB: Votes received on the first ballot at a convention. Fractional totals have been rounded to the nearest whole number.

FB%: Percentage of all votes cast on the first ballot.

ConLB: Votes received on the last ballot at a multi-ballot convention. (The number of the last ballot is indicated in brackets.) Fractional votes have been rounded to the nearest whole number.

LB%: Percentage of all votes cast on the last ballot.

PriW: Number of primary elections won by a candidate.

PriV: Votes received in a party's primary elections.

PriV%: Percentage of all votes cast in a party's primary elections.

General election

Candidate: Any candidate in the field who received support in the general election. Candidates are ranked in order of EV, then PV.

EV: Electoral votes.

EV%: Percentage of all electoral votes cast. Percentages for each double-ballot election (1789-1800) are based on the number of electors, not the number of electoral votes.

SC: States carried. (If two or more candidates tied for the electoral-vote lead in a given state, each is credited with a state carried.)

PV: Popular votes.

PV%: Percentage of all popular votes cast.

State popular votes

State: Alphabetical listing of states that cast popular votes in the election.

Total PV: Number of popular votes cast.

Candidates: Candidates are listed from left to right in order of PV.

State electoral votes

State: Alphabetical listing of states that cast electoral votes.
Total EV: Number of electoral votes cast.
Candidates: Candidates are listed from left to right in order of EV.

Scenarios

1% to a candidate: Electoral-vote count that would occur if a candidate's share of each state's popular votes were increased by one percentage point, while his chief opponent's share were decreased by one percentage point in each state. (This scenario is shown for the top two candidates in the national PV count.)

10K to a candidate: Electoral-vote count that would occur if a candidate were given an additional 10,000 popular votes in each state, while his chief opponent had 10,000 votes taken away in each state. (This scenario is shown for the top two candidates in the national PV count.)

1964 allocation: Electoral-vote count that would occur if each state were allocated the same number of electoral votes as in 1964, the first election in which all 51 states (including the District of Columbia) participated.

2020 allocation: Electoral-vote count that would occur if each state were allocated the same number of electoral votes as in 2020.

1789

Basics

Incumbent	none
Prior streak	n.a.
Prior 5	n.a.
Population	3,812,757
States	10
Electoral votes	69
Popular votes	n.a.

Field

Candidate	PI	Age	State	Position	N	W	CS
George Washington (F)	5.6	57.69	Va.	Former general	X	X	96.18
John Adams (F)	4.4	54.01	Mass.	Former ambassador	—	—	64.00
John Jay (F)	4.1	43.89	N.Y.	Cabinet member	—	—	51.15
Robert Harrison (F)	2.3	44.00	Md.	State judge	—	—	45.73
John Rutledge (F)	4.5	50.12	S.C.	Former governor	—	—	45.73
John Hancock (F)	4.3	52.77	Mass.	Governor	—	—	35.97
George Clinton (DR)	2.6	50.27	N.Y.	Governor	—	—	31.09
Samuel Huntington (F)	4.7	58.33	Conn.	Governor	—	—	26.29
John Milton (F)	3.1	49.00	Ga.	State official	—	—	26.29
James Armstrong (F)	4.0	61.00	Ga.	State official	—	—	21.42
Benjamin Lincoln (F)	4.8	56.77	Mass.	Former general	—	—	21.42
Edward Telfair (DR)	4.8	54.00	Ga.	Former governor	—	—	21.42

General election

Candidate	EV	EV%	SC	PV	PV%
Washington	69	100.00%	10	—	—
Adams	34	49.28%	2	—	—
Jay	9	13.04%	1	—	—
Harrison	6	8.70%	1	—	—
Rutledge	6	8.70%	0	—	—
Hancock	4	5.80%	0	—	—
Clinton	3	4.35%	0	—	—
Huntington	2	2.90%	0	—	—
Milton	2	2.90%	0	—	—
Armstrong	1	1.45%	0	—	—
Lincoln	1	1.45%	0	—	—
Telfair	1	1.45%	0	—	—

State electoral votes

State	Total EV	W	A	J	H	R	H	C	H	M	A	L	T
Connecticut	7	7	5	0	0	0	0	0	2	0	0	0	0
Delaware	3	3	0	3	0	0	0	0	0	0	0	0	0
Georgia	5	5	0	0	0	0	0	0	0	2	1	1	1
Maryland	6	6	0	0	6	0	0	0	0	0	0	0	0
Massachusetts	10	10	10	0	0	0	0	0	0	0	0	0	0
New Hampshire	5	5	5	0	0	0	0	0	0	0	0	0	0

State	Total EV	W	A	J	H	R	H	C	H	M	A	L	T
New Jersey	6	6	1	5	0	0	0	0	0	0	0	0	0
New York	0	0	0	0	0	0	0	0	0	0	0	0	0
Pennsylvania	10	10	8	0	0	0	2	0	0	0	0	0	0
South Carolina	7	7	0	0	0	6	1	0	0	0	0	0	0
Virginia	10	10	5	1	0	0	1	3	0	0	0	0	0
Total	69	69	34	9	6	6	4	3	2	2	1	1	1

Scenarios

1964 allocation...............................Washington 117, Adams 56, Jay 18, Harrison 10, others 33
2020 allocation...............................Washington 107, Adams 45, Jay 16, Harrison 10, others 36

1792

Basics

Incumbent .... George Washington (F)
Prior streak .... F (1)
Prior 5 .... F (1)
Population 4,172,906
States 15
Electoral votes 132
Popular votes .... n.a.

Field

Candidate	PI	Age	State	Position	N	W	CS
George Washington (F)	9.7	60.69	Va.	President	X	X	96.18
John Adams (F)	6.4	57.01	Mass.	Vice president	—	—	67.23
George Clinton (DR)	3.2	53.27	N.Y.	Governor	—	—	59.98
Thomas Jefferson (DR)	6.7	49.55	Va.	Cabinet member	—	—	26.68
Aaron Burr (DR)	4.7	36.73	N.Y.	Senator	—	—	19.07

General election

Candidate	EV	EV%	SC	PV	PV%
Washington	132	100.00%	15	—	—
Adams	77	58.33%	8	—	—
Clinton	50	37.88%	4	—	—
Jefferson	4	3.03%	1	—	—
Burr	1	0.76%	0	—	—

State electoral votes

State	Total EV	Washington	Adams	Clinton	Jefferson	Burr
Connecticut	9	9	9	0	0	0
Delaware	3	3	3	0	0	0
Georgia	4	4	0	4	0	0
Kentucky	4	4	0	0	4	0
Maryland	8	8	8	0	0	0
Massachusetts	16	16	16	0	0	0
New Hampshire	6	6	6	0	0	0
New Jersey	7	7	7	0	0	0
New York	12	12	0	12	0	0
North Carolina	12	12	0	12	0	0
Pennsylvania	15	15	14	1	0	0
Rhode Island	4	4	4	0	0	0
South Carolina	8	8	7	0	0	1
Vermont	3	3	3	0	0	0
Virginia	21	21	0	21	0	0
Total	132	132	77	50	4	1

Scenarios

1964 allocation .... Washington 189, Adams 97, Clinton 82, Jefferson 9, Burr 1
2020 allocation .... Washington 166, Adams 83, Clinton 74, Jefferson 8, Burr 1

1796

Basics

Incumbent .... George Washington (F)
Prior streak .... F (2)
Prior 5 .... F (2)
Population 4,706,570
States 16
Electoral votes 138
Popular votes .... n.a.

Field

Candidate	PI	Age	State	Position	N	W	CS
John Adams (F)	5.7	61.01	Mass.	Vice president	X	X	77.27
Thomas Jefferson (DR)	6.9	53.55	Va.	Former Cabinet member	X	—	74.00
Thomas Pinckney (F)	4.1	46.02	S.C.	Ambassador	—	—	61.70
Aaron Burr (DR)	4.7	40.73	N.Y.	Senator	—	—	54.24
Samuel Adams (DR)	3.7	74.10	Mass.	Governor	—	—	50.36
Oliver Ellsworth (F)	4.8	51.51	Conn.	Supreme Court justice	—	—	43.29
George Clinton (DR)	3.0	57.27	N.Y.	Former governor	—	—	33.54
John Jay (F)	5.1	50.89	N.Y.	Governor	—	—	28.66
James Iredell (F)	3.6	45.07	N.C.	Supreme Court justice	—	—	23.85
John Henry (DR)	4.7	46.00	Md.	Senator	—	—	21.42
Samuel Johnston (F)	6.5	62.88	N.C.	Former senator	—	—	21.42
George Washington (F)	9.1	64.69	Va.	President	—	—	21.42
Charles C. Pinckney (F)	3.9	50.68	S.C.	Ambassador	—	—	18.98

General election

Candidate	EV	EV%	SC	PV	PV%
J. Adams	71	51.45%	9	—	—
Jefferson	68	49.28%	7	—	—
T. Pinckney	59	42.75%	5	—	—
Burr	30	21.74%	2	—	—
S. Adams	15	10.87%	0	—	—
Ellsworth	11	7.97%	2	—	—
Clinton	7	5.07%	1	—	—
Jay	5	3.62%	0	—	—
Iredell	3	2.17%	0	—	—
Henry	2	1.45%	0	—	—
Johnston	2	1.45%	0	—	—
Washington	2	1.45%	0	—	—
C. Pinckney	1	0.73%	0	—	—

State electoral votes

State	Total EV	A	J	P	B	A	E	C	J	I	H	J	W	P
Connecticut	9	9	0	4	0	0	0	0	5	0	0	0	0	0
Delaware	3	3	0	3	0	0	0	0	0	0	0	0	0	0
Georgia	4	0	4	0	0	0	0	4	0	0	0	0	0	0
Kentucky	4	0	4	0	4	0	0	0	0	0	0	0	0	0

State	Total EV	A	J	P	B	A	E	C	J	I	H	J	W	P
Maryland	10	7	4	4	3	0	0	0	0	0	2	0	0	0
Massachusetts	16	16	0	13	0	0	1	0	0	0	0	2	0	0
New Hampshire	6	6	0	0	0	0	6	0	0	0	0	0	0	0
New Jersey	7	7	0	7	0	0	0	0	0	0	0	0	0	0
New York	12	12	0	12	0	0	0	0	0	0	0	0	0	0
North Carolina	12	1	11	1	6	0	0	0	0	3	0	0	1	1
Pennsylvania	15	1	14	2	13	0	0	0	0	0	0	0	0	0
Rhode Island	4	4	0	0	0	0	4	0	0	0	0	0	0	0
South Carolina	8	0	8	8	0	0	0	0	0	0	0	0	0	0
Tennessee	3	0	3	0	3	0	0	0	0	0	0	0	0	0
Vermont	4	4	0	4	0	0	0	0	0	0	0	0	0	0
Virginia	21	1	20	1	1	15	0	3	0	0	0	0	1	0
Total	138	71	68	59	30	15	11	7	5	3	2	2	2	1

Scenarios

1964 allocation............................J. Adams 107, T. Pinckney 99, Jefferson 94, Burr 56, others 44
2020 allocation............................ Jefferson 93, J. Adams 85, T. Pinckney 79, Burr 48, others 49

1800

Basics

Incumbent	John Adams (F)
Prior streak	F (3)
Prior 5	F (3)
Population	5,308,483
States	16
Electoral votes	138
Popular votes	n.a.

Field

Candidate	PI	Age	State	Position	N	W	CS
Thomas Jefferson (DR)	7.6	57.55	Va.	Vice president	X	X	77.84
John Adams (F)	7.2	65.01	Mass.	President	X	—	73.21
Aaron Burr (DR)	4.9	44.73	N.Y.	Former senator	—	—	65.31
Charles C. Pinckney (F)	4.4	54.68	S.C.	Former ambassador	—	—	63.01
John Jay (F)	3.3	54.89	N.Y.	Governor	—	—	18.98

General election

Candidate	EV	EV%	SC	PV	PV%
Jefferson	73	52.90%	9	—	—
Burr	73	52.90%	9	—	—
Adams	65	47.10%	8	—	—
Pinckney	64	46.38%	7	—	—
Jay	1	0.73%	0	—	—

NOTE: Jefferson was elected president by the House of Representatives on the 36th ballot. The final vote was 10 states for Jefferson, 4 states for Burr, 2 states abstaining.

State electoral votes

State	Total EV	Jefferson	Burr	Adams	Pinckney	Jay
Connecticut	9	0	0	9	9	0
Delaware	3	0	0	3	3	0
Georgia	4	4	4	0	0	0
Kentucky	4	4	4	0	0	0
Maryland	10	5	5	5	5	0
Massachusetts	16	0	0	16	16	0
New Hampshire	6	0	0	6	6	0
New Jersey	7	0	0	7	7	0
New York	12	12	12	0	0	0
North Carolina	12	8	8	4	4	0
Pennsylvania	15	8	8	7	7	0
Rhode Island	4	0	0	4	3	1
South Carolina	8	8	8	0	0	0
Tennessee	3	3	3	0	0	0
Vermont	4	0	0	4	4	0
Virginia	21	21	21	0	0	0
Total	138	73	73	65	64	1

Scenarios

1964 allocation .... Jefferson 124, Burr 124, Adams 76, Pinckney 75, Jay 1
2020 allocation .... Jefferson 112, Burr 112, Adams 65, Pinckney 64, Jay 1

1804

Basics

Incumbent ....Thomas Jefferson (DR)
Prior streak ....DR (1)
Prior 5 ....F (3), DR (1)
Population 6,010,004
States 17
Electoral votes 176
Popular votes .... n.a.

Field

Candidate	PI	Age	State	Position	N	W	CS
Thomas Jefferson (DR)	9.2	61.55	Va.	President	X	X	93.05
Charles C. Pinckney (F)	5.1	58.68	S.C.	Former ambassador	X	—	59.38

General election

Candidate	EV	EV%	SC	PV	PV%
Jefferson	162	92.05%	15	—	—
Pinckney	14	7.96%	2	—	—

State electoral votes

State	Total EV	Jefferson	Pinckney
Connecticut	9	0	9
Delaware	3	0	3
Georgia	6	6	0
Kentucky	8	8	0
Maryland	11	9	2
Massachusetts	19	19	0
New Hampshire	7	7	0
New Jersey	8	8	0
New York	19	19	0
North Carolina	14	14	0
Ohio	3	3	0
Pennsylvania	20	20	0
Rhode Island	4	4	0
South Carolina	10	10	0
Tennessee	5	5	0
Vermont	6	6	0
Virginia	24	24	0
Total	176	162	14

Scenarios

1964 allocation ....Jefferson 213, Pinckney 13
2020 allocation ....Jefferson 183, Pinckney 12

1808

Basics

Incumbent ....Thomas Jefferson (DR)
Prior streak ....DR (2)
Prior 5...F (3), DR (2)
Population..6,804,233
States 17
Electoral votes 175
Popular votes ....n.a.

Field

Candidate	PI	Age	State	Position	N	W	CS
James Madison (DR)	6.8	57.63	Va.	Cabinet member	X	X	84.36
Charles C. Pinckney (F)	3.9	62.68	S.C.	Former nominee	X	—	66.03
George Clinton (DR)	4.0	69.27	N.Y.	Vice president	—	—	28.01

General election

Candidate	EV	EV%	SC	PV	PV%
Madison	122	69.71%	12	—	—
Pinckney	47	26.86%	5	—	—
Clinton	6	3.43%	0	—	—

State electoral votes

State	Total EV	Madison	Pinckney	Clinton
Connecticut	9	0	9	0
Delaware	3	0	3	0
Georgia	6	6	0	0
Kentucky	7	7	0	0
Maryland	11	9	2	0
Massachusetts	19	0	19	0
New Hampshire	7	0	7	0
New Jersey	8	8	0	0
New York	19	13	0	6
North Carolina	14	11	3	0
Ohio	3	3	0	0
Pennsylvania	20	20	0	0
Rhode Island	4	0	4	0
South Carolina	10	10	0	0
Tennessee	5	5	0	0
Vermont	6	6	0	0
Virginia	24	24	0	0
Total	175	122	47	6

Scenarios

1964 allocation...Madison 174, Pinckney 38, Clinton 14
2020 allocation... Madison 152, Pinckney 34, Clinton 9

1812

Basics

Incumbent .... James Madison (DR)
Prior streak ....DR (3)
Prior 5 ....DR (3), F (2)
Population.. 7,666,314
States 18
Electoral votes 217
Popular votes ....n.a.

Field

Candidate	PI	Age	State	Position	N	W	CS
James Madison (DR)	8.7	61.63	Va.	President	X	X	80.17
DeWitt Clinton (F-DR)	3.7	43.67	N.Y.	Mayor	X	—	71.10

General election

Candidate	EV	EV%	SC	PV	PV%
Madison	128	58.99%	11	—	—
Clinton	89	41.01%	7	—	—

State electoral votes

State	Total EV	Madison	Clinton
Connecticut	9	0	9
Delaware	4	0	4
Georgia	8	8	0
Kentucky	12	12	0
Louisiana	3	3	0
Maryland	11	6	5
Massachusetts	22	0	22
New Hampshire	8	0	8
New Jersey	8	0	8
New York	29	0	29
North Carolina	15	15	0
Ohio	7	7	0
Pennsylvania	25	25	0
Rhode Island	4	0	4
South Carolina	11	11	0
Tennessee	8	8	0
Vermont	8	8	0
Virginia	25	25	0
Total	217	128	89

Scenarios

1964 allocation.. Madison 138, Clinton 98
2020 allocation.. Madison 126, Clinton 77

1816

Basics

Incumbent .... James Madison (DR)
Prior streak .... DR (4)
Prior 5 .... DR (4), F (1)
Population 8,596,011
States 19
Electoral votes 217
Popular votes .... n.a.

Field

Candidate	PI	Age	State	Position	N	W	CS
James Monroe (DR)	7.3	58.51	Va.	Cabinet member	X	X	90.10
Rufus King (F)	7.1	61.61	N.Y.	Senator	X	—	62.07

General election

Candidate	EV	EV%	SC	PV	PV%
Monroe	183	84.33%	16	—	—
King	34	15.67%	3	—	—

State electoral votes

State	Total EV	Monroe	King
Connecticut	9	0	9
Delaware	3	0	3
Georgia	8	8	0
Indiana	3	3	0
Kentucky	12	12	0
Louisiana	3	3	0
Maryland	8	8	0
Massachusetts	22	0	22
New Hampshire	8	8	0
New Jersey	8	8	0
New York	29	29	0
North Carolina	15	15	0
Ohio	8	8	0
Pennsylvania	25	25	0
Rhode Island	4	4	0
South Carolina	11	11	0
Tennessee	8	8	0
Vermont	8	8	0
Virginia	25	25	0
Total	217	183	34

Scenarios

1964 allocation .... Monroe 224, King 25
2020 allocation .... Monroe 193, King 21

1820

Basics

Incumbent ....James Monroe (DR)
Prior streak ....DR (5)
Prior 5...DR (5)
Population... 9,638,453
States 24
Electoral votes 232
Popular votes ....n.a.

Field

Candidate	PI	Age	State	Position	N	W	CS
James Monroe (DR)	8.7	62.51	Va.	President	X	X	96.04
John Quincy Adams (DR)	5.0	53.31	Mass.	Cabinet member	—	—	17.96

General election

Candidate	EV	EV%	SC	PV	PV%
Monroe	231	99.57%	24	—	—
Adams	1	0.43%	0	—	—

State electoral votes

State	Total EV	Monroe	Adams
Alabama	3	3	0
Connecticut	9	9	0
Delaware	4	4	0
Georgia	8	8	0
Illinois	3	3	0
Indiana	3	3	0
Kentucky	12	12	0
Louisiana	3	3	0
Maine	9	9	0
Maryland	11	11	0
Massachusetts	15	15	0
Mississippi	2	2	0
Missouri	3	3	0
New Hampshire	8	7	1
New Jersey	8	8	0
New York	29	29	0
North Carolina	15	15	0
Ohio	8	8	0
Pennsylvania	24	24	0
Rhode Island	4	4	0
South Carolina	11	11	0
Tennessee	7	7	0
Vermont	8	8	0
Virginia	25	25	0
Total	232	231	1

Scenarios

1824

Basics

Incumbent	James Monroe (DR)
Prior streak	DR (6)
Prior 5	DR (5)
Population	10,818,874
States	24
Electoral votes	261
Popular votes	365,833

Field

Candidate	PI	Age	State	Position	N	W	CS
Andrew Jackson (DR)	5.9	57.63	Tenn.	Senator	X	—	69.65
John Quincy Adams (DR)	5.6	57.31	Mass.	Cabinet member	X	X	67.41
William Crawford (DR)	5.4	52.69	Ga.	Cabinet member	—	—	46.97
Henry Clay (DR)	3.7	47.55	Ky.	Representative	—	—	46.84

General election

Candidate	EV	EV%	SC	PV	PV%
Jackson	99	37.93%	11	151,271	41.35%
Adams	84	32.18%	7	113,122	30.92%
Crawford	41	15.71%	3	40,856	11.17%
Clay	37	14.18%	3	47,531	12.99%

NOTE: Adams was elected president by the House of Representatives on the first ballot. The final vote was 13 states for Adams, 7 states for Jackson, 4 states for Crawford.

State popular votes

State	Total PV	Jackson	Adams	Clay	Crawford	Other
Alabama	13,603	9,429	2,422	96	1,656	—
Connecticut	10,647	—	7,494	—	1,965	1,188
Delaware	—	—	—	—	—	—
Georgia	—	—	—	—	—	—
Illinois	4,671	1,272	1,516	1,036	847	—
Indiana	15,838	7,444	3,071	5,316	—	7
Kentucky	23,338	6,356	—	16,982	—	—
Louisiana	—	—	—	—	—	—
Maine	12,625	—	10,289	—	2,336	—
Maryland	33,214	14,523	14,632	695	3,364	—
Massachusetts	42,056	—	30,687	—	—	11,369
Mississippi	4,894	3,121	1,654	—	119	—
Missouri	3,432	1,166	159	2,042	32	33
New Hampshire	10,032	—	9,389	—	643	—
New Jersey	19,837	10,332	8,309	—	1,196	—
New York	—	—	—	—	—	—
North Carolina	36,109	20,231	—	—	15,622	256
Ohio	50,024	18,489	12,280	19,255	—	—
Pennsylvania	47,073	35,736	5,441	1,690	4,206	—

State	Total PV	Jackson	Adams	Clay	Crawford	Other
Rhode Island	2,344	—	2,144	—	—	200
South Carolina	—	—	—	—	—	—
Tennessee	20,725	20,197	216	—	312	—
Vermont	—	—	—	—	—	—
Virginia	15,371	2,975	3,419	419	8,558	—
Total	365,833	151,271	113,122	47,531	40,856	13,053

State electoral votes

State	Total EV	Jackson	Adams	Crawford	Clay
Alabama	5	5	0	0	0
Connecticut	8	0	8	0	0
Delaware	3	0	1	2	0
Georgia	9	0	0	9	0
Illinois	3	2	1	0	0
Indiana	5	5	0	0	0
Kentucky	14	0	0	0	14
Louisiana	5	3	2	0	0
Maine	9	0	9	0	0
Maryland	11	7	3	1	0
Massachusetts	15	0	15	0	0
Mississippi	3	3	0	0	0
Missouri	3	0	0	0	3
New Hampshire	8	0	8	0	0
New Jersey	8	8	0	0	0
New York	36	1	26	5	4
North Carolina	15	15	0	0	0
Ohio	16	0	0	0	16
Pennsylvania	28	28	0	0	0
Rhode Island	4	0	4	0	0
South Carolina	11	11	0	0	0
Tennessee	11	11	0	0	0
Vermont	7	0	7	0	0
Virginia	24	0	0	24	0
Total	261	99	84	41	37

Scenarios

1% to Jackson	Jackson 99, Adams 84, Crawford 41, Clay 37
1% to Adams	Jackson 99, Adams 84, Crawford 41, Clay 37
10K to Jackson	Jackson 142, Adams 59, Crawford 42, Clay 18
10K to Adams	Adams 159, Jackson 52, Crawford 32, Clay 18
1964 allocation	Jackson 138, Adams 85, Clay 52, Crawford 33
2020 allocation	Jackson 120, Adams 68, Clay 39, Crawford 36

1828

Basics

Incumbent ....John Quincy Adams (NR)
Prior streak...DR (7)
Prior 5...DR (5)
Population..12,143,862
States 24
Electoral votes 261
Popular votes 1,148,018

Field

Candidate	PI	Age	State	Position	N	W	CS
Andrew Jackson (DR)	6.9	61.63	Tenn.	Former senator	X	X	84.82
John Quincy Adams (NR)	7.7	61.31	Mass.	President	X	—	68.27

General election

Candidate	EV	EV%	SC	PV	PV%
Jackson	178	68.20%	15	642,553	55.97%
Adams	83	31.80%	9	500,897	43.63%

State popular votes

State	Total PV	Jackson	Adams	Other
Alabama	18,618	16,736	1,878	4
Connecticut	19,378	4,448	13,829	1,101
Delaware	—	—	—	—
Georgia	20,004	19,362	642	—
Illinois	14,222	9,560	4,662	—
Indiana	39,210	22,201	17,009	—
Kentucky	70,776	39,308	31,468	—
Louisiana	8,687	4,605	4,082	—
Maine	34,789	13,927	20,773	89
Maryland	45,796	22,782	23,014	—
Massachusetts	39,074	6,012	29,836	3,226
Mississippi	8,344	6,763	1,581	—
Missouri	11,654	8,232	3,422	—
New Hampshire	44,035	20,212	23,823	—
New Jersey	45,570	21,809	23,753	8
New York	270,975	139,412	131,563	—
North Carolina	51,747	37,814	13,918	15
Ohio	131,049	67,596	63,453	—
Pennsylvania	152,220	101,457	50,763	—
Rhode Island	3,580	820	2,755	5
South Carolina	—	—	—	—
Tennessee	46,533	44,293	2,240	—
Vermont	32,833	8,350	24,363	120
Virginia	38,924	26,854	12,070	—
Total	1,148,018	642,553	500,897	4,568

State electoral votes

State	Total EV	Jackson	Adams
Alabama	5	5	0
Connecticut	8	0	8
Delaware	3	0	3
Georgia	9	9	0
Illinois	3	3	0
Indiana	5	5	0
Kentucky	14	14	0
Louisiana	5	5	0
Maine	9	1	8
Maryland	11	5	6
Massachusetts	15	0	15
Mississippi	3	3	0
Missouri	3	3	0
New Hampshire	8	0	8
New Jersey	8	0	8
New York	36	20	16
North Carolina	15	15	0
Ohio	16	16	0
Pennsylvania	28	28	0
Rhode Island	4	0	4
South Carolina	11	11	0
Tennessee	11	11	0
Vermont	7	0	7
Virginia	24	24	0
Total	261	178	83

Scenarios

1% to Jackson .... Jackson 179, Adams 82
1% to Adams .... Jackson 178, Adams 83
10K to Jackson .... Jackson 227, Adams 34
10K to Adams .... Adams 179, Jackson 82
1964 allocation .... Jackson 227, Adams 81
2020 allocation .... Jackson 195, Adams 68

1832

Basics

Incumbent ....Andrew Jackson (D)
Prior streak ....DR (8)
Prior 5 ....DR (5)
Population 13,614,424
States 24
Electoral votes 286
Popular votes 1,293,973

Field

Candidate	PI	Age	State	Position	N	W	CS
Andrew Jackson (D)	7.8	65.63	Tenn.	President	X	X	87.20
Henry Clay (NR)	6.4	55.55	Ky.	Senator	X	—	62.61
William Wirt (AM)	3.9	59.98	Md.	Former Cabinet member	—	—	35.63
John Floyd (D)	4.2	49.52	Va.	Governor	—	—	22.71

Democratic nomination

Candidate	ConFB	FB%	ConLB	LB%	PriW	PriV	PriV%
Jackson	283	100.00%	—	—	—	—	—

National Republican nomination

Candidate	ConFB	FB%	ConLB	LB%	PriW	PriV	PriV%
Clay	167	99.41%	—	—	—	—	—

General election

Candidate	EV	EV%	SC	PV	PV%
Jackson	219	76.57%	16	701,780	54.24%
Clay	49	17.13%	6	484,205	37.42%
Floyd	11	3.85%	1	0	0.00%
Wirt	7	2.45%	1	100,715	7.78%

State popular votes

State	Total PV	Jackson	Clay	Wirt	Other
Alabama	14,291	14,286	5	—	—
Connecticut	32,833	11,269	18,155	3,409	—
Delaware	8,386	4,110	4,276	—	—
Georgia	20,750	20,750	—	—	—
Illinois	21,481	14,609	6,745	97	30
Indiana	57,152	31,652	25,473	27	—
Kentucky	79,741	36,292	43,449	—	—
Louisiana	6,337	3,908	2,429	—	—
Maine	62,153	33,978	27,331	844	—
Maryland	38,316	19,156	19,160	—	—
Massachusetts	67,619	13,933	31,963	14,692	7,031
Mississippi	5,750	5,750	—	—	—
Missouri	5,192	5,192	—	—	—

State	Total PV	Jackson	Clay	Wirt	Other
New Hampshire	43,793	24,855	18,938	—	—
New Jersey	47,760	23,826	23,466	468	—
New York	323,393	168,497	154,896	—	—
North Carolina	29,799	25,261	4,538	—	—
Ohio	158,350	81,246	76,566	538	—
Pennsylvania	157,679	90,973	—	66,706	—
Rhode Island	5,747	2,051	2,871	819	6
South Carolina	—	—	—	—	—
Tennessee	29,425	28,078	1,347	—	—
Vermont	32,344	7,865	11,161	13,112	206
Virginia	45,682	34,243	11,436	3	—
Total	1,293,973	701,780	484,205	100,715	7,273

State electoral votes

State	Total EV	Jackson	Clay	Floyd	Wirt
Alabama	7	7	0	0	0
Connecticut	8	0	8	0	0
Delaware	3	0	3	0	0
Georgia	11	11	0	0	0
Illinois	5	5	0	0	0
Indiana	9	9	0	0	0
Kentucky	15	0	15	0	0
Louisiana	5	5	0	0	0
Maine	10	10	0	0	0
Maryland	8	3	5	0	0
Massachusetts	14	0	14	0	0
Mississippi	4	4	0	0	0
Missouri	4	4	0	0	0
New Hampshire	7	7	0	0	0
New Jersey	8	8	0	0	0
New York	42	42	0	0	0
North Carolina	15	15	0	0	0
Ohio	21	21	0	0	0
Pennsylvania	30	30	0	0	0
Rhode Island	4	0	4	0	0
South Carolina	11	0	0	11	0
Tennessee	15	15	0	0	0
Vermont	7	0	0	0	7
Virginia	23	23	0	0	0
Total	286	219	49	11	7

Scenarios

1% to Jackson	Jackson 224, Clay 44, Floyd 11, Wirt 7
1% to Clay	Jackson 211, Clay 57, Floyd 11, Wirt 7
10K to Jackson	Jackson 275, Floyd 11, Clay 0, Wirt 0
10K to Clay	Clay 173, Jackson 102, Floyd 11, Wirt 0
1964 allocation	Jackson 253, Clay 44, Floyd 8, Wirt 3
2020 allocation	Jackson 212, Clay 39, Floyd 9, Wirt 3

1836

Basics

Incumbent ....Andrew Jackson (D)
Prior streak ....D (1)
Prior 5...DR (4), D (1)
Population...15,244,368
States 26
Electoral votes 294
Popular votes 1,503,534

Field

Candidate	PI	Age	State	Position	N	W	CS
Martin Van Buren (D)	6.8	53.91	N.Y.	Vice president	X	X	80.26
William Henry Harrison (W)	4.9	63.73	Ohio	Former senator	X	—	64.80
Hugh White (W)	6.3	63.01	Tenn.	Senator	X	—	54.62
Daniel Webster (W)	5.0	54.79	Mass.	Senator	—	—	26.29
Willie Person Mangum (W)	5.4	44.48	N.C.	Senator	—	—	22.34

Democratic nomination

Candidate	ConFB	FB%	ConLB	LB%	PriW	PriV	PriV%
Van Buren	265	100.00%	—	—	—	—	—

Whig nomination

(No convention)

General election

Candidate	EV	EV%	SC	PV	PV%
Van Buren	170	57.82%	15	764,176	50.83%
Harrison	73	24.83%	7	550,816	36.64%
White	26	8.84%	2	146,107	9.72%
Webster	14	4.76%	1	41,201	2.74%
Mangum	11	3.74%	1	0	0.00%

State popular votes

State	Total PV	Van Buren	Harrison	White	Webster	Other
Alabama	37,296	20,638	—	16,658	—	—
Arkansas	3,714	2,380	—	1,334	—	—
Connecticut	38,093	19,294	18,799	—	—	—
Delaware	8,895	4,154	4,736	—	—	5
Georgia	47,259	22,778	—	24,481	—	—
Illinois	33,589	18,369	15,220	—	—	—
Indiana	74,423	33,084	41,339	—	—	—
Kentucky	70,090	33,229	36,861	—	—	—
Louisiana	7,425	3,842	—	3,583	—	—
Maine	38,740	22,825	14,803	—	—	1,112
Maryland	48,119	22,267	25,852	—	—	—
Massachusetts	74,732	33,486	—	—	41,201	45

State	Total PV	Van Buren	Harrison	White	Webster	Other
Michigan	12,052	6,507	5,545	—	—	—
Mississippi	20,079	10,297	—	9,782	—	—
Missouri	18,332	10,995	—	7,337	—	—
New Hampshire	24,925	18,697	6,228	—	—	—
New Jersey	51,729	25,592	26,137	—	—	—
New York	305,343	166,795	138,548	—	—	—
North Carolina	50,153	26,631	—	23,521	—	1
Ohio	202,931	97,122	105,809	—	—	—
Pennsylvania	178,701	91,466	87,235	—	—	—
Rhode Island	5,673	2,962	2,710	—	—	1
South Carolina	—	—	—	—	—	—
Tennessee	62,197	26,170	—	36,027	—	—
Vermont	35,099	14,040	20,994	—	—	65
Virginia	53,945	30,556	—	23,384	—	5
Total	1,503,534	764,176	550,816	146,107	41,201	1,234

State electoral votes

State	Total EV	Van Buren	Harrison	White	Webster	Mangum
Alabama	7	7	0	0	0	0
Arkansas	3	3	0	0	0	0
Connecticut	8	8	0	0	0	0
Delaware	3	0	3	0	0	0
Georgia	11	0	0	11	0	0
Illinois	5	5	0	0	0	0
Indiana	9	0	9	0	0	0
Kentucky	15	0	15	0	0	0
Louisiana	5	5	0	0	0	0
Maine	10	10	0	0	0	0
Maryland	10	0	10	0	0	0
Massachusetts	14	0	0	0	14	0
Michigan	3	3	0	0	0	0
Mississippi	4	4	0	0	0	0
Missouri	4	4	0	0	0	0
New Hampshire	7	7	0	0	0	0
New Jersey	8	0	8	0	0	0
New York	42	42	0	0	0	0
North Carolina	15	15	0	0	0	0
Ohio	21	0	21	0	0	0
Pennsylvania	30	30	0	0	0	0
Rhode Island	4	4	0	0	0	0
South Carolina	11	0	0	0	0	11
Tennessee	15	0	0	15	0	0
Vermont	7	0	7	0	0	0
Virginia	23	23	0	0	0	0
Total	294	170	73	26	14	11

Scenarios

1% to Van Buren.................... Van Buren 178, Harrison 65, White 26, Webster 14, Mangum 11
1% to Harrison....................... Van Buren 162, Harrison 81, White 26, Webster 14, Mangum 11
10K to Van Buren ....Van Buren 283, Mangum 11, Harrison 0, Webster 0, White 0
10K to Harrison...................... Harrison 140, White 79, Van Buren 50, Webster 14, Mangum 11
1964 allocation.........................Van Buren 209, Harrison 81, White 23, Webster 14, Mangum 8
2020 allocation..........................Van Buren 171, Harrison 67, White 27, Webster 11, Mangum 9

1840

Basics

Incumbent ....Martin Van Buren (D)
Prior streak ....D (2)
Prior 5..DR (3), D (2)
Population..17,069,453
States 26
Electoral votes 294
Popular votes 2,411,808

Field

Candidate	PI	Age	State	Position	N	W	CS
William Henry Harrison (W)	8.7	67.73	Ohio	Former senator	X	X	87.90
Martin Van Buren (D)	9.1	57.91	N.Y.	President	X	—	65.49
Henry Clay (W)	6.7	63.55	Ky.	Former nominee	—	—	42.42
Winfield Scott (W)	5.8	54.39	N.J.	General	—	—	27.88

Democratic nomination

Candidate	ConFB	FB%	ConLB	LB%	PriW	PriV	PriV%
Van Buren	244	100.00%	—	—	—	—	—

Whig nomination

Candidate	ConFB	FB%	ConLB[5]	LB%	PriW	PriV	PriV%
Harrison	91	35.83%	148	58.27%	—	—	—
Clay	103	40.55%	90	35.43%	—	—	—
Scott	57	22.44%	16	6.30%	—	—	—

General election

Candidate	EV	EV%	SC	PV	PV%
Harrison	234	79.59%	19	1,275,390	52.88%
Van Buren	60	20.41%	7	1,128,854	46.81%

State popular votes

State	Total PV	Harrison	Van Buren	Other
Alabama	62,511	28,515	33,996	—
Arkansas	11,839	5,160	6,679	—
Connecticut	56,879	31,598	25,281	—
Delaware	10,852	5,967	4,872	13
Georgia	72,322	40,339	31,983	—
Illinois	93,175	45,574	47,441	160
Indiana	117,605	65,280	51,696	629
Kentucky	91,104	58,488	32,616	—
Louisiana	18,912	11,296	7,616	—
Maine	92,802	46,612	46,190	—
Maryland	62,280	33,528	28,752	—
Massachusetts	126,825	72,852	52,355	1,618
Michigan	44,029	22,933	21,096	—

State	Total PV	Harrison	Van Buren	Other
Mississippi	36,525	19,515	17,010	—
Missouri	52,923	22,954	29,969	—
New Hampshire	59,956	26,310	32,774	872
New Jersey	64,454	33,351	31,034	69
New York	441,543	226,001	212,733	2,809
North Carolina	80,735	46,567	34,168	—
Ohio	272,890	148,043	123,944	903
Pennsylvania	287,695	144,023	143,672	—
Rhode Island	8,631	5,213	3,263	155
South Carolina	—	—	—	—
Tennessee	108,145	60,194	47,951	—
Vermont	50,782	32,440	18,006	336
Virginia	86,394	42,637	43,757	—
Total	2,411,808	1,275,390	1,128,854	7,564

State electoral votes

State	Total EV	Harrison	Van Buren
Alabama	7	0	7
Arkansas	3	0	3
Connecticut	8	8	0
Delaware	3	3	0
Georgia	11	11	0
Illinois	5	0	5
Indiana	9	9	0
Kentucky	15	15	0
Louisiana	5	5	0
Maine	10	10	0
Maryland	10	10	0
Massachusetts	14	14	0
Michigan	3	3	0
Mississippi	4	4	0
Missouri	4	0	4
New Hampshire	7	0	7
New Jersey	8	8	0
New York	42	42	0
North Carolina	15	15	0
Ohio	21	21	0
Pennsylvania	30	30	0
Rhode Island	4	4	0
South Carolina	11	0	11
Tennessee	15	15	0
Vermont	7	7	0
Virginia	23	0	23
Total	294	234	60

Scenarios

1% to Harrison	Harrison 257, Van Buren 37
1% to Van Buren	Harrison 194, Van Buren 100
10K to Harrison	Harrison 283, Van Buren 11
10K to Van Buren	Van Buren 244, Harrison 50
1964 allocation	Harrison 257, Van Buren 78
2020 allocation	Harrison 214, Van Buren 71

1844

Basics

Incumbent .... John Tyler (I)
Prior streak .... W (1)
Prior 5 .... D (2), DR (2), W (1)
Population 19,295,947
States 26
Electoral votes 275
Popular votes 2,703,659

Field

Candidate	PI	Age	State	Position	N	W	CS
James Polk (D)	6.7	49.00	Tenn.	Former governor	X	X	81.33
Henry Clay (W)	5.6	67.55	Ky.	Former nominee	X	—	71.05
Martin Van Buren (D)	8.7	61.91	N.Y.	Former president	—	—	50.00
Lewis Cass (D)	5.1	62.06	Mich.	Former Cabinet member	—	—	34.91
James Birney (LTY)	2.6	52.74	Mich.	Movement leader	—	—	17.35
Richard Johnson (D)	5.6	64.04	Ky.	Former vice president	—	—	17.19

Democratic nomination

Candidate	ConFB	FB%	ConLB[9]	LB%	PriW	PriV	PriV%
Polk	0	0.00%	231	86.84%	—	—	—
Cass	83	31.20%	29	10.90%	—	—	—
Van Buren	146	54.89%	0	0.00%	—	—	—
Johnson	24	9.02%	0	0.00%	—	—	—

Whig nomination

Candidate	ConFB	FB%	ConLB	LB%	PriW	PriV	PriV%
Clay	275	100.00%	—	—	—	—	—

General election

Candidate	EV	EV%	SC	PV	PV%
Polk	170	61.82%	15	1,339,494	49.54%
Clay	105	38.18%	11	1,300,004	48.08%
Birney	0	0.00%	0	62,103	2.30%

State popular votes

State	Total PV	Polk	Clay	Birney	Other
Alabama	63,403	37,401	26,002	—	—
Arkansas	15,150	9,546	5,604	—	—
Connecticut	64,616	29,841	32,832	1,943	—
Delaware	12,247	5,970	6,271	—	6
Georgia	86,247	44,147	42,100	—	—
Illinois	109,057	58,795	45,854	3,469	939
Indiana	140,157	70,183	67,866	2,108	—
Kentucky	113,237	51,988	61,249	—	—
Louisiana	26,865	13,782	13,083	—	—

State	Total PV	Polk	Clay	Birney	Other
Maine	84,933	45,719	34,378	4,836	—
Maryland	68,690	32,706	35,984	—	—
Massachusetts	132,037	53,039	67,062	10,830	1,106
Michigan	55,560	27,737	24,185	3,638	—
Mississippi	45,004	25,846	19,158	—	—
Missouri	72,522	41,322	31,200	—	—
New Hampshire	49,187	27,160	17,866	4,161	—
New Jersey	75,944	37,495	38,318	131	—
New York	485,882	237,588	232,482	15,812	—
North Carolina	82,521	39,287	43,232	—	2
Ohio	312,300	149,127	155,091	8,082	—
Pennsylvania	331,645	167,311	161,195	3,139	—
Rhode Island	12,194	4,867	7,322	—	5
South Carolina	—	—	—	—	—
Tennessee	119,957	59,917	60,040	—	—
Vermont	48,765	18,041	26,770	3,954	—
Virginia	95,539	50,679	44,860	—	—
Total	2,703,659	1,339,494	1,300,004	62,103	2,058

State electoral votes

State	Total EV	Polk	Clay
Alabama	9	9	0
Arkansas	3	3	0
Connecticut	6	0	6
Delaware	3	0	3
Georgia	10	10	0
Illinois	9	9	0
Indiana	12	12	0
Kentucky	12	0	12
Louisiana	6	6	0
Maine	9	9	0
Maryland	8	0	8
Massachusetts	12	0	12
Michigan	5	5	0
Mississippi	6	6	0
Missouri	7	7	0
New Hampshire	6	6	0
New Jersey	7	0	7
New York	36	36	0
North Carolina	11	0	11
Ohio	23	0	23
Pennsylvania	26	26	0
Rhode Island	4	0	4
South Carolina	9	9	0
Tennessee	13	0	13
Vermont	6	0	6
Virginia	17	17	0
Total	275	170	105

Scenarios

1% to Polk .... Polk 213, Clay 62
1% to Clay .... Clay 179, Polk 96
10K to Polk .... Polk 275, Clay 0
10K to Clay .... Clay 266, Polk 9
1964 allocation .... Polk 217, Clay 118
2020 allocation .... Polk 181, Clay 104

1848

Basics

Incumbent ....James Polk (D)
Prior streak ....D (1)
Prior 5 ....D (3), W (1), DR (1)
Population 21,812,860
States 30
Electoral votes 290
Popular votes 2,879,184

Field

Candidate	PI	Age	State	Position	N	W	CS
Zachary Taylor (W)	4.1	63.94	La.	General	X	X	78.93
Lewis Cass (D)	6.9	66.06	Mich.	Senator	X	—	71.66
Martin Van Buren (FS)	7.1	65.91	N.Y.	Former president	—	—	42.02
Henry Clay (W)	5.1	71.55	Ky.	Former nominee	—	—	37.63
Winfield Scott (W)	5.0	62.39	N.J.	General	—	—	27.96
James Buchanan (D)	8.2	57.52	Pa.	Cabinet member	—	—	25.17
Levi Woodbury (D)	7.0	58.86	N.H.	Supreme Court justice	—	—	24.61
Daniel Webster (W)	7.0	66.79	Mass.	Senator	—	—	16.31

Democratic nomination

Candidate	ConFB	FB%	ConLB[4]	LB%	PriW	PriV	PriV%
Cass	125	43.10%	179	61.72%	—	—	—
Woodbury	53	18.28%	38	13.10%	—	—	—
Buchanan	55	18.97%	33	11.38%	—	—	—

Whig nomination

Candidate	ConFB	FB%	ConLB[4]	LB%	PriW	PriV	PriV%
Taylor	111	39.64%	171	61.07%	—	—	—
Scott	43	15.36%	63	22.50%	—	—	—
Clay	97	34.64%	32	11.43%	—	—	—
Webster	22	7.86%	14	5.00%	—	—	—

General election

Candidate	EV	EV%	SC	PV	PV%
Taylor	163	56.21%	15	1,361,393	47.28%
Cass	127	43.79%	15	1,223,460	42.49%
Van Buren	0	0.00%	0	291,501	10.12%
Clay	0	0.00%	0	89	0.00%

State popular votes

State	Total PV	Taylor	Cass	Van Buren	Other
Alabama	61,659	30,482	31,173	—	4
Arkansas	16,888	7,587	9,301	—	—
Connecticut	62,398	30,318	27,051	5,005	24
Delaware	12,432	6,440	5,910	82	—

State	Total PV	Taylor	Cass	Van Buren	Other
Florida	7,203	4,120	3,083	—	—
Georgia	92,317	47,532	44,785	—	—
Illinois	124,596	52,853	55,952	15,702	89
Indiana	152,394	69,668	74,695	8,031	—
Iowa	22,271	9,930	11,238	1,103	—
Kentucky	116,865	67,145	49,720	—	—
Louisiana	33,866	18,487	15,379	—	—
Maine	87,625	35,273	40,195	12,157	—
Maryland	72,359	37,702	34,528	129	—
Massachusetts	134,748	61,072	35,281	38,333	62
Michigan	65,082	23,947	30,742	10,393	—
Mississippi	52,456	25,911	26,545	—	—
Missouri	72,748	32,671	40,077	—	—
New Hampshire	50,104	14,781	27,763	7,560	—
New Jersey	77,745	40,015	36,901	829	—
New York	455,944	218,583	114,319	120,497	2,545
North Carolina	79,826	44,054	35,772	—	—
Ohio	328,987	138,656	154,782	35,523	26
Pennsylvania	369,092	185,730	172,186	11,176	—
Rhode Island	11,049	6,705	3,613	726	5
South Carolina	—	—	—	—	—
Tennessee	122,463	64,321	58,142	—	—
Texas	17,000	5,281	11,644	—	75
Vermont	47,897	23,117	10,943	13,837	—
Virginia	92,004	45,265	46,739	—	—
Wisconsin	39,166	13,747	15,001	10,418	—
Total	2,879,184	1,361,393	1,223,460	291,501	2,830

State electoral votes

State	Total EV	Taylor	Cass
Alabama	9	0	9
Arkansas	3	0	3
Connecticut	6	6	0
Delaware	3	3	0
Florida	3	3	0
Georgia	10	10	0
Illinois	9	0	9
Indiana	12	0	12
Iowa	4	0	4
Kentucky	12	12	0
Louisiana	6	6	0
Maine	9	0	9
Maryland	8	8	0
Massachusetts	12	12	0
Michigan	5	0	5
Mississippi	6	0	6
Missouri	7	0	7
New Hampshire	6	0	6
New Jersey	7	7	0
New York	36	36	0
North Carolina	11	11	0
Ohio	23	0	23

State	Total EV	Taylor	Cass
Pennsylvania	26	26	0
Rhode Island	4	4	0
South Carolina	9	0	9
Tennessee	13	13	0
Texas	4	0	4
Vermont	6	6	0
Virginia	17	0	17
Wisconsin	4	0	4
Total	290	163	127

Scenarios

1% to Taylor .... Taylor 195, Cass 95
1% to Cass .... Taylor 163, Cass 127
10K to Taylor .... Taylor 281, Cass 9
10K to Cass .... Cass 242, Taylor 48
1964 allocation .... Taylor 200, Cass 195
2020 allocation .... Taylor 188, Cass 180

1852

Basics

Incumbent	Millard Fillmore (W)
Prior streak	W (1)
Prior 5	D (3), W (2)
Population	24,647,585
States	31
Electoral votes	296
Popular votes	3,161,830

Field

Candidate	PI	Age	State	Position	N	W	CS
Franklin Pierce (D)	7.0	47.94	N.H.	Former senator	X	X	89.52
Winfield Scott (W)	4.2	66.39	N.J.	General	X	—	63.01
Millard Fillmore (W)	9.1	52.82	N.Y.	President	—	—	45.85
Lewis Cass (D)	6.9	70.06	Mich.	Senator	—	—	42.18
James Buchanan (D)	7.9	61.52	Pa.	Former Cabinet member	—	—	35.79
John Hale (FS)	5.4	46.59	N.H.	Senator	—	—	25.71
Daniel Webster (W)	6.0	70.79	Mass.	Cabinet member	—	—	18.52
William Marcy (D)	5.9	65.89	N.Y.	Former Cabinet member	—	—	17.50
Stephen Douglas (D)	6.9	39.52	Ill.	Senator	—	—	15.51
Joseph Lane (D)	3.1	50.88	Ore.	Territorial delegate	—	—	13.59

Democratic nomination

Candidate	ConFB	FB%	ConLB[49]	LB%	PriW	PriV	PriV%
Pierce	0	0.00%	279	96.88%	—	—	—
Cass	116	40.28%	2	0.69%	—	—	—
Douglas	20	6.94%	2	0.69%	—	—	—
Buchanan	93	32.29%	0	0.00%	—	—	—
Marcy	27	9.38%	0	0.00%	—	—	—
Lane	13	4.51%	0	0.00%	—	—	—

Whig nomination

Candidate	ConFB	FB%	ConLB[53]	LB%	PriW	PriV	PriV%
Scott	131	44.26%	159	53.72%	—	—	—
Fillmore	133	44.93%	112	37.84%	—	—	—
Webster	29	9.80%	21	7.10%	—	—	—

General election

Candidate	EV	EV%	SC	PV	PV%
Pierce	254	85.81%	27	1,607,510	50.84%
Scott	42	14.19%	4	1,386,942	43.87%
Hale	0	0.00%	0	155,210	4.91%
Webster	0	0.00%	0	6,994	0.22%

State popular votes

State	Total PV	Pierce	Scott	Hale	Other
Alabama	44,147	26,881	15,061	—	2,205
Arkansas	19,577	12,173	7,404	—	—
California	76,810	40,721	35,972	61	56
Connecticut	66,781	33,249	30,359	3,161	12
Delaware	12,673	6,318	6,293	62	—
Florida	7,193	4,318	2,875	—	—
Georgia	62,626	40,516	16,660	—	5,450
Illinois	154,974	80,378	64,733	9,863	—
Indiana	183,176	95,340	80,907	6,929	—
Iowa	35,364	17,763	15,856	1,606	139
Kentucky	111,643	53,949	57,428	266	—
Louisiana	35,902	18,647	17,255	—	—
Maine	82,182	41,609	32,543	8,030	—
Maryland	75,120	40,022	35,077	21	—
Massachusetts	127,103	44,569	52,683	28,023	1,828
Michigan	82,939	41,842	33,860	7,237	—
Mississippi	44,454	26,896	17,558	—	—
Missouri	68,801	38,817	29,984	—	—
New Hampshire	50,535	28,503	15,486	6,546	—
New Jersey	83,926	44,301	38,551	336	738
New York	522,294	262,083	234,882	25,329	—
North Carolina	78,891	39,788	39,043	—	60
Ohio	352,903	169,193	152,577	31,133	—
Pennsylvania	387,920	198,568	179,182	8,500	1,670
Rhode Island	17,005	8,735	7,626	644	—
South Carolina	—	—	—	—	—
Tennessee	115,486	56,900	58,586	—	—
Texas	20,223	14,857	5,356	—	10
Vermont	43,838	13,044	22,173	8,621	—
Virginia	132,604	73,872	58,732	—	—
Wisconsin	64,740	33,658	22,240	8,842	—
Total	3,161,830	1,607,510	1,386,942	155,210	12,168

State electoral votes

State	Total EV	Pierce	Scott
Alabama	9	9	0
Arkansas	4	4	0
California	4	4	0
Connecticut	6	6	0
Delaware	3	3	0
Florida	3	3	0
Georgia	10	10	0
Illinois	11	11	0
Indiana	13	13	0
Iowa	4	4	0
Kentucky	12	0	12
Louisiana	6	6	0
Maine	8	8	0
Maryland	8	8	0
Massachusetts	13	0	13

State	Total EV	Pierce	Scott
Michigan	6	6	0
Mississippi	7	7	0
Missouri	9	9	0
New Hampshire	5	5	0
New Jersey	7	7	0
New York	35	35	0
North Carolina	10	10	0
Ohio	23	23	0
Pennsylvania	27	27	0
Rhode Island	4	4	0
South Carolina	8	8	0
Tennessee	12	0	12
Texas	4	4	0
Vermont	5	0	5
Virginia	15	15	0
Wisconsin	5	5	0
Total	296	254	42

Scenarios

1% to Pierce...Pierce 266, Scott 30
1% to Scott..Pierce 241, Scott 55
10K to Pierce...Pierce 296, Scott 0
10K to Scott ....Scott 243, Pierce 53
1964 allocation...Pierce 398, Scott 37
2020 allocation...Pierce 390, Scott 33

1856

Basics

Incumbent .... Franklin Pierce (D)
Prior streak .... D (1)
Prior 5 .... D (3), W (2)
Population 27,838,856
States 31
Electoral votes 296
Popular votes 4,054,647

Field

Candidate	PI	Age	State	Position	N	W	CS
James Buchanan (D)	5.1	65.52	Pa.	Former Cabinet member	X	X	79.35
John Fremont (R)	5.3	43.78	Calif.	Former senator	X	—	68.16
Millard Fillmore (AW)	7.4	56.82	N.Y.	Former president	—	—	45.15
Franklin Pierce (D)	8.1	51.94	N.H.	President	—	—	43.05
Stephen Douglas (D)	7.1	43.52	Ill.	Senator	—	—	18.86
John McLean (R)	4.2	71.64	Ohio	Supreme Court justice	—	—	15.19

Democratic nomination

Candidate	ConFB	FB%	ConLB[17]	LB%	PriW	PriV	PriV%
Buchanan	136	45.78%	296	100.00%	—	—	—
Pierce	123	41.39%	0	0.00%	—	—	—
Douglas	33	11.15%	0	0.00%	—	—	—

Republican nomination

Candidate	ConFB	FB%	ConLB	LB%	PriW	PriV	PriV%
Fremont	520	91.71%	—	—	—	—	—
McLean	37	6.53%	—	—	—	—	—

General election

Candidate	EV	EV%	SC	PV	PV%
Buchanan	174	58.78%	19	1,836,072	45.28%
Fremont	114	38.51%	11	1,342,345	33.11%
Fillmore	8	2.70%	1	873,053	21.53%

State popular votes

State	Total PV	Buchanan	Fremont	Fillmore	Other
Alabama	75,291	46,739	—	28,552	—
Arkansas	32,642	21,910	—	10,732	—
California	110,255	53,342	20,704	36,195	14
Connecticut	80,360	35,028	42,717	2,615	—
Delaware	14,598	8,004	310	6,275	9
Florida	11,191	6,358	—	4,833	—
Georgia	99,020	56,581	—	42,439	—
Illinois	239,334	105,528	96,275	37,531	—
Indiana	235,401	118,670	94,375	22,356	—

State	Total PV	Buchanan	Fremont	Fillmore	Other
Iowa	92,310	37,568	45,073	9,669	—
Kentucky	142,058	74,642	—	67,416	—
Louisiana	42,873	22,164	—	20,709	—
Maine	109,689	39,140	67,279	3,270	—
Maryland	86,860	39,123	285	47,452	—
Massachusetts	170,048	39,244	108,172	19,626	3,006
Michigan	125,558	52,136	71,762	1,660	—
Mississippi	59,647	35,456	—	24,191	—
Missouri	106,486	57,964	—	48,522	—
New Hampshire	69,774	31,891	37,473	410	—
New Jersey	99,396	46,943	28,338	24,115	—
New York	596,486	195,878	276,004	124,604	—
North Carolina	84,963	48,243	—	36,720	—
Ohio	386,640	170,874	187,497	28,121	148
Pennsylvania	460,937	230,772	147,963	82,202	—
Rhode Island	19,822	6,680	11,467	1,675	—
South Carolina	—	—	—	—	—
Tennessee	133,582	69,704	—	63,878	—
Texas	48,005	31,995	—	16,010	—
Vermont	50,675	10,569	39,561	545	—
Virginia	150,233	90,083	—	60,150	—
Wisconsin	120,513	52,843	67,090	580	—
Total	4,054,647	1,836,072	1,342,345	873,053	3,177

State electoral votes

State	Total EV	Buchanan	Fremont	Fillmore
Alabama	9	9	0	0
Arkansas	4	4	0	0
California	4	4	0	0
Connecticut	6	0	6	0
Delaware	3	3	0	0
Florida	3	3	0	0
Georgia	10	10	0	0
Illinois	11	11	0	0
Indiana	13	13	0	0
Iowa	4	0	4	0
Kentucky	12	12	0	0
Louisiana	6	6	0	0
Maine	8	0	8	0
Maryland	8	0	0	8
Massachusetts	13	0	13	0
Michigan	6	0	6	0
Mississippi	7	7	0	0
Missouri	9	9	0	0
New Hampshire	5	0	5	0
New Jersey	7	7	0	0
New York	35	0	35	0
North Carolina	10	10	0	0
Ohio	23	0	23	0
Pennsylvania	27	27	0	0
Rhode Island	4	0	4	0
South Carolina	8	8	0	0

State	Total EV	Buchanan	Fremont	Fillmore
Tennessee	12	12	0	0
Texas	4	4	0	0
Vermont	5	0	5	0
Virginia	15	15	0	0
Wisconsin	5	0	5	0
Total	296	174	114	8

Scenarios

1% to Buchanan...Buchanan 174, Fremont 114, Fillmore 8
1% to Fremont..Buchanan 174, Fremont 114, Fillmore 8
10K to Buchanan.. Buchanan 235, Fremont 61, Fillmore 0
10K to Fremont.. Fremont 135, Buchanan 111, Fillmore 50
1964 allocation...Buchanan 277, Fremont 148, Fillmore 10
2020 allocation...Buchanan 301, Fremont 112, Fillmore 10

1860

Basics

Incumbent ....James Buchanan (D)
Prior streak ....D (2)
Prior 5 ....D (3), W (2)
Population 31,443,321
States 33
Electoral votes 303
Popular votes 4,685,561

Field

Candidate	PI	Age	State	Position	N	W	CS
Abraham Lincoln (R)	6.2	51.72	Ill.	Former representative	X	X	78.38
John Breckinridge (D/SD)	4.7	39.79	Ky.	Vice president	X	—	60.76
Stephen Douglas (D)	7.0	47.52	Ill.	Senator	X	—	57.06
John Bell (CU)	4.6	64.70	Tenn.	Former senator	—	—	46.37
William Seward (R)	8.2	59.46	N.Y.	Senator	—	—	39.70
Robert Hunter (D)	7.0	51.53	Va.	Senator	—	—	21.10
James Guthrie (D)	3.9	67.91	Ky.	Former Cabinet member	—	—	19.34
Simon Cameron (R)	7.8	61.65	Pa.	Senator	—	—	18.62
Salmon Chase (R)	8.7	52.80	Ohio	Former governor	—	—	18.38
Edward Bates (R)	5.2	67.16	Mo.	Former representative	—	—	18.22
Andrew Johnson (D)	6.9	51.84	Tenn.	Senator	—	—	13.19

Democratic nomination

Candidate	ConFB	FB%	ConLB[59]	LB%	PriW	PriV	PriV%
Douglas	146	48.02%	191	62.87%	—	—	—
Breckinridge	0	0.00%	8	2.48%	—	—	—
Guthrie	36	11.72%	6	1.82%	—	—	—
Hunter	42	13.86%	0	0.00%	—	—	—
Johnson	12	3.96%	0	0.00%	—	—	—

Republican nomination

Candidate	ConFB	FB%	ConLB[3]	LB%	PriW	PriV	PriV%
Lincoln	102	21.89%	340	72.96%	—	—	—
Seward	174	37.23%	122	26.07%	—	—	—
Chase	49	10.52%	2	0.43%	—	—	—
Cameron	51	10.84%	0	0.00%	—	—	—
Bates	48	10.30%	0	0.00%	—	—	—

General election

Candidate	EV	EV%	SC	PV	PV%
Lincoln	180	59.41%	18	1,865,908	39.82%
Breckinridge	72	23.76%	11	848,019	18.10%
Bell	39	12.87%	3	590,901	12.61%
Douglas	12	3.96%	1	1,380,202	29.46%

State popular votes

State	Total PV	Lincoln	Douglas	Breckinridge	Bell	Other
Alabama	90,122	—	13,618	48,669	27,835	—
Arkansas	54,152	—	5,357	28,732	20,063	—
California	119,827	38,733	37,999	33,969	9,111	15
Connecticut	74,819	43,488	15,431	14,372	1,528	—
Delaware	16,115	3,822	1,066	7,339	3,888	—
Florida	13,301	—	223	8,277	4,801	—
Georgia	106,717	—	11,581	52,176	42,960	—
Illinois	339,666	172,171	160,215	2,331	4,914	35
Indiana	272,143	139,033	115,509	12,295	5,306	—
Iowa	128,739	70,302	55,639	1,035	1,763	—
Kentucky	146,216	1,364	25,651	53,143	66,058	—
Louisiana	50,510	—	7,625	22,681	20,204	—
Maine	100,918	62,811	29,693	6,368	2,046	—
Maryland	92,502	2,294	5,966	42,482	41,760	—
Massachusetts	169,876	106,684	34,370	6,163	22,331	328
Michigan	154,758	88,481	65,057	805	415	—
Minnesota	34,804	22,069	11,920	748	50	17
Mississippi	69,095	—	3,282	40,768	25,045	—
Missouri	165,563	17,028	58,801	31,362	58,372	—
New Hampshire	65,943	37,519	25,887	2,125	412	—
New Jersey	121,215	58,346	62,869	—	—	—
New York	675,156	362,646	312,510	—	—	—
North Carolina	96,712	—	2,737	48,846	45,129	—
Ohio	442,866	231,709	187,421	11,406	12,194	136
Oregon	14,758	5,329	4,136	5,075	218	—
Pennsylvania	476,442	268,030	16,765	178,871	12,776	—
Rhode Island	19,951	12,244	7,707	—	—	—
South Carolina	—	—	—	—	—	—
Tennessee	146,106	—	11,281	65,097	69,728	—
Texas	62,855	—	18	47,454	15,383	—
Vermont	44,644	33,808	8,649	218	1,969	—
Virginia	166,891	1,887	16,198	74,325	74,481	—
Wisconsin	152,179	86,110	65,021	887	161	—
Total	4,685,561	1,865,908	1,380,202	848,019	590,901	531

State electoral votes

State	Total EV	Lincoln	Breckinridge	Bell	Douglas
Alabama	9	0	9	0	0
Arkansas	4	0	4	0	0
California	4	4	0	0	0
Connecticut	6	6	0	0	0
Delaware	3	0	3	0	0
Florida	3	0	3	0	0
Georgia	10	0	10	0	0
Illinois	11	11	0	0	0
Indiana	13	13	0	0	0
Iowa	4	4	0	0	0
Kentucky	12	0	0	12	0
Louisiana	6	0	6	0	0
Maine	8	8	0	0	0

State	Total EV	Lincoln	Breckinridge	Bell	Douglas
Maryland	8	0	8	0	0
Massachusetts	13	13	0	0	0
Michigan	6	6	0	0	0
Minnesota	4	4	0	0	0
Mississippi	7	0	7	0	0
Missouri	9	0	0	0	9
New Hampshire	5	5	0	0	0
New Jersey	7	4	0	0	3
New York	35	35	0	0	0
North Carolina	10	0	10	0	0
Ohio	23	23	0	0	0
Oregon	3	3	0	0	0
Pennsylvania	27	27	0	0	0
Rhode Island	4	4	0	0	0
South Carolina	8	0	8	0	0
Tennessee	12	0	0	12	0
Texas	4	0	4	0	0
Vermont	5	5	0	0	0
Virginia	15	0	0	15	0
Wisconsin	5	5	0	0	0
Total	303	180	72	39	12

Scenarios

1% to Lincoln .... Lincoln 179, Breckinridge 72, Bell 48, Douglas 4
1% to Douglas .... Lincoln 175, Breckinridge 72, Bell 39, Douglas 17
10K to Lincoln .... Lincoln 186, Breckinridge 69, Bell 48, Douglas 0
10K to Douglas .... Lincoln 141, Breckinridge 66, Douglas 57, Bell 39
1964 allocation .... Lincoln 282, Breckinridge 118, Bell 32, Douglas 19
2020 allocation .... Lincoln 243, Breckinridge 149, Bell 32, Douglas 16

1864

Basics

Incumbent	Abraham Lincoln (R)
Prior streak	R (1)
Prior 5	D (3), R (1), W (1)
Population	34,558,173
States	25
Electoral votes	233
Popular votes	4,030,986

Field

Candidate	PI	Age	State	Position	N	W	CS
Abraham Lincoln (R)	8.9	55.72	Ill.	President	X	X	92.17
George McClellan (D)	4.7	37.91	N.J.	General	X	—	61.66
Thomas Seymour (D)	6.8	57.09	Conn.	Former governor	—	—	23.41
Horatio Seymour (D)	8.0	54.42	N.Y.	Governor	—	—	14.23
Ulysses Grant (R)	5.6	42.51	Ill.	General	—	—	13.35

Democratic nomination

Candidate	ConFB	FB%	ConLB	LB%	PriW	PriV	PriV%
McClellan	174	76.99%	—	—	—	—	—
T. Seymour	38	16.81%	—	—	—	—	—
H. Seymour	12	5.31%	—	—	—	—	—

Republican nomination

Candidate	ConFB	FB%	ConLB	LB%	PriW	PriV	PriV%
Lincoln	494	95.18%	—	—	—	—	—
Grant	22	4.24%	—	—	—	—	—

General election

Candidate	EV	EV%	SC	PV	PV%
Lincoln	212	90.99%	22	2,220,845	55.09%
McClellan	21	9.01%	3	1,809,449	44.89%

State popular votes

State	Total PV	Lincoln	McClellan	Other
California	105,890	62,053	43,837	—
Connecticut	86,958	44,673	42,285	—
Delaware	16,922	8,155	8,767	—
Illinois	348,236	189,512	158,724	—
Indiana	280,117	149,887	130,230	—
Iowa	138,025	88,500	49,525	—
Kansas	21,580	17,089	3,836	655
Kentucky	92,088	27,787	64,301	—
Maine	115,099	68,104	46,995	—
Maryland	72,892	40,153	32,739	—
Massachusetts	175,493	126,742	48,745	6

State	Total PV	Lincoln	McClellan	Other
Michigan	160,023	88,551	71,472	—
Minnesota	42,433	25,031	17,376	26
Missouri	104,346	72,750	31,596	—
Nevada	16,420	9,826	6,594	—
New Hampshire	69,630	36,596	33,034	—
New Jersey	128,747	60,723	68,024	—
New York	730,721	368,735	361,986	—
Ohio	471,283	265,674	205,609	—
Oregon	18,350	9,888	8,457	5
Pennsylvania	572,707	296,391	276,316	—
Rhode Island	23,067	14,349	8,718	—
Vermont	55,740	42,419	13,321	—
West Virginia	34,877	23,799	11,078	—
Wisconsin	149,342	83,458	65,884	—
Total	4,030,986	2,220,845	1,809,449	692

State electoral votes

State	Total EV	Lincoln	McClellan
California	5	5	0
Connecticut	6	6	0
Delaware	3	0	3
Illinois	16	16	0
Indiana	13	13	0
Iowa	8	8	0
Kansas	3	3	0
Kentucky	11	0	11
Maine	7	7	0
Maryland	7	7	0
Massachusetts	12	12	0
Michigan	8	8	0
Minnesota	4	4	0
Missouri	11	11	0
Nevada	2	2	0
New Hampshire	5	5	0
New Jersey	7	0	7
New York	33	33	0
Ohio	21	21	0
Oregon	3	3	0
Pennsylvania	26	26	0
Rhode Island	4	4	0
Vermont	5	5	0
West Virginia	5	5	0
Wisconsin	8	8	0
Total	233	212	21

Scenarios

1% to Lincoln	Lincoln 212, McClellan 21
1% to McClellan	Lincoln 179, McClellan 54
10K to Lincoln	Lincoln 222, McClellan 11
10K to McClellan	McClellan 127, Lincoln 106
1964 allocation	Lincoln 311, McClellan 29
2020 allocation	Lincoln 272, McClellan 25

1868

Basics

Incumbent ....Andrew Johnson (D)
Prior streak..R (2)
Prior 5.. R (2), D (2), W (1)
Population...37,981,591
States 34
Electoral votes 294
Popular votes 5,722,440

Field

Candidate	PI	Age	State	Position	N	W	CS
Ulysses Grant (R)	6.3	46.51	Ill.	General	X	X	85.63
Horatio Seymour (D)	7.5	58.42	N.Y.	Former governor	X	—	67.61
George Pendleton (D)	6.7	43.29	Ohio	Former representative	—	—	36.43
Andrew Johnson (D)	7.4	59.84	Tenn.	President	—	—	26.37
Sanford Church (D)	5.0	53.54	N.Y.	Former state official	—	—	18.54
Winfield Hancock (D)	6.0	44.71	Pa.	General	—	—	18.46
Asa Packer (D)	6.0	62.84	Pa.	Former representative	—	—	16.55
James English (D)	7.0	56.64	Conn.	Governor	—	—	13.99
James Doolittle (D)	7.9	53.83	Wis.	Senator	—	—	13.27
Joel Parker (D)	6.7	51.94	N.J.	Former governor	—	—	13.27

Democratic nomination

Candidate	ConFB	FB%	ConLB[22]	LB%	PriW	PriV	PriV%
Seymour	0	0.00%	317	100.00%	—	—	—
Pendleton	105	33.12%	0	0.00%	—	—	—
Johnson	65	20.51%	0	0.00%	—	—	—
Church	34	10.73%	0	0.00%	—	—	—
Hancock	34	10.57%	0	0.00%	—	—	—
Packer	26	8.20%	0	0.00%	—	—	—
English	16	5.05%	0	0.00%	—	—	—
Doolittle	13	4.10%	0	0.00%	—	—	—
Parker	13	4.10%	0	0.00%	—	—	—

Republican nomination

Candidate	ConFB	FB%	ConLB	LB%	PriW	PriV	PriV%
Grant	650	100.00%	—	—	—	—	—

General election

Candidate	EV	EV%	SC	PV	PV%
Grant	214	72.79%	26	3,013,650	52.66%
Seymour	80	27.21%	8	2,708,744	47.34%

State popular votes

State	Total PV	Grant	Seymour	Other
Alabama	149,594	76,667	72,921	6
Arkansas	41,190	22,112	19,078	—
California	108,656	54,588	54,068	—
Connecticut	98,570	50,789	47,781	—
Delaware	18,571	7,614	10,957	—
Florida	—	—	—	—
Georgia	159,816	57,109	102,707	—
Illinois	449,420	250,304	199,116	—
Indiana	343,528	176,548	166,980	—
Iowa	194,439	120,399	74,040	—
Kansas	43,630	30,027	13,600	3
Kentucky	155,455	39,566	115,889	—
Louisiana	113,488	33,263	80,225	—
Maine	112,962	70,502	42,460	—
Maryland	92,795	30,438	62,357	—
Massachusetts	195,508	136,379	59,103	26
Michigan	225,632	128,563	97,069	—
Minnesota	71,620	43,545	28,075	—
Missouri	152,488	86,860	65,628	—
Nebraska	15,291	9,772	5,519	—
Nevada	11,689	6,474	5,215	—
New Hampshire	68,304	37,718	30,575	11
New Jersey	163,133	80,132	83,001	—
New York	849,771	419,888	429,883	—
North Carolina	181,498	96,939	84,559	—
Ohio	518,665	280,159	238,506	—
Oregon	22,086	10,961	11,125	—
Pennsylvania	655,662	342,280	313,382	—
Rhode Island	19,511	13,017	6,494	—
South Carolina	107,538	62,301	45,237	—
Tennessee	82,757	56,628	26,129	—
Vermont	56,224	44,173	12,051	—
West Virginia	49,321	29,015	20,306	—
Wisconsin	193,628	108,920	84,708	—
Total	5,722,440	3,013,650	2,708,744	46

State electoral votes

State	Total EV	Grant	Seymour
Alabama	8	8	0
Arkansas	5	5	0
California	5	5	0
Connecticut	6	6	0
Delaware	3	0	3
Florida	3	3	0
Georgia	9	0	9
Illinois	16	16	0
Indiana	13	13	0
Iowa	8	8	0
Kansas	3	3	0
Kentucky	11	0	11

State	Total EV	Grant	Seymour
Louisiana	7	0	7
Maine	7	7	0
Maryland	7	0	7
Massachusetts	12	12	0
Michigan	8	8	0
Minnesota	4	4	0
Missouri	11	11	0
Nebraska	3	3	0
Nevada	3	3	0
New Hampshire	5	5	0
New Jersey	7	0	7
New York	33	0	33
North Carolina	9	9	0
Ohio	21	21	0
Oregon	3	0	3
Pennsylvania	26	26	0
Rhode Island	4	4	0
South Carolina	6	6	0
Tennessee	10	10	0
Vermont	5	5	0
West Virginia	5	5	0
Wisconsin	8	8	0
Total	294	214	80

Scenarios

1% to Grant...Grant 257, Seymour 37
1% to Seymour..Grant 209, Seymour 85
10K to Grant ....Grant 260, Seymour 34
10K to Seymour... Seymour 159, Grant 135
1964 allocation... Grant 319, Seymour 110
2020 allocation...Grant 310, Seymour 95

1872

Basics

Incumbent .... Ulysses Grant (R)
Prior streak .... R (3)
Prior 5 .... R (3), D (2)
Population 41,705,136
States 35
Electoral votes 349
Popular votes 6,470,674

Field

Candidate	PI	Age	State	Position	N	W	CS
Ulysses Grant (R)	9.0	50.51	Ill.	President	X	X	89.28
Horace Greeley (D-LR)	4.8	61.74	N.Y.	Journalist	X	—	58.76
Thomas Hendricks (D)	8.2	53.15	Ind.	Former senator	—	—	43.62
Gratz Brown (D-LR)	7.8	46.43	Mo.	Governor	—	—	27.03
Charles Jenkins (D)	5.1	67.82	Ga.	Former governor	—	—	11.89
David Davis (D)	5.1	57.65	Ill.	Supreme Court justice	—	—	10.97

Democratic nomination

Candidate	ConFB	FB%	ConLB	LB%	PriW	PriV	PriV%
Greeley	686	93.72%	—	—	—	—	—

Republican nomination

Candidate	ConFB	FB%	ConLB	LB%	PriW	PriV	PriV%
Grant	752	100.00%	—	—	—	—	—

General election

Candidate	EV	EV%	SC	PV	PV%
Grant	286	81.95%	29	3,598,468	55.61%
Hendricks	42	12.03%	4	0	0.00%
Brown	18	5.16%	2	0	0.00%
Jenkins	2	0.57%	0	0	0.00%
Davis	1	0.29%	0	0	0.00%
Greeley	—	—	—	2,835,315	43.82%

NOTE: Greeley died on November 29, 1872, which was after the general election, but before the tabulation of electoral votes. His electors scattered their votes among four candidates.

State popular votes

State	Total PV	Grant	Greeley	Other
Alabama	169,716	90,272	79,444	—
Arkansas	79,300	41,373	37,927	—
California	95,785	54,007	40,717	1,061
Connecticut	95,992	50,307	45,685	—
Delaware	21,822	11,129	10,205	488
Florida	33,190	17,763	15,427	—
Georgia	138,906	62,550	76,356	—

State	Total PV	Grant	Greeley	Other
Illinois	429,971	241,936	184,884	3,151
Indiana	349,779	186,147	163,632	—
Iowa	216,365	131,566	71,189	13,610
Kansas	100,512	66,805	32,970	737
Kentucky	191,552	88,970	100,208	2,374
Louisiana	128,692	71,663	57,029	—
Maine	90,523	61,426	29,097	—
Maryland	134,447	66,760	67,687	—
Massachusetts	192,650	133,455	59,195	—
Michigan	221,569	138,768	78,651	4,150
Minnesota	91,339	56,040	35,131	168
Mississippi	129,457	82,175	47,282	—
Missouri	273,059	119,196	151,434	2,429
Nebraska	25,932	18,329	7,603	—
Nevada	14,649	8,413	6,236	—
New Hampshire	68,906	37,168	31,425	313
New Jersey	168,467	91,666	76,801	—
New York	829,692	440,758	387,279	1,655
North Carolina	165,163	94,772	70,130	261
Ohio	529,435	281,852	244,320	3,263
Oregon	20,107	11,818	7,742	547
Pennsylvania	561,629	349,589	212,040	—
Rhode Island	18,994	13,665	5,329	—
South Carolina	95,452	72,290	22,699	463
Tennessee	179,046	85,655	93,391	—
Texas	115,700	47,910	67,675	115
Vermont	52,959	41,480	10,926	553
Virginia	185,195	93,463	91,647	85
West Virginia	62,467	32,320	29,532	615
Wisconsin	192,255	105,012	86,390	853
Total	6,470,674	3,598,468	2,835,315	36,891

State electoral votes

State	Total EV	Grant	Hendricks	Brown	Jenkins	Davis
Alabama	10	10	0	0	0	0
Arkansas	0	0	0	0	0	0
California	6	6	0	0	0	0
Connecticut	6	6	0	0	0	0
Delaware	3	3	0	0	0	0
Florida	4	4	0	0	0	0
Georgia	8	0	0	6	2	0
Illinois	21	21	0	0	0	0
Indiana	15	15	0	0	0	0
Iowa	11	11	0	0	0	0
Kansas	5	5	0	0	0	0
Kentucky	12	0	8	4	0	0
Louisiana	0	0	0	0	0	0
Maine	7	7	0	0	0	0
Maryland	8	0	8	0	0	0
Massachusetts	13	13	0	0	0	0
Michigan	11	11	0	0	0	0
Minnesota	5	5	0	0	0	0

State	Total EV	Grant	Hendricks	Brown	Jenkins	Davis
Mississippi	8	8	0	0	0	0
Missouri	15	0	6	8	0	1
Nebraska	3	3	0	0	0	0
Nevada	3	3	0	0	0	0
New Hampshire	5	5	0	0	0	0
New Jersey	9	9	0	0	0	0
New York	35	35	0	0	0	0
North Carolina	10	10	0	0	0	0
Ohio	22	22	0	0	0	0
Oregon	3	3	0	0	0	0
Pennsylvania	29	29	0	0	0	0
Rhode Island	4	4	0	0	0	0
South Carolina	7	7	0	0	0	0
Tennessee	12	0	12	0	0	0
Texas	8	0	8	0	0	0
Vermont	5	5	0	0	0	0
Virginia	11	11	0	0	0	0
West Virginia	5	5	0	0	0	0
Wisconsin	10	10	0	0	0	0
Total	349	286	42	18	2	1

NOTE: Congress invalidated the electoral votes of Arkansas and Louisiana.

Scenarios

1% to Grant .... Grant 294, Hendricks 34, Brown 18, Jenkins 2, Davis 1
1% to Greeley .... Grant 275, Hendricks 53, Brown 18, Jenkins 2, Davis 1
10K to Grant .... Grant 334, Brown 8, Hendricks 6, Davis 1, Jenkins 0
10K to Greeley .... Grant 204, Hendricks 124, Brown 18, Jenkins 2, Davis 1
1964 allocation .... Grant 378, Hendricks 57, Brown 18, Jenkins 3, Davis 1
2020 allocation .... Grant 355, Hendricks 68, Brown 20, Jenkins 4, Davis 1

1876

Basics

Incumbent .... Ulysses Grant (R)
Prior streak .... R (4)
Prior 5 .... R (4), D (1)
Population 45,750,932
States 38
Electoral votes 369
Popular votes 8,411,618

Field

Candidate	PI	Age	State	Position	N	W	CS
Rutherford Hayes (R)	8.3	54.08	Ohio	Governor	X	X	77.12
Samuel Tilden (D)	7.2	62.73	N.Y.	Governor	X	—	75.14
James Blaine (R)	5.1	46.75	Maine	Representative	—	—	47.05
Thomas Hendricks (D)	7.9	57.15	Ind.	Governor	—	—	25.17
Oliver Morton (R)	8.2	53.24	Ind.	Senator	—	—	23.09
Benjamin Bristow (R)	4.0	44.37	Ky.	Cabinet member	—	—	21.90
Roscoe Conkling (R)	8.2	47.01	N.Y.	Senator	—	—	20.46
Winfield Hancock (D)	6.5	52.71	Pa.	General	—	—	18.14
John Hartranft (R)	7.6	45.88	Pa.	Governor	—	—	16.15
William Allen (D)	6.9	72.87	Ohio	Former governor	—	—	15.83
Thomas Bayard (D)	7.1	48.01	Del.	Senator	—	—	13.59

Democratic nomination

Candidate	ConFB	FB%	ConLB[2]	LB%	PriW	PriV	PriV%
Tilden	402	54.40%	535	72.49%	—	—	—
Hendricks	141	19.04%	85	11.52%	—	—	—
Hancock	75	10.16%	58	7.86%	—	—	—
Allen	54	7.32%	54	7.32%	—	—	—
Bayard	33	4.47%	4	0.54%	—	—	—

Republican nomination

Candidate	ConFB	FB%	ConLB[7]	LB%	PriW	PriV	PriV%
Hayes	61	8.07%	384	50.79%	—	—	—
Blaine	285	37.70%	351	46.43%	—	—	—
Bristow	113	14.95%	21	2.78%	—	—	—
Morton	124	16.40%	0	0.00%	—	—	—
Conkling	99	13.10%	0	0.00%	—	—	—
Hartranft	58	7.67%	0	0.00%	—	—	—

General election

Candidate	EV	EV%	SC	PV	PV%
Hayes	185	50.14%	21	4,033,497	47.95%
Tilden	184	49.86%	17	4,288,191	50.98%

State popular votes

State	Total PV	Tilden	Hayes	Other
Alabama	171,699	102,989	68,708	2
Arkansas	96,946	58,086	38,649	211
California	155,784	76,460	79,258	66
Colorado	—	—	—	—
Connecticut	122,134	61,927	59,033	1,174
Delaware	24,133	13,381	10,752	—
Florida	46,776	22,927	23,849	—
Georgia	180,690	130,157	50,533	—
Illinois	554,368	258,611	278,232	17,525
Indiana	430,020	213,516	206,971	9,533
Iowa	293,398	112,121	171,326	9,951
Kansas	124,134	37,902	78,324	7,908
Kentucky	259,614	159,696	97,156	2,762
Louisiana	145,823	70,508	75,315	—
Maine	117,045	49,917	66,300	828
Maryland	163,759	91,779	71,980	—
Massachusetts	259,619	108,777	150,063	779
Michigan	318,426	141,665	166,901	9,860
Minnesota	124,119	48,816	72,982	2,321
Mississippi	164,776	112,173	52,603	—
Missouri	350,610	202,086	145,027	3,497
Nebraska	49,258	17,343	31,915	—
Nevada	19,691	9,308	10,383	—
New Hampshire	80,143	38,510	41,540	93
New Jersey	220,193	115,962	103,517	714
New York	1,015,503	521,949	489,207	4,347
North Carolina	233,911	125,427	108,484	—
Ohio	658,650	323,182	330,698	4,770
Oregon	29,873	14,157	15,207	509
Pennsylvania	758,973	366,204	384,157	8,612
Rhode Island	26,499	10,712	15,787	—
South Carolina	182,683	90,897	91,786	—
Tennessee	222,743	133,177	89,566	—
Texas	151,431	106,372	45,013	46
Vermont	64,460	20,254	44,092	114
Virginia	236,288	140,770	95,518	—
West Virginia	99,647	56,546	41,997	1,104
Wisconsin	257,799	123,927	130,668	3,204
Total	8,411,618	4,288,191	4,033,497	89,930

State electoral votes

State	Total EV	Hayes	Tilden
Alabama	10	0	10
Arkansas	6	0	6
California	6	6	0
Colorado	3	3	0
Connecticut	6	0	6
Delaware	3	0	3
Florida	4	4	0
Georgia	11	0	11

State	Total EV	Hayes	Tilden
Illinois	21	21	0
Indiana	15	0	15
Iowa	11	11	0
Kansas	5	5	0
Kentucky	12	0	12
Louisiana	8	8	0
Maine	7	7	0
Maryland	8	0	8
Massachusetts	13	13	0
Michigan	11	11	0
Minnesota	5	5	0
Mississippi	8	0	8
Missouri	15	0	15
Nebraska	3	3	0
Nevada	3	3	0
New Hampshire	5	5	0
New Jersey	9	0	9
New York	35	0	35
North Carolina	10	0	10
Ohio	22	22	0
Oregon	3	3	0
Pennsylvania	29	29	0
Rhode Island	4	4	0
South Carolina	7	7	0
Tennessee	12	0	12
Texas	8	0	8
Vermont	5	5	0
Virginia	11	0	11
West Virginia	5	0	5
Wisconsin	10	10	0
Total	369	185	184

Scenarios

1% to Hayes	Hayes 200, Tilden 169
1% to Tilden	Tilden 223, Hayes 146
10K to Hayes	Hayes 247, Tilden 122
10K to Tilden	Tilden 316, Hayes 53
1964 allocation	Hayes 261, Tilden 218
2020 allocation	Hayes 260, Tilden 211

1880

Basics

Incumbent .... Rutherford Hayes (R)
Prior streak .... R (5)
Prior 5 .... R (5)
Population 50,189,209
States 38
Electoral votes 369
Popular votes 9,220,197

Field

Candidate	PI	Age	State	Position	N	W	CS
James Garfield (R)	6.6	48.95	Ohio	Representative	X	X	79.77
Winfield Hancock (D)	5.6	56.71	Pa.	General	X	—	72.24
Ulysses Grant (R)	8.5	58.51	Ill.	Former president	—	—	42.34
James Blaine (R)	7.3	50.75	Maine	Senator	—	—	40.02
Thomas Bayard (D)	7.1	52.01	Del.	Senator	—	—	26.61
James Weaver (GBK)	4.2	47.39	Iowa	Representative	—	—	20.66
John Sherman (R)	8.1	57.48	Ohio	Cabinet member	—	—	19.82
Henry Payne (D)	5.6	69.92	Ohio	Former representative	—	—	18.78
Allen Thurman (D)	7.7	66.97	Ohio	Senator	—	—	17.43
Stephen Field (D)	2.3	63.99	Calif.	Supreme Court justice	—	—	17.03
William Morrison (D)	6.5	56.13	Ill.	Representative	—	—	16.71
Thomas Hendricks (D)	7.4	61.15	Ind.	Former governor	—	—	15.35
Samuel Tilden (D)	8.0	66.73	N.Y.	Former nominee	—	—	14.07
George Edmunds (R)	7.3	52.75	Vt.	Senator	—	—	13.59
Elihu Washburne (R)	4.4	64.11	Ill.	Former ambassador	—	—	13.19

Democratic nomination

Candidate	ConFB	FB%	ConLB[2]	LB%	PriW	PriV	PriV%
Hancock	171	23.17%	705	95.53%	—	—	—
Hendricks	50	6.71%	30	4.07%	—	—	—
Bayard	154	20.80%	2	0.27%	—	—	—
Tilden	38	5.15%	1	0.14%	—	—	—
Payne	81	10.98%	0	0.00%	—	—	—
Thurman	69	9.28%	0	0.00%	—	—	—
Field	65	8.81%	0	0.00%	—	—	—
Morrison	62	8.40%	0	0.00%	—	—	—

Republican nomination

Candidate	ConFB	FB%	ConLB[36]	LB%	PriW	PriV	PriV%
Garfield	0	0.00%	399	52.78%	—	—	—
Grant	304	40.21%	306	40.48%	—	—	—
Blaine	284	37.57%	42	5.56%	—	—	—
Washburne	30	3.97%	5	0.66%	—	—	—
Sherman	93	12.30%	3	0.40%	—	—	—
Edmunds	34	4.50%	0	0.00%	—	—	—

General election

Candidate	EV	EV%	SC	PV	PV%
Garfield	214	58.00%	19	4,453,611	48.30%
Hancock	155	42.01%	19	4,445,256	48.21%
Weaver	0	0.00%	0	306,921	3.33%

State popular votes

State	Total PV	Garfield	Hancock	Weaver	Other
Alabama	151,902	56,350	91,130	4,422	—
Arkansas	108,870	42,436	60,775	4,116	1,543
California	164,218	80,282	80,426	3,381	129
Colorado	53,546	27,450	24,647	1,435	14
Connecticut	132,798	67,071	64,411	868	448
Delaware	29,458	14,148	15,181	129	—
Florida	51,618	23,654	27,964	—	—
Georgia	157,451	54,470	102,981	—	—
Illinois	622,305	318,036	277,321	26,358	590
Indiana	470,758	232,169	225,523	13,066	—
Iowa	323,140	183,904	105,845	32,327	1,064
Kansas	201,054	121,520	59,789	19,710	35
Kentucky	266,884	106,059	149,068	11,499	258
Louisiana	104,462	38,978	65,047	437	—
Maine	143,903	74,052	65,211	4,409	231
Maryland	173,049	78,515	93,706	828	—
Massachusetts	282,505	165,198	111,960	4,548	799
Michigan	353,076	185,335	131,596	34,895	1,250
Minnesota	150,806	93,939	53,314	3,267	286
Mississippi	117,068	34,844	75,750	5,797	677
Missouri	397,289	153,647	208,600	35,042	—
Nebraska	87,355	54,979	28,523	3,853	—
Nevada	18,343	8,732	9,611	—	—
New Hampshire	86,361	44,856	40,797	528	180
New Jersey	245,928	120,555	122,565	2,617	191
New York	1,103,945	555,544	534,511	12,373	1,517
North Carolina	240,946	115,616	124,204	1,126	—
Ohio	724,984	375,048	340,867	6,456	2,613
Oregon	40,841	20,619	19,955	267	—
Pennsylvania	874,783	444,704	407,428	20,667	1,984
Rhode Island	29,235	18,195	10,779	236	25
South Carolina	169,793	57,954	111,236	567	36
Tennessee	243,263	107,677	129,569	6,017	—
Texas	240,659	57,225	155,963	27,471	—
Vermont	65,098	45,567	18,316	1,215	—
Virginia	212,660	83,634	128,647	—	379
West Virginia	112,641	46,243	57,390	9,008	—
Wisconsin	267,202	144,406	114,650	7,986	160
Total	9,220,197	4,453,611	4,445,256	306,921	14,409

State electoral votes

State	Total EV	Garfield	Hancock
Alabama	10	0	10
Arkansas	6	0	6

State	Total EV	Garfield	Hancock
California	6	1	5
Colorado	3	3	0
Connecticut	6	6	0
Delaware	3	0	3
Florida	4	0	4
Georgia	11	0	11
Illinois	21	21	0
Indiana	15	15	0
Iowa	11	11	0
Kansas	5	5	0
Kentucky	12	0	12
Louisiana	8	0	8
Maine	7	7	0
Maryland	8	0	8
Massachusetts	13	13	0
Michigan	11	11	0
Minnesota	5	5	0
Mississippi	8	0	8
Missouri	15	0	15
Nebraska	3	3	0
Nevada	3	0	3
New Hampshire	5	5	0
New Jersey	9	0	9
New York	35	35	0
North Carolina	10	0	10
Ohio	22	22	0
Oregon	3	3	0
Pennsylvania	29	29	0
Rhode Island	4	4	0
South Carolina	7	0	7
Tennessee	12	0	12
Texas	8	0	8
Vermont	5	5	0
Virginia	11	0	11
West Virginia	5	0	5
Wisconsin	10	10	0
Total	369	214	155

Scenarios

1884

Basics

Incumbent ....Chester Arthur (R)
Prior streak ....R (6)
Prior 5...R (5)
Population..54,959,987
States 38
Electoral votes 401
Popular votes 10,058,373

Field

Candidate	PI	Age	State	Position	N	W	CS
Grover Cleveland (D)	7.5	47.62	N.Y.	Governor	X	X	78.78
James Blaine (R)	6.7	54.75	Maine	Former senator	X	—	73.26
Chester Arthur (R)	8.8	55.07	N.Y.	President	—	—	37.07
Thomas Bayard (D)	6.2	56.01	Del.	Senator	—	—	26.53
George Edmunds (R)	7.0	56.75	Vt.	Senator	—	—	19.02
Allen Thurman (D)	7.4	70.97	Ohio	Former senator	—	—	18.54
Samuel Randall (D)	6.3	56.06	Pa.	Representative	—	—	17.58
John Logan (R)	8.1	58.73	Ill.	Senator	—	—	16.15
Joseph McDonald (D)	7.3	65.17	Ind.	Former senator	—	—	15.43
Thomas Hendricks (D)	6.4	65.15	Ind.	Former governor	—	—	14.39

Democratic nomination

Candidate	ConFB	FB%	ConLB[2]	LB%	PriW	PriV	PriV%
Cleveland	392	47.81%	683	83.29%	—	—	—
Bayard	170	20.73%	82	9.94%	—	—	—
Hendricks	1	0.12%	46	5.55%	—	—	—
Thurman	88	10.73%	4	0.49%	—	—	—
Randall	78	9.51%	4	0.49%	—	—	—
McDonald	56	6.83%	2	0.24%	—	—	—

Republican nomination

Candidate	ConFB	FB%	ConLB[4]	LB%	PriW	PriV	PriV%
Blaine	335	40.79%	541	65.98%	—	—	—
Arthur	278	33.90%	207	25.24%	—	—	—
Edmunds	93	11.34%	41	5.00%	—	—	—
Logan	64	7.74%	7	0.85%	—	—	—

General election

Candidate	EV	EV%	SC	PV	PV%
Cleveland	219	54.61%	20	4,915,586	48.87%
Blaine	182	45.39%	18	4,852,916	48.25%

State popular votes

State	Total PV	Cleveland	Blaine	Other
Alabama	153,624	92,736	59,444	1,444
Arkansas	125,779	72,734	51,198	1,847
California	196,988	89,288	102,369	5,331
Colorado	66,519	27,723	36,084	2,712
Connecticut	137,221	67,167	65,879	4,175
Delaware	29,984	16,957	12,953	74
Florida	59,990	31,769	28,031	190
Georgia	143,610	94,667	48,603	340
Illinois	672,670	312,351	337,469	22,850
Indiana	495,423	245,041	238,511	11,871
Iowa	393,542	177,316	197,089	19,137
Kansas	250,991	90,111	154,410	6,470
Kentucky	276,503	152,894	118,822	4,787
Louisiana	109,399	62,594	46,347	458
Maine	130,489	52,153	72,217	6,119
Maryland	185,838	96,941	85,748	3,149
Massachusetts	303,383	122,352	146,724	34,307
Michigan	401,186	189,361	192,669	19,156
Minnesota	190,236	70,135	111,819	8,282
Mississippi	120,688	77,653	43,035	—
Missouri	441,268	236,023	203,081	2,164
Nebraska	134,202	54,391	76,912	2,899
Nevada	12,779	5,577	7,176	26
New Hampshire	84,586	39,198	43,254	2,134
New Jersey	260,853	127,747	123,436	9,670
New York	1,167,003	563,048	562,001	41,954
North Carolina	268,356	142,905	125,021	430
Ohio	784,620	368,280	400,092	16,248
Oregon	52,683	24,598	26,845	1,240
Pennsylvania	899,563	392,915	474,350	32,298
Rhode Island	32,771	12,391	19,030	1,350
South Carolina	92,812	69,845	21,730	1,237
Tennessee	259,978	133,770	124,101	2,107
Texas	326,458	226,375	93,345	6,738
Vermont	59,409	17,331	39,514	2,564
Virginia	284,977	145,491	139,356	130
West Virginia	132,145	67,311	63,096	1,738
Wisconsin	319,847	146,447	161,155	12,245
Total	10,058,373	4,915,586	4,852,916	289,871

State electoral votes

State	Total EV	Cleveland	Blaine
Alabama	10	10	0
Arkansas	7	7	0
California	8	0	8
Colorado	3	0	3
Connecticut	6	6	0
Delaware	3	3	0
Florida	4	4	0
Georgia	12	12	0

State	Total EV	Cleveland	Blaine
Illinois	22	0	22
Indiana	15	15	0
Iowa	13	0	13
Kansas	9	0	9
Kentucky	13	13	0
Louisiana	8	8	0
Maine	6	0	6
Maryland	8	8	0
Massachusetts	14	0	14
Michigan	13	0	13
Minnesota	7	0	7
Mississippi	9	9	0
Missouri	16	16	0
Nebraska	5	0	5
Nevada	3	0	3
New Hampshire	4	0	4
New Jersey	9	9	0
New York	36	36	0
North Carolina	11	11	0
Ohio	23	0	23
Oregon	3	0	3
Pennsylvania	30	0	30
Rhode Island	4	0	4
South Carolina	9	9	0
Tennessee	12	12	0
Texas	13	13	0
Vermont	4	0	4
Virginia	12	12	0
West Virginia	6	6	0
Wisconsin	11	0	11
Total	401	219	182

Scenarios

1% to Cleveland	Cleveland 232, Blaine 169
1% to Blaine	Blaine 248, Cleveland 153
10K to Cleveland	Cleveland 281, Blaine 120
10K to Blaine	Blaine 312, Cleveland 89
1964 allocation	Cleveland 250, Blaine 229
2020 allocation	Cleveland 257, Blaine 214

1888

Basics

Incumbent .... Grover Cleveland (D)
Prior streak .... D (1)
Prior 5 .... R (4), D (1)
Population 60,184,257
States 38
Electoral votes 401
Popular votes 11,395,705

Field

Candidate	PI	Age	State	Position	N	W	CS
Benjamin Harrison (R)	7.9	55.20	Ind.	Former senator	X	X	79.71
Grover Cleveland (D)	9.2	51.62	N.Y.	President	X	—	72.27
John Sherman (R)	7.7	65.48	Ohio	Senator	—	—	31.96
Walter Gresham (R)	5.7	56.63	Ind.	Federal judge	—	—	20.30
Russell Alger (R)	7.8	52.68	Mich.	Former governor	—	—	19.58
Chauncey Depew (R)	4.9	54.52	N.Y.	Business executive	—	—	19.50
Clinton Fisk (PRO)	3.8	59.90	N.J.	Former general	—	—	17.02
William Boyd Allison (R)	7.6	59.67	Iowa	Senator	—	—	16.95
James Blaine (R)	6.3	58.75	Maine	Former nominee	—	—	13.35

Democratic nomination

Candidate	ConFB	FB%	ConLB	LB%	PriW	PriV	PriV%
Cleveland	822	100.00%	—	—	—	—	—

Republican nomination

Candidate	ConFB	FB%	ConLB[8]	LB%	PriW	PriV	PriV%
Harrison	85	10.22%	544	65.39%	—	—	—
Sherman	229	27.52%	118	14.18%	—	—	—
Alger	84	10.10%	100	12.02%	—	—	—
Gresham	107	12.86%	59	7.09%	—	—	—
Blaine	35	4.21%	5	0.60%	—	—	—
Depew	99	11.90%	0	0.00%	—	—	—
Allison	72	8.65%	0	0.00%	—	—	—

General election

Candidate	EV	EV%	SC	PV	PV%
Harrison	233	58.11%	20	5,449,825	47.82%
Cleveland	168	41.90%	18	5,539,118	48.61%
Fisk	0	0.00%	0	249,913	2.19%

State popular votes

State	Total PV	Cleveland	Harrison	Fisk	Other
Alabama	175,085	117,314	57,177	594	—
Arkansas	157,058	86,062	59,752	614	10,630
California	251,339	117,729	124,816	5,761	3,033

State	Total PV	Cleveland	Harrison	Fisk	Other
Colorado	91,946	37,549	50,772	2,182	1,443
Connecticut	153,978	74,920	74,584	4,234	240
Delaware	29,764	16,414	12,950	399	1
Florida	66,500	39,557	26,529	414	—
Georgia	142,936	100,493	40,499	1,808	136
Illinois	747,813	348,351	370,475	21,703	7,284
Indiana	536,988	260,990	263,366	9,939	2,693
Iowa	404,694	179,876	211,607	3,550	9,661
Kansas	331,133	102,739	182,845	6,774	38,775
Kentucky	344,868	183,830	155,138	5,223	677
Louisiana	115,891	85,032	30,660	160	39
Maine	128,253	50,472	73,730	2,691	1,360
Maryland	210,941	106,188	99,986	4,767	—
Massachusetts	344,243	151,590	183,892	8,701	60
Michigan	475,356	213,469	236,387	20,945	4,555
Minnesota	263,162	104,372	142,492	15,201	1,097
Mississippi	115,786	85,451	30,095	240	—
Missouri	521,359	261,943	236,252	4,539	18,625
Nebraska	202,630	80,552	108,417	9,435	4,226
Nevada	12,573	5,303	7,229	41	—
New Hampshire	90,770	43,382	45,734	1,596	58
New Jersey	303,801	151,508	144,360	7,933	—
New York	1,321,897	635,965	650,338	30,231	5,363
North Carolina	285,946	148,336	134,784	2,789	37
Ohio	839,357	395,456	416,054	24,356	3,491
Oregon	61,889	26,518	33,291	1,676	404
Pennsylvania	997,568	446,633	526,091	20,947	3,897
Rhode Island	40,775	17,530	21,969	1,251	25
South Carolina	79,997	65,824	13,736	—	437
Tennessee	304,313	158,779	139,511	5,975	48
Texas	363,479	236,290	93,991	4,739	28,459
Vermont	63,476	16,788	45,193	1,460	35
Virginia	304,087	152,004	150,399	1,684	—
West Virginia	159,440	78,677	78,171	1,084	1,508
Wisconsin	354,614	155,232	176,553	14,277	8,552
Total	11,395,705	5,539,118	5,449,825	249,913	156,849

State electoral votes

State	Total EV	Harrison	Cleveland
Alabama	10	0	10
Arkansas	7	0	7
California	8	8	0
Colorado	3	3	0
Connecticut	6	0	6
Delaware	3	0	3
Florida	4	0	4
Georgia	12	0	12
Illinois	22	22	0
Indiana	15	15	0
Iowa	13	13	0
Kansas	9	9	0
Kentucky	13	0	13

State	Total EV	Harrison	Cleveland
Louisiana	8	0	8
Maine	6	6	0
Maryland	8	0	8
Massachusetts	14	14	0
Michigan	13	13	0
Minnesota	7	7	0
Mississippi	9	0	9
Missouri	16	0	16
Nebraska	5	5	0
Nevada	3	3	0
New Hampshire	4	4	0
New Jersey	9	0	9
New York	36	36	0
North Carolina	11	0	11
Ohio	23	23	0
Oregon	3	3	0
Pennsylvania	30	30	0
Rhode Island	4	4	0
South Carolina	9	0	9
Tennessee	12	0	12
Texas	13	0	13
Vermont	4	4	0
Virginia	12	0	12
West Virginia	6	0	6
Wisconsin	11	11	0
Total	401	233	168

Scenarios

1% to Harrison ....Harrison 257, Cleveland 144
1% to Cleveland ....Cleveland 219, Harrison 182
10K to Harrison ....Harrison 304, Cleveland 97
10K to Cleveland ....Cleveland 244, Harrison 157
1964 allocation ....Harrison 285, Cleveland 194
2020 allocation ....Harrison 254, Cleveland 217

1892

Basics

Incumbent .... Benjamin Harrison (R)
Prior streak .... R (1)
Prior 5 .... R (4), D (1)
Population 65,428,309
States 44
Electoral votes 444
Popular votes 12,071,548

Field

Candidate	PI	Age	State	Position	N	W	CS
Grover Cleveland (D)	9.1	55.62	N.Y.	Former president	X	X	80.73
Benjamin Harrison (R)	8.5	59.20	Ind.	President	X	—	68.40
James Weaver (POP)	4.1	59.39	Iowa	Former representative	—	—	38.80
James Blaine (R)	3.7	62.75	Maine	Former nominee	—	—	26.05
William McKinley (R)	8.2	49.76	Ohio	Governor	—	—	26.05
David Hill (D)	8.5	49.17	N.Y.	Senator	—	—	19.98
Horace Boies (D)	6.3	64.90	Iowa	Governor	—	—	19.02
John Bidwell (PRO)	0.4	73.24	Calif.	Movement leader	—	—	17.19
Arthur Gorman (D)	7.4	53.64	Md.	Senator	—	—	13.19

Democratic nomination

Candidate	ConFB	FB%	ConLB	LB%	PriW	PriV	PriV%
Cleveland	617	67.84%	—	—	—	—	—
Hill	114	12.53%	—	—	—	—	—
Boies	103	11.32%	—	—	—	—	—
Gorman	37	4.01%	—	—	—	—	—

Republican nomination

Candidate	ConFB	FB%	ConLB	LB%	PriW	PriV	PriV%
Harrison	535	59.07%	—	—	—	—	—
Blaine	182	20.11%	—	—	—	—	—
McKinley	182	20.09%	—	—	—	—	—

General election

Candidate	EV	EV%	SC	PV	PV%
Cleveland	277	62.39%	24	5,554,617	46.01%
Harrison	145	32.66%	17	5,186,793	42.97%
Weaver	22	4.96%	5	1,029,357	8.53%
Bidwell	0	0.00%	0	270,979	2.25%

State popular votes

State	Total PV	Cleveland	Harrison	Weaver	Bidwell	Other
Alabama	232,543	138,135	9,184	84,984	240	—
Arkansas	148,117	87,834	47,072	11,831	113	1,267
California	269,585	118,151	118,027	25,311	8,096	—

State	Total PV	Cleveland	Harrison	Weaver	Bidwell	Other
Colorado	93,881	—	38,620	53,584	1,677	—
Connecticut	164,593	82,395	77,030	809	4,026	333
Delaware	37,235	18,581	18,077	—	564	13
Florida	35,567	30,154	—	4,843	570	—
Georgia	223,961	129,386	48,305	42,937	988	2,345
Idaho	19,407	—	8,599	10,520	288	—
Illinois	873,667	426,281	399,308	22,207	25,871	—
Indiana	553,613	262,740	255,615	22,208	13,050	—
Iowa	443,159	196,367	219,795	20,595	6,402	—
Kansas	323,591	—	156,134	162,888	4,569	—
Kentucky	340,864	175,461	135,462	23,500	6,441	—
Louisiana	118,287	87,922	27,903	2,462	—	—
Maine	116,013	48,024	62,878	2,045	3,062	4
Maryland	213,275	113,866	92,736	796	5,877	—
Massachusetts	391,028	176,813	202,814	3,210	7,539	652
Michigan	466,917	202,396	222,708	20,031	20,857	925
Minnesota	267,461	101,055	122,836	29,336	14,234	—
Mississippi	52,519	40,030	1,398	10,118	973	—
Missouri	541,583	268,400	227,646	41,204	4,333	—
Montana	44,461	17,690	18,871	7,338	562	—
Nebraska	200,205	24,956	87,213	83,134	4,902	—
Nevada	10,826	703	2,811	7,226	86	—
New Hampshire	89,328	42,081	45,658	292	1,297	—
New Jersey	337,485	170,987	156,059	969	8,133	1,337
New York	1,336,793	654,868	609,350	16,429	38,190	17,956
North Carolina	280,270	132,951	100,346	44,336	2,637	—
North Dakota	36,118	—	17,519	17,700	899	—
Ohio	850,164	404,115	405,187	14,850	26,012	—
Oregon	78,378	14,243	35,002	26,875	2,258	—
Pennsylvania	1,003,000	452,264	516,011	8,714	25,123	888
Rhode Island	53,196	24,336	26,975	228	1,654	3
South Carolina	70,504	54,680	13,345	2,407	—	72
South Dakota	70,513	9,081	34,888	26,544	—	—
Tennessee	265,732	136,468	100,537	23,918	4,809	—
Texas	422,447	239,148	77,478	99,688	2,165	3,968
Vermont	55,793	16,325	37,992	42	1,424	10
Virginia	292,238	164,136	113,098	12,275	2,729	—
Washington	87,968	29,802	36,459	19,165	2,542	—
West Virginia	171,079	84,467	80,292	4,167	2,153	—
Wisconsin	371,481	177,325	171,101	9,919	13,136	—
Wyoming	16,703	—	8,454	7,722	498	29
Total	12,071,548	5,554,617	5,186,793	1,029,357	270,979	29,802

State electoral votes

State	Total EV	Cleveland	Harrison	Weaver
Alabama	11	11	0	0
Arkansas	8	8	0	0
California	9	8	1	0
Colorado	4	0	0	4
Connecticut	6	6	0	0
Delaware	3	3	0	0
Florida	4	4	0	0

State	Total EV	Cleveland	Harrison	Weaver
Georgia	13	13	0	0
Idaho	3	0	0	3
Illinois	24	24	0	0
Indiana	15	15	0	0
Iowa	13	0	13	0
Kansas	10	0	0	10
Kentucky	13	13	0	0
Louisiana	8	8	0	0
Maine	6	0	6	0
Maryland	8	8	0	0
Massachusetts	15	0	15	0
Michigan	14	5	9	0
Minnesota	9	0	9	0
Mississippi	9	9	0	0
Missouri	17	17	0	0
Montana	3	0	3	0
Nebraska	8	0	8	0
Nevada	3	0	0	3
New Hampshire	4	0	4	0
New Jersey	10	10	0	0
New York	36	36	0	0
North Carolina	11	11	0	0
North Dakota	3	1	1	1
Ohio	23	1	22	0
Oregon	4	0	3	1
Pennsylvania	32	0	32	0
Rhode Island	4	0	4	0
South Carolina	9	9	0	0
South Dakota	4	0	4	0
Tennessee	12	12	0	0
Texas	15	15	0	0
Vermont	4	0	4	0
Virginia	12	12	0	0
Washington	4	0	4	0
West Virginia	6	6	0	0
Wisconsin	12	12	0	0
Wyoming	3	0	3	0
Total	444	277	145	22

Scenarios

1% to Cleveland	Cleveland 299, Harrison 123, Weaver 22
1% to Harrison	Cleveland 239, Harrison 183, Weaver 22
10K to Cleveland	Cleveland 325, Harrison 85, Weaver 34
10K to Harrison	Harrison 226, Cleveland 212, Weaver 6
1964 allocation	Cleveland 334, Harrison 151, Weaver 23
2020 allocation	Cleveland 344, Harrison 127, Weaver 28

1896

Basics

Incumbent .... Grover Cleveland (D)
Prior streak .... D (1)
Prior 5 .... R (3), D (2)
Population 70,614,681
States 45
Electoral votes 447
Popular votes 13,904,866

Field

Candidate	PI	Age	State	Position	N	W	CS
William McKinley (R)	8.2	53.76	Ohio	Former governor	X	X	81.24
William J. Bryan (D-POP)	4.6	36.62	Nebr.	Former representative	X	—	70.98
Richard Bland (D)	5.5	61.20	Mo.	Former representative	—	—	30.20
Robert Pattison (D)	7.2	45.90	Pa.	Former governor	—	—	18.30
Thomas Reed (R)	5.2	57.04	Maine	Representative	—	—	17.27
Joseph Blackburn (D)	6.2	58.08	Ky.	Senator	—	—	17.03
Horace Boies (D)	6.3	68.90	Iowa	Former governor	—	—	15.75
Matthew Quay (R)	7.5	63.09	Pa.	Senator	—	—	15.35
Levi Morton (R)	7.8	72.46	N.Y.	Governor	—	—	15.03
John R. McLean (D)	5.0	48.12	Ohio	Journalist	—	—	14.63
Claude Matthews (D)	7.3	50.88	Ind.	Governor	—	—	13.19

Democratic nomination

Candidate	ConFB	FB%	ConLB[5]	LB%	PriW	PriV	PriV%
Bryan	137	14.73%	652	70.11%	—	—	—
Pattison	97	10.43%	95	10.22%	—	—	—
Bland	235	25.27%	11	1.18%	—	—	—
Blackburn	82	8.82%	0	0.00%	—	—	—
Boies	67	7.20%	0	0.00%	—	—	—
McLean	54	5.81%	0	0.00%	—	—	—
Matthews	37	3.98%	0	0.00%	—	—	—

Republican nomination

Candidate	ConFB	FB%	ConLB	LB%	PriW	PriV	PriV%
McKinley	662	71.59%	—	—	—	—	—
Reed	85	9.15%	—	—	—	—	—
Quay	62	6.66%	—	—	—	—	—
Morton	58	6.28%	—	—	—	—	—

General election

Candidate	EV	EV%	SC	PV	PV%
McKinley	271	60.63%	23	7,105,076	51.10%
Bryan	176	39.37%	22	6,370,897	45.82%

State popular votes

State	Total PV	McKinley	Bryan	Other
Alabama	194,580	55,673	130,298	8,609
Arkansas	149,396	37,512	110,103	1,781
California	298,695	146,688	123,143	28,864
Colorado	189,539	26,271	161,005	2,263
Connecticut	174,394	110,285	56,740	7,369
Delaware	31,540	16,883	13,425	1,232
Florida	46,468	11,298	30,683	4,487
Georgia	163,309	60,107	94,733	8,469
Idaho	29,631	6,324	23,135	172
Illinois	1,090,766	607,130	465,593	18,043
Indiana	637,089	323,754	305,538	7,797
Iowa	521,550	289,293	223,744	8,513
Kansas	336,085	159,484	173,049	3,552
Kentucky	445,928	218,171	217,894	9,863
Louisiana	101,046	22,037	77,175	1,834
Maine	118,419	80,403	34,587	3,429
Maryland	250,249	136,959	104,150	9,140
Massachusetts	401,269	278,976	105,414	16,879
Michigan	545,583	293,336	237,164	15,083
Minnesota	341,762	193,503	139,735	8,524
Mississippi	69,591	4,819	63,355	1,417
Missouri	674,032	304,940	363,667	5,425
Montana	53,330	10,509	42,628	193
Nebraska	223,181	103,064	115,007	5,110
Nevada	10,314	1,938	7,802	574
New Hampshire	83,670	57,444	21,271	4,955
New Jersey	371,014	221,367	133,675	15,972
New York	1,423,876	819,838	551,369	52,669
North Carolina	331,337	155,122	174,408	1,807
North Dakota	47,391	26,335	20,686	370
Ohio	1,014,295	525,991	474,882	13,422
Oregon	97,335	48,700	46,739	1,896
Pennsylvania	1,194,355	728,300	427,125	38,930
Rhode Island	54,785	37,437	14,459	2,889
South Carolina	68,938	9,313	58,801	824
South Dakota	82,937	41,040	41,225	672
Tennessee	320,903	148,683	167,168	5,052
Texas	515,987	163,413	267,803	84,771
Utah	78,098	13,491	64,607	—
Vermont	63,831	51,127	10,179	2,525
Virginia	294,674	135,379	154,708	4,587
Washington	93,435	39,153	51,646	2,636
West Virginia	201,757	105,379	94,480	1,898
Wisconsin	447,409	268,135	165,523	13,751
Wyoming	21,093	10,072	10,376	645
Total	13,904,866	7,105,076	6,370,897	428,893

State electoral votes

State	Total EV	McKinley	Bryan
Alabama	11	0	11
Arkansas	8	0	8
California	9	8	1
Colorado	4	0	4
Connecticut	6	6	0
Delaware	3	3	0
Florida	4	0	4
Georgia	13	0	13
Idaho	3	0	3
Illinois	24	24	0
Indiana	15	15	0
Iowa	13	13	0
Kansas	10	0	10
Kentucky	13	12	1
Louisiana	8	0	8
Maine	6	6	0
Maryland	8	8	0
Massachusetts	15	15	0
Michigan	14	14	0
Minnesota	9	9	0
Mississippi	9	0	9
Missouri	17	0	17
Montana	3	0	3
Nebraska	8	0	8
Nevada	3	0	3
New Hampshire	4	4	0
New Jersey	10	10	0
New York	36	36	0
North Carolina	11	0	11
North Dakota	3	3	0
Ohio	23	23	0
Oregon	4	4	0
Pennsylvania	32	32	0
Rhode Island	4	4	0
South Carolina	9	0	9
South Dakota	4	0	4
Tennessee	12	0	12
Texas	15	0	15
Utah	3	0	3
Vermont	4	4	0
Virginia	12	0	12
Washington	4	0	4
West Virginia	6	6	0
Wisconsin	12	12	0
Wyoming	3	0	3
Total	447	271	176

Scenarios

1% to McKinley ....McKinley 278, Bryan 169
1% to Bryan ....McKinley 260, Bryan 187
10K to McKinley ....McKinley 345, Bryan 102
10K to Bryan ....McKinley 228, Bryan 219
1964 allocation ....McKinley 317, Bryan 194
2020 allocation ....McKinley 271, Bryan 234

1900

Basics

Incumbent ....William McKinley (R)
Prior streak ....R (1)
Prior 5.. R (3), D (2)
Population..76,212,168
States 45
Electoral votes 447
Popular votes 13,972,525

Field

Candidate	PI	Age	State	Position	N	W	CS
William McKinley (R)	8.9	57.76	Ohio	President	X	X	82.89
William Jennings Bryan (D)	5.6	40.62	Nebr.	Former nominee	X	—	69.53

Democratic nomination

Candidate	ConFB	FB%	ConLB	LB%	PriW	PriV	PriV%
Bryan	936	100.00%	—	—	—	—	—

Republican nomination

Candidate	ConFB	FB%	ConLB	LB%	PriW	PriV	PriV%
McKinley	926	100.00%	—	—	—	—	—

General election

Candidate	EV	EV%	SC	PV	PV%
McKinley	292	65.32%	28	7,219,193	51.67%
Bryan	155	34.68%	17	6,357,698	45.50%

State popular votes

State	Total PV	McKinley	Bryan	Other
Alabama	160,477	55,634	96,368	8,475
Arkansas	127,966	44,800	81,242	1,924
California	302,399	164,755	124,985	12,659
Colorado	220,895	92,701	122,705	5,489
Connecticut	180,195	102,572	74,014	3,609
Delaware	41,989	22,535	18,852	602
Florida	39,777	7,463	28,273	4,041
Georgia	121,410	34,260	81,180	5,970
Idaho	56,760	27,198	28,260	1,302
Illinois	1,131,898	597,985	503,061	30,852
Indiana	664,094	336,063	309,584	18,447
Iowa	530,345	307,799	209,261	13,285
Kansas	353,766	185,955	162,601	5,210
Kentucky	467,580	226,801	234,889	5,890
Louisiana	67,906	14,234	53,668	4
Maine	107,698	66,413	37,822	3,463
Maryland	264,386	136,151	122,237	5,998

State	Total PV	McKinley	Bryan	Other
Massachusetts	414,804	238,866	156,997	18,941
Michigan	543,789	316,014	211,432	16,343
Minnesota	316,311	190,461	112,901	12,949
Mississippi	59,055	5,707	51,706	1,642
Missouri	683,658	314,092	351,922	17,644
Montana	63,856	25,409	37,311	1,136
Nebraska	241,430	121,835	114,013	5,582
Nevada	10,196	3,849	6,347	—
New Hampshire	92,364	54,799	35,489	2,076
New Jersey	401,050	221,707	164,808	14,535
New York	1,548,043	822,013	678,462	47,568
North Carolina	292,518	132,997	157,733	1,788
North Dakota	57,783	35,898	20,524	1,361
Ohio	1,040,073	543,918	474,882	21,273
Oregon	84,216	46,526	33,385	4,305
Pennsylvania	1,173,210	712,665	424,232	36,313
Rhode Island	56,548	33,784	19,812	2,952
South Carolina	50,698	3,525	47,173	—
South Dakota	96,169	54,574	39,538	2,057
Tennessee	273,860	123,108	145,240	5,512
Texas	424,334	131,174	267,945	25,215
Utah	93,071	47,089	44,949	1,033
Vermont	56,212	42,569	12,849	794
Virginia	264,208	115,769	146,079	2,360
Washington	107,523	57,455	44,833	5,235
West Virginia	220,796	119,829	98,807	2,160
Wisconsin	442,501	265,760	159,163	17,578
Wyoming	24,708	14,482	10,164	62
Total	13,972,525	7,219,193	6,357,698	395,634

State electoral votes

State	Total EV	McKinley	Bryan
Alabama	11	0	11
Arkansas	8	0	8
California	9	9	0
Colorado	4	0	4
Connecticut	6	6	0
Delaware	3	3	0
Florida	4	0	4
Georgia	13	0	13
Idaho	3	0	3
Illinois	24	24	0
Indiana	15	15	0
Iowa	13	13	0
Kansas	10	10	0
Kentucky	13	0	13
Louisiana	8	0	8
Maine	6	6	0
Maryland	8	8	0
Massachusetts	15	15	0
Michigan	14	14	0
Minnesota	9	9	0

State	Total EV	McKinley	Bryan
Mississippi	9	0	9
Missouri	17	0	17
Montana	3	0	3
Nebraska	8	8	0
Nevada	3	0	3
New Hampshire	4	4	0
New Jersey	10	10	0
New York	36	36	0
North Carolina	11	0	11
North Dakota	3	3	0
Ohio	23	23	0
Oregon	4	4	0
Pennsylvania	32	32	0
Rhode Island	4	4	0
South Carolina	9	0	9
South Dakota	4	4	0
Tennessee	12	0	12
Texas	15	0	15
Utah	3	3	0
Vermont	4	4	0
Virginia	12	0	12
Washington	4	4	0
West Virginia	6	6	0
Wisconsin	12	12	0
Wyoming	3	3	0
Total	447	292	155

Scenarios

1% to McKinley...McKinley 308, Bryan 139
1% to Bryan ....McKinley 292, Bryan 155
10K to McKinley ....McKinley 314, Bryan 133
10K to Bryan ....McKinley 244, Bryan 203
1964 allocation..McKinley 345, Bryan 166
2020 allocation..McKinley 305, Bryan 200

1904

Basics

Incumbent .... Theodore Roosevelt (R)
Prior streak .... R (2)
Prior 5 .... R (3), D (2)
Population 82,166,000
States 45
Electoral votes 476
Popular votes 13,519,039

Field

Candidate	PI	Age	State	Position	N	W	CS
Theodore Roosevelt (R)	8.8	46.01	N.Y.	President	X	X	85.72
Alton Parker (D)	4.9	52.47	N.Y.	State judge	X	—	66.33
William Randolph Hearst (D)	5.5	41.51	N.Y.	Journalist	—	—	24.45
Eugene Debs (SOC)	2.9	48.99	Ind.	Movement leader	—	—	19.53
Francis Cockrell (D)	7.0	70.08	Mo.	Senator	—	—	13.35

Democratic nomination

Candidate	ConFB	FB%	ConLB	LB%	PriW	PriV	PriV%
Parker	679	67.90%	—	—	—	—	—
Hearst	181	18.10%	—	—	—	—	—
Cockrell	42	4.20%	—	—	—	—	—

Republican nomination

Candidate	ConFB	FB%	ConLB	LB%	PriW	PriV	PriV%
Roosevelt	994	100.00%	—	—	—	—	—

General election

Candidate	EV	EV%	SC	PV	PV%
Roosevelt	336	70.59%	32	7,625,599	56.41%
Parker	140	29.41%	13	5,083,501	37.60%
Debs	0	0.00%	0	402,490	2.98%

State popular votes

State	Total PV	Roosevelt	Parker	Debs	Other
Alabama	108,785	22,472	79,797	853	5,663
Arkansas	116,328	46,760	64,434	1,816	3,318
California	331,768	205,226	89,294	29,535	7,713
Colorado	243,667	134,661	100,105	4,304	4,597
Connecticut	191,136	111,089	72,909	4,543	2,595
Delaware	43,856	23,705	19,347	146	658
Florida	39,302	8,314	27,046	2,337	1,605
Georgia	130,986	24,004	83,466	196	23,320
Idaho	72,577	47,783	18,480	4,949	1,365
Illinois	1,076,495	632,645	327,606	69,225	47,019
Indiana	682,206	368,289	274,356	12,023	27,538

State	Total PV	Roosevelt	Parker	Debs	Other
Iowa	485,703	307,907	149,141	14,847	13,808
Kansas	329,047	213,455	86,164	15,869	13,559
Kentucky	435,946	205,457	217,170	3,599	9,720
Louisiana	53,908	5,205	47,708	995	—
Maine	96,036	64,438	27,648	2,103	1,847
Maryland	224,229	109,497	109,446	2,247	3,039
Massachusetts	445,100	257,813	165,746	13,604	7,937
Michigan	520,443	361,863	134,163	8,942	15,475
Minnesota	292,860	216,651	55,187	11,692	9,330
Mississippi	58,721	3,280	53,480	462	1,499
Missouri	643,861	321,449	296,312	13,009	13,091
Montana	63,568	33,994	21,816	5,675	2,083
Nebraska	225,732	138,558	52,921	7,412	26,841
Nevada	12,115	6,864	3,982	925	344
New Hampshire	90,151	54,157	34,071	1,090	833
New Jersey	432,547	245,164	164,566	9,587	13,230
New York	1,617,765	859,533	683,981	36,883	37,368
North Carolina	207,818	82,442	124,091	124	1,161
North Dakota	70,179	52,595	14,273	2,009	1,302
Ohio	1,004,395	600,095	344,674	36,260	23,366
Oregon	89,656	60,309	17,327	7,479	4,541
Pennsylvania	1,236,738	840,949	337,998	21,863	35,928
Rhode Island	68,656	41,605	24,839	956	1,256
South Carolina	55,890	2,570	53,320	—	—
South Dakota	101,395	72,083	21,969	3,138	4,205
Tennessee	242,750	105,363	131,653	1,354	4,380
Texas	233,609	51,307	167,088	2,788	12,426
Utah	101,626	62,446	33,413	5,767	—
Vermont	51,888	40,459	9,777	859	793
Virginia	130,410	48,180	80,649	202	1,379
Washington	145,151	101,540	28,098	10,023	5,490
West Virginia	239,986	132,620	100,855	1,573	4,938
Wisconsin	443,440	280,314	124,205	28,240	10,681
Wyoming	30,614	20,489	8,930	987	208
Total	13,519,039	7,625,599	5,083,501	402,490	407,449

State electoral votes

State	Total EV	Roosevelt	Parker
Alabama	11	0	11
Arkansas	9	0	9
California	10	10	0
Colorado	5	5	0
Connecticut	7	7	0
Delaware	3	3	0
Florida	5	0	5
Georgia	13	0	13
Idaho	3	3	0
Illinois	27	27	0
Indiana	15	15	0
Iowa	13	13	0
Kansas	10	10	0
Kentucky	13	0	13

State	Total EV	Roosevelt	Parker
Louisiana	9	0	9
Maine	6	6	0
Maryland	8	1	7
Massachusetts	16	16	0
Michigan	14	14	0
Minnesota	11	11	0
Mississippi	10	0	10
Missouri	18	18	0
Montana	3	3	0
Nebraska	8	8	0
Nevada	3	3	0
New Hampshire	4	4	0
New Jersey	12	12	0
New York	39	39	0
North Carolina	12	0	12
North Dakota	4	4	0
Ohio	23	23	0
Oregon	4	4	0
Pennsylvania	34	34	0
Rhode Island	4	4	0
South Carolina	9	0	9
South Dakota	4	4	0
Tennessee	12	0	12
Texas	18	0	18
Utah	3	3	0
Vermont	4	4	0
Virginia	12	0	12
Washington	5	5	0
West Virginia	7	7	0
Wisconsin	13	13	0
Wyoming	3	3	0
Total	476	336	140

Scenarios

1% to Roosevelt .... Roosevelt 342, Parker 134
1% to Parker .... Roosevelt 336, Parker 140
10K to Roosevelt .... Roosevelt 370, Parker 106
10K to Parker .... Roosevelt 319, Parker 157
1964 allocation .... Roosevelt 365, Parker 146
2020 allocation .... Roosevelt 328, Parker 177

1908

Basics

Incumbent .... Theodore Roosevelt (R)
Prior streak .... R (3)
Prior 5 .... R (4), D (1)
Population 88,710,000
States 46
Electoral votes 483
Popular votes 14,884,098

Field

Candidate	PI	Age	State	Position	N	W	CS
William Howard Taft (R)	6.0	51.13	Ohio	Cabinet member	X	X	83.31
William Jennings Bryan (D)	5.2	48.62	Nebr.	Former nominee	X	—	68.65
Eugene Debs (SOC)	2.9	52.99	Ind.	Movement leader	—	—	19.04
Philander Knox (R)	8.2	55.49	Pa.	Senator	—	—	15.51
Charles Evans Hughes (R)	7.4	46.56	N.Y.	Governor	—	—	15.43
Joseph Cannon (R)	5.3	72.49	Ill.	Representative	—	—	14.71
George Gray (D)	6.3	68.49	Del.	Former senator	—	—	14.71
John Johnson (D)	6.8	47.26	Minn.	Governor	—	—	13.67
Charles Fairbanks (R)	8.8	56.48	Ind.	Vice president	—	—	13.27

Democratic nomination

Candidate	ConFB	FB%	ConLB	LB%	PriW	PriV	PriV%
Bryan	889	88.67%	—	—	—	—	—
Gray	60	5.94%	—	—	—	—	—
Johnson	46	4.59%	—	—	—	—	—

Republican nomination

Candidate	ConFB	FB%	ConLB	LB%	PriW	PriV	PriV%
Taft	702	71.63%	—	—	—	—	—
Knox	68	6.94%	—	—	—	—	—
Hughes	67	6.84%	—	—	—	—	—
Cannon	58	5.92%	—	—	—	—	—
Fairbanks	40	4.08%	—	—	—	—	—

General election

Candidate	EV	EV%	SC	PV	PV%
Taft	321	66.46%	29	7,676,598	51.58%
Bryan	162	33.54%	17	6,406,874	43.05%
Debs	0	0.00%	0	420,436	2.83%

State popular votes

State	Total PV	Taft	Bryan	Debs	Other
Alabama	105,152	25,561	74,391	1,450	3,750
Arkansas	151,845	56,684	87,020	5,842	2,299
California	386,625	214,398	127,492	28,659	16,076

State	Total PV	Taft	Bryan	Debs	Other
Colorado	263,858	123,693	126,644	7,960	5,561
Connecticut	189,903	112,815	68,255	5,113	3,720
Delaware	48,007	25,014	22,055	239	699
Florida	49,360	10,654	31,104	3,747	3,855
Georgia	132,794	41,692	72,413	584	18,105
Idaho	97,293	52,621	36,162	6,400	2,110
Illinois	1,155,254	629,932	450,810	34,711	39,801
Indiana	721,117	348,993	338,262	13,476	20,386
Iowa	494,770	275,210	200,771	8,287	10,502
Kansas	376,043	197,316	161,209	12,420	5,098
Kentucky	490,719	235,711	244,092	4,093	6,823
Louisiana	75,117	8,958	63,568	2,514	77
Maine	106,335	66,987	35,403	1,758	2,187
Maryland	238,531	116,513	115,908	2,323	3,787
Massachusetts	456,905	265,966	155,533	10,778	24,628
Michigan	538,124	333,313	174,619	11,527	18,665
Minnesota	331,328	195,846	109,411	14,528	11,543
Mississippi	66,904	4,363	60,287	978	1,276
Missouri	715,841	347,203	346,574	15,431	6,633
Montana	69,233	32,471	29,511	5,920	1,331
Nebraska	266,799	126,997	131,099	3,524	5,179
Nevada	24,526	10,775	11,212	2,103	436
New Hampshire	89,595	53,144	33,655	1,299	1,497
New Jersey	467,111	265,298	182,522	10,249	9,042
New York	1,638,350	870,070	667,468	38,451	62,361
North Carolina	252,554	114,887	136,928	372	367
North Dakota	94,524	57,680	32,884	2,421	1,539
Ohio	1,121,552	572,312	502,721	33,795	12,724
Oklahoma	254,260	110,473	122,362	21,425	—
Oregon	110,539	62,454	37,792	7,322	2,971
Pennsylvania	1,267,450	745,779	448,782	33,914	38,975
Rhode Island	72,317	43,942	24,706	1,365	2,304
South Carolina	66,379	3,945	62,288	100	46
South Dakota	114,775	67,536	40,266	2,846	4,127
Tennessee	257,180	117,977	135,608	1,870	1,725
Texas	292,913	65,605	216,662	7,779	2,867
Utah	108,757	61,165	42,610	4,890	92
Vermont	52,680	39,552	11,496	—	1,632
Virginia	137,065	52,572	82,946	255	1,292
Washington	183,570	106,062	58,383	14,177	4,948
West Virginia	258,098	137,869	111,410	3,679	5,140
Wisconsin	454,438	247,744	166,662	28,147	11,885
Wyoming	37,608	20,846	14,918	1,715	129
Total	14,884,098	7,676,598	6,406,874	420,436	380,190

State electoral votes

State	Total EV	Taft	Bryan
Alabama	11	0	11
Arkansas	9	0	9
California	10	10	0
Colorado	5	0	5
Connecticut	7	7	0

State	Total EV	Taft	Bryan
Delaware	3	3	0
Florida	5	0	5
Georgia	13	0	13
Idaho	3	3	0
Illinois	27	27	0
Indiana	15	15	0
Iowa	13	13	0
Kansas	10	10	0
Kentucky	13	0	13
Louisiana	9	0	9
Maine	6	6	0
Maryland	8	2	6
Massachusetts	16	16	0
Michigan	14	14	0
Minnesota	11	11	0
Mississippi	10	0	10
Missouri	18	18	0
Montana	3	3	0
Nebraska	8	0	8
Nevada	3	0	3
New Hampshire	4	4	0
New Jersey	12	12	0
New York	39	39	0
North Carolina	12	0	12
North Dakota	4	4	0
Ohio	23	23	0
Oklahoma	7	0	7
Oregon	4	4	0
Pennsylvania	34	34	0
Rhode Island	4	4	0
South Carolina	9	0	9
South Dakota	4	4	0
Tennessee	12	0	12
Texas	18	0	18
Utah	3	3	0
Vermont	4	4	0
Virginia	12	0	12
Washington	5	5	0
West Virginia	7	7	0
Wisconsin	13	13	0
Wyoming	3	3	0
Total	483	321	162

Scenarios

1% to Taft...Taft 354, Bryan 129
1% to Bryan..Taft 288, Bryan 195
10K to Taft...Taft 375, Bryan 108
10K to Bryan..Taft 263, Bryan 220
1964 allocation..Taft 353, Bryan 167
2020 allocation..Taft 310, Bryan 203

1912

Basics

Incumbent .... William Howard Taft (R)
Prior streak .... R (4)
Prior 5 .... R (4), D (1)
Population 95,335,000
States 48
Electoral votes 531
Popular votes 15,043,030

Field

Candidate	PI	Age	State	Position	N	W	CS
Woodrow Wilson (D)	6.6	55.84	N.J.	Governor	X	X	86.26
Theodore Roosevelt (R/P)	10.0	54.01	N.Y.	Former president	—	—	66.37
William Howard Taft (R)	8.2	55.13	Ohio	President	X	—	55.09
Champ Clark (D)	3.7	62.65	Mo.	Representative	—	—	42.45
Eugene Debs (SOC)	1.5	56.99	Ind.	Movement leader	—	—	29.16
Judson Harmon (D)	5.6	66.74	Ohio	Governor	—	—	20.47
Oscar Underwood (D)	3.0	50.49	Ala.	Representative	—	—	16.41
Robert La Follette (R)	6.3	57.38	Wis.	Senator	—	—	15.18

Democratic nomination

Candidate	ConFB	FB%	ConLB[46]	LB%	PriW	PriV	PriV%
Wilson	324	29.62%	990	90.49%	5	435,169	44.64%
Clark	441	40.27%	84	7.68%	5	405,537	41.60%
Harmon	148	13.53%	12	1.10%	1	116,294	11.93%
Underwood	118	10.74%	0	0.00%	0	0	0.00%

Republican nomination

Candidate	ConFB	FB%	ConLB	LB%	PriW	PriV	PriV%
Taft	556	51.58%	—	—	1	766,326	33.89%
Roosevelt	107	9.93%	—	—	9	1,164,765	51.51%
La Follette	41	3.80%	—	—	2	327,357	14.48%

NOTE: A total of 348 delegates, most of them Roosevelt supporters, abstained.

General election

Candidate	EV	EV%	SC	PV	PV%
Wilson	435	81.92%	40	6,294,327	41.84%
Roosevelt	88	16.57%	6	4,120,207	27.39%
Taft	8	1.51%	2	3,486,343	23.18%
Debs	0	0.00%	0	900,370	5.99%

State popular votes

State	Total PV	Wilson	Roosevelt	Taft	Debs	Other
Alabama	117,959	82,438	22,680	9,807	3,029	5
Arizona	23,687	10,324	6,949	2,986	3,163	265
Arkansas	125,104	68,814	21,644	25,585	8,153	908

State	Total PV	Wilson	Roosevelt	Taft	Debs	Other
California	677,877	283,436	283,610	3,847	79,201	27,783
Colorado	265,954	113,912	71,752	58,386	16,366	5,538
Connecticut	190,404	74,561	34,129	68,324	10,056	3,334
Delaware	48,690	22,631	8,886	15,997	556	620
Florida	51,911	36,417	4,555	4,279	4,806	1,854
Georgia	121,470	93,087	21,985	5,191	1,058	149
Idaho	105,754	33,921	25,527	32,810	11,960	1,536
Illinois	1,146,173	405,048	386,478	253,593	81,278	19,776
Indiana	654,474	281,890	162,007	151,267	36,931	22,379
Iowa	492,353	185,322	161,819	119,805	16,967	8,440
Kansas	365,560	143,663	120,210	74,845	26,779	63
Kentucky	453,707	219,585	102,766	115,520	11,647	4,189
Louisiana	79,248	60,871	9,283	3,833	5,261	—
Maine	129,641	51,113	48,495	26,545	2,541	947
Maryland	231,981	112,674	57,789	54,956	3,996	2,566
Massachusetts	488,056	173,408	142,228	155,948	12,616	3,856
Michigan	547,971	150,201	213,243	151,434	23,060	10,033
Minnesota	334,219	106,426	125,856	64,334	27,505	10,098
Mississippi	64,483	57,324	3,549	1,560	2,050	—
Missouri	698,566	330,746	124,375	207,821	28,466	7,158
Montana	80,256	28,129	22,709	18,575	10,811	32
Nebraska	249,483	109,008	72,681	54,226	10,185	3,383
Nevada	20,115	7,986	5,620	3,196	3,313	—
New Hampshire	87,961	34,724	17,794	32,927	1,981	535
New Jersey	433,663	178,638	145,679	89,066	15,948	4,332
New Mexico	48,807	20,437	8,347	17,164	2,859	—
New York	1,588,315	655,573	390,093	455,487	63,434	23,728
North Carolina	243,776	144,407	69,135	29,129	987	118
North Dakota	86,474	29,549	25,726	22,990	6,966	1,243
Ohio	1,037,114	424,834	229,807	278,168	90,164	14,141
Oklahoma	253,694	119,143	—	90,726	41,630	2,195
Oregon	137,040	47,064	37,600	34,673	13,343	4,360
Pennsylvania	1,217,736	395,637	444,894	273,360	83,614	20,231
Rhode Island	77,894	30,412	16,878	27,703	2,049	852
South Carolina	50,403	48,355	1,293	536	164	55
South Dakota	116,327	48,942	58,811	—	4,664	3,910
Tennessee	251,933	133,021	54,041	60,475	3,564	832
Texas	300,961	218,921	26,715	28,310	24,884	2,131
Utah	112,272	36,576	24,174	42,013	8,999	510
Vermont	62,804	15,350	22,129	23,303	928	1,094
Virginia	136,975	90,332	21,776	23,288	820	759
Washington	322,799	86,840	113,698	70,445	40,134	11,682
West Virginia	268,728	113,097	79,112	56,754	15,248	4,517
Wisconsin	399,975	164,230	62,448	130,596	33,476	9,225
Wyoming	42,283	15,310	9,232	14,560	2,760	421
Total	15,043,030	6,294,327	4,120,207	3,486,343	900,370	241,783

State electoral votes

State	Total EV	Wilson	Roosevelt	Taft
Alabama	12	12	0	0
Arizona	3	3	0	0
Arkansas	9	9	0	0

State	Total EV	Wilson	Roosevelt	Taft
California	13	2	11	0
Colorado	6	6	0	0
Connecticut	7	7	0	0
Delaware	3	3	0	0
Florida	6	6	0	0
Georgia	14	14	0	0
Idaho	4	4	0	0
Illinois	29	29	0	0
Indiana	15	15	0	0
Iowa	13	13	0	0
Kansas	10	10	0	0
Kentucky	13	13	0	0
Louisiana	10	10	0	0
Maine	6	6	0	0
Maryland	8	8	0	0
Massachusetts	18	18	0	0
Michigan	15	0	15	0
Minnesota	12	0	12	0
Mississippi	10	10	0	0
Missouri	18	18	0	0
Montana	4	4	0	0
Nebraska	8	8	0	0
Nevada	3	3	0	0
New Hampshire	4	4	0	0
New Jersey	14	14	0	0
New Mexico	3	3	0	0
New York	45	45	0	0
North Carolina	12	12	0	0
North Dakota	5	5	0	0
Ohio	24	24	0	0
Oklahoma	10	10	0	0
Oregon	5	5	0	0
Pennsylvania	38	0	38	0
Rhode Island	5	5	0	0
South Carolina	9	9	0	0
South Dakota	5	0	5	0
Tennessee	12	12	0	0
Texas	20	20	0	0
Utah	4	0	0	4
Vermont	4	0	0	4
Virginia	12	12	0	0
Washington	7	0	7	0
West Virginia	8	8	0	0
Wisconsin	13	13	0	0
Wyoming	3	3	0	0
Total	531	435	88	8

Scenarios

1% to Wilson..Wilson 446, Roosevelt 77, Taft 8
1% to Roosevelt ....Wilson 404, Roosevelt 119, Taft 8
10K to Wilson ....Wilson 471, Roosevelt 60, Taft 0
10K to Roosevelt..Wilson 349, Roosevelt 162, Taft 20
1964 allocation..Wilson 414, Roosevelt 107, Taft 7
2020 allocation ....Wilson 411, Roosevelt 108, Taft 9

1916

Basics

Incumbent ....Woodrow Wilson (D)
Prior streak ....D (1)
Prior 5.. R (4), D (1)
Population..101,961,000
States 48
Electoral votes 531
Popular votes 18,535,445

Field

Candidate	PI	Age	State	Position	N	W	CS
Woodrow Wilson (D)	8.6	59.84	N.J.	President	X	X	78.07
Charles Evans Hughes (R)	8.0	54.56	N.Y.	Supreme Court justice	X	—	73.55
Allan Benson (SOC)	2.7	44.99	N.Y.	Journalist	—	—	20.19
Albert Cummins (R)	5.3	66.71	Iowa	Senator	—	—	17.15
John Weeks (R)	6.5	56.56	Mass.	Senator	—	—	16.35
Charles Fairbanks (R)	4.7	64.48	Ind.	Former vice president	—	—	16.32
Elihu Root (R)	6.0	71.71	N.Y.	Former senator	—	—	16.23
Theodore Burton (R)	5.3	64.87	Ohio	Former senator	—	—	16.00
Lawrence Sherman (R)	6.1	57.98	Ill.	Senator	—	—	15.63
Theodore Roosevelt (R)	9.6	58.01	N.Y.	Former president	—	—	14.78
Henry Ford (R)	3.8	53.26	Mich.	Business executive	—	—	13.29
Robert La Follette (R)	5.2	61.38	Wis.	Senator	—	—	12.89

Democratic nomination

Candidate	ConFB	FB%	ConLB	LB%	PriW	PriV	PriV%
Wilson	1,092	100.00%	—	—	20	1,173,220	98.78%

Republican nomination

Candidate	ConFB	FB%	ConLB[3]	LB%	PriW	PriV	PriV%
Hughes	254	25.68%	950	96.20%	2	80,737	4.20%
Roosevelt	65	6.59%	19	1.87%	1	80,019	4.16%
Weeks	105	10.64%	3	0.30%	0	0	0.00%
La Follette	25	2.53%	3	0.30%	2	133,426	6.94%
Root	103	10.44%	0	0.00%	0	0	0.00%
Cummins	85	8.61%	0	0.00%	5	191,950	9.98%
Burton	78	7.85%	0	0.00%	2	122,165	6.35%
Fairbanks	75	7.55%	0	0.00%	1	176,078	9.16%
Sherman	66	6.69%	0	0.00%	1	155,945	8.11%
Ford	32	3.24%	0	0.00%	1	131,889	6.86%

General election

Candidate	EV	EV%	SC	PV	PV%
Wilson	277	52.17%	30	9,126,063	49.24%
Hughes	254	47.83%	18	8,547,030	46.11%
Benson	0	0.00%	0	590,070	3.18%

State popular votes

State	Total PV	Wilson	Hughes	Benson	Other
Alabama	131,142	99,409	28,809	1,925	999
Arizona	58,019	33,170	20,522	3,174	1,153
Arkansas	168,348	112,186	47,148	6,999	2,015
California	999,250	465,936	462,516	42,898	27,900
Colorado	294,375	178,816	102,308	10,049	3,202
Connecticut	213,874	99,786	106,514	5,179	2,395
Delaware	51,810	24,753	26,011	480	566
Florida	80,734	55,984	14,611	5,353	4,786
Georgia	158,690	125,845	11,225	967	20,653
Idaho	134,615	70,054	55,368	8,066	1,127
Illinois	2,192,707	950,229	1,152,549	61,394	28,535
Indiana	718,853	334,063	341,005	21,860	21,925
Iowa	518,738	221,699	280,439	10,976	5,624
Kansas	629,813	314,588	277,658	24,685	12,882
Kentucky	520,078	269,990	241,854	4,734	3,500
Louisiana	92,974	79,875	6,466	284	6,349
Maine	136,314	64,033	69,508	2,177	596
Maryland	262,039	138,359	117,347	2,674	3,659
Massachusetts	531,822	247,885	268,784	11,058	4,095
Michigan	646,873	283,993	337,952	16,012	8,916
Minnesota	387,367	179,155	179,544	20,117	8,551
Mississippi	86,679	80,422	4,253	1,484	520
Missouri	786,773	398,032	369,339	14,612	4,790
Montana	178,009	101,104	66,933	9,634	338
Nebraska	287,315	158,827	117,771	7,141	3,576
Nevada	33,314	17,776	12,127	3,065	346
New Hampshire	89,127	43,781	43,725	1,318	303
New Jersey	494,442	211,018	268,982	10,405	4,037
New Mexico	66,879	33,693	31,097	1,977	112
New York	1,706,305	759,426	879,238	45,944	21,697
North Carolina	289,837	168,383	120,890	509	55
North Dakota	115,390	55,206	53,471	5,716	997
Ohio	1,165,091	604,161	514,753	38,092	8,085
Oklahoma	292,327	148,123	97,233	45,091	1,880
Oregon	261,650	120,087	126,813	9,711	5,039
Pennsylvania	1,297,189	521,784	703,823	42,638	28,944
Rhode Island	87,816	40,394	44,858	1,914	650
South Carolina	63,950	61,845	1,550	135	420
South Dakota	128,942	59,191	64,217	3,760	1,774
Tennessee	272,190	153,280	116,223	2,542	145
Texas	372,467	286,514	64,999	18,969	1,985
Utah	143,145	84,145	54,137	4,460	403
Vermont	64,475	22,708	40,250	798	719
Virginia	153,993	102,825	49,358	1,060	750
Washington	380,994	183,388	167,208	22,800	7,598
West Virginia	289,671	140,403	143,124	6,144	—
Wisconsin	447,134	191,363	220,822	27,631	7,318
Wyoming	51,906	28,376	21,698	1,459	373
Total	18,535,445	9,126,063	8,547,030	590,070	272,282

State electoral votes

State	Total EV	Wilson	Hughes
Alabama	12	12	0
Arizona	3	3	0
Arkansas	9	9	0
California	13	13	0
Colorado	6	6	0
Connecticut	7	0	7
Delaware	3	0	3
Florida	6	6	0
Georgia	14	14	0
Idaho	4	4	0
Illinois	29	0	29
Indiana	15	0	15
Iowa	13	0	13
Kansas	10	10	0
Kentucky	13	13	0
Louisiana	10	10	0
Maine	6	0	6
Maryland	8	8	0
Massachusetts	18	0	18
Michigan	15	0	15
Minnesota	12	0	12
Mississippi	10	10	0
Missouri	18	18	0
Montana	4	4	0
Nebraska	8	8	0
Nevada	3	3	0
New Hampshire	4	4	0
New Jersey	14	0	14
New Mexico	3	3	0
New York	45	0	45
North Carolina	12	12	0
North Dakota	5	5	0
Ohio	24	24	0
Oklahoma	10	10	0
Oregon	5	0	5
Pennsylvania	38	0	38
Rhode Island	5	0	5
South Carolina	9	9	0
South Dakota	5	0	5
Tennessee	12	12	0
Texas	20	20	0
Utah	4	4	0
Vermont	4	0	4
Virginia	12	12	0
Washington	7	7	0
West Virginia	8	1	7
Wisconsin	13	0	13
Wyoming	3	3	0
Total	531	277	254

Scenarios

1% to Wilson..Wilson 311, Hughes 220
1% to Hughes ....Hughes 276, Wilson 255
10K to Wilson ....Wilson 346, Hughes 185
10K to Hughes ....Hughes 299, Wilson 232
1964 allocation...Wilson 296, Hughes 232
2020 allocation...Wilson 346, Hughes 182

1920

Basics

Incumbent ....Woodrow Wilson (D)
Prior streak ....D (2)
Prior 5 ....R (3), D (2)
Population 106,021,537
States 48
Electoral votes 531
Popular votes 26,768,457

Field

Candidate	PI	Age	State	Position	N	W	CS
Warren Harding (R)	6.0	55.00	Ohio	Senator	X	X	88.37
James Cox (D)	5.9	50.59	Ohio	Governor	X	—	64.01
Leonard Wood (R)	4.3	60.06	N.H.	General	—	—	31.95
William Gibbs McAdoo (D)	6.3	57.00	N.Y.	Former Cabinet member	—	—	27.41
Mitchell Palmer (D)	4.9	48.49	Pa.	Cabinet member	—	—	27.09
Frank Lowden (R)	6.3	59.77	Ill.	Governor	—	—	25.31
Hiram Johnson (R)	5.8	54.16	Calif.	Senator	—	—	24.20
Eugene Debs (SOC)	0.1	64.99	Ind.	Movement leader	—	—	20.94
Alfred Smith (D)	6.5	46.84	N.Y.	Governor	—	—	15.99
William Sproul (R)	6.4	50.13	Pa.	Governor	—	—	15.09
Nicholas Murray Butler (R)	5.9	58.58	N.Y.	College president	—	—	14.25
Edward Edwards (D)	6.6	56.92	N.J.	Governor	—	—	13.28
John Davis (D)	3.7	47.55	W.Va.	Ambassador	—	—	12.87
Herbert Hoover (R)	2.6	46.23	Calif.	Business executive	—	—	12.56

Democratic nomination

Candidate	ConFB	FB%	ConLB[44]	LB%	PriW	PriV	PriV%
Cox	134	12.25%	700	63.94%	1	86,194	15.08%
McAdoo	266	24.31%	270	24.68%	3	74,987	13.12%
Davis	32	2.93%	52	4.75%	0	0	0.00%
Palmer	254	23.22%	1	0.09%	1	91,543	16.01%
Smith	109	9.96%	0	0.00%	0	0	0.00%
Edwards	42	3.84%	0	0.00%	2	28,470	4.98%

Republican nomination

Candidate	ConFB	FB%	ConLB[10]	LB%	PriW	PriV	PriV%
Harding	66	6.66%	645	65.52%	1	144,762	4.54%
Wood	288	29.22%	182	18.45%	8	710,863	22.31%
Johnson	134	13.57%	81	8.21%	7	965,651	30.31%
Lowden	212	21.49%	28	2.85%	1	389,127	12.21%
Hoover	6	0.56%	11	1.07%	0	303,212	9.52%
Butler	70	7.06%	2	0.20%	0	0	0.00%
Sproul	84	8.54%	0	0.00%	0	0	0.00%

General election

Candidate	EV	EV%	SC	PV	PV%
Harding	404	76.08%	37	16,151,916	60.34%
Cox	127	23.92%	11	9,134,074	34.12%
Debs	0	0.00%	0	915,511	3.42%

State popular votes

State	Total PV	Harding	Cox	Debs	Other
Alabama	233,951	74,719	156,064	2,402	766
Arizona	66,803	37,016	29,546	222	19
Arkansas	183,637	71,117	107,409	5,111	—
California	943,463	624,992	229,191	64,076	25,204
Colorado	292,053	173,248	104,936	8,046	5,823
Connecticut	365,518	229,238	120,721	10,350	5,209
Delaware	94,875	52,858	39,911	988	1,118
Florida	145,684	44,853	90,515	5,189	5,127
Georgia	149,558	42,981	106,112	465	—
Idaho	138,359	91,351	46,930	38	40
Illinois	2,094,714	1,420,480	534,395	74,747	65,092
Indiana	1,262,974	696,370	511,364	24,713	30,527
Iowa	894,959	634,674	227,804	16,981	15,500
Kansas	570,243	369,268	185,464	15,511	—
Kentucky	918,636	452,480	456,497	6,409	3,250
Louisiana	126,397	38,539	87,519	—	339
Maine	197,840	136,355	58,961	2,214	310
Maryland	428,443	236,117	180,626	8,876	2,824
Massachusetts	993,718	681,153	276,691	32,267	3,607
Michigan	1,048,411	762,865	233,450	28,947	23,149
Minnesota	735,838	519,421	142,994	56,106	17,317
Mississippi	82,351	11,576	69,136	1,639	—
Missouri	1,332,140	727,252	574,699	20,342	9,847
Montana	179,006	109,430	57,372	—	12,204
Nebraska	382,743	247,498	119,608	9,600	6,037
Nevada	27,194	15,479	9,851	1,864	—
New Hampshire	159,092	95,196	62,662	1,234	—
New Jersey	910,251	615,333	258,761	27,385	8,772
New Mexico	105,412	57,634	46,668	2	1,108
New York	2,898,513	1,871,167	781,238	203,201	42,907
North Carolina	538,649	232,819	305,367	446	17
North Dakota	205,786	160,082	37,422	8,282	—
Ohio	2,021,653	1,182,022	780,037	57,147	2,447
Oklahoma	485,678	243,840	216,122	25,716	—
Oregon	238,522	143,592	80,019	9,801	5,110
Pennsylvania	1,851,248	1,218,215	503,202	70,021	59,810
Rhode Island	167,981	107,463	55,062	4,351	1,105
South Carolina	66,808	2,610	64,170	28	—
South Dakota	182,237	110,692	35,938	—	35,607
Tennessee	428,036	219,229	206,558	2,249	—
Texas	486,109	114,658	287,920	8,124	75,407
Utah	145,828	81,555	56,639	3,159	4,475
Vermont	89,961	68,212	20,919	—	830
Virginia	231,000	87,456	141,670	808	1,066

State	Total PV	Harding	Cox	Debs	Other
Washington	398,715	223,137	84,298	8,913	82,367
West Virginia	509,936	282,007	220,785	5,618	1,526
Wisconsin	701,281	498,576	113,422	80,635	8,648
Wyoming	56,253	35,091	17,429	1,288	2,445
Total	26,768,457	16,151,916	9,134,074	915,511	566,956

State electoral votes

State	Total EV	Harding	Cox
Alabama	12	0	12
Arizona	3	3	0
Arkansas	9	0	9
California	13	13	0
Colorado	6	6	0
Connecticut	7	7	0
Delaware	3	3	0
Florida	6	0	6
Georgia	14	0	14
Idaho	4	4	0
Illinois	29	29	0
Indiana	15	15	0
Iowa	13	13	0
Kansas	10	10	0
Kentucky	13	0	13
Louisiana	10	0	10
Maine	6	6	0
Maryland	8	8	0
Massachusetts	18	18	0
Michigan	15	15	0
Minnesota	12	12	0
Mississippi	10	0	10
Missouri	18	18	0
Montana	4	4	0
Nebraska	8	8	0
Nevada	3	3	0
New Hampshire	4	4	0
New Jersey	14	14	0
New Mexico	3	3	0
New York	45	45	0
North Carolina	12	0	12
North Dakota	5	5	0
Ohio	24	24	0
Oklahoma	10	10	0
Oregon	5	5	0
Pennsylvania	38	38	0
Rhode Island	5	5	0
South Carolina	9	0	9
South Dakota	5	5	0
Tennessee	12	12	0
Texas	20	0	20
Utah	4	4	0
Vermont	4	4	0
Virginia	12	0	12

State	Total EV	Harding	Cox
Washington	7	7	0
West Virginia	8	8	0
Wisconsin	13	13	0
Wyoming	3	3	0
Total	531	404	127

Scenarios

1% to Harding...Harding 417, Cox 114
1% to Cox ....Harding 404, Cox 127
10K to Harding ....Harding 417, Cox 114
10K to Cox..Harding 377, Cox 154
1964 allocation..Harding 402, Cox 126
2020 allocation..Harding 371, Cox 157

1924

Basics

Incumbent ....Calvin Coolidge (R)
Prior streak ....R (1)
Prior 5 ....R (3), D (2)
Population 114,109,000
States 48
Electoral votes 531
Popular votes 29,099,121

Field

Candidate	PI	Age	State	Position	N	W	CS
Calvin Coolidge (R)	9.1	52.33	Mass.	President	X	X	85.63
John Davis (D)	4.4	51.55	W.Va.	Former ambassador	X	—	63.46
Robert La Follette (R/P)	2.2	69.38	Wis.	Senator	—	—	46.37
William Gibbs McAdoo (D)	3.6	61.00	Calif.	Former Cabinet member	—	—	43.53
Alfred Smith (D)	7.0	50.84	N.Y.	Governor	—	—	23.54
Hiram Johnson (R)	5.4	58.16	Calif.	Senator	—	—	16.26
Oscar Underwood (D)	4.5	62.49	Ala.	Senator	—	—	15.57
James Cox (D)	7.5	54.59	Ohio	Former nominee	—	—	15.17
Thomas Walsh (D)	4.0	65.39	Mont.	Senator	—	—	13.17
Pat Harrison (D)	3.4	43.17	Miss.	Senator	—	—	12.40

Democratic nomination

Candidate	ConFB	FB%	ConLB[103]	LB%	PriW	PriV	PriV%
Davis	31	2.82%	844	76.87%	0	0	0.00%
Underwood	43	3.87%	103	9.34%	0	0	0.00%
Walsh	0	0.00%	58	5.28%	0	0	0.00%
McAdoo	432	39.30%	12	1.05%	9	456,733	59.79%
Smith	241	21.95%	8	0.68%	0	16,459	2.16%
Cox	59	5.37%	0	0.00%	1	74,183	9.71%
Harrison	44	3.96%	0	0.00%	0	0	0.00%

Republican nomination

Candidate	ConFB	FB%	ConLB	LB%	PriW	PriV	PriV%
Coolidge	1,065	96.03%	—	—	15	2,410,363	68.38%
La Follette	34	3.07%	—	—	1	82,492	2.34%
Johnson	10	0.90%	—	—	1	1,007,833	28.59%

General election

Candidate	EV	EV%	SC	PV	PV%
Coolidge	382	71.94%	35	15,724,310	54.04%
Davis	136	25.61%	12	8,386,532	28.82%
La Follette	13	2.45%	1	4,827,184	16.59%

State popular votes

State	Total PV	Coolidge	Davis	La Follette	Other
Alabama	166,593	45,005	112,966	8,084	538
Arizona	73,961	30,516	26,235	17,210	—
Arkansas	138,540	40,583	84,790	13,167	—
California	1,281,778	733,250	105,514	424,649	18,365
Colorado	342,260	195,171	75,238	69,945	1,906
Connecticut	400,396	246,322	110,184	42,416	1,474
Delaware	90,885	52,441	33,445	4,979	20
Florida	109,158	30,633	62,083	8,625	7,817
Georgia	166,635	30,300	123,262	12,687	386
Idaho	147,690	69,791	23,951	53,948	—
Illinois	2,470,067	1,453,321	576,975	432,027	7,744
Indiana	1,272,390	703,042	492,245	71,700	5,403
Iowa	976,770	537,458	160,382	274,448	4,482
Kansas	662,456	407,671	156,320	98,461	4
Kentucky	816,070	398,966	375,593	38,465	3,046
Louisiana	121,951	24,670	93,218	—	4,063
Maine	192,192	138,440	41,964	11,382	406
Maryland	358,630	162,414	148,072	47,157	987
Massachusetts	1,129,837	703,476	280,831	141,225	4,305
Michigan	1,160,419	874,631	152,359	122,014	11,415
Minnesota	822,146	420,759	55,913	339,192	6,282
Mississippi	112,442	8,494	100,474	3,474	—
Missouri	1,310,085	648,488	574,962	83,986	2,649
Montana	174,177	74,138	33,805	65,876	358
Nebraska	463,559	218,985	137,299	105,681	1,594
Nevada	26,921	11,243	5,909	9,769	—
New Hampshire	164,769	98,575	57,201	8,993	—
New Jersey	1,088,054	676,277	298,043	109,028	4,706
New Mexico	112,830	54,745	48,542	9,543	—
New York	3,263,939	1,820,058	950,796	474,913	18,172
North Carolina	481,608	190,754	284,190	6,651	13
North Dakota	199,081	94,931	13,858	89,922	370
Ohio	2,016,296	1,176,130	477,887	358,008	4,271
Oklahoma	527,928	225,755	255,798	41,141	5,234
Oregon	279,488	142,579	67,589	68,403	917
Pennsylvania	2,144,850	1,401,481	409,192	307,567	26,610
Rhode Island	210,115	125,286	76,606	7,628	595
South Carolina	50,755	1,123	49,008	623	1
South Dakota	203,868	101,299	27,214	75,355	—
Tennessee	301,030	130,831	159,339	10,666	194
Texas	657,054	130,794	483,381	42,879	—
Utah	156,990	77,327	47,001	32,662	—
Vermont	102,917	80,498	16,124	5,964	331
Virginia	223,603	73,328	139,717	10,369	189
Washington	421,549	220,224	42,842	150,727	7,756
West Virginia	583,662	288,635	257,232	36,723	1,072
Wisconsin	840,827	311,614	68,115	453,678	7,420
Wyoming	79,900	41,858	12,868	25,174	—
Total	29,099,121	15,724,310	8,386,532	4,827,184	161,095

State electoral votes

State	Total EV	Coolidge	Davis	La Follette
Alabama	12	0	12	0
Arizona	3	3	0	0
Arkansas	9	0	9	0
California	13	13	0	0
Colorado	6	6	0	0
Connecticut	7	7	0	0
Delaware	3	3	0	0
Florida	6	0	6	0
Georgia	14	0	14	0
Idaho	4	4	0	0
Illinois	29	29	0	0
Indiana	15	15	0	0
Iowa	13	13	0	0
Kansas	10	10	0	0
Kentucky	13	13	0	0
Louisiana	10	0	10	0
Maine	6	6	0	0
Maryland	8	8	0	0
Massachusetts	18	18	0	0
Michigan	15	15	0	0
Minnesota	12	12	0	0
Mississippi	10	0	10	0
Missouri	18	18	0	0
Montana	4	4	0	0
Nebraska	8	8	0	0
Nevada	3	3	0	0
New Hampshire	4	4	0	0
New Jersey	14	14	0	0
New Mexico	3	3	0	0
New York	45	45	0	0
North Carolina	12	0	12	0
North Dakota	5	5	0	0
Ohio	24	24	0	0
Oklahoma	10	0	10	0
Oregon	5	5	0	0
Pennsylvania	38	38	0	0
Rhode Island	5	5	0	0
South Carolina	9	0	9	0
South Dakota	5	5	0	0
Tennessee	12	0	12	0
Texas	20	0	20	0
Utah	4	4	0	0
Vermont	4	4	0	0
Virginia	12	0	12	0
Washington	7	7	0	0
West Virginia	8	8	0	0
Wisconsin	13	0	0	13
Wyoming	3	3	0	0
Total	531	382	136	13

Scenarios

1% to Coolidge...Coolidge 382, Davis 136, La Follette 13
1% to Davis..Coolidge 382, Davis 136, La Follette 13
10K to Coolidge...Coolidge 382, Davis 136, La Follette 13
10K to Davis...Coolidge 353, Davis 156, La Follette 22
1964 allocation..Coolidge 380, Davis 136, La Follette 12
2020 allocation..Coolidge 351, Davis 167, La Follette 10

1928

Basics

Incumbent ....Calvin Coolidge (R)
Prior streak ....R (2)
Prior 5 ....R (3), D (2)
Population 120,509,000
States 48
Electoral votes 531
Popular votes 36,801,510

Field

Candidate	PI	Age	State	Position	N	W	CS
Herbert Hoover (R)	4.0	54.23	Calif.	Cabinet member	X	X	90.41
Alfred Smith (D)	6.9	54.84	N.Y.	Governor	X	—	63.06
Frank Lowden (R)	5.7	67.77	Ill.	Former governor	—	—	20.32
James Reed (D)	4.8	66.98	Mo.	Senator	—	—	16.09
James Watson (R)	5.1	64.00	Ind.	Senator	—	—	13.57
Charles Curtis (R)	4.1	68.77	Kan.	Senator	—	—	13.53
Walter George (D)	4.4	50.76	Ga.	Senator	—	—	12.87
Cordell Hull (D)	3.7	57.08	Tenn.	Representative	—	—	12.75
George Norris (R)	4.3	67.31	Nebr.	Senator	—	—	12.58
Thomas Walsh (D)	3.5	69.39	Mont.	Senator	—	—	10.95

Democratic nomination

Candidate	ConFB	FB%	ConLB	LB%	PriW	PriV	PriV%
Smith	850	77.24%	—	—	9	499,452	39.51%
George	53	4.77%	—	—	0	0	0.00%
Reed	52	4.73%	—	—	1	207,367	16.40%
Hull	51	4.62%	—	—	0	0	0.00%
Walsh	0	0.00%	—	—	0	59,871	4.74%

Republican nomination

Candidate	ConFB	FB%	ConLB	LB%	PriW	PriV	PriV%
Hoover	837	76.86%	—	—	7	2,020,325	49.15%
Lowden	74	6.80%	—	—	2	1,283,535	31.23%
Curtis	64	5.88%	—	—	0	0	0.00%
Watson	45	4.13%	—	—	1	228,795	5.57%
Norris	24	2.20%	—	—	2	259,548	6.32%

General election

Candidate	EV	EV%	SC	PV	PV%
Hoover	444	83.62%	40	21,432,823	58.24%
Smith	87	16.38%	8	15,004,336	40.77%

State popular votes

State	Total PV	Hoover	Smith	Other
Alabama	248,981	120,725	127,796	460
Arizona	91,254	52,533	38,537	184
Arkansas	197,726	77,784	119,196	746
California	1,796,656	1,162,323	614,365	19,968
Colorado	392,242	253,872	133,131	5,239
Connecticut	553,118	296,641	252,085	4,392
Delaware	104,602	68,860	35,354	388
Florida	253,672	144,168	101,764	7,740
Georgia	231,592	101,800	129,604	188
Idaho	154,230	99,848	53,074	1,308
Illinois	3,107,489	1,769,141	1,313,817	24,531
Indiana	1,421,314	848,290	562,691	10,333
Iowa	1,009,189	623,570	379,011	6,608
Kansas	713,200	513,672	193,003	6,525
Kentucky	940,521	558,064	381,070	1,387
Louisiana	215,833	51,160	164,655	18
Maine	262,170	179,923	81,179	1,068
Maryland	528,348	301,479	223,626	3,243
Massachusetts	1,577,823	775,566	792,758	9,499
Michigan	1,372,082	965,396	396,762	9,924
Minnesota	970,976	560,977	396,451	13,548
Mississippi	151,568	27,030	124,538	—
Missouri	1,500,845	834,080	662,684	4,081
Montana	194,108	113,300	78,578	2,230
Nebraska	547,128	345,745	197,950	3,433
Nevada	32,417	18,327	14,090	—
New Hampshire	196,757	115,404	80,715	638
New Jersey	1,549,381	926,050	616,517	6,814
New Mexico	118,077	69,708	48,211	158
New York	4,405,626	2,193,344	2,089,863	122,419
North Carolina	635,150	348,923	286,227	—
North Dakota	239,845	131,419	106,648	1,778
Ohio	2,508,346	1,627,546	864,210	16,590
Oklahoma	618,427	394,046	219,174	5,207
Oregon	319,942	205,341	109,223	5,378
Pennsylvania	3,150,612	2,055,382	1,067,586	27,644
Rhode Island	237,194	117,522	118,973	699
South Carolina	68,605	5,858	62,700	47
South Dakota	261,857	157,603	102,660	1,594
Tennessee	353,192	195,388	157,143	661
Texas	708,999	367,036	341,032	931
Utah	176,603	94,618	80,985	1,000
Vermont	135,191	90,404	44,440	347
Virginia	305,364	164,609	140,146	609
Washington	500,840	335,844	156,772	8,224
West Virginia	642,752	375,551	263,784	3,417
Wisconsin	1,016,831	544,205	450,259	22,367
Wyoming	82,835	52,748	29,299	788
Total	36,801,510	21,432,823	15,004,336	364,351

State electoral votes

State	Total EV	Hoover	Smith
Alabama	12	0	12
Arizona	3	3	0
Arkansas	9	0	9
California	13	13	0
Colorado	6	6	0
Connecticut	7	7	0
Delaware	3	3	0
Florida	6	6	0
Georgia	14	0	14
Idaho	4	4	0
Illinois	29	29	0
Indiana	15	15	0
Iowa	13	13	0
Kansas	10	10	0
Kentucky	13	13	0
Louisiana	10	0	10
Maine	6	6	0
Maryland	8	8	0
Massachusetts	18	0	18
Michigan	15	15	0
Minnesota	12	12	0
Mississippi	10	0	10
Missouri	18	18	0
Montana	4	4	0
Nebraska	8	8	0
Nevada	3	3	0
New Hampshire	4	4	0
New Jersey	14	14	0
New Mexico	3	3	0
New York	45	45	0
North Carolina	12	12	0
North Dakota	5	5	0
Ohio	24	24	0
Oklahoma	10	10	0
Oregon	5	5	0
Pennsylvania	38	38	0
Rhode Island	5	0	5
South Carolina	9	0	9
South Dakota	5	5	0
Tennessee	12	12	0
Texas	20	20	0
Utah	4	4	0
Vermont	4	4	0
Virginia	12	12	0
Washington	7	7	0
West Virginia	8	8	0
Wisconsin	13	13	0
Wyoming	3	3	0
Total	531	444	87

Scenarios

1932

Basics

Incumbent .... Herbert Hoover (R)
Prior streak .... R (3)
Prior 5 .... R (3), D (2)
Population 124,840,471
States 48
Electoral votes 531
Popular votes 39,747,783

Field

Candidate	PI	Age	State	Position	N	W	CS
Franklin Roosevelt (D)	8.3	50.75	N.Y.	Governor	X	X	91.94
Herbert Hoover (R)	7.3	58.23	Calif.	President	X	—	61.28
Alfred Smith (D)	6.6	58.84	N.Y.	Former nominee	—	—	23.23
Joseph France (R)	5.6	59.06	Md.	Former senator	—	—	19.88
Norman Thomas (SOC)	3.0	47.95	N.Y.	Movement leader	—	—	17.13
John Nance Garner (D)	3.3	63.94	Texas	Representative	—	—	16.36
William Murray (D)	5.1	62.95	Okla.	Governor	—	—	12.73
George White (D)	6.1	60.20	Ohio	Governor	—	—	12.70
Jacob Coxey (R/FL)	2.5	78.54	Ohio	Mayor	—	—	10.92

Democratic nomination

Candidate	ConFB	FB%	ConLB[4]	LB%	PriW	PriV	PriV%
Roosevelt	666	57.73%	945	81.89%	9	1,314,366	44.51%
Smith	202	17.48%	191	16.51%	2	406,162	13.76%
White	52	4.51%	3	0.26%	0	834	0.03%
Garner	90	7.82%	0	0.00%	1	249,816	8.46%
Murray	23	1.99%	0	0.00%	1	226,392	7.67%

Republican nomination

Candidate	ConFB	FB%	ConLB	LB%	PriW	PriV	PriV%
Hoover	1,127	97.62%	—	—	2	781,165	33.28%
France	4	0.35%	—	—	7	1,137,948	48.49%
Coxey	0	0.00%	—	—	1	100,844	4.30%

General election

Candidate	EV	EV%	SC	PV	PV%
Roosevelt	472	88.89%	42	22,818,740	57.41%
Hoover	59	11.11%	6	15,760,425	39.65%
Thomas	0	0.00%	0	884,685	2.23%
Coxey	0	0.00%	0	7,431	0.02%

State popular votes

State	Total PV	Roosevelt	Hoover	Thomas	Other
Alabama	245,303	207,910	34,675	2,030	688
Arizona	118,251	79,264	36,104	2,618	265

State	Total PV	Roosevelt	Hoover	Thomas	Other
Arkansas	216,569	186,829	27,465	1,166	1,109
California	2,266,972	1,324,157	847,902	63,299	31,614
Colorado	457,696	250,877	189,617	13,591	3,611
Connecticut	594,183	281,632	288,420	20,480	3,651
Delaware	112,901	54,319	57,073	1,376	133
Florida	276,943	206,307	69,170	775	691
Georgia	255,590	234,118	19,863	461	1,148
Idaho	186,520	109,479	71,312	526	5,203
Illinois	3,407,926	1,882,304	1,432,756	67,258	25,608
Indiana	1,576,927	862,054	677,184	21,388	16,301
Iowa	1,036,687	598,019	414,433	20,467	3,768
Kansas	791,978	424,204	349,498	18,276	—
Kentucky	983,059	580,574	394,716	3,853	3,916
Louisiana	268,804	249,418	18,853	—	533
Maine	298,444	128,907	166,631	2,489	417
Maryland	511,054	314,314	184,184	10,489	2,067
Massachusetts	1,580,114	800,148	736,959	34,305	8,702
Michigan	1,664,765	871,700	739,894	39,205	13,966
Minnesota	1,002,843	600,806	363,959	25,476	12,602
Mississippi	146,034	140,168	5,180	686	—
Missouri	1,609,894	1,025,406	564,713	16,374	3,401
Montana	216,479	127,286	78,078	7,891	3,224
Nebraska	570,135	359,082	201,177	9,876	—
Nevada	41,430	28,756	12,674	—	—
New Hampshire	205,520	100,680	103,629	947	264
New Jersey	1,630,063	806,630	775,684	42,998	4,751
New Mexico	151,606	95,089	54,217	1,776	524
New York	4,688,614	2,534,959	1,937,963	177,397	38,295
North Carolina	711,498	497,566	208,344	5,588	—
North Dakota	256,290	178,350	71,772	3,521	2,647
Ohio	2,609,728	1,301,695	1,227,319	64,094	16,620
Oklahoma	704,633	516,468	188,165	—	—
Oregon	368,751	213,871	136,019	15,450	3,411
Pennsylvania	2,859,021	1,295,948	1,453,540	91,119	18,414
Rhode Island	266,170	146,604	115,266	3,138	1,162
South Carolina	104,407	102,347	1,978	82	—
South Dakota	288,438	183,515	99,212	1,551	4,160
Tennessee	390,273	259,473	126,752	1,796	2,252
Texas	863,406	760,348	97,959	4,450	649
Utah	206,578	116,750	84,795	4,087	946
Vermont	136,980	56,266	78,984	1,533	197
Virginia	297,942	203,979	89,637	2,382	1,944
Washington	614,814	353,260	208,645	17,080	35,829
West Virginia	743,774	405,124	330,731	5,133	2,786
Wisconsin	1,114,814	707,410	347,741	53,379	6,284
Wyoming	96,962	54,370	39,583	2,829	180
Total	39,747,783	22,818,740	15,760,425	884,685	283,933

State electoral votes

State	Total EV	Roosevelt	Hoover
Alabama	11	11	0
Arizona	3	3	0
Arkansas	9	9	0
California	22	22	0
Colorado	6	6	0
Connecticut	8	0	8
Delaware	3	0	3
Florida	7	7	0
Georgia	12	12	0
Idaho	4	4	0
Illinois	29	29	0
Indiana	14	14	0
Iowa	11	11	0
Kansas	9	9	0
Kentucky	11	11	0
Louisiana	10	10	0
Maine	5	0	5
Maryland	8	8	0
Massachusetts	17	17	0
Michigan	19	19	0
Minnesota	11	11	0
Mississippi	9	9	0
Missouri	15	15	0
Montana	4	4	0
Nebraska	7	7	0
Nevada	3	3	0
New Hampshire	4	0	4
New Jersey	16	16	0
New Mexico	3	3	0
New York	47	47	0
North Carolina	13	13	0
North Dakota	4	4	0
Ohio	26	26	0
Oklahoma	11	11	0
Oregon	5	5	0
Pennsylvania	36	0	36
Rhode Island	4	4	0
South Carolina	8	8	0
South Dakota	4	4	0
Tennessee	11	11	0
Texas	23	23	0
Utah	4	4	0
Vermont	3	0	3
Virginia	11	11	0
Washington	8	8	0
West Virginia	8	8	0
Wisconsin	12	12	0
Wyoming	3	3	0
Total	531	472	59

Scenarios

1% to Roosevelt ....Roosevelt 484, Hoover 47
1% to Hoover ....Roosevelt 456, Hoover 75
10K to Roosevelt ....Roosevelt 487, Hoover 44
10K to Hoover ....Roosevelt 466, Hoover 65
1964 allocation ....Roosevelt 477, Hoover 51
2020 allocation ....Roosevelt 487, Hoover 41

1936

Basics

Incumbent ....Franklin Roosevelt (D)
Prior streak ....D (1)
Prior 5...R (3), D (2)
Population...128,053,180
States 48
Electoral votes 531
Popular votes 45,646,991

Field

Candidate	PI	Age	State	Position	N	W	CS
Franklin Roosevelt (D)	10.0	54.75	N.Y.	President	X	X	95.88
Alfred Landon (R)	4.8	49.14	Kan.	Governor	X	—	57.76
William Borah (R)	3.3	71.34	Idaho	Senator	—	—	20.02
William Lemke (U)	1.8	58.22	N.D.	Representative	—	—	16.26
Frank Knox (R)	3.5	62.83	Ill.	Journalist	—	—	12.97

Democratic nomination

Candidate	ConFB	FB%	ConLB	LB%	PriW	PriV	PriV%
Roosevelt	1,100	100.00%	—	—	12	4,814,978	92.92%

Republican nomination

Candidate	ConFB	FB%	ConLB	LB%	PriW	PriV	PriV%
Landon	984	98.11%	—	—	2	729,908	21.99%
Borah	19	1.89%	—	—	5	1,474,152	44.41%
Knox	0	0.00%	—	—	1	493,562	14.87%

General election

Candidate	EV	EV%	SC	PV	PV%
Roosevelt	523	98.49%	46	27,750,866	60.80%
Landon	8	1.51%	2	16,679,683	36.54%
Lemke	0	0.00%	0	892,361	1.96%

State popular votes

State	Total PV	Roosevelt	Landon	Lemke	Other
Alabama	275,744	238,196	35,358	551	1,639
Arizona	124,163	86,722	33,433	3,307	701
Arkansas	179,431	146,765	32,049	4	613
California	2,638,882	1,766,836	836,431	—	35,615
Colorado	488,685	295,021	181,267	9,962	2,435
Connecticut	690,723	382,129	278,685	21,805	8,104
Delaware	127,603	69,702	54,014	442	3,445
Florida	327,436	249,117	78,248	—	71
Georgia	293,170	255,363	36,943	136	728
Idaho	199,617	125,683	66,256	7,678	—
Illinois	3,956,522	2,282,999	1,570,393	89,439	13,691

State	Total PV	Roosevelt	Landon	Lemke	Other
Indiana	1,650,897	934,974	691,570	19,407	4,946
Iowa	1,142,737	621,756	487,977	29,687	3,317
Kansas	865,507	464,520	397,727	494	2,766
Kentucky	926,214	541,944	369,702	12,501	2,067
Louisiana	329,778	292,894	36,791	—	93
Maine	304,240	126,333	168,823	7,581	1,503
Maryland	624,896	389,612	231,435	—	3,849
Massachusetts	1,840,357	942,716	768,613	118,639	10,389
Michigan	1,805,098	1,016,794	699,733	75,795	12,776
Minnesota	1,129,975	698,811	350,461	74,296	6,407
Mississippi	162,142	157,333	4,467	—	342
Missouri	1,828,635	1,111,043	697,891	14,630	5,071
Montana	230,502	159,690	63,598	5,539	1,675
Nebraska	608,023	347,445	247,731	12,847	—
Nevada	43,848	31,925	11,923	—	—
New Hampshire	218,114	108,460	104,642	4,819	193
New Jersey	1,820,437	1,083,850	720,322	9,407	6,858
New Mexico	169,135	106,037	61,727	924	447
New York	5,596,398	3,293,222	2,180,670	—	122,506
North Carolina	839,475	616,141	223,294	2	38
North Dakota	273,716	163,148	72,751	36,708	1,109
Ohio	3,012,660	1,747,140	1,127,855	132,212	5,453
Oklahoma	749,740	501,069	245,122	—	3,549
Oregon	414,021	266,733	122,706	21,831	2,751
Pennsylvania	4,138,105	2,353,788	1,690,300	67,467	26,550
Rhode Island	310,278	164,338	125,031	19,569	1,340
South Carolina	115,437	113,791	1,646	—	—
South Dakota	296,452	160,137	125,977	10,338	—
Tennessee	475,533	327,083	146,516	296	1,638
Texas	843,482	734,485	103,874	3,281	1,842
Utah	216,679	150,248	64,555	1,121	755
Vermont	143,689	62,124	81,023	—	542
Virginia	334,590	234,980	98,336	233	1,041
Washington	692,338	459,579	206,892	17,463	8,404
West Virginia	829,945	502,582	325,358	—	2,005
Wisconsin	1,258,560	802,984	380,828	60,297	14,451
Wyoming	103,382	62,624	38,739	1,653	366
Total	45,646,991	27,750,866	16,679,683	892,361	324,081

State electoral votes

State	Total EV	Roosevelt	Landon
Alabama	11	11	0
Arizona	3	3	0
Arkansas	9	9	0
California	22	22	0
Colorado	6	6	0
Connecticut	8	8	0
Delaware	3	3	0
Florida	7	7	0
Georgia	12	12	0
Idaho	4	4	0
Illinois	29	29	0

State	Total EV	Roosevelt	Landon
Indiana	14	14	0
Iowa	11	11	0
Kansas	9	9	0
Kentucky	11	11	0
Louisiana	10	10	0
Maine	5	0	5
Maryland	8	8	0
Massachusetts	17	17	0
Michigan	19	19	0
Minnesota	11	11	0
Mississippi	9	9	0
Missouri	15	15	0
Montana	4	4	0
Nebraska	7	7	0
Nevada	3	3	0
New Hampshire	4	4	0
New Jersey	16	16	0
New Mexico	3	3	0
New York	47	47	0
North Carolina	13	13	0
North Dakota	4	4	0
Ohio	26	26	0
Oklahoma	11	11	0
Oregon	5	5	0
Pennsylvania	36	36	0
Rhode Island	4	4	0
South Carolina	8	8	0
South Dakota	4	4	0
Tennessee	11	11	0
Texas	23	23	0
Utah	4	4	0
Vermont	3	0	3
Virginia	11	11	0
Washington	8	8	0
West Virginia	8	8	0
Wisconsin	12	12	0
Wyoming	3	3	0
Total	531	523	8

Scenarios

1% to Roosevelt ....Roosevelt 523, Landon 8
1% to Landon.. Roosevelt 519, Landon 12
10K to Roosevelt..Roosevelt 526, Landon 5
10K to Landon .... Roosevelt 516, Landon 15
1964 allocation..Roosevelt 521, Landon 7
2020 allocation..Roosevelt 521, Landon 7

1940

Basics

Incumbent ....Franklin Roosevelt (D)
Prior streak ....D (2)
Prior 5 .... R (3), D (2)
Population 132,164,569
States 48
Electoral votes 531
Popular votes 49,817,149

Field

Candidate	PI	Age	State	Position	N	W	CS
Franklin Roosevelt (D)	9.6	58.75	N.Y.	President	X	X	89.94
Wendell Willkie (R)	4.7	48.70	N.Y.	Business executive	X	—	63.60
Thomas Dewey (R)	4.0	38.61	N.Y.	District attorney	—	—	41.51
Robert Taft (R)	5.8	51.15	Ohio	Senator	—	—	32.24
John Nance Garner (D)	3.5	71.94	Texas	Vice president	—	—	15.20
Arthur Vandenberg (R)	5.8	56.61	Mich.	Senator	—	—	15.17
Arthur James (R)	7.1	57.30	Pa.	Governor	—	—	14.48
James Farley (D)	6.3	52.42	N.Y.	Cabinet member	—	—	13.95
Joseph Martin (R)	5.1	55.99	Mass.	Representative	—	—	12.63

Democratic nomination

Candidate	ConFB	FB%	ConLB	LB%	PriW	PriV	PriV%
Roosevelt	946	86.04%	—	—	7	3,204,054	71.70%
Farley	73	6.63%	—	—	0	0	0.00%
Garner	61	5.55%	—	—	0	426,641	9.55%

Republican nomination

Candidate	ConFB	FB%	ConLB[6]	LB%	PriW	PriV	PriV%
Willkie	105	10.50%	655	65.50%	0	21,140	0.66%
Taft	189	18.90%	318	31.80%	1	516,428	16.00%
Dewey	360	36.00%	11	1.10%	6	1,605,754	49.75%
Vandenberg	76	7.60%	0	0.00%	0	100,651	3.12%
James	74	7.40%	0	0.00%	0	8,172	0.25%
Martin	44	4.40%	0	0.00%	0	0	0.00%

General election

Candidate	EV	EV%	SC	PV	PV%
Roosevelt	449	84.56%	38	27,243,218	54.69%
Willkie	82	15.44%	10	22,334,940	44.83%

State popular votes

State	Total PV	Roosevelt	Willkie	Other
Alabama	294,219	250,726	42,184	1,309
Arizona	150,039	95,267	54,030	742
Arkansas	200,429	157,213	42,122	1,094

State	Total PV	Roosevelt	Willkie	Other
California	3,268,791	1,877,618	1,351,419	39,754
Colorado	549,004	265,554	279,576	3,874
Connecticut	781,502	417,621	361,819	2,062
Delaware	136,374	74,599	61,440	335
Florida	485,640	359,334	126,158	148
Georgia	312,686	265,194	46,495	997
Idaho	235,168	127,842	106,553	773
Illinois	4,217,935	2,149,934	2,047,240	20,761
Indiana	1,782,747	874,063	899,466	9,218
Iowa	1,215,432	578,802	632,370	4,260
Kansas	860,297	364,725	489,169	6,403
Kentucky	970,163	557,322	410,384	2,457
Louisiana	372,305	319,751	52,446	108
Maine	320,840	156,478	163,951	411
Maryland	660,104	384,546	269,534	6,024
Massachusetts	2,026,993	1,076,522	939,700	10,771
Michigan	2,085,929	1,032,991	1,039,917	13,021
Minnesota	1,251,188	644,196	596,274	10,718
Mississippi	175,824	168,267	7,364	193
Missouri	1,833,729	958,476	871,009	4,244
Montana	247,873	145,698	99,579	2,596
Nebraska	615,878	263,677	352,201	—
Nevada	53,174	31,945	21,229	—
New Hampshire	235,419	125,292	110,127	—
New Jersey	1,972,552	1,016,808	945,475	10,269
New Mexico	183,258	103,699	79,315	244
New York	6,301,596	3,251,918	3,027,478	22,200
North Carolina	822,648	609,015	213,633	—
North Dakota	280,775	124,036	154,590	2,149
Ohio	3,319,912	1,733,139	1,586,773	—
Oklahoma	826,212	474,313	348,872	3,027
Oregon	481,240	258,415	219,555	3,270
Pennsylvania	4,078,714	2,171,035	1,889,848	17,831
Rhode Island	321,152	182,181	138,654	317
South Carolina	99,830	95,470	4,360	—
South Dakota	308,427	131,362	177,065	—
Tennessee	522,823	351,601	169,153	2,069
Texas	1,041,168	840,151	199,152	1,865
Utah	247,819	154,277	93,151	391
Vermont	143,062	64,269	78,371	422
Virginia	346,608	235,961	109,363	1,284
Washington	793,833	462,145	322,123	9,565
West Virginia	868,076	495,662	372,414	—
Wisconsin	1,405,522	704,821	679,206	21,495
Wyoming	112,240	59,287	52,633	320
Total	49,817,149	27,243,218	22,334,940	238,991

State electoral votes

State	Total EV	Roosevelt	Willkie
Alabama	11	11	0
Arizona	3	3	0
Arkansas	9	9	0

State	Total EV	Roosevelt	Willkie
California	22	22	0
Colorado	6	0	6
Connecticut	8	8	0
Delaware	3	3	0
Florida	7	7	0
Georgia	12	12	0
Idaho	4	4	0
Illinois	29	29	0
Indiana	14	0	14
Iowa	11	0	11
Kansas	9	0	9
Kentucky	11	11	0
Louisiana	10	10	0
Maine	5	0	5
Maryland	8	8	0
Massachusetts	17	17	0
Michigan	19	0	19
Minnesota	11	11	0
Mississippi	9	9	0
Missouri	15	15	0
Montana	4	4	0
Nebraska	7	0	7
Nevada	3	3	0
New Hampshire	4	4	0
New Jersey	16	16	0
New Mexico	3	3	0
New York	47	47	0
North Carolina	13	13	0
North Dakota	4	0	4
Ohio	26	26	0
Oklahoma	11	11	0
Oregon	5	5	0
Pennsylvania	36	36	0
Rhode Island	4	4	0
South Carolina	8	8	0
South Dakota	4	0	4
Tennessee	11	11	0
Texas	23	23	0
Utah	4	4	0
Vermont	3	0	3
Virginia	11	11	0
Washington	8	8	0
West Virginia	8	8	0
Wisconsin	12	12	0
Wyoming	3	3	0
Total	531	449	82

Scenarios

1% to Roosevelt .... Roosevelt 482, Willkie 49
1% to Willkie .... Roosevelt 437, Willkie 94
10K to Roosevelt .... Roosevelt 482, Willkie 49
10K to Willkie .... Roosevelt 436, Willkie 95
1964 allocation .... Roosevelt 452, Willkie 76
2020 allocation .... Roosevelt 462, Willkie 66

1944

Basics

Incumbent ....Franklin Roosevelt (D)
Prior streak ....D (3)
Prior 5 ....D (3), R (2)
Population 138,397,345
States 48
Electoral votes 531
Popular votes 47,976,649

Field

Candidate	PI	Age	State	Position	N	W	CS
Franklin Roosevelt (D)	9.4	62.75	N.Y.	President	X	X	88.61
Thomas Dewey (R)	6.3	42.61	N.Y.	Governor	X	—	64.76
Douglas MacArthur (R)	3.9	64.77	Wis.	General	—	—	15.89
Harry Byrd (D)	5.1	57.39	Va.	Senator	—	—	14.55

Democratic nomination

Candidate	ConFB	FB%	ConLB	LB%	PriW	PriV	PriV%
Roosevelt	1,086	92.35%	—	—	7	1,324,006	70.89%
Byrd	89	7.57%	—	—	0	0	0.00%

Republican nomination

Candidate	ConFB	FB%	ConLB	LB%	PriW	PriV	PriV%
Dewey	1,056	99.72%	—	—	3	262,746	11.57%
MacArthur	1	0.09%	—	—	2	662,127	29.15%

General election

Candidate	EV	EV%	SC	PV	PV%
Roosevelt	432	81.36%	36	25,612,610	53.39%
Dewey	99	18.64%	12	22,014,160	45.89%

State popular votes

State	Total PV	Roosevelt	Dewey	Other
Alabama	244,743	198,918	44,540	1,285
Arizona	137,634	80,926	56,287	421
Arkansas	212,954	148,965	63,551	438
California	3,520,875	1,988,564	1,512,965	19,346
Colorado	505,039	234,331	268,731	1,977
Connecticut	831,990	435,146	390,527	6,317
Delaware	125,361	68,166	56,747	448
Florida	482,803	339,377	143,215	211
Georgia	328,108	268,187	56,506	3,415
Idaho	208,321	107,399	100,137	785
Illinois	4,036,061	2,079,479	1,939,314	17,268
Indiana	1,672,091	781,403	875,891	14,797
Iowa	1,052,599	499,876	547,267	5,456

State	Total PV	Roosevelt	Dewey	Other
Kansas	733,776	287,458	442,096	4,222
Kentucky	867,924	472,589	392,448	2,887
Louisiana	349,383	281,564	67,750	69
Maine	296,400	140,631	155,434	335
Maryland	608,439	315,490	292,949	—
Massachusetts	1,960,665	1,035,296	921,350	4,019
Michigan	2,205,223	1,106,899	1,084,423	13,901
Minnesota	1,125,504	589,864	527,416	8,224
Mississippi	180,234	168,621	11,613	—
Missouri	1,571,697	807,356	761,175	3,166
Montana	207,355	112,556	93,163	1,636
Nebraska	563,126	233,246	329,880	—
Nevada	54,234	29,623	24,611	—
New Hampshire	229,625	119,663	109,916	46
New Jersey	1,963,761	987,874	961,335	14,552
New Mexico	152,225	81,389	70,688	148
New York	6,316,790	3,304,238	2,987,647	24,905
North Carolina	790,554	527,399	263,155	—
North Dakota	220,182	100,144	118,535	1,503
Ohio	3,153,056	1,570,763	1,582,293	—
Oklahoma	722,636	401,549	319,424	1,663
Oregon	480,147	248,635	225,365	6,147
Pennsylvania	3,794,793	1,940,479	1,835,054	19,260
Rhode Island	299,276	175,356	123,487	433
South Carolina	103,382	90,601	4,554	8,227
South Dakota	232,076	96,711	135,365	—
Tennessee	510,692	308,707	200,311	1,674
Texas	1,150,334	821,605	191,423	137,306
Utah	248,319	150,088	97,891	340
Vermont	125,361	53,820	71,527	14
Virginia	388,485	242,276	145,243	966
Washington	856,328	486,774	361,689	7,865
West Virginia	715,596	392,777	322,819	—
Wisconsin	1,339,152	650,413	674,532	14,207
Wyoming	101,340	49,419	51,921	—
Total	47,976,649	25,612,610	22,014,160	349,879

State electoral votes

State	Total EV	Roosevelt	Dewey
Alabama	11	11	0
Arizona	4	4	0
Arkansas	9	9	0
California	25	25	0
Colorado	6	0	6
Connecticut	8	8	0
Delaware	3	3	0
Florida	8	8	0
Georgia	12	12	0
Idaho	4	4	0
Illinois	28	28	0
Indiana	13	0	13
Iowa	10	0	10

State	Total EV	Roosevelt	Dewey
Kansas	8	0	8
Kentucky	11	11	0
Louisiana	10	10	0
Maine	5	0	5
Maryland	8	8	0
Massachusetts	16	16	0
Michigan	19	19	0
Minnesota	11	11	0
Mississippi	9	9	0
Missouri	15	15	0
Montana	4	4	0
Nebraska	6	0	6
Nevada	3	3	0
New Hampshire	4	4	0
New Jersey	16	16	0
New Mexico	4	4	0
New York	47	47	0
North Carolina	14	14	0
North Dakota	4	0	4
Ohio	25	0	25
Oklahoma	10	10	0
Oregon	6	6	0
Pennsylvania	35	35	0
Rhode Island	4	4	0
South Carolina	8	8	0
South Dakota	4	0	4
Tennessee	12	12	0
Texas	23	23	0
Utah	4	4	0
Vermont	3	0	3
Virginia	11	11	0
Washington	8	8	0
West Virginia	8	8	0
Wisconsin	12	0	12
Wyoming	3	0	3
Total	531	432	99

Scenarios

1% to Roosevelt ....Roosevelt 469, Dewey 62
1% to Dewey .... Roosevelt 397, Dewey 134
10K to Roosevelt..Roosevelt 472, Dewey 59
10K to Dewey.. Roosevelt 410, Dewey 121
1964 allocation..Roosevelt 432, Dewey 96
2020 allocation..Roosevelt 447, Dewey 81

1948

Basics

Incumbent .... Harry Truman (D)
Prior streak .... D (4)
Prior 5 .... D (4), R (1)
Population 146,631,302
States 48
Electoral votes 531
Popular votes 48,691,494

Field

Candidate	PI	Age	State	Position	N	W	CS
Harry Truman (D)	7.6	64.48	Mo.	President	X	X	79.72
Thomas Dewey (R)	6.6	46.61	N.Y.	Former nominee	X	—	69.67
Strom Thurmond (SRD)	2.2	45.91	S.C.	Governor	—	—	34.75
Richard Russell (D)	4.4	51.00	Ga.	Senator	—	—	22.93
Robert Taft (R)	5.6	59.15	Ohio	Senator	—	—	22.57
Harold Stassen (R)	4.5	41.55	Minn.	Former governor	—	—	22.01
Earl Warren (R)	5.7	57.62	Calif.	Governor	—	—	19.04
Henry Wallace (D/P)	3.1	60.07	Iowa	Former vice president	—	—	17.65
Arthur Vandenberg (R)	5.1	64.61	Mich.	Senator	—	—	13.55
Dwight Green (R)	6.5	51.81	Ill.	Governor	—	—	13.05

Democratic nomination

Candidate	ConFB	FB%	ConLB	LB%	PriW	PriV	PriV%
Truman	926	75.04%	—	—	8	1,375,452	63.92%
Russell	266	21.56%	—	—	0	0	0.00%
Wallace	0	0.00%	—	—	0	4,416	0.21%

Republican nomination

Candidate	ConFB	FB%	ConLB[3]	LB%	PriW	PriV	PriV%
Dewey	434	39.67%	1,094	100.00%	2	304,394	11.47%
Taft	224	20.48%	0	0.00%	0	37,974	1.43%
Stassen	157	14.35%	0	0.00%	4	449,713	16.95%
Vandenberg	62	5.67%	0	0.00%	0	18,924	0.71%
Warren	59	5.39%	0	0.00%	1	771,295	29.07%
Green	56	5.12%	0	0.00%	0	0	0.00%

General election

Candidate	EV	EV%	SC	PV	PV%
Truman	303	57.06%	28	24,105,810	49.51%
Dewey	189	35.59%	16	21,970,064	45.12%
Thurmond	39	7.35%	4	1,169,156	2.40%
Wallace	0	0.00%	0	1,157,172	2.38%

State popular votes

State	Total PV	Truman	Dewey	Thurmond	Wallace	Other
Alabama	214,980	—	40,930	171,443	1,522	1,085
Arizona	177,065	95,251	77,597	—	3,310	907
Arkansas	242,475	149,659	50,959	40,068	751	1,038
California	4,021,538	1,913,134	1,895,269	1,228	190,381	21,526
Colorado	515,237	267,288	239,714	—	6,115	2,120
Connecticut	883,518	423,297	437,754	—	13,713	8,754
Delaware	139,073	67,813	69,588	—	1,050	622
Florida	577,643	281,988	194,280	89,755	11,620	—
Georgia	418,844	254,646	76,691	85,135	1,636	736
Idaho	214,816	107,370	101,514	—	4,972	960
Illinois	3,984,046	1,994,715	1,961,103	—	—	28,228
Indiana	1,656,212	807,831	821,079	—	9,649	17,653
Iowa	1,038,264	522,380	494,018	—	12,125	9,741
Kansas	788,819	351,902	423,039	—	4,603	9,275
Kentucky	822,658	466,756	341,210	10,411	1,567	2,714
Louisiana	416,336	136,344	72,657	204,290	3,035	10
Maine	264,787	111,916	150,234	—	1,884	753
Maryland	596,748	286,521	294,814	2,489	9,983	2,941
Massachusetts	2,107,146	1,151,788	909,370	—	38,157	7,831
Michigan	2,109,609	1,003,448	1,038,595	—	46,515	21,051
Minnesota	1,212,226	692,966	483,617	—	27,866	7,777
Mississippi	192,190	19,384	5,043	167,538	225	—
Missouri	1,578,628	917,315	655,039	42	3,998	2,234
Montana	224,278	119,071	96,770	—	7,313	1,124
Nebraska	488,940	224,165	264,774	—	—	1
Nevada	62,117	31,291	29,357	—	1,469	—
New Hampshire	231,440	107,995	121,299	7	1,970	169
New Jersey	1,949,555	895,455	981,124	—	42,683	30,293
New Mexico	187,063	105,464	80,303	—	1,037	259
New York	6,177,337	2,780,204	2,841,163	—	509,559	46,411
North Carolina	791,209	459,070	258,572	69,652	3,915	—
North Dakota	220,716	95,812	115,139	374	8,391	1,000
Ohio	2,936,071	1,452,791	1,445,684	—	37,596	—
Oklahoma	721,599	452,782	268,817	—	—	—
Oregon	524,080	243,147	260,904	—	14,978	5,051
Pennsylvania	3,735,348	1,752,426	1,902,197	—	55,161	25,564
Rhode Island	327,702	188,736	135,787	—	2,619	560
South Carolina	142,571	34,423	5,386	102,607	154	1
South Dakota	250,105	117,653	129,651	—	2,801	—
Tennessee	550,283	270,402	202,914	73,815	1,864	1,288
Texas	1,147,245	750,700	282,240	106,909	3,764	3,632
Utah	276,306	149,151	124,402	—	2,679	74
Vermont	123,382	45,557	75,926	—	1,279	620
Virginia	419,256	200,786	172,070	43,393	2,047	960
Washington	905,058	476,165	386,314	—	31,692	10,887
West Virginia	748,750	429,188	316,251	—	3,311	—
Wisconsin	1,276,800	647,310	590,959	—	25,282	13,249
Wyoming	101,425	52,354	47,947	—	931	193
Total	48,691,494	24,105,810	21,970,064	1,169,156	1,157,172	289,292

State electoral votes

State	Total EV	Truman	Dewey	Thurmond
Alabama	11	0	0	11
Arizona	4	4	0	0
Arkansas	9	9	0	0
California	25	25	0	0
Colorado	6	6	0	0
Connecticut	8	0	8	0
Delaware	3	0	3	0
Florida	8	8	0	0
Georgia	12	12	0	0
Idaho	4	4	0	0
Illinois	28	28	0	0
Indiana	13	0	13	0
Iowa	10	10	0	0
Kansas	8	0	8	0
Kentucky	11	11	0	0
Louisiana	10	0	0	10
Maine	5	0	5	0
Maryland	8	0	8	0
Massachusetts	16	16	0	0
Michigan	19	0	19	0
Minnesota	11	11	0	0
Mississippi	9	0	0	9
Missouri	15	15	0	0
Montana	4	4	0	0
Nebraska	6	0	6	0
Nevada	3	3	0	0
New Hampshire	4	0	4	0
New Jersey	16	0	16	0
New Mexico	4	4	0	0
New York	47	0	47	0
North Carolina	14	14	0	0
North Dakota	4	0	4	0
Ohio	25	25	0	0
Oklahoma	10	10	0	0
Oregon	6	0	6	0
Pennsylvania	35	0	35	0
Rhode Island	4	4	0	0
South Carolina	8	0	0	8
South Dakota	4	0	4	0
Tennessee	12	11	0	1
Texas	23	23	0	0
Utah	4	4	0	0
Vermont	3	0	3	0
Virginia	11	11	0	0
Washington	8	8	0	0
West Virginia	8	8	0	0
Wisconsin	12	12	0	0
Wyoming	3	3	0	0
Total	531	303	189	39

Scenarios

1% to Truman...Truman 401, Dewey 91, Thurmond 39
1% to Dewey .... Dewey 267, Truman 225, Thurmond 39
10K to Truman .... Truman 353, Dewey 139, Thurmond 39
10K to Dewey.. Dewey 253, Truman 239, Thurmond 39
1964 allocation.. Truman 311, Dewey 181, Thurmond 36
2020 allocation.. Truman 350, Dewey 145, Thurmond 33

1952

Basics

Incumbent	Harry Truman (D)
Prior streak	D (5)
Prior 5	D (5)
Population	157,552,740
States	48
Electoral votes	531
Popular votes	61,550,918

Field

Candidate	PI	Age	State	Position	N	W	CS
Dwight Eisenhower (R)	5.6	62.05	N.Y.	General	X	X	89.56
Adlai Stevenson (D)	6.7	52.74	Ill.	Governor	X	—	63.90
Estes Kefauver (D)	4.4	49.27	Tenn.	Senator	—	—	38.77
Robert Taft (R)	4.6	63.15	Ohio	Senator	—	—	32.33
Richard Russell (D)	5.1	55.00	Ga.	Senator	—	—	23.13
Earl Warren (R)	6.2	61.62	Calif.	Governor	—	—	18.38
Averell Harriman (D)	5.8	60.96	N.Y.	Former Cabinet member	—	—	15.10
Harold Stassen (R)	3.9	45.55	Pa.	College president	—	—	13.39
Robert Kerr (D)	5.3	56.14	Okla.	Senator	—	—	12.90
Alben Barkley (D)	4.2	74.94	Ky.	Vice president	—	—	12.74

Democratic nomination

Candidate	ConFB	FB%	ConLB[3]	LB%	PriW	PriV	PriV%
Stevenson	273	22.20%	618	50.20%	0	78,583	1.60%
Kefauver	340	27.64%	276	22.40%	12	3,169,448	64.32%
Russell	268	21.79%	261	21.22%	1	369,671	7.50%
Barkley	49	3.94%	68	5.49%	0	0	0.00%
Harriman	124	10.04%	0	0.00%	0	17,820	0.36%
Kerr	65	5.29%	0	0.00%	0	42,467	0.86%

Republican nomination

Candidate	ConFB	FB%	ConLB	LB%	PriW	PriV	PriV%
Eisenhower	845	70.07%	—	—	5	2,114,588	27.11%
Taft	280	23.22%	—	—	6	2,794,736	35.82%
Warren	77	6.39%	—	—	1	1,349,036	17.29%
Stassen	0	0.00%	—	—	1	881,702	11.30%

General election

Candidate	EV	EV%	SC	PV	PV%
Eisenhower	442	83.24%	39	33,777,945	54.88%
Stevenson	89	16.76%	9	27,314,992	44.38%

State popular votes

State	Total PV	Eisenhower	Stevenson	Other
Alabama	426,120	149,231	275,075	1,814
Arizona	260,570	152,042	108,528	—
Arkansas	404,800	177,155	226,300	1,345
California	5,141,849	2,897,310	2,197,548	46,991
Colorado	630,103	379,782	245,504	4,817
Connecticut	1,096,911	611,012	481,649	4,250
Delaware	174,025	90,059	83,315	651
Florida	989,337	544,036	444,950	351
Georgia	655,785	198,961	456,823	1
Idaho	276,254	180,707	95,081	466
Illinois	4,481,058	2,457,327	2,013,920	9,811
Indiana	1,955,049	1,136,259	801,530	17,260
Iowa	1,268,773	808,906	451,513	8,354
Kansas	896,166	616,302	273,296	6,568
Kentucky	993,148	495,029	495,729	2,390
Louisiana	651,952	306,925	345,027	—
Maine	351,786	232,353	118,806	627
Maryland	902,074	499,424	395,337	7,313
Massachusetts	2,383,398	1,292,325	1,083,525	7,548
Michigan	2,798,592	1,551,529	1,230,657	16,406
Minnesota	1,379,483	763,211	608,458	7,814
Mississippi	285,532	112,966	172,566	—
Missouri	1,892,062	959,429	929,830	2,803
Montana	265,037	157,394	106,213	1,430
Nebraska	609,660	421,603	188,057	—
Nevada	82,190	50,502	31,688	—
New Hampshire	272,950	166,287	106,663	—
New Jersey	2,418,554	1,373,613	1,015,902	29,039
New Mexico	238,608	132,170	105,661	777
New York	7,128,239	3,952,813	3,104,601	70,825
North Carolina	1,210,910	558,107	652,803	—
North Dakota	270,127	191,712	76,694	1,721
Ohio	3,700,758	2,100,391	1,600,367	—
Oklahoma	948,984	518,045	430,939	—
Oregon	695,059	420,815	270,579	3,665
Pennsylvania	4,580,969	2,415,789	2,146,269	18,911
Rhode Island	414,498	210,935	203,293	270
South Carolina	341,087	9,793	173,004	158,290
South Dakota	294,283	203,857	90,426	—
Tennessee	892,553	446,147	443,710	2,696
Texas	2,075,946	1,102,878	969,228	3,840
Utah	329,554	194,190	135,364	—
Vermont	153,557	109,717	43,355	485
Virginia	619,689	349,037	268,677	1,975
Washington	1,102,708	599,107	492,845	10,756
West Virginia	873,548	419,970	453,578	—
Wisconsin	1,607,370	979,744	622,175	5,451
Wyoming	129,253	81,049	47,934	270
Total	61,550,918	33,777,945	27,314,992	457,981

State electoral votes

State	Total EV	Eisenhower	Stevenson
Alabama	11	0	11
Arizona	4	4	0
Arkansas	8	0	8
California	32	32	0
Colorado	6	6	0
Connecticut	8	8	0
Delaware	3	3	0
Florida	10	10	0
Georgia	12	0	12
Idaho	4	4	0
Illinois	27	27	0
Indiana	13	13	0
Iowa	10	10	0
Kansas	8	8	0
Kentucky	10	0	10
Louisiana	10	0	10
Maine	5	5	0
Maryland	9	9	0
Massachusetts	16	16	0
Michigan	20	20	0
Minnesota	11	11	0
Mississippi	8	0	8
Missouri	13	13	0
Montana	4	4	0
Nebraska	6	6	0
Nevada	3	3	0
New Hampshire	4	4	0
New Jersey	16	16	0
New Mexico	4	4	0
New York	45	45	0
North Carolina	14	0	14
North Dakota	4	4	0
Ohio	25	25	0
Oklahoma	8	8	0
Oregon	6	6	0
Pennsylvania	32	32	0
Rhode Island	4	4	0
South Carolina	8	0	8
South Dakota	4	4	0
Tennessee	11	11	0
Texas	24	24	0
Utah	4	4	0
Vermont	3	3	0
Virginia	12	12	0
Washington	9	9	0
West Virginia	8	0	8
Wisconsin	12	12	0
Wyoming	3	3	0
Total	531	442	89

Scenarios

1% to Eisenhower..Eisenhower 452, Stevenson 79
1% to Stevenson .... Eisenhower 414, Stevenson 117
10K to Eisenhower ....Eisenhower 452, Stevenson 79
10K to Stevenson.. Eisenhower 421, Stevenson 110
1964 allocation..Eisenhower 446, Stevenson 82
2020 allocation ....Eisenhower 446, Stevenson 82

1956

Basics

Incumbent ....Dwight Eisenhower (R)
Prior streak ....R (1)
Prior 5...D (4), R (1)
Population..168,903,031
States 48
Electoral votes 531
Popular votes 62,026,908

Field

Candidate	PI	Age	State	Position	N	W	CS
Dwight Eisenhower (R)	8.7	66.05	N.Y.	President	X	X	91.03
Adlai Stevenson (D)	7.6	56.74	Ill.	Former nominee	X	—	62.52
Estes Kefauver (D)	5.1	53.27	Tenn.	Senator	—	—	21.72
Averell Harriman (D)	7.4	64.96	N.Y.	Governor	—	—	17.64
Lyndon Johnson (D)	4.5	48.18	Texas	Senator	—	—	12.89
Frank Lausche (D)	5.7	60.96	Ohio	Governor	—	—	11.62
Walter Jones (D)	1.9	68.04	Ala.	State judge	—	—	10.62

Democratic nomination

Candidate	ConFB	FB%	ConLB	LB%	PriW	PriV	PriV%
Stevenson	906	66.00%	—	—	7	3,058,470	52.33%
Harriman	210	15.31%	—	—	0	2,281	0.04%
Johnson	80	5.83%	—	—	0	0	0.00%
Lausche	6	0.40%	—	—	1	276,923	4.74%
Kefauver	0	0.00%	—	—	9	2,283,172	39.07%

Republican nomination

Candidate	ConFB	FB%	ConLB	LB%	PriW	PriV	PriV%
Eisenhower	1,323	100.00%	—	—	15	5,007,970	85.93%

General election

Candidate	EV	EV%	SC	PV	PV%
Eisenhower	457	86.06%	41	35,590,472	57.38%
Stevenson	73	13.75%	7	26,022,752	41.95%
Jones	1	0.19%	0	0	0.00%

State popular votes

State	Total PV	Eisenhower	Stevenson	Other
Alabama	496,861	195,694	280,844	20,323
Arizona	290,173	176,990	112,880	303
Arkansas	406,572	186,287	213,277	7,008
California	5,466,355	3,027,668	2,420,135	18,552
Colorado	657,074	394,479	257,997	4,598
Connecticut	1,117,121	711,837	405,079	205
Delaware	177,988	98,057	79,421	510

State	Total PV	Eisenhower	Stevenson	Other
Florida	1,125,762	643,849	480,371	1,542
Georgia	669,655	222,778	444,688	2,189
Idaho	272,989	166,979	105,868	142
Illinois	4,407,407	2,623,327	1,775,682	8,398
Indiana	1,974,607	1,182,811	783,908	7,888
Iowa	1,234,564	729,187	501,858	3,519
Kansas	866,243	566,878	296,317	3,048
Kentucky	1,053,805	572,192	476,453	5,160
Louisiana	617,544	329,047	243,977	44,520
Maine	351,706	249,238	102,468	—
Maryland	932,827	559,738	372,613	476
Massachusetts	2,348,506	1,393,197	948,190	7,119
Michigan	3,080,468	1,713,647	1,359,898	6,923
Minnesota	1,340,005	719,302	617,525	3,178
Mississippi	248,104	60,685	144,453	42,966
Missouri	1,832,562	914,289	918,273	—
Montana	271,171	154,933	116,238	—
Nebraska	577,137	378,108	199,029	—
Nevada	96,689	56,049	40,640	—
New Hampshire	266,994	176,519	90,364	111
New Jersey	2,484,312	1,606,942	850,337	27,033
New Mexico	253,926	146,788	106,098	1,040
New York	7,095,971	4,345,506	2,747,944	2,521
North Carolina	1,165,592	575,062	590,530	—
North Dakota	253,991	156,766	96,742	483
Ohio	3,702,265	2,262,610	1,439,655	—
Oklahoma	859,350	473,769	385,581	—
Oregon	736,132	406,393	329,204	535
Pennsylvania	4,576,503	2,585,252	1,981,769	9,482
Rhode Island	387,609	225,819	161,790	—
South Carolina	300,583	75,700	136,372	88,511
South Dakota	293,857	171,569	122,288	—
Tennessee	939,404	462,288	456,507	20,609
Texas	1,955,168	1,080,619	859,958	14,591
Utah	333,995	215,631	118,364	—
Vermont	152,978	110,390	42,549	39
Virginia	697,978	386,459	267,760	43,759
Washington	1,150,889	620,430	523,002	7,457
West Virginia	830,831	449,297	381,534	—
Wisconsin	1,550,558	954,844	586,768	8,946
Wyoming	124,127	74,573	49,554	—
Total	62,026,908	35,590,472	26,022,752	413,684

State electoral votes

State	Total EV	Eisenhower	Stevenson	Jones
Alabama	11	0	10	1
Arizona	4	4	0	0
Arkansas	8	0	8	0
California	32	32	0	0
Colorado	6	6	0	0
Connecticut	8	8	0	0
Delaware	3	3	0	0

State	Total EV	Eisenhower	Stevenson	Jones
Florida	10	10	0	0
Georgia	12	0	12	0
Idaho	4	4	0	0
Illinois	27	27	0	0
Indiana	13	13	0	0
Iowa	10	10	0	0
Kansas	8	8	0	0
Kentucky	10	10	0	0
Louisiana	10	10	0	0
Maine	5	5	0	0
Maryland	9	9	0	0
Massachusetts	16	16	0	0
Michigan	20	20	0	0
Minnesota	11	11	0	0
Mississippi	8	0	8	0
Missouri	13	0	13	0
Montana	4	4	0	0
Nebraska	6	6	0	0
Nevada	3	3	0	0
New Hampshire	4	4	0	0
New Jersey	16	16	0	0
New Mexico	4	4	0	0
New York	45	45	0	0
North Carolina	14	0	14	0
North Dakota	4	4	0	0
Ohio	25	25	0	0
Oklahoma	8	8	0	0
Oregon	6	6	0	0
Pennsylvania	32	32	0	0
Rhode Island	4	4	0	0
South Carolina	8	0	8	0
South Dakota	4	4	0	0
Tennessee	11	11	0	0
Texas	24	24	0	0
Utah	4	4	0	0
Vermont	3	3	0	0
Virginia	12	12	0	0
Washington	9	9	0	0
West Virginia	8	8	0	0
Wisconsin	12	12	0	0
Wyoming	3	3	0	0
Total	531	457	73	1

Scenarios

1% to Eisenhower	Eisenhower 484, Stevenson 46, Jones 1
1% to Stevenson	Eisenhower 446, Stevenson 84, Jones 1
10K to Eisenhower	Eisenhower 484, Stevenson 46, Jones 1
10K to Stevenson	Eisenhower 440, Stevenson 90, Jones 1
1964 allocation	Eisenhower 460, Stevenson 67, Jones 1
2020 allocation	Eisenhower 457, Stevenson 70, Jones 1

1960

Basics

Incumbent .... Dwight Eisenhower (R)
Prior streak .... R (2)
Prior 5 .... D (3), R (2)
Population 179,323,175
States 50
Electoral votes 537
Popular votes 68,838,219

Field

Candidate	PI	Age	State	Position	N	W	CS
John Kennedy (D)	6.2	43.43	Mass.	Senator	X	X	79.58
Richard Nixon (R)	8.0	47.81	Calif.	Vice president	X	—	72.12
Lyndon Johnson (D)	8.1	52.18	Texas	Senator	—	—	23.50
Harry Byrd (D)	6.9	73.39	Va.	Senator	—	—	19.25
Hubert Humphrey (D)	7.1	49.43	Minn.	Senator	—	—	14.46
Stuart Symington (D)	6.9	59.35	Mo.	Senator	—	—	13.00
Adlai Stevenson (D)	7.2	60.74	Ill.	Former nominee	—	—	12.86

Democratic nomination

Candidate	ConFB	FB%	ConLB	LB%	PriW	PriV	PriV%
Kennedy	806	52.99%	—	—	10	1,847,259	32.48%
Johnson	409	26.89%	—	—	0	15,691	0.28%
Symington	86	5.65%	—	—	0	29,557	0.52%
Stevenson	80	5.23%	—	—	0	51,665	0.91%
Humphrey	42	2.73%	—	—	2	590,410	10.38%

Republican nomination

Candidate	ConFB	FB%	ConLB	LB%	PriW	PriV	PriV%
Nixon	1,321	99.25%	—	—	11	4,975,938	89.85%

General election

Candidate	EV	EV%	SC	PV	PV%
Kennedy	303	56.43%	22	34,226,731	49.72%
Nixon	219	40.78%	26	34,108,157	49.55%
Byrd	15	2.79%	2	116,248	0.17%

NOTE: The popular votes listed for Byrd were cast for unpledged electors who declared their support for him after the general election.

State popular votes

State	Total PV	Kennedy	Nixon	Other
Alabama	570,225	324,050	237,981	8,194
Alaska	60,762	29,809	30,953	—
Arizona	398,491	176,781	221,241	469
Arkansas	428,509	215,049	184,508	28,952
California	6,506,578	3,224,099	3,259,722	22,757

State	Total PV	Kennedy	Nixon	Other
Colorado	736,236	330,629	402,242	3,365
Connecticut	1,222,883	657,055	565,813	15
Delaware	196,683	99,590	96,373	720
Florida	1,544,176	748,700	795,476	—
Georgia	733,349	458,638	274,472	239
Hawaii	184,705	92,410	92,295	—
Idaho	300,450	138,853	161,597	—
Illinois	4,757,409	2,377,846	2,368,988	10,575
Indiana	2,135,360	952,358	1,175,120	7,882
Iowa	1,273,810	550,565	722,381	864
Kansas	928,825	363,213	561,474	4,138
Kentucky	1,124,462	521,855	602,607	—
Louisiana	807,891	407,339	230,980	169,572
Maine	421,767	181,159	240,608	—
Maryland	1,055,349	565,808	489,538	3
Massachusetts	2,469,480	1,487,174	976,750	5,556
Michigan	3,318,097	1,687,269	1,620,428	10,400
Minnesota	1,541,887	779,933	757,915	4,039
Mississippi	298,171	108,362	73,561	116,248
Missouri	1,934,422	972,201	962,221	—
Montana	277,579	134,891	141,841	847
Nebraska	613,095	232,542	380,553	—
Nevada	107,267	54,880	52,387	—
New Hampshire	295,761	137,772	157,989	—
New Jersey	2,773,111	1,385,415	1,363,324	24,372
New Mexico	311,107	156,027	153,733	1,347
New York	7,291,079	3,830,085	3,446,419	14,575
North Carolina	1,368,556	713,136	655,420	—
North Dakota	278,431	123,963	154,310	158
Ohio	4,161,859	1,944,248	2,217,611	—
Oklahoma	903,150	370,111	533,039	—
Oregon	776,421	367,402	408,060	959
Pennsylvania	5,006,541	2,556,282	2,439,956	10,303
Rhode Island	405,535	258,032	147,502	1
South Carolina	386,688	198,129	188,558	1
South Dakota	306,487	128,070	178,417	—
Tennessee	1,051,792	481,453	556,577	13,762
Texas	2,311,084	1,167,567	1,121,310	22,207
Utah	374,709	169,248	205,361	100
Vermont	167,324	69,186	98,131	7
Virginia	771,449	362,327	404,521	4,601
Washington	1,241,572	599,298	629,273	13,001
West Virginia	837,781	441,786	395,995	—
Wisconsin	1,729,082	830,805	895,175	3,102
Wyoming	140,782	63,331	77,451	—
Total	68,838,219	34,226,731	34,108,157	503,331

State electoral votes

State	Total EV	Kennedy	Nixon	Byrd
Alabama	11	5	0	6
Alaska	3	0	3	0

State	Total EV	Kennedy	Nixon	Byrd
Arizona	4	0	4	0
Arkansas	8	8	0	0
California	32	0	32	0
Colorado	6	0	6	0
Connecticut	8	8	0	0
Delaware	3	3	0	0
Florida	10	0	10	0
Georgia	12	12	0	0
Hawaii	3	3	0	0
Idaho	4	0	4	0
Illinois	27	27	0	0
Indiana	13	0	13	0
Iowa	10	0	10	0
Kansas	8	0	8	0
Kentucky	10	0	10	0
Louisiana	10	10	0	0
Maine	5	0	5	0
Maryland	9	9	0	0
Massachusetts	16	16	0	0
Michigan	20	20	0	0
Minnesota	11	11	0	0
Mississippi	8	0	0	8
Missouri	13	13	0	0
Montana	4	0	4	0
Nebraska	6	0	6	0
Nevada	3	3	0	0
New Hampshire	4	0	4	0
New Jersey	16	16	0	0
New Mexico	4	4	0	0
New York	45	45	0	0
North Carolina	14	14	0	0
North Dakota	4	0	4	0
Ohio	25	0	25	0
Oklahoma	8	0	7	1
Oregon	6	0	6	0
Pennsylvania	32	32	0	0
Rhode Island	4	4	0	0
South Carolina	8	8	0	0
South Dakota	4	0	4	0
Tennessee	11	0	11	0
Texas	24	24	0	0
Utah	4	0	4	0
Vermont	3	0	3	0
Virginia	12	0	12	0
Washington	9	0	9	0
West Virginia	8	8	0	0
Wisconsin	12	0	12	0
Wyoming	3	0	3	0
Total	537	303	219	15

Scenarios

1964

Basics

Incumbent .... Lyndon Johnson (D)
Prior streak .... D (1)
Prior 5 .... D (3), R (2)
Population 191,888,791
States 51
Electoral votes 538
Popular votes 70,644,592

Field

Candidate	PI	Age	State	Position	N	W	CS
Lyndon Johnson (D)	9.3	56.18	Texas	President	X	X	93.24
Barry Goldwater (R)	6.6	55.83	Ariz.	Senator	X	—	60.59
Nelson Rockefeller (R)	7.6	56.32	N.Y.	Governor	—	—	20.93
William Scranton (R)	6.9	47.29	Pa.	Governor	—	—	19.42
George Wallace (D)	6.4	45.19	Ala.	Governor	—	—	13.23
Henry Cabot Lodge (R)	4.8	62.33	Mass.	Former v.p. nominee	—	—	12.05
Richard Nixon (R)	6.7	51.81	N.Y.	Former nominee	—	—	11.00

Democratic nomination

Candidate	ConFB	FB%	ConLB	LB%	PriW	PriV	PriV%
Johnson	2,318	100.00%	—	—	8	1,106,999	17.72%
Wallace	0	0.00%	—	—	0	672,984	10.77%

Republican nomination

Candidate	ConFB	FB%	ConLB	LB%	PriW	PriV	PriV%
Goldwater	883	67.51%	—	—	5	2,267,079	38.20%
Scranton	214	16.36%	—	—	1	245,401	4.14%
Rockefeller	114	8.72%	—	—	2	1,304,204	21.97%
Lodge	2	0.15%	—	—	3	386,661	6.52%
Nixon	0	0.00%	—	—	0	197,212	3.32%

General election

Candidate	EV	EV%	SC	PV	PV%
Johnson	486	90.34%	45	43,129,566	61.05%
Goldwater	52	9.67%	6	27,178,188	38.47%

State popular votes

State	Total PV	Johnson	Goldwater	Other
Alabama	689,818	—	479,085	210,733
Alaska	67,259	44,329	22,930	—
Arizona	480,770	237,753	242,535	482
Arkansas	560,426	314,197	243,264	2,965
California	7,057,586	4,171,877	2,879,108	6,601
Colorado	776,986	476,024	296,767	4,195
Connecticut	1,218,578	826,269	390,996	1,313

State	Total PV	Johnson	Goldwater	Other
Delaware	201,320	122,704	78,078	538
District of Columbia	198,597	169,796	28,801	—
Florida	1,854,481	948,540	905,941	—
Georgia	1,139,335	522,556	616,584	195
Hawaii	207,271	163,249	44,022	—
Idaho	292,477	148,920	143,557	—
Illinois	4,702,841	2,796,833	1,905,946	62
Indiana	2,091,606	1,170,848	911,118	9,640
Iowa	1,184,539	733,030	449,148	2,361
Kansas	857,901	464,028	386,579	7,294
Kentucky	1,046,105	669,659	372,977	3,469
Louisiana	896,293	387,068	509,225	—
Maine	380,965	262,264	118,701	—
Maryland	1,116,457	730,912	385,495	50
Massachusetts	2,344,798	1,786,422	549,727	8,649
Michigan	3,203,102	2,136,615	1,060,152	6,335
Minnesota	1,554,462	991,117	559,624	3,721
Mississippi	409,146	52,618	356,528	—
Missouri	1,817,879	1,164,344	653,535	—
Montana	278,628	164,246	113,032	1,350
Nebraska	584,154	307,307	276,847	—
Nevada	135,433	79,339	56,094	—
New Hampshire	288,093	184,064	104,029	—
New Jersey	2,847,663	1,868,231	964,174	15,258
New Mexico	328,645	194,015	132,838	1,792
New York	7,166,275	4,913,102	2,243,559	9,614
North Carolina	1,424,983	800,139	624,844	—
North Dakota	258,389	149,784	108,207	398
Ohio	3,969,196	2,498,331	1,470,865	—
Oklahoma	932,499	519,834	412,665	—
Oregon	786,305	501,017	282,779	2,509
Pennsylvania	4,822,690	3,130,954	1,673,657	18,079
Rhode Island	390,091	315,463	74,615	13
South Carolina	524,779	215,723	309,048	8
South Dakota	293,118	163,010	130,108	—
Tennessee	1,143,946	634,947	508,965	34
Texas	2,626,811	1,663,185	958,566	5,060
Utah	401,413	219,628	181,785	—
Vermont	163,089	108,127	54,942	20
Virginia	1,042,267	558,038	481,334	2,895
Washington	1,258,556	779,881	470,366	8,309
West Virginia	792,040	538,087	253,953	—
Wisconsin	1,691,815	1,050,424	638,495	2,896
Wyoming	142,716	80,718	61,998	—
Total	70,644,592	43,129,566	27,178,188	336,838

State electoral votes

State	Total EV	Johnson	Goldwater
Alabama	10	0	10
Alaska	3	3	0
Arizona	5	0	5
Arkansas	6	6	0

State	Total EV	Johnson	Goldwater
California	40	40	0
Colorado	6	6	0
Connecticut	8	8	0
Delaware	3	3	0
District of Columbia	3	3	0
Florida	14	14	0
Georgia	12	0	12
Hawaii	4	4	0
Idaho	4	4	0
Illinois	26	26	0
Indiana	13	13	0
Iowa	9	9	0
Kansas	7	7	0
Kentucky	9	9	0
Louisiana	10	0	10
Maine	4	4	0
Maryland	10	10	0
Massachusetts	14	14	0
Michigan	21	21	0
Minnesota	10	10	0
Mississippi	7	0	7
Missouri	12	12	0
Montana	4	4	0
Nebraska	5	5	0
Nevada	3	3	0
New Hampshire	4	4	0
New Jersey	17	17	0
New Mexico	4	4	0
New York	43	43	0
North Carolina	13	13	0
North Dakota	4	4	0
Ohio	26	26	0
Oklahoma	8	8	0
Oregon	6	6	0
Pennsylvania	29	29	0
Rhode Island	4	4	0
South Carolina	8	0	8
South Dakota	4	4	0
Tennessee	11	11	0
Texas	25	25	0
Utah	4	4	0
Vermont	3	3	0
Virginia	12	12	0
Washington	9	9	0
West Virginia	7	7	0
Wisconsin	12	12	0
Wyoming	3	3	0
Total	538	486	52

Scenarios

1968

Basics

Incumbent .... Lyndon Johnson (D)
Prior streak .... D (2)
Prior 5 .... D (3), R (2)
Population 200,706,052
States 51
Electoral votes 538
Popular votes 73,211,875

Field

Candidate	PI	Age	State	Position	N	W	CS
Richard Nixon (R)	6.2	55.81	N.Y.	Former nominee	X	X	78.01
Hubert Humphrey (D)	7.8	57.43	Minn.	Vice president	X	—	69.19
George Wallace (D/AI)	5.4	49.19	Ala.	Former governor	—	—	45.41
Eugene McCarthy (D)	6.9	52.59	Minn.	Senator	—	—	33.16
Ronald Reagan (R)	7.3	57.73	Calif.	Governor	—	—	28.22
Nelson Rockefeller (R)	7.1	60.32	N.Y.	Governor	—	—	21.48
Robert Kennedy (D)	6.6	42.95	N.Y.	Senator	—	—	19.18
James Rhodes (R)	6.6	59.13	Ohio	Governor	—	—	16.17
George McGovern (D)	6.0	46.29	S.D.	Senator	—	—	12.79
Lyndon Johnson (D)	8.7	60.18	Texas	President	—	—	11.53

Democratic nomination

Candidate	ConFB	FB%	ConLB	LB%	PriW	PriV	PriV%
Humphrey	1,759	67.10%	—	—	0	166,463	2.21%
McCarthy	601	22.92%	—	—	6	2,914,933	38.69%
McGovern	147	5.59%	—	—	0	0	0.00%
Wallace	1	0.02%	—	—	0	33,520	0.45%
Johnson	0	0.00%	—	—	1	383,048	5.08%
Kennedy	—	—	—	—	5	2,304,542	30.58%

Republican nomination

Candidate	ConFB	FB%	ConLB	LB%	PriW	PriV	PriV%
Nixon	692	51.91%	—	—	9	1,679,443	37.54%
Rockefeller	277	20.78%	—	—	1	164,340	3.67%
Reagan	182	13.65%	—	—	1	1,696,270	37.92%
Rhodes	55	4.13%	—	—	1	614,492	13.74%

General election

Candidate	EV	EV%	SC	PV	PV%
Nixon	301	55.95%	32	31,785,480	43.42%
Humphrey	191	35.50%	14	31,275,166	42.72%
Wallace	46	8.55%	5	9,906,473	13.53%
McCarthy	0	0.00%	0	25,552	0.04%

State popular votes

State	Total PV	Nixon	Humphrey	Wallace	Other
Alabama	1,049,922	146,923	196,579	691,425	14,995
Alaska	83,035	37,600	35,411	10,024	—
Arizona	486,936	266,721	170,514	46,573	3,128
Arkansas	619,969	190,759	188,228	240,982	—
California	7,251,587	3,467,664	3,244,318	487,270	52,335
Colorado	811,199	409,345	335,174	60,813	5,867
Connecticut	1,256,232	556,721	621,561	76,650	1,300
Delaware	214,367	96,714	89,194	28,459	—
District of Columbia	170,578	31,012	139,566	—	—
Florida	2,187,805	886,804	676,794	624,207	—
Georgia	1,250,266	380,111	334,440	535,550	165
Hawaii	236,218	91,425	141,324	3,469	—
Idaho	291,183	165,369	89,273	36,541	—
Illinois	4,619,749	2,174,774	2,039,814	390,958	14,203
Indiana	2,123,597	1,067,885	806,659	243,108	5,945
Iowa	1,167,931	619,106	476,699	66,422	5,704
Kansas	872,783	478,674	302,996	88,921	2,192
Kentucky	1,055,893	462,411	397,541	193,098	2,843
Louisiana	1,097,450	257,535	309,615	530,300	—
Maine	392,936	169,254	217,312	6,370	—
Maryland	1,235,039	517,995	538,310	178,734	—
Massachusetts	2,331,752	766,844	1,469,218	87,088	8,602
Michigan	3,306,250	1,370,665	1,593,082	331,968	10,535
Minnesota	1,588,506	658,643	857,738	68,931	3,194
Mississippi	654,509	88,516	150,644	415,349	—
Missouri	1,809,502	811,932	791,444	206,126	—
Montana	274,404	138,835	114,117	20,015	1,437
Nebraska	536,851	321,163	170,784	44,904	—
Nevada	154,218	73,188	60,598	20,432	—
New Hampshire	297,298	154,903	130,589	11,173	633
New Jersey	2,875,395	1,325,467	1,264,206	262,187	23,535
New Mexico	327,350	169,692	130,081	25,737	1,840
New York	6,791,688	3,007,932	3,378,470	358,864	46,422
North Carolina	1,587,493	627,192	464,113	496,188	—
North Dakota	247,882	138,669	94,769	14,244	200
Ohio	3,959,698	1,791,014	1,700,586	467,495	603
Oklahoma	943,086	449,697	301,658	191,731	—
Oregon	819,622	408,433	358,866	49,683	2,640
Pennsylvania	4,747,928	2,090,017	2,259,405	378,582	19,924
Rhode Island	385,000	122,359	246,518	15,678	445
South Carolina	666,978	254,062	197,486	215,430	—
South Dakota	281,264	149,841	118,023	13,400	—
Tennessee	1,248,617	472,592	351,233	424,792	—
Texas	3,079,216	1,227,844	1,266,804	584,269	299
Utah	422,568	238,728	156,665	26,906	269
Vermont	161,404	85,142	70,255	5,104	903
Virginia	1,361,491	590,319	442,387	321,833	6,952

State	Total PV	Nixon	Humphrey	Wallace	Other
Washington	1,304,281	588,510	616,037	96,990	2,744
West Virginia	754,206	307,555	374,091	72,560	—
Wisconsin	1,691,538	809,997	748,804	127,835	4,902
Wyoming	127,205	70,927	45,173	11,105	—
Total	73,211,875	31,785,480	31,275,166	9,906,473	244,756

State electoral votes

State	Total EV	Nixon	Humphrey	Wallace
Alabama	10	0	0	10
Alaska	3	3	0	0
Arizona	5	5	0	0
Arkansas	6	0	0	6
California	40	40	0	0
Colorado	6	6	0	0
Connecticut	8	0	8	0
Delaware	3	3	0	0
District of Columbia	3	0	3	0
Florida	14	14	0	0
Georgia	12	0	0	12
Hawaii	4	0	4	0
Idaho	4	4	0	0
Illinois	26	26	0	0
Indiana	13	13	0	0
Iowa	9	9	0	0
Kansas	7	7	0	0
Kentucky	9	9	0	0
Louisiana	10	0	0	10
Maine	4	0	4	0
Maryland	10	0	10	0
Massachusetts	14	0	14	0
Michigan	21	0	21	0
Minnesota	10	0	10	0
Mississippi	7	0	0	7
Missouri	12	12	0	0
Montana	4	4	0	0
Nebraska	5	5	0	0
Nevada	3	3	0	0
New Hampshire	4	4	0	0
New Jersey	17	17	0	0
New Mexico	4	4	0	0
New York	43	0	43	0
North Carolina	13	12	0	1
North Dakota	4	4	0	0
Ohio	26	26	0	0
Oklahoma	8	8	0	0
Oregon	6	6	0	0
Pennsylvania	29	0	29	0
Rhode Island	4	0	4	0
South Carolina	8	8	0	0
South Dakota	4	4	0	0
Tennessee	11	11	0	0
Texas	25	0	25	0

State	Total EV	Nixon	Humphrey	Wallace
Utah	4	4	0	0
Vermont	3	3	0	0
Virginia	12	12	0	0
Washington	9	0	9	0
West Virginia	7	0	7	0
Wisconsin	12	12	0	0
Wyoming	3	3	0	0
Total	538	301	191	46

Scenarios

1% to Nixon .... Nixon 336, Humphrey 156, Wallace 46
1% to Humphrey .... Nixon 289, Humphrey 203, Wallace 46
10K to Nixon .... Nixon 301, Humphrey 191, Wallace 46
10K to Humphrey .... Nixon 289, Humphrey 203, Wallace 46
1964 allocation .... Nixon 301, Humphrey 191, Wallace 46
2020 allocation .... Nixon 319, Humphrey 173, Wallace 46

1972

Basics

Incumbent .... Richard Nixon (R)
Prior streak .... R (1)
Prior 5 .... R (3), D (2)
Population 209,896,021
States 51
Electoral votes 538
Popular votes 77,718,554

Field

Candidate	PI	Age	State	Position	N	W	CS
Richard Nixon (R)	8.8	59.81	Calif.	President	X	X	95.25
George McGovern (D)	6.4	50.29	S.D.	Senator	X	—	58.46
George Wallace (D)	6.5	53.19	Ala.	Governor	—	—	26.62
Hubert Humphrey (D)	6.5	61.43	Minn.	Former nominee	—	—	25.90
Edmund Muskie (D)	7.2	58.60	Maine	Senator	—	—	17.06
Henry Jackson (D)	6.3	60.42	Wash.	Senator	—	—	15.37
John Ashbrook (R)	4.2	44.11	Ohio	Representative	—	—	13.02
Shirley Chisholm (D)	4.5	47.92	N.Y.	Representative	—	—	12.62
Paul McCloskey (R)	4.7	45.09	Calif.	Representative	—	—	11.31
John Hospers (LIB)	3.3	54.40	Calif.	Movement leader	—	—	10.62
Wilbur Mills (D)	4.3	63.44	Ark.	Representative	—	—	10.36
Sam Yorty (D)	4.3	63.08	Calif.	Mayor	—	—	10.30

Democratic nomination

Candidate	ConFB	FB%	ConLB	LB%	PriW	PriV	PriV%
McGovern	1,728	57.31%	—	—	8	4,053,451	25.34%
Jackson	525	17.41%	—	—	0	505,198	3.16%
Wallace	382	12.66%	—	—	5	3,755,424	23.48%
Chisholm	152	5.04%	—	—	1	430,703	2.69%
Humphrey	67	2.21%	—	—	4	4,121,372	25.77%
Mills	34	1.12%	—	—	0	37,401	0.23%
Muskie	24	0.81%	—	—	2	1,840,217	11.51%
Yorty	0	0.00%	—	—	0	79,446	0.50%

Republican nomination

Candidate	ConFB	FB%	ConLB	LB%	PriW	PriV	PriV%
Nixon	1,347	99.93%	—	—	18	5,378,704	86.92%
McCloskey	1	0.07%	—	—	0	132,731	2.15%
Ashbrook	0	0.00%	—	—	0	311,543	5.03%

General election

Candidate	EV	EV%	SC	PV	PV%
Nixon	520	96.65%	49	47,169,911	60.69%
McGovern	17	3.16%	2	29,170,383	37.53%
Hospers	1	0.19%	0	3,673	0.01%

State popular votes

State	Total PV	Nixon	McGovern	Other
Alabama	1,006,111	728,701	256,923	20,487
Alaska	95,219	55,349	32,967	6,903
Arizona	622,926	402,812	198,540	21,574
Arkansas	651,320	448,541	199,892	2,887
California	8,367,862	4,602,096	3,475,847	289,919
Colorado	953,884	597,189	329,980	26,715
Connecticut	1,384,277	810,763	555,498	18,016
Delaware	235,516	140,357	92,283	2,876
District of Columbia	163,421	35,226	127,627	568
Florida	2,583,283	1,857,759	718,117	7,407
Georgia	1,174,772	881,496	289,529	3,747
Hawaii	270,274	168,865	101,409	—
Idaho	310,379	199,384	80,826	30,169
Illinois	4,723,236	2,788,179	1,913,472	21,585
Indiana	2,125,529	1,405,154	708,568	11,807
Iowa	1,225,944	706,207	496,206	23,531
Kansas	916,095	619,812	270,287	25,996
Kentucky	1,067,499	676,446	371,159	19,894
Louisiana	1,051,491	686,852	298,142	66,497
Maine	417,042	256,458	160,584	—
Maryland	1,353,812	829,305	505,781	18,726
Massachusetts	2,458,756	1,112,078	1,332,540	14,138
Michigan	3,489,727	1,961,721	1,459,435	68,571
Minnesota	1,741,652	898,269	802,346	41,037
Mississippi	645,963	505,125	126,782	14,056
Missouri	1,855,803	1,153,852	697,147	4,804
Montana	317,603	183,976	120,197	13,430
Nebraska	576,289	406,298	169,991	—
Nevada	181,766	115,750	66,016	—
New Hampshire	334,055	213,724	116,435	3,896
New Jersey	2,997,229	1,845,502	1,102,211	49,516
New Mexico	386,241	235,606	141,084	9,551
New York	7,165,919	4,192,778	2,951,084	22,057
North Carolina	1,518,612	1,054,889	438,705	25,018
North Dakota	280,514	174,109	100,384	6,021
Ohio	4,094,787	2,441,827	1,558,889	94,071
Oklahoma	1,029,900	759,025	247,147	23,728
Oregon	927,946	486,686	392,760	48,500
Pennsylvania	4,592,106	2,714,521	1,796,951	80,634
Rhode Island	415,808	220,383	194,645	780
South Carolina	673,960	477,044	186,824	10,092
South Dakota	307,415	166,476	139,945	994
Tennessee	1,201,182	813,147	357,293	30,742
Texas	3,471,281	2,298,896	1,154,289	18,096
Utah	478,476	323,643	126,284	28,549
Vermont	186,947	117,149	68,174	1,624
Virginia	1,457,019	988,493	438,887	29,639

State	Total PV	Nixon	McGovern	Other
Washington	1,470,847	837,135	568,334	65,378
West Virginia	762,399	484,964	277,435	—
Wisconsin	1,852,890	989,430	810,174	53,286
Wyoming	145,570	100,464	44,358	748
Total	77,718,554	47,169,911	29,170,383	1,378,260

State electoral votes

State	Total EV	Nixon	McGovern	Hospers
Alabama	9	9	0	0
Alaska	3	3	0	0
Arizona	6	6	0	0
Arkansas	6	6	0	0
California	45	45	0	0
Colorado	7	7	0	0
Connecticut	8	8	0	0
Delaware	3	3	0	0
District of Columbia	3	0	3	0
Florida	17	17	0	0
Georgia	12	12	0	0
Hawaii	4	4	0	0
Idaho	4	4	0	0
Illinois	26	26	0	0
Indiana	13	13	0	0
Iowa	8	8	0	0
Kansas	7	7	0	0
Kentucky	9	9	0	0
Louisiana	10	10	0	0
Maine	4	4	0	0
Maryland	10	10	0	0
Massachusetts	14	0	14	0
Michigan	21	21	0	0
Minnesota	10	10	0	0
Mississippi	7	7	0	0
Missouri	12	12	0	0
Montana	4	4	0	0
Nebraska	5	5	0	0
Nevada	3	3	0	0
New Hampshire	4	4	0	0
New Jersey	17	17	0	0
New Mexico	4	4	0	0
New York	41	41	0	0
North Carolina	13	13	0	0
North Dakota	3	3	0	0
Ohio	25	25	0	0
Oklahoma	8	8	0	0
Oregon	6	6	0	0
Pennsylvania	27	27	0	0
Rhode Island	4	4	0	0
South Carolina	8	8	0	0
South Dakota	4	4	0	0
Tennessee	10	10	0	0
Texas	26	26	0	0

State	Total EV	Nixon	McGovern	Hospers
Utah	4	4	0	0
Vermont	3	3	0	0
Virginia	12	11	0	1
Washington	9	9	0	0
West Virginia	6	6	0	0
Wisconsin	11	11	0	0
Wyoming	3	3	0	0
Total	538	520	17	1

Scenarios

1% to Nixon..Nixon 520, McGovern 17, Hospers 1
1% to McGovern..Nixon 520, McGovern 17, Hospers 1
10K to Nixon...Nixon 520, McGovern 17, Hospers 1
10K to McGovern..Nixon 520, McGovern 17, Hospers 1
1964 allocation...Nixon 520, McGovern 17, Hospers 1
2020 allocation...Nixon 523, McGovern 14, Hospers 1

1976

Basics

Incumbent ....Gerald Ford (R)
Prior streak ....R (2)
Prior 5 ....R (3), D (2)
Population 218,035,164
States 51
Electoral votes 538
Popular votes 81,555,889

Field

Candidate	PI	Age	State	Position	N	W	CS
Jimmy Carter (D)	7.4	52.08	Ga.	Former governor	X	X	79.23
Gerald Ford (R)	6.6	63.30	Mich.	President	X	—	72.98
Ronald Reagan (R)	6.7	65.73	Calif.	Former governor	—	—	47.60
Jerry Brown (D)	6.2	38.57	Calif.	Governor	—	—	21.16
Morris Udall (D)	4.3	54.38	Ariz.	Representative	—	—	18.22
George Wallace (D)	5.6	57.19	Ala.	Governor	—	—	17.84
Henry Jackson (D)	6.2	64.42	Wash.	Senator	—	—	14.30
Frank Church (D)	6.5	52.27	Idaho	Senator	—	—	13.23
Sargent Shriver (D)	4.2	60.98	Md.	Former v.p. nominee	—	—	11.14
Fred Harris (D)	6.9	45.97	Okla.	Former senator	—	—	10.94
Birch Bayh (D)	6.9	48.78	Ind.	Senator	—	—	10.32
Hubert Humphrey (D)	5.5	65.43	Minn.	Former nominee	—	—	10.29

Democratic nomination

Candidate	ConFB	FB%	ConLB	LB%	PriW	PriV	PriV%
Carter	2,239	74.42%	—	—	17	6,235,609	38.85%
Udall	330	10.95%	—	—	0	1,611,754	10.04%
Brown	301	9.99%	—	—	3	2,449,374	15.26%
Wallace	57	1.90%	—	—	0	1,995,388	12.43%
Church	19	0.63%	—	—	4	830,818	5.18%
Jackson	10	0.33%	—	—	1	1,134,375	7.07%
Humphrey	10	0.33%	—	—	0	61,992	0.39%
Harris	9	0.30%	—	—	0	234,568	1.46%
Shriver	0	0.00%	—	—	0	304,399	1.90%
Bayh	0	0.00%	—	—	0	86,438	0.54%

Republican nomination

Candidate	ConFB	FB%	ConLB	LB%	PriW	PriV	PriV%
Ford	1,187	52.55%	—	—	16	5,529,899	53.31%
Reagan	1,070	47.37%	—	—	10	4,758,325	45.87%

General election

Candidate	EV	EV%	SC	PV	PV%
Carter	297	55.20%	24	40,830,763	50.07%
Ford	240	44.61%	27	39,147,793	48.00%
Reagan	1	0.19%	0	0	0.00%

State popular votes

State	Total PV	Carter	Ford	Other
Alabama	1,182,850	659,170	504,070	19,610
Alaska	123,574	44,058	71,555	7,961
Arizona	742,719	295,602	418,642	28,475
Arkansas	767,535	498,604	267,903	1,028
California	7,867,117	3,742,284	3,882,244	242,589
Colorado	1,081,554	460,353	584,367	36,834
Connecticut	1,381,526	647,895	719,261	14,370
Delaware	235,834	122,596	109,831	3,407
District of Columbia	168,830	137,818	27,873	3,139
Florida	3,150,631	1,636,000	1,469,531	45,100
Georgia	1,467,458	979,409	483,743	4,306
Hawaii	291,301	147,375	140,003	3,923
Idaho	344,071	126,549	204,151	13,371
Illinois	4,718,914	2,271,295	2,364,269	83,350
Indiana	2,220,362	1,014,714	1,183,958	21,690
Iowa	1,279,306	619,931	632,863	26,512
Kansas	957,845	430,421	502,752	24,672
Kentucky	1,167,142	615,717	531,852	19,573
Louisiana	1,278,439	661,365	587,446	29,628
Maine	483,216	232,279	236,320	14,617
Maryland	1,439,897	759,612	672,661	7,624
Massachusetts	2,547,558	1,429,475	1,030,276	87,807
Michigan	3,653,749	1,696,714	1,893,742	63,293
Minnesota	1,949,931	1,070,440	819,395	60,096
Mississippi	769,361	381,309	366,846	21,206
Missouri	1,953,600	998,387	927,443	27,770
Montana	328,734	149,259	173,703	5,772
Nebraska	607,668	233,692	359,705	14,271
Nevada	201,876	92,479	101,273	8,124
New Hampshire	339,618	147,635	185,935	6,048
New Jersey	3,014,472	1,444,653	1,509,688	60,131
New Mexico	418,409	201,148	211,419	5,842
New York	6,534,170	3,389,558	3,100,791	43,821
North Carolina	1,678,914	927,365	741,960	9,589
North Dakota	297,188	136,078	153,470	7,640
Ohio	4,111,873	2,011,621	2,000,505	99,747
Oklahoma	1,092,251	532,442	545,708	14,101
Oregon	1,029,876	490,407	492,120	47,349
Pennsylvania	4,620,787	2,328,677	2,205,604	86,506
Rhode Island	411,170	227,636	181,249	2,285
South Carolina	802,583	450,807	346,149	5,627
South Dakota	300,678	147,068	151,505	2,105
Tennessee	1,476,345	825,879	633,969	16,497
Texas	4,071,884	2,082,319	1,953,300	36,265
Utah	541,198	182,110	337,908	21,180
Vermont	187,765	80,954	102,085	4,726
Virginia	1,697,094	813,896	836,554	46,644

State	Total PV	Carter	Ford	Other
Washington	1,555,534	717,323	777,732	60,479
West Virginia	750,964	435,914	314,760	290
Wisconsin	2,104,175	1,040,232	1,004,987	58,956
Wyoming	156,343	62,239	92,717	1,387
Total	81,555,889	40,830,763	39,147,793	1,577,333

State electoral votes

State	Total EV	Carter	Ford	Reagan
Alabama	9	9	0	0
Alaska	3	0	3	0
Arizona	6	0	6	0
Arkansas	6	6	0	0
California	45	0	45	0
Colorado	7	0	7	0
Connecticut	8	0	8	0
Delaware	3	3	0	0
District of Columbia	3	3	0	0
Florida	17	17	0	0
Georgia	12	12	0	0
Hawaii	4	4	0	0
Idaho	4	0	4	0
Illinois	26	0	26	0
Indiana	13	0	13	0
Iowa	8	0	8	0
Kansas	7	0	7	0
Kentucky	9	9	0	0
Louisiana	10	10	0	0
Maine	4	0	4	0
Maryland	10	10	0	0
Massachusetts	14	14	0	0
Michigan	21	0	21	0
Minnesota	10	10	0	0
Mississippi	7	7	0	0
Missouri	12	12	0	0
Montana	4	0	4	0
Nebraska	5	0	5	0
Nevada	3	0	3	0
New Hampshire	4	0	4	0
New Jersey	17	0	17	0
New Mexico	4	0	4	0
New York	41	41	0	0
North Carolina	13	13	0	0
North Dakota	3	0	3	0
Ohio	25	25	0	0
Oklahoma	8	0	8	0
Oregon	6	0	6	0
Pennsylvania	27	27	0	0
Rhode Island	4	4	0	0
South Carolina	8	8	0	0
South Dakota	4	0	4	0
Tennessee	10	10	0	0
Texas	26	26	0	0

State	Total EV	Carter	Ford	Reagan
Utah	4	0	4	0
Vermont	3	0	3	0
Virginia	12	0	12	0
Washington	9	0	8	1
West Virginia	6	6	0	0
Wisconsin	11	11	0	0
Wyoming	3	0	3	0
Total	538	297	240	1

Scenarios

1% to Carter...Carter 410, Ford 127, Reagan 1
1% to Ford..Ford 283, Carter 254, Reagan 1
10K to Carter ....Carter 337, Ford 200, Reagan 1
10K to Ford..Ford 279, Carter 258, Reagan 1
1964 allocation..Carter 302, Ford 235, Reagan 1
2020 allocation..Carter 292, Ford 245, Reagan 1

1980

Basics

Incumbent ....Jimmy Carter (D)
Prior streak .... D (1)
Prior 5.. D (3), R (2)
Population...226,542,199
States 51
Electoral votes 538
Popular votes 86,513,813

Field

Candidate	PI	Age	State	Position	N	W	CS
Ronald Reagan (R)	5.7	69.73	Calif.	Former governor	X	X	91.16
Jimmy Carter (D)	9.0	56.08	Ga.	President	X	—	60.93
Edward Kennedy (D)	6.8	48.69	Mass.	Senator	—	—	39.18
John Anderson (R/NU)	4.7	58.71	Ill.	Representative	—	—	38.97
George H.W. Bush (R)	5.2	56.39	Texas	Former ambassador	—	—	24.15
Jerry Brown (D)	6.4	42.57	Calif.	Governor	—	—	11.84
Howard Baker (R)	7.7	54.96	Tenn.	Senator	—	—	10.51
Phil Crane (R)	4.7	49.99	Ill.	Representative	—	—	10.46
John Connally (R)	7.4	63.68	Texas	Former governor	—	—	10.38

Democratic nomination

Candidate	ConFB	FB%	ConLB	LB%	PriW	PriV	PriV%
Carter	2,123	63.74%	—	—	23	9,593,335	51.17%
Kennedy	1,150	34.54%	—	—	10	6,963,625	37.15%
Brown	1	0.03%	—	—	0	573,994	3.06%

Republican nomination

Candidate	ConFB	FB%	ConLB	LB%	PriW	PriV	PriV%
Reagan	1,939	97.24%	—	—	29	7,709,793	60.76%
Anderson	37	1.86%	—	—	0	1,572,174	12.39%
Bush	13	0.65%	—	—	5	2,963,509	23.35%
Baker	0	0.00%	—	—	0	106,819	0.84%
Crane	0	0.00%	—	—	0	97,793	0.77%
Connally	0	0.00%	—	—	0	80,662	0.64%

General election

Candidate	EV	EV%	SC	PV	PV%
Reagan	489	90.89%	44	43,904,153	50.75%
Carter	49	9.11%	7	35,483,883	41.02%
Anderson	0	0.00%	0	5,720,060	6.61%

State popular votes

State	Total PV	Reagan	Carter	Anderson	Other
Alabama	1,341,929	654,192	636,730	16,481	34,526
Alaska	158,445	86,112	41,842	11,155	19,336
Arizona	873,945	529,688	246,843	76,952	20,462
Arkansas	837,582	403,164	398,041	22,468	13,909
California	8,587,063	4,524,858	3,083,661	739,833	238,711
Colorado	1,184,415	652,264	367,973	130,633	33,545
Connecticut	1,406,285	677,210	541,732	171,807	15,536
Delaware	235,900	111,252	105,754	16,288	2,606
District of Columbia	175,237	23,545	131,113	16,337	4,242
Florida	3,686,930	2,046,951	1,419,475	189,692	30,812
Georgia	1,596,695	654,168	890,733	36,055	15,739
Hawaii	303,287	130,112	135,879	32,021	5,275
Idaho	437,431	290,699	110,192	27,058	9,482
Illinois	4,749,721	2,358,049	1,981,413	346,754	63,505
Indiana	2,242,033	1,255,656	844,197	111,639	30,541
Iowa	1,317,661	676,026	508,672	115,633	17,330
Kansas	979,795	566,812	326,150	68,231	18,602
Kentucky	1,294,627	635,274	616,417	31,127	11,809
Louisiana	1,548,591	792,853	708,453	26,345	20,940
Maine	523,011	238,522	220,974	53,327	10,188
Maryland	1,540,496	680,606	726,161	119,537	14,192
Massachusetts	2,522,890	1,057,631	1,053,802	382,539	28,918
Michigan	3,909,725	1,915,225	1,661,532	275,223	57,745
Minnesota	2,051,980	873,268	954,174	174,990	49,548
Mississippi	892,620	441,089	429,281	12,036	10,214
Missouri	2,099,824	1,074,181	931,182	77,920	16,541
Montana	363,952	206,814	118,032	29,281	9,825
Nebraska	640,854	419,937	166,851	44,993	9,073
Nevada	247,885	155,017	66,666	17,651	8,551
New Hampshire	383,990	221,705	108,864	49,693	3,728
New Jersey	2,975,684	1,546,557	1,147,364	234,632	47,131
New Mexico	456,971	250,779	167,826	29,459	8,907
New York	6,201,959	2,893,831	2,728,372	467,801	111,955
North Carolina	1,855,833	915,018	875,635	52,800	12,380
North Dakota	301,545	193,695	79,189	23,640	5,021
Ohio	4,283,603	2,206,545	1,752,414	254,472	70,172
Oklahoma	1,149,708	695,570	402,026	38,284	13,828
Oregon	1,181,516	571,044	456,890	112,389	41,193
Pennsylvania	4,561,501	2,261,872	1,937,540	292,921	69,168
Rhode Island	416,072	154,793	198,342	59,819	3,118
South Carolina	894,071	441,841	430,385	14,153	7,692
South Dakota	327,703	198,343	103,855	21,431	4,074
Tennessee	1,617,616	787,761	783,051	35,991	10,813
Texas	4,541,636	2,510,705	1,881,147	111,613	38,171
Utah	604,222	439,687	124,266	30,284	9,985
Vermont	213,299	94,628	81,952	31,761	4,958
Virginia	1,866,032	989,609	752,174	95,418	28,831

State	Total PV	Reagan	Carter	Anderson	Other
Washington	1,742,394	865,244	650,193	185,073	41,884
West Virginia	737,715	334,206	367,462	31,691	4,356
Wisconsin	2,273,221	1,088,845	981,584	160,657	42,135
Wyoming	176,713	110,700	49,427	12,072	4,514
Total	86,513,813	43,904,153	35,483,883	5,720,060	1,405,717

State electoral votes

State	Total EV	Reagan	Carter
Alabama	9	9	0
Alaska	3	3	0
Arizona	6	6	0
Arkansas	6	6	0
California	45	45	0
Colorado	7	7	0
Connecticut	8	8	0
Delaware	3	3	0
District of Columbia	3	0	3
Florida	17	17	0
Georgia	12	0	12
Hawaii	4	0	4
Idaho	4	4	0
Illinois	26	26	0
Indiana	13	13	0
Iowa	8	8	0
Kansas	7	7	0
Kentucky	9	9	0
Louisiana	10	10	0
Maine	4	4	0
Maryland	10	0	10
Massachusetts	14	14	0
Michigan	21	21	0
Minnesota	10	0	10
Mississippi	7	7	0
Missouri	12	12	0
Montana	4	4	0
Nebraska	5	5	0
Nevada	3	3	0
New Hampshire	4	4	0
New Jersey	17	17	0
New Mexico	4	4	0
New York	41	41	0
North Carolina	13	13	0
North Dakota	3	3	0
Ohio	25	25	0
Oklahoma	8	8	0
Oregon	6	6	0
Pennsylvania	27	27	0
Rhode Island	4	0	4
South Carolina	8	8	0
South Dakota	4	4	0
Tennessee	10	10	0
Texas	26	26	0

State	Total EV	Reagan	Carter
Utah	4	4	0
Vermont	3	3	0
Virginia	12	12	0
Washington	9	9	0
West Virginia	6	0	6
Wisconsin	11	11	0
Wyoming	3	3	0
Total	538	489	49

Scenarios

1% to Reagan..Reagan 493, Carter 45
1% to Carter...Reagan 426, Carter 112
10K to Reagan...Reagan 493, Carter 45
10K to Carter ....Reagan 416, Carter 122
1964 allocation...Reagan 488, Carter 50
2020 allocation...Reagan 486, Carter 52

1984

Basics

Incumbent ....Ronald Reagan (R)
Prior streak...R (1)
Prior 5... R (3), D (2)
Population..235,824,902
States 51
Electoral votes 538
Popular votes 92,652,842

Field

Candidate	PI	Age	State	Position	N	W	CS
Ronald Reagan (R)	8.1	73.73	Calif.	President	X	X	95.13
Walter Mondale (D)	7.8	56.82	Minn.	Former vice president	X	—	58.83
Gary Hart (D)	6.3	47.93	Colo.	Senator	—	—	37.76
Jesse Jackson (D)	3.3	43.07	Ill.	Movement leader	—	—	23.30
John Glenn (D)	6.8	63.29	Ohio	Senator	—	—	12.08
George McGovern (D)	6.2	62.29	S.D.	Former nominee	—	—	11.14
Alan Cranston (D)	7.0	70.37	Calif.	Senator	—	—	10.17

Democratic nomination

Candidate	ConFB	FB%	ConLB	LB%	PriW	PriV	PriV%
Mondale	2,191	55.71%	—	—	10	6,811,214	37.82%
Hart	1,201	30.52%	—	—	16	6,503,968	36.12%
Jackson	466	11.84%	—	—	2	3,282,380	18.23%
McGovern	4	0.10%	—	—	0	334,801	1.86%
Glenn	2	0.05%	—	—	0	617,473	3.43%
Cranston	0	0.00%	—	—	0	51,437	0.29%

Republican nomination

Candidate	ConFB	FB%	ConLB	LB%	PriW	PriV	PriV%
Reagan	2,233	99.91%	—	—	25	6,484,987	98.62%

General election

Candidate	EV	EV%	SC	PV	PV%
Reagan	525	97.58%	49	54,455,075	58.77%
Mondale	13	2.42%	2	37,577,185	40.56%

State popular votes

State	Total PV	Reagan	Mondale	Other
Alabama	1,441,713	872,849	551,899	16,965
Alaska	207,605	138,377	62,007	7,221
Arizona	1,025,897	681,416	333,854	10,627
Arkansas	884,406	534,774	338,646	10,986
California	9,505,423	5,467,009	3,922,519	115,895
Colorado	1,295,380	821,817	454,975	18,588
Connecticut	1,466,900	890,877	569,597	6,426

State	Total PV	Reagan	Mondale	Other
Delaware	254,572	152,190	101,656	726
District of Columbia	211,288	29,009	180,408	1,871
Florida	4,180,051	2,730,350	1,448,816	885
Georgia	1,776,120	1,068,722	706,628	770
Hawaii	335,846	185,050	147,154	3,642
Idaho	411,144	297,523	108,510	5,111
Illinois	4,819,088	2,707,103	2,086,499	25,486
Indiana	2,233,069	1,377,230	841,481	14,358
Iowa	1,319,805	703,088	605,620	11,097
Kansas	1,021,991	677,296	333,149	11,546
Kentucky	1,369,345	821,702	539,539	8,104
Louisiana	1,706,822	1,037,299	651,586	17,937
Maine	553,144	336,500	214,515	2,129
Maryland	1,675,873	879,918	787,935	8,020
Massachusetts	2,559,453	1,310,936	1,239,606	8,911
Michigan	3,801,658	2,251,571	1,529,638	20,449
Minnesota	2,084,449	1,032,603	1,036,364	15,482
Mississippi	941,104	582,377	352,192	6,535
Missouri	2,122,783	1,274,188	848,583	12
Montana	384,377	232,450	146,742	5,185
Nebraska	652,090	460,054	187,866	4,170
Nevada	286,667	188,770	91,655	6,242
New Hampshire	389,066	267,051	120,395	1,620
New Jersey	3,217,862	1,933,630	1,261,323	22,909
New Mexico	514,370	307,101	201,769	5,500
New York	6,806,810	3,664,763	3,119,609	22,438
North Carolina	2,175,361	1,346,481	824,287	4,593
North Dakota	308,971	200,336	104,429	4,206
Ohio	4,547,619	2,678,560	1,825,440	43,619
Oklahoma	1,255,676	861,530	385,080	9,066
Oregon	1,226,527	685,700	536,479	4,348
Pennsylvania	4,844,903	2,584,323	2,228,131	32,449
Rhode Island	410,492	212,080	197,106	1,306
South Carolina	968,529	615,539	344,459	8,531
South Dakota	317,867	200,267	116,113	1,487
Tennessee	1,711,994	990,212	711,714	10,068
Texas	5,397,571	3,433,428	1,949,276	14,867
Utah	629,656	469,105	155,369	5,182
Vermont	234,561	135,865	95,730	2,966
Virginia	2,146,635	1,337,078	796,250	13,307
Washington	1,883,910	1,051,670	807,352	24,888
West Virginia	735,742	405,483	328,125	2,134
Wisconsin	2,211,689	1,198,584	995,740	17,365
Wyoming	188,968	133,241	53,370	2,357
Total	92,652,842	54,455,075	37,577,185	620,582

State electoral votes

State	Total EV	Reagan	Mondale
Alabama	9	9	0
Alaska	3	3	0
Arizona	7	7	0
Arkansas	6	6	0

State	Total EV	Reagan	Mondale
California	47	47	0
Colorado	8	8	0
Connecticut	8	8	0
Delaware	3	3	0
District of Columbia	3	0	3
Florida	21	21	0
Georgia	12	12	0
Hawaii	4	4	0
Idaho	4	4	0
Illinois	24	24	0
Indiana	12	12	0
Iowa	8	8	0
Kansas	7	7	0
Kentucky	9	9	0
Louisiana	10	10	0
Maine	4	4	0
Maryland	10	10	0
Massachusetts	13	13	0
Michigan	20	20	0
Minnesota	10	0	10
Mississippi	7	7	0
Missouri	11	11	0
Montana	4	4	0
Nebraska	5	5	0
Nevada	4	4	0
New Hampshire	4	4	0
New Jersey	16	16	0
New Mexico	5	5	0
New York	36	36	0
North Carolina	13	13	0
North Dakota	3	3	0
Ohio	23	23	0
Oklahoma	8	8	0
Oregon	7	7	0
Pennsylvania	25	25	0
Rhode Island	4	4	0
South Carolina	8	8	0
South Dakota	3	3	0
Tennessee	11	11	0
Texas	29	29	0
Utah	5	5	0
Vermont	3	3	0
Virginia	12	12	0
Washington	10	10	0
West Virginia	6	6	0
Wisconsin	11	11	0
Wyoming	3	3	0
Total	538	525	13

Scenarios

1988

Basics

Incumbent ....Ronald Reagan (R)
Prior streak ....R (2)
Prior 5 ....R (4), D (1)
Population 244,498,982
States 51
Electoral votes 538
Popular votes 91,594,809

Field

Candidate	PI	Age	State	Position	N	W	CS
George H.W. Bush (R)	6.5	64.39	Texas	Vice president	X	X	87.86
Michael Dukakis (D)	6.7	54.99	Mass.	Governor	X	—	65.32
Jesse Jackson (D)	3.6	47.07	Ill.	Movement leader	—	—	33.32
Bob Dole (R)	7.0	65.28	Kan.	Senator	—	—	21.51
Al Gore (D)	6.8	40.59	Tenn.	Senator	—	—	18.19
Pat Robertson (R)	4.5	58.61	Va.	Movement leader	—	—	15.41
Richard Gephardt (D)	4.0	47.75	Mo.	Representative	—	—	13.63
Paul Simon (D)	7.1	59.92	Ill.	Senator	—	—	12.66
Jack Kemp (R)	5.2	53.30	N.Y.	Representative	—	—	11.63
Gary Hart (D)	6.7	51.93	Colo.	Former senator	—	—	11.02
Lloyd Bentsen (D)	7.6	67.72	Texas	Senator	—	—	10.62
Pete du Pont (R)	6.6	53.78	Del.	Former governor	—	—	10.25
Bruce Babbitt (D)	6.2	50.35	Ariz.	Former governor	—	—	10.20

Democratic nomination

Candidate	ConFB	FB%	ConLB	LB%	PriW	PriV	PriV%
Dukakis	2,876	69.12%	—	—	22	9,817,185	42.75%
Jackson	1,219	29.28%	—	—	6	6,685,699	29.12%
Gephardt	2	0.05%	—	—	2	1,388,356	6.05%
Hart	1	0.02%	—	—	0	389,003	1.69%
Bentsen	1	0.02%	—	—	0	0	0.00%
Gore	0	0.00%	—	—	5	3,134,516	13.65%
Simon	0	0.00%	—	—	1	1,018,136	4.43%
Babbitt	0	0.00%	—	—	0	77,780	0.34%

Republican nomination

Candidate	ConFB	FB%	ConLB	LB%	PriW	PriV	PriV%
Bush	2,277	100.00%	—	—	35	8,254,654	67.86%
Dole	0	0.00%	—	—	1	2,333,268	19.18%
Robertson	0	0.00%	—	—	0	1,097,442	9.02%
Kemp	0	0.00%	—	—	0	331,333	2.72%
Du Pont	0	0.00%	—	—	0	49,781	0.41%

General election

Candidate	EV	EV%	SC	PV	PV%
Bush	426	79.18%	40	48,886,106	53.37%
Dukakis	111	20.63%	11	41,809,065	45.65%
Bentsen	1	0.19%	0	0	0.00%

State popular votes

State	Total PV	Bush	Dukakis	Other
Alabama	1,378,476	815,576	549,506	13,394
Alaska	200,116	119,251	72,584	8,281
Arizona	1,171,873	702,541	454,029	15,303
Arkansas	827,738	466,578	349,237	11,923
California	9,887,065	5,054,917	4,702,233	129,915
Colorado	1,372,394	728,177	621,453	22,764
Connecticut	1,443,394	750,241	676,584	16,569
Delaware	249,891	139,639	108,647	1,605
District of Columbia	192,877	27,590	159,407	5,880
Florida	4,302,313	2,618,885	1,656,701	26,727
Georgia	1,809,672	1,081,331	714,792	13,549
Hawaii	354,461	158,625	192,364	3,472
Idaho	408,968	253,881	147,272	7,815
Illinois	4,559,120	2,310,939	2,215,940	32,241
Indiana	2,168,621	1,297,763	860,643	10,215
Iowa	1,225,614	545,355	670,557	9,702
Kansas	993,044	554,049	422,636	16,359
Kentucky	1,322,517	734,281	580,368	7,868
Louisiana	1,628,202	883,702	717,460	27,040
Maine	555,035	307,131	243,569	4,335
Maryland	1,714,358	876,167	826,304	11,887
Massachusetts	2,632,805	1,194,644	1,401,406	36,755
Michigan	3,669,163	1,965,486	1,675,783	27,894
Minnesota	2,096,790	962,337	1,109,471	24,982
Mississippi	931,527	557,890	363,921	9,716
Missouri	2,093,713	1,084,953	1,001,619	7,141
Montana	365,674	190,412	168,936	6,326
Nebraska	661,465	397,956	259,235	4,274
Nevada	350,067	206,040	132,738	11,289
New Hampshire	451,074	281,537	163,696	5,841
New Jersey	3,099,553	1,743,192	1,320,352	36,009
New Mexico	521,287	270,341	244,497	6,449
New York	6,485,683	3,081,871	3,347,882	55,930
North Carolina	2,134,370	1,237,258	890,167	6,945
North Dakota	297,261	166,559	127,739	2,963
Ohio	4,393,699	2,416,549	1,939,629	37,521
Oklahoma	1,171,036	678,367	483,423	9,246
Oregon	1,201,694	560,126	616,206	25,362
Pennsylvania	4,536,251	2,300,087	2,194,944	41,220
Rhode Island	404,620	177,761	225,123	1,736
South Carolina	986,009	606,443	370,554	9,012
South Dakota	312,991	165,415	145,560	2,016
Tennessee	1,636,250	947,233	679,794	9,223
Texas	5,427,410	3,036,829	2,352,748	37,833

State	Total PV	Bush	Dukakis	Other
Utah	647,008	428,442	207,343	11,223
Vermont	243,328	124,331	115,775	3,222
Virginia	2,191,609	1,309,162	859,799	22,648
Washington	1,865,253	903,835	933,516	27,902
West Virginia	653,311	310,065	341,016	2,230
Wisconsin	2,191,608	1,047,499	1,126,794	17,315
Wyoming	176,551	106,867	67,113	2,571
Total	91,594,809	48,886,106	41,809,065	899,638

State electoral votes

State	Total EV	Bush	Dukakis	Bentsen
Alabama	9	9	0	0
Alaska	3	3	0	0
Arizona	7	7	0	0
Arkansas	6	6	0	0
California	47	47	0	0
Colorado	8	8	0	0
Connecticut	8	8	0	0
Delaware	3	3	0	0
District of Columbia	3	0	3	0
Florida	21	21	0	0
Georgia	12	12	0	0
Hawaii	4	0	4	0
Idaho	4	4	0	0
Illinois	24	24	0	0
Indiana	12	12	0	0
Iowa	8	0	8	0
Kansas	7	7	0	0
Kentucky	9	9	0	0
Louisiana	10	10	0	0
Maine	4	4	0	0
Maryland	10	10	0	0
Massachusetts	13	0	13	0
Michigan	20	20	0	0
Minnesota	10	0	10	0
Mississippi	7	7	0	0
Missouri	11	11	0	0
Montana	4	4	0	0
Nebraska	5	5	0	0
Nevada	4	4	0	0
New Hampshire	4	4	0	0
New Jersey	16	16	0	0
New Mexico	5	5	0	0
New York	36	0	36	0
North Carolina	13	13	0	0
North Dakota	3	3	0	0
Ohio	23	23	0	0
Oklahoma	8	8	0	0
Oregon	7	0	7	0
Pennsylvania	25	25	0	0
Rhode Island	4	0	4	0
South Carolina	8	8	0	0

State	Total EV	Bush	Dukakis	Bentsen
South Dakota	3	3	0	0
Tennessee	11	11	0	0
Texas	29	29	0	0
Utah	5	5	0	0
Vermont	3	3	0	0
Virginia	12	12	0	0
Washington	10	0	10	0
West Virginia	6	0	5	1
Wisconsin	11	0	11	0
Wyoming	3	3	0	0
Total	538	426	111	1

Scenarios

1% to Bush ....Bush 436, Dukakis 101, Bentsen 1
1% to Dukakis ....Bush 426, Dukakis 111, Bentsen 1
10K to Bush ....Bush 426, Dukakis 111, Bentsen 1
10K to Dukakis ....Bush 420, Dukakis 117, Bentsen 1
1964 allocation ....Bush 417, Dukakis 120, Bentsen 1
2020 allocation ....Bush 437, Dukakis 100, Bentsen 1

1992

Basics

Incumbent .... George H.W. Bush (R)
Prior streak .... R (3)
Prior 5 .... R (4), D (1)
Population 256,514,224
States 51
Electoral votes 538
Popular votes 104,425,014

Field

Candidate	PI	Age	State	Position	N	W	CS
Bill Clinton (D)	6.5	46.20	Ark.	Governor	X	X	82.15
George H.W. Bush (R)	8.2	68.39	Texas	President	X	—	66.86
Ross Perot (I)	2.9	62.35	Texas	Business executive	—	—	43.78
Jerry Brown (D)	6.8	54.57	Calif.	Former governor	—	—	24.83
Pat Buchanan (R)	5.2	54.00	Va.	Journalist	—	—	23.85
Paul Tsongas (D)	7.0	51.71	Mass.	Former senator	—	—	21.82
Bob Kerrey (D)	6.4	49.18	Nebr.	Senator	—	—	10.95
Tom Harkin (D)	6.9	52.95	Iowa	Senator	—	—	10.83

Democratic nomination

Candidate	ConFB	FB%	ConLB	LB%	PriW	PriV	PriV%
Clinton	3,372	78.64%	—	—	31	10,503,503	51.73%
Brown	596	13.90%	—	—	2	4,081,036	20.10%
Tsongas	209	4.87%	—	—	5	3,666,618	18.06%
Kerrey	0	0.00%	—	—	1	321,913	1.59%
Harkin	0	0.00%	—	—	0	281,584	1.39%

Republican nomination

Candidate	ConFB	FB%	ConLB	LB%	PriW	PriV	PriV%
Bush	2,166	98.01%	—	—	38	9,199,504	72.41%
Buchanan	18	0.81%	—	—	0	2,899,508	22.82%

General election

Candidate	EV	EV%	SC	PV	PV%
Clinton	370	68.77%	33	44,909,326	43.01%
Bush	168	31.23%	18	39,103,882	37.45%
Perot	0	0.00%	0	19,741,657	18.91%

State popular votes

State	Total PV	Clinton	Bush	Perot	Other
Alabama	1,688,060	690,080	804,283	183,109	10,588
Alaska	258,506	78,294	102,000	73,481	4,731
Arizona	1,486,975	543,050	572,086	353,741	18,098
Arkansas	950,653	505,823	337,324	99,132	8,374
California	11,131,721	5,121,325	3,630,574	2,296,006	83,816

State	Total PV	Clinton	Bush	Perot	Other
Colorado	1,569,180	629,681	562,850	366,010	10,639
Connecticut	1,616,332	682,318	578,313	348,771	6,930
Delaware	289,735	126,054	102,313	59,213	2,155
District of Columbia	227,572	192,619	20,698	9,681	4,574
Florida	5,314,392	2,072,698	2,173,310	1,053,067	15,317
Georgia	2,321,125	1,008,966	995,252	309,657	7,250
Hawaii	372,842	179,310	136,822	53,003	3,707
Idaho	482,142	137,013	202,645	130,395	12,089
Illinois	5,050,157	2,453,350	1,734,096	840,515	22,196
Indiana	2,305,871	848,420	989,375	455,934	12,142
Iowa	1,354,607	586,353	504,891	253,468	9,895
Kansas	1,157,335	390,434	449,951	312,358	4,592
Kentucky	1,492,900	665,104	617,178	203,944	6,674
Louisiana	1,790,017	815,971	733,386	211,478	29,182
Maine	679,499	263,420	206,504	206,820	2,755
Maryland	1,985,046	988,571	707,094	281,414	7,967
Massachusetts	2,773,700	1,318,662	805,049	630,731	19,258
Michigan	4,274,673	1,871,182	1,554,940	824,813	23,738
Minnesota	2,347,948	1,020,997	747,841	562,506	16,604
Mississippi	981,793	400,258	487,793	85,626	8,116
Missouri	2,391,565	1,053,873	811,159	518,741	7,792
Montana	410,611	154,507	144,207	107,225	4,672
Nebraska	737,546	216,864	343,678	174,104	2,900
Nevada	506,318	189,148	175,828	132,580	8,762
New Hampshire	537,943	209,040	202,484	121,337	5,082
New Jersey	3,343,594	1,436,206	1,356,865	521,829	28,694
New Mexico	569,986	261,617	212,824	91,895	3,650
New York	6,926,925	3,444,450	2,346,649	1,090,721	45,105
North Carolina	2,611,850	1,114,042	1,134,661	357,864	5,283
North Dakota	308,133	99,168	136,244	71,084	1,637
Ohio	4,939,967	1,984,942	1,894,310	1,036,426	24,289
Oklahoma	1,390,359	473,066	592,929	319,878	4,486
Oregon	1,462,643	621,314	475,757	354,091	11,481
Pennsylvania	4,959,810	2,239,164	1,791,841	902,667	26,138
Rhode Island	453,477	213,299	131,601	105,045	3,532
South Carolina	1,202,527	479,514	577,507	138,872	6,634
South Dakota	336,254	124,888	136,718	73,295	1,353
Tennessee	1,982,638	933,521	841,300	199,968	7,849
Texas	6,154,018	2,281,815	2,496,071	1,354,781	21,351
Utah	743,999	183,429	322,632	203,400	34,538
Vermont	289,701	133,592	88,122	65,991	1,996
Virginia	2,558,665	1,038,650	1,150,517	348,639	20,859
Washington	2,288,230	993,037	731,234	541,780	22,179
West Virginia	683,762	331,001	241,974	108,829	1,958
Wisconsin	2,531,114	1,041,066	930,855	544,479	14,714
Wyoming	200,598	68,160	79,347	51,263	1,828
Total	104,425,014	44,909,326	39,103,882	19,741,657	670,149

State electoral votes

State	Total EV	Clinton	Bush
Alabama	9	0	9
Alaska	3	0	3
Arizona	8	0	8
Arkansas	6	6	0
California	54	54	0
Colorado	8	8	0
Connecticut	8	8	0
Delaware	3	3	0
District of Columbia	3	3	0
Florida	25	0	25
Georgia	13	13	0
Hawaii	4	4	0
Idaho	4	0	4
Illinois	22	22	0
Indiana	12	0	12
Iowa	7	7	0
Kansas	6	0	6
Kentucky	8	8	0
Louisiana	9	9	0
Maine	4	4	0
Maryland	10	10	0
Massachusetts	12	12	0
Michigan	18	18	0
Minnesota	10	10	0
Mississippi	7	0	7
Missouri	11	11	0
Montana	3	3	0
Nebraska	5	0	5
Nevada	4	4	0
New Hampshire	4	4	0
New Jersey	15	15	0
New Mexico	5	5	0
New York	33	33	0
North Carolina	14	0	14
North Dakota	3	0	3
Ohio	21	21	0
Oklahoma	8	0	8
Oregon	7	7	0
Pennsylvania	23	23	0
Rhode Island	4	4	0
South Carolina	8	0	8
South Dakota	3	0	3
Tennessee	11	11	0
Texas	32	0	32
Utah	5	0	5
Vermont	3	3	0
Virginia	13	0	13

State	Total EV	Clinton	Bush
Washington	11	11	0
West Virginia	5	5	0
Wisconsin	11	11	0
Wyoming	3	0	3
Total	538	370	168

Scenarios

1% to Clinton .... Clinton 417, Bush 121
1% to Bush .... Clinton 332, Bush 206
10K to Clinton .... Clinton 376, Bush 162
10K to Bush .... Clinton 346, Bush 192
1964 allocation .... Clinton 389, Bush 149
2020 allocation .... Clinton 357, Bush 181

1996

Basics

Incumbent .... Bill Clinton (D)
Prior streak .... D (1)
Prior 5 .... R (3), D (2)
Population 269,394,284
States 51
Electoral votes 538
Popular votes 96,277,223

Field

Candidate	PI	Age	State	Position	N	W	CS
Bill Clinton (D)	8.5	50.20	Ark.	President	X	X	84.08
Bob Dole (R)	6.8	73.28	Kan.	Senator	X	—	67.01
Ross Perot (REF)	2.6	66.35	Texas	Business executive	—	—	36.87
Pat Buchanan (R)	5.0	58.00	Va.	Journalist	—	—	23.11
Steve Forbes (R)	3.6	49.29	N.J.	Journalist	—	—	16.96
Lyndon LaRouche (D)	3.6	74.15	Va.	Movement leader	—	—	13.27
Lamar Alexander (R)	7.8	56.33	Tenn.	Former governor	—	—	11.97
Alan Keyes (R)	3.2	46.23	Md.	Former ambassador	—	—	11.81
Richard Lugar (R)	6.5	64.58	Ind.	Senator	—	—	10.51
Phil Gramm (R)	8.4	54.32	Texas	Senator	—	—	10.30

Democratic nomination

Candidate	ConFB	FB%	ConLB	LB%	PriW	PriV	PriV%
Clinton	4,277	99.72%	—	—	34	9,706,802	88.57%
LaRouche	0	0.00%	—	—	0	596,422	5.44%

Republican nomination

Candidate	ConFB	FB%	ConLB	LB%	PriW	PriV	PriV%
Dole	1,928	96.88%	—	—	39	8,791,000	58.30%
Buchanan	43	2.16%	—	—	1	3,184,099	21.12%
Gramm	2	0.10%	—	—	0	70,002	0.46%
Keyes	1	0.05%	—	—	0	449,459	2.98%
Forbes	0	0.00%	—	—	2	1,750,109	11.61%
Alexander	0	0.00%	—	—	0	494,317	3.28%
Lugar	0	0.00%	—	—	0	127,111	0.84%

General election

Candidate	EV	EV%	SC	PV	PV%
Clinton	379	70.45%	32	47,402,357	49.24%
Dole	159	29.55%	19	39,198,755	40.71%
Perot	0	0.00%	0	8,085,402	8.40%

State popular votes

State	Total PV	Clinton	Dole	Perot	Other
Alabama	1,534,349	662,165	769,044	92,149	10,991
Alaska	241,620	80,380	122,746	26,333	12,161
Arizona	1,404,405	653,288	622,073	112,072	16,972
Arkansas	884,262	475,171	325,416	69,884	13,791
California	10,019,484	5,119,835	3,828,380	697,847	373,422
Colorado	1,510,704	671,152	691,848	99,629	48,075
Connecticut	1,392,614	735,740	483,109	139,523	34,242
Delaware	270,845	140,355	99,062	28,719	2,709
District of Columbia	185,726	158,220	17,339	3,611	6,556
Florida	5,303,794	2,546,870	2,244,536	483,870	28,518
Georgia	2,299,071	1,053,849	1,080,843	146,337	18,042
Hawaii	360,120	205,012	113,943	27,358	13,807
Idaho	491,719	165,443	256,595	62,518	7,163
Illinois	4,311,391	2,341,744	1,587,021	346,408	36,218
Indiana	2,135,431	887,424	1,006,693	224,299	17,015
Iowa	1,234,075	620,258	492,644	105,159	16,014
Kansas	1,074,300	387,659	583,245	92,639	10,757
Kentucky	1,388,708	636,614	623,283	120,396	8,415
Louisiana	1,783,959	927,837	712,586	123,293	20,243
Maine	605,897	312,788	186,378	85,970	20,761
Maryland	1,780,870	966,207	681,530	115,812	17,321
Massachusetts	2,556,786	1,571,763	718,107	227,217	39,699
Michigan	3,848,844	1,989,653	1,481,212	336,670	41,309
Minnesota	2,192,640	1,120,438	766,476	257,704	48,022
Mississippi	893,857	394,022	439,838	52,222	7,775
Missouri	2,158,065	1,025,935	890,016	217,188	24,926
Montana	407,261	167,922	179,652	55,229	4,458
Nebraska	677,415	236,761	363,467	71,278	5,909
Nevada	464,279	203,974	199,244	43,986	17,075
New Hampshire	499,175	246,214	196,532	48,390	8,039
New Jersey	3,075,807	1,652,329	1,103,078	262,134	58,266
New Mexico	556,074	273,495	232,751	32,257	17,571
New York	6,316,129	3,756,177	1,933,492	503,458	123,002
North Carolina	2,515,807	1,107,849	1,225,938	168,059	13,961
North Dakota	266,411	106,905	125,050	32,515	1,941
Ohio	4,534,434	2,148,222	1,859,883	483,207	43,122
Oklahoma	1,206,713	488,105	582,315	130,788	5,505
Oregon	1,377,760	649,641	538,152	121,221	68,746
Pennsylvania	4,506,118	2,215,819	1,801,169	430,984	58,146
Rhode Island	390,284	233,050	104,683	43,723	8,828
South Carolina	1,151,689	506,283	573,458	64,386	7,562
South Dakota	323,826	139,333	150,543	31,250	2,700
Tennessee	1,894,105	909,146	863,530	105,918	15,511
Texas	5,611,644	2,459,683	2,736,167	378,537	37,257
Utah	665,629	221,633	361,911	66,461	15,624
Vermont	258,449	137,894	80,352	31,024	9,179
Virginia	2,416,642	1,091,060	1,138,350	159,861	27,371

State	Total PV	Clinton	Dole	Perot	Other
Washington	2,253,837	1,123,323	840,712	201,003	88,799
West Virginia	636,459	327,812	233,946	71,639	3,062
Wisconsin	2,196,169	1,071,971	845,029	227,339	51,830
Wyoming	211,571	77,934	105,388	25,928	2,321
Total	96,277,223	47,402,357	39,198,755	8,085,402	1,590,709

State electoral votes

State	Total EV	Clinton	Dole
Alabama	9	0	9
Alaska	3	0	3
Arizona	8	8	0
Arkansas	6	6	0
California	54	54	0
Colorado	8	0	8
Connecticut	8	8	0
Delaware	3	3	0
District of Columbia	3	3	0
Florida	25	25	0
Georgia	13	0	13
Hawaii	4	4	0
Idaho	4	0	4
Illinois	22	22	0
Indiana	12	0	12
Iowa	7	7	0
Kansas	6	0	6
Kentucky	8	8	0
Louisiana	9	9	0
Maine	4	4	0
Maryland	10	10	0
Massachusetts	12	12	0
Michigan	18	18	0
Minnesota	10	10	0
Mississippi	7	0	7
Missouri	11	11	0
Montana	3	0	3
Nebraska	5	0	5
Nevada	4	4	0
New Hampshire	4	4	0
New Jersey	15	15	0
New Mexico	5	5	0
New York	33	33	0
North Carolina	14	0	14
North Dakota	3	0	3
Ohio	21	21	0
Oklahoma	8	0	8
Oregon	7	7	0
Pennsylvania	23	23	0
Rhode Island	4	4	0
South Carolina	8	0	8
South Dakota	3	0	3
Tennessee	11	11	0
Texas	32	0	32

State	Total EV	Clinton	Dole
Utah	5	0	5
Vermont	3	3	0
Virginia	13	0	13
Washington	11	11	0
West Virginia	5	5	0
Wisconsin	11	11	0
Wyoming	3	0	3
Total	538	379	159

Scenarios

1% to Clinton ....Clinton 413, Dole 125
1% to Dole...Clinton 367, Dole 171
10K to Clinton ....Clinton 388, Dole 150
10K to Dole ....Clinton 367, Dole 171
1964 allocation..Clinton 386, Dole 152
2020 allocation..Clinton 369, Dole 169

2000

Basics

Incumbent .... Bill Clinton (D)
Prior streak .... D (2)
Prior 5 .... R (3), D (2)
Population 281,424,603
States 51
Electoral votes 537
Popular votes 105,405,100

Field

Candidate	PI	Age	State	Position	N	W	CS
George W. Bush (R)	7.9	54.32	Texas	Governor	X	X	77.21
Al Gore (D)	8.8	52.59	Tenn.	Vice president	X	—	74.51
John McCain (R)	6.2	64.17	Ariz.	Senator	—	—	29.92
Bill Bradley (D)	7.1	57.26	N.J.	Former senator	—	—	22.10
Ralph Nader (GRN)	1.3	66.68	Conn.	Movement leader	—	—	18.76
Alan Keyes (R)	3.7	50.23	Md.	Former ambassador	—	—	13.04
Steve Forbes (R)	4.0	53.29	N.J.	Journalist	—	—	10.52
Gary Bauer (R)	5.1	54.49	Va.	Movement leader	—	—	10.19

Democratic nomination

Candidate	ConFB	FB%	ConLB	LB%	PriW	PriV	PriV%
Gore	4,339	100.00%	—	—	39	11,081,274	75.56%
Bradley	0	0.00%	—	—	0	2,958,074	20.17%

Republican nomination

Candidate	ConFB	FB%	ConLB	LB%	PriW	PriV	PriV%
Bush	2,066	100.00%	—	—	36	12,390,575	60.08%
McCain	0	0.00%	—	—	7	6,848,293	33.21%
Keyes	0	0.00%	—	—	0	1,043,465	5.06%
Forbes	0	0.00%	—	—	0	177,685	0.86%
Bauer	0	0.00%	—	—	0	64,344	0.31%

General election

Candidate	EV	EV%	SC	PV	PV%
Bush	271	50.47%	30	50,456,002	47.87%
Gore	266	49.53%	21	50,999,897	48.39%
Nader	0	0.00%	0	2,882,955	2.74%

State popular votes

State	Total PV	Gore	Bush	Nader	Other
Alabama	1,666,272	692,611	941,173	18,323	14,165
Alaska	285,560	79,004	167,398	28,747	10,411
Arizona	1,532,016	685,341	781,652	45,645	19,378
Arkansas	921,781	422,768	472,940	13,421	12,652
California	10,965,856	5,861,203	4,567,429	418,707	118,517

State	Total PV	Gore	Bush	Nader	Other
Colorado	1,741,368	738,227	883,748	91,434	27,959
Connecticut	1,459,525	816,015	561,094	64,452	17,964
Delaware	327,622	180,068	137,288	8,307	1,959
District of Columbia	201,894	171,923	18,073	10,576	1,322
Florida	5,963,110	2,912,253	2,912,790	97,488	40,579
Georgia	2,596,804	1,116,230	1,419,720	13,432	47,422
Hawaii	367,951	205,286	137,845	21,623	3,197
Idaho	501,621	138,637	336,937	12,292	13,755
Illinois	4,742,123	2,589,026	2,019,421	103,759	29,917
Indiana	2,199,302	901,980	1,245,836	18,531	32,955
Iowa	1,315,563	638,517	634,373	29,374	13,299
Kansas	1,072,218	399,276	622,332	36,086	14,524
Kentucky	1,544,187	638,898	872,492	23,192	9,605
Louisiana	1,765,656	792,344	927,871	20,473	24,968
Maine	651,817	319,951	286,616	37,127	8,123
Maryland	2,025,480	1,145,782	813,797	53,768	12,133
Massachusetts	2,702,984	1,616,487	878,502	173,564	34,431
Michigan	4,232,501	2,170,418	1,953,139	84,165	24,779
Minnesota	2,438,685	1,168,266	1,109,659	126,696	34,064
Mississippi	994,184	404,614	572,844	8,122	8,604
Missouri	2,359,892	1,111,138	1,189,924	38,515	20,315
Montana	410,997	137,126	240,178	24,437	9,256
Nebraska	697,019	231,780	433,862	24,540	6,837
Nevada	608,970	279,978	301,575	15,008	12,409
New Hampshire	569,081	266,348	273,559	22,198	6,976
New Jersey	3,187,226	1,788,850	1,284,173	94,554	19,649
New Mexico	598,605	286,783	286,417	21,251	4,154
New York	6,821,999	4,107,697	2,403,374	244,030	66,898
North Carolina	2,911,262	1,257,692	1,631,163	—	22,407
North Dakota	288,256	95,284	174,852	9,486	8,634
Ohio	4,705,457	2,186,190	2,351,209	117,857	50,201
Oklahoma	1,234,229	474,276	744,337	—	15,616
Oregon	1,533,968	720,342	713,577	77,357	22,692
Pennsylvania	4,913,119	2,485,967	2,281,127	103,392	42,633
Rhode Island	409,112	249,508	130,555	25,052	3,997
South Carolina	1,382,717	565,561	785,937	20,200	11,019
South Dakota	316,269	118,804	190,700	—	6,765
Tennessee	2,076,181	981,720	1,061,949	19,781	12,731
Texas	6,407,637	2,433,746	3,799,639	137,994	36,258
Utah	770,754	203,053	515,096	35,850	16,755
Vermont	294,308	149,022	119,775	20,374	5,137
Virginia	2,739,447	1,217,290	1,437,490	59,398	25,269
Washington	2,487,433	1,247,652	1,108,864	103,002	27,915
West Virginia	648,124	295,497	336,475	10,680	5,472
Wisconsin	2,598,607	1,242,987	1,237,279	94,070	24,271
Wyoming	218,351	60,481	147,947	4,625	5,298
Total	105,405,100	50,999,897	50,456,002	2,882,955	1,066,246

State electoral votes

State	Total EV	Bush	Gore
Alabama	9	9	0
Alaska	3	3	0
Arizona	8	8	0
Arkansas	6	6	0
California	54	0	54
Colorado	8	8	0
Connecticut	8	0	8
Delaware	3	0	3
District of Columbia	2	0	2
Florida	25	25	0
Georgia	13	13	0
Hawaii	4	0	4
Idaho	4	4	0
Illinois	22	0	22
Indiana	12	12	0
Iowa	7	0	7
Kansas	6	6	0
Kentucky	8	8	0
Louisiana	9	9	0
Maine	4	0	4
Maryland	10	0	10
Massachusetts	12	0	12
Michigan	18	0	18
Minnesota	10	0	10
Mississippi	7	7	0
Missouri	11	11	0
Montana	3	3	0
Nebraska	5	5	0
Nevada	4	4	0
New Hampshire	4	4	0
New Jersey	15	0	15
New Mexico	5	0	5
New York	33	0	33
North Carolina	14	14	0
North Dakota	3	3	0
Ohio	21	21	0
Oklahoma	8	8	0
Oregon	7	0	7
Pennsylvania	23	0	23
Rhode Island	4	0	4
South Carolina	8	8	0
South Dakota	3	3	0
Tennessee	11	11	0
Texas	32	32	0
Utah	5	5	0
Vermont	3	0	3
Virginia	13	13	0

State	Total EV	Bush	Gore
Washington	11	0	11
West Virginia	5	5	0
Wisconsin	11	0	11
Wyoming	3	3	0
Total	537	271	266

Scenarios

1% to Bush ....Bush 301, Gore 236
1% to Gore ....Gore 295, Bush 242
10K to Bush..Bush 301, Gore 236
10K to Gore ....Gore 295, Bush 242
1964 allocation...Gore 279, Bush 259
2020 allocation ....Bush 285, Gore 253

2004

Basics

Incumbent ....George W. Bush (R)
Prior streak ....R (1)
Prior 5 .... R (3), D (2)
Population 292,805,298
States 51
Electoral votes 538
Popular votes 122,295,345

Field

Candidate	PI	Age	State	Position	N	W	CS
George W. Bush (R)	9.3	58.32	Texas	President	X	X	78.71
John Kerry (D)	6.6	60.89	Mass.	Senator	X	—	73.65
John Edwards (D)	7.8	51.39	N.C.	Senator	—	—	22.22
Howard Dean (D)	6.0	55.96	Vt.	Former governor	—	—	13.32
Wesley Clark (D)	4.2	59.86	Ark.	Former general	—	—	12.00
Joseph Lieberman (D)	7.2	62.69	Conn.	Senator	—	—	11.04
Richard Gephardt (D)	3.9	63.75	Mo.	Representative	—	—	10.23

Democratic nomination

Candidate	ConFB	FB%	ConLB	LB%	PriW	PriV	PriV%
Kerry	4,253	98.40%	—	—	33	9,753,562	61.06%
Edwards	0	0.00%	—	—	1	3,089,104	19.34%
Dean	0	0.00%	—	—	2	883,808	5.53%
Clark	0	0.00%	—	—	1	532,512	3.33%
Lieberman	0	0.00%	—	—	0	277,050	1.73%
Gephardt	0	0.00%	—	—	0	62,036	0.39%

Republican nomination

Candidate	ConFB	FB%	ConLB	LB%	PriW	PriV	PriV%
Bush	2,508	99.96%	—	—	27	7,784,653	98.04%

General election

Candidate	EV	EV%	SC	PV	PV%
Bush	286	53.16%	31	62,040,610	50.73%
Kerry	251	46.65%	20	59,028,439	48.27%
Edwards	1	0.19%	0	0	0.00%

State popular votes

State	Total PV	Bush	Kerry	Other
Alabama	1,883,449	1,176,394	693,933	13,122
Alaska	312,598	190,889	111,025	10,684
Arizona	2,012,585	1,104,294	893,524	14,767
Arkansas	1,054,945	572,898	469,953	12,094
California	12,421,852	5,509,826	6,745,485	166,541
Colorado	2,130,330	1,101,255	1,001,732	27,343

State	Total PV	Bush	Kerry	Other
Connecticut	1,578,769	693,826	857,488	27,455
Delaware	375,190	171,660	200,152	3,378
District of Columbia	227,586	21,256	202,970	3,360
Florida	7,609,810	3,964,522	3,583,544	61,744
Georgia	3,301,875	1,914,254	1,366,149	21,472
Hawaii	429,013	194,191	231,708	3,114
Idaho	598,447	409,235	181,098	8,114
Illinois	5,274,322	2,345,946	2,891,550	36,826
Indiana	2,468,002	1,479,438	969,011	19,553
Iowa	1,506,908	751,957	741,898	13,053
Kansas	1,187,756	736,456	434,993	16,307
Kentucky	1,795,882	1,069,439	712,733	13,710
Louisiana	1,943,106	1,102,169	820,299	20,638
Maine	740,752	330,201	396,842	13,709
Maryland	2,386,678	1,024,703	1,334,493	27,482
Massachusetts	2,912,388	1,071,109	1,803,800	37,479
Michigan	4,839,252	2,313,746	2,479,183	46,323
Minnesota	2,828,387	1,346,695	1,445,014	36,678
Mississippi	1,152,145	684,981	458,094	9,070
Missouri	2,731,364	1,455,713	1,259,171	16,480
Montana	450,445	266,063	173,710	10,672
Nebraska	778,186	512,814	254,328	11,044
Nevada	829,587	418,690	397,190	13,707
New Hampshire	677,738	331,237	340,511	5,990
New Jersey	3,611,691	1,670,003	1,911,430	30,258
New Mexico	756,304	376,930	370,942	8,432
New York	7,391,036	2,962,567	4,314,280	114,189
North Carolina	3,501,007	1,961,166	1,525,849	13,992
North Dakota	312,833	196,651	111,052	5,130
Ohio	5,627,908	2,859,768	2,741,167	26,973
Oklahoma	1,463,758	959,792	503,966	—
Oregon	1,836,782	866,831	943,163	26,788
Pennsylvania	5,769,590	2,793,847	2,938,095	37,648
Rhode Island	437,134	169,046	259,760	8,328
South Carolina	1,617,730	937,974	661,699	18,057
South Dakota	388,215	232,584	149,244	6,387
Tennessee	2,437,319	1,384,375	1,036,477	16,467
Texas	7,410,765	4,526,917	2,832,704	51,144
Utah	927,844	663,742	241,199	22,903
Vermont	312,309	121,180	184,067	7,062
Virginia	3,198,367	1,716,959	1,454,742	26,666
Washington	2,859,084	1,304,894	1,510,201	43,989
West Virginia	755,887	423,778	326,541	5,568
Wisconsin	2,997,007	1,478,120	1,489,504	29,383
Wyoming	243,428	167,629	70,776	5,023
Total	122,295,345	62,040,610	59,028,439	1,226,296

State electoral votes

State	Total EV	Bush	Kerry	Edwards
Alabama	9	9	0	0
Alaska	3	3	0	0
Arizona	10	10	0	0
Arkansas	6	6	0	0
California	55	0	55	0
Colorado	9	9	0	0
Connecticut	7	0	7	0
Delaware	3	0	3	0
District of Columbia	3	0	3	0
Florida	27	27	0	0
Georgia	15	15	0	0
Hawaii	4	0	4	0
Idaho	4	4	0	0
Illinois	21	0	21	0
Indiana	11	11	0	0
Iowa	7	7	0	0
Kansas	6	6	0	0
Kentucky	8	8	0	0
Louisiana	9	9	0	0
Maine	4	0	4	0
Maryland	10	0	10	0
Massachusetts	12	0	12	0
Michigan	17	0	17	0
Minnesota	10	0	9	1
Mississippi	6	6	0	0
Missouri	11	11	0	0
Montana	3	3	0	0
Nebraska	5	5	0	0
Nevada	5	5	0	0
New Hampshire	4	0	4	0
New Jersey	15	0	15	0
New Mexico	5	5	0	0
New York	31	0	31	0
North Carolina	15	15	0	0
North Dakota	3	3	0	0
Ohio	20	20	0	0
Oklahoma	7	7	0	0
Oregon	7	0	7	0
Pennsylvania	21	0	21	0
Rhode Island	4	0	4	0
South Carolina	8	8	0	0
South Dakota	3	3	0	0
Tennessee	11	11	0	0
Texas	34	34	0	0
Utah	5	5	0	0
Vermont	3	0	3	0
Virginia	13	13	0	0

State	Total EV	Bush	Kerry	Edwards
Washington	11	0	11	0
West Virginia	5	5	0	0
Wisconsin	10	0	10	0
Wyoming	3	3	0	0
Total	538	286	251	1

Scenarios

1% to Bush...Bush 300, Kerry 237, Edwards 1
1% to Kerry...Bush 274, Kerry 263, Edwards 1
10K to Bush..Bush 300, Kerry 237, Edwards 1
10K to Kerry..Bush 274, Kerry 263, Edwards 1
1964 allocation..Kerry 269, Bush 268, Edwards 1
2020 allocation..Bush 292, Kerry 245, Edwards 1

2008

Basics

Incumbent ....George W. Bush (R)
Prior streak ....R (2)
Prior 5 ....R (3), D (2)
Population 304,093,966
States 51
Electoral votes 538
Popular votes 131,313,820

Field

Candidate	PI	Age	State	Position	N	W	CS
Barack Obama (D)	6.8	47.24	Ill.	Senator	X	X	84.03
John McCain (R)	5.9	72.17	Ariz.	Senator	X	—	68.78
Hillary Clinton (D)	7.0	61.02	N.Y.	Senator	—	—	43.42
Mitt Romney (R)	6.1	61.64	Mass.	Former governor	—	—	23.13
Mike Huckabee (R)	7.3	53.19	Ark.	Former governor	—	—	22.10
Ron Paul (R/TC)	4.8	73.20	Texas	Representative	—	—	13.62
Rudy Giuliani (R)	3.9	64.43	N.Y.	Former mayor	—	—	11.71
John Edwards (D)	8.9	55.39	N.C.	Former senator	—	—	11.63
Fred Thompson (R)	7.2	66.20	Tenn.	Former senator	—	—	10.81
Bill Richardson (D)	5.9	60.96	N.M.	Governor	—	—	10.17

Democratic nomination

Candidate	ConFB	FB%	ConLB	LB%	PriW	PriV	PriV%
Obama	3,189	72.15%	—	—	21	17,423,182	47.28%
Clinton	1,011	22.87%	—	—	19	17,714,951	48.08%
Edwards	0	0.00%	—	—	0	1,000,862	2.72%
Richardson	0	0.00%	—	—	0	104,616	0.28%

Republican nomination

Candidate	ConFB	FB%	ConLB	LB%	PriW	PriV	PriV%
McCain	2,341	98.36%	—	—	33	9,776,631	47.02%
Paul	17	0.71%	—	—	0	1,169,863	5.63%
Romney	2	0.08%	—	—	3	4,544,125	21.86%
Huckabee	0	0.00%	—	—	5	4,194,460	20.18%
Giuliani	0	0.00%	—	—	0	591,395	2.84%
Thompson	0	0.00%	—	—	0	282,185	1.36%

General election

Candidate	EV	EV%	SC	PV	PV%
Obama	365	67.84%	29	69,498,516	52.93%
McCain	173	32.16%	22	59,948,323	45.65%
Paul	0	0.00%	0	38,105	0.03%

State popular votes

State	Total PV	Obama	McCain	Other
Alabama	2,099,819	813,479	1,266,546	19,794
Alaska	326,197	123,594	193,841	8,762
Arizona	2,293,475	1,034,707	1,230,111	28,657
Arkansas	1,086,617	422,310	638,017	26,290
California	13,561,900	8,274,473	5,011,781	275,646
Colorado	2,401,462	1,288,633	1,073,629	39,200
Connecticut	1,646,797	997,772	629,428	19,597
Delaware	412,412	255,459	152,374	4,579
District of Columbia	265,853	245,800	17,367	2,686
Florida	8,390,744	4,282,074	4,045,624	63,046
Georgia	3,924,486	1,844,123	2,048,759	31,604
Hawaii	453,568	325,871	120,566	7,131
Idaho	655,122	236,440	403,012	15,670
Illinois	5,522,371	3,419,348	2,031,179	71,844
Indiana	2,751,054	1,374,039	1,345,648	31,367
Iowa	1,537,123	828,940	682,379	25,804
Kansas	1,235,872	514,765	699,655	21,452
Kentucky	1,826,620	751,985	1,048,462	26,173
Louisiana	1,960,761	782,989	1,148,275	29,497
Maine	731,163	421,923	295,273	13,967
Maryland	2,631,596	1,629,467	959,862	42,267
Massachusetts	3,080,985	1,904,097	1,108,854	68,034
Michigan	5,001,766	2,872,579	2,048,639	80,548
Minnesota	2,910,369	1,573,354	1,275,409	61,606
Mississippi	1,289,865	554,662	724,597	10,606
Missouri	2,925,205	1,441,911	1,445,814	37,480
Montana	490,302	231,667	242,763	15,872
Nebraska	801,281	333,319	452,979	14,983
Nevada	967,848	533,736	412,827	21,285
New Hampshire	710,970	384,826	316,534	9,610
New Jersey	3,868,237	2,215,422	1,613,207	39,608
New Mexico	830,158	472,422	346,832	10,904
New York	7,640,931	4,804,945	2,752,771	83,215
North Carolina	4,310,789	2,142,651	2,128,474	39,664
North Dakota	316,621	141,278	168,601	6,742
Ohio	5,708,350	2,940,044	2,677,820	90,486
Oklahoma	1,462,661	502,496	960,165	—
Oregon	1,827,864	1,037,291	738,475	52,098
Pennsylvania	6,013,272	3,276,363	2,655,885	81,024
Rhode Island	471,766	296,571	165,391	9,804
South Carolina	1,920,969	862,449	1,034,896	23,624
South Dakota	381,975	170,924	203,054	7,997
Tennessee	2,599,749	1,087,437	1,479,178	33,134
Texas	8,077,795	3,528,633	4,479,328	69,834
Utah	952,370	327,670	596,030	28,670
Vermont	325,046	219,262	98,974	6,810
Virginia	3,723,260	1,959,532	1,725,005	38,723
Washington	3,036,878	1,750,848	1,229,216	56,814

State	Total PV	Obama	McCain	Other
West Virginia	713,451	303,857	397,466	12,128
Wisconsin	2,983,417	1,677,211	1,262,393	43,813
Wyoming	254,658	82,868	164,958	6,832
Total	131,313,820	69,498,516	59,948,323	1,866,981

State electoral votes

State	Total EV	Obama	McCain
Alabama	9	0	9
Alaska	3	0	3
Arizona	10	0	10
Arkansas	6	0	6
California	55	55	0
Colorado	9	9	0
Connecticut	7	7	0
Delaware	3	3	0
District of Columbia	3	3	0
Florida	27	27	0
Georgia	15	0	15
Hawaii	4	4	0
Idaho	4	0	4
Illinois	21	21	0
Indiana	11	11	0
Iowa	7	7	0
Kansas	6	0	6
Kentucky	8	0	8
Louisiana	9	0	9
Maine	4	4	0
Maryland	10	10	0
Massachusetts	12	12	0
Michigan	17	17	0
Minnesota	10	10	0
Mississippi	6	0	6
Missouri	11	0	11
Montana	3	0	3
Nebraska	5	1	4
Nevada	5	5	0
New Hampshire	4	4	0
New Jersey	15	15	0
New Mexico	5	5	0
New York	31	31	0
North Carolina	15	15	0
North Dakota	3	0	3
Ohio	20	20	0
Oklahoma	7	0	7
Oregon	7	7	0
Pennsylvania	21	21	0
Rhode Island	4	4	0
South Carolina	8	0	8
South Dakota	3	0	3
Tennessee	11	0	11
Texas	34	0	34
Utah	5	0	5

State	Total EV	Obama	McCain
Vermont	3	3	0
Virginia	13	13	0
Washington	11	11	0
West Virginia	5	0	5
Wisconsin	10	10	0
Wyoming	3	0	3
Total	538	365	173

Scenarios

1% to Obama ....Obama 376, McCain 162
1% to McCain ....Obama 339, McCain 199
10K to Obama ....Obama 379, McCain 159
10K to McCain ....Obama 350, McCain 188
1964 allocation ....Obama 371, McCain 167
2020 allocation ....Obama 359, McCain 179

2012

Basics

Incumbent	Barack Obama (D)
Prior streak	D (1)
Prior 5	D (3), R (2)
Population	313,914,040
States	51
Electoral votes	538
Popular votes	129,085,403

Field

Candidate	PI	Age	State	Position	N	W	CS
Barack Obama (D)	8.3	51.24	Ill.	President	X	X	81.59
Mitt Romney (R)	5.9	65.64	Mass.	Former governor	X	—	70.93
Rick Santorum (R)	7.3	54.48	Pa.	Former senator	—	—	22.25
Newt Gingrich (R)	4.3	69.37	Ga.	Former representative	—	—	18.59
Ron Paul (R)	4.6	77.20	Texas	Representative	—	—	18.11
Jon Huntsman (R)	6.7	52.60	Utah	Former governor	—	—	10.27
Rick Perry (R)	7.5	62.66	Texas	Governor	—	—	10.14
Michele Bachmann (R)	4.3	56.57	Minn.	Representative	—	—	10.11

Democratic nomination

Candidate	ConFB	FB%	ConLB	LB%	PriW	PriV	PriV%
Obama	5,425	97.70%	—	—	30	8,415,194	91.40%

Republican nomination

Candidate	ConFB	FB%	ConLB	LB%	PriW	PriV	PriV%
Romney	2,061	90.16%	—	—	31	9,841,300	52.43%
Paul	190	8.31%	—	—	0	2,016,389	10.74%
Santorum	9	0.39%	—	—	6	3,805,655	20.28%
Huntsman	1	0.04%	—	—	0	83,131	0.44%
Bachmann	1	0.04%	—	—	0	35,084	0.19%
Gingrich	0	0.00%	—	—	2	2,687,243	14.32%
Perry	0	0.00%	—	—	0	42,245	0.23%

General election

Candidate	EV	EV%	SC	PV	PV%
Obama	332	61.71%	27	65,915,796	51.06%
Romney	206	38.29%	24	60,933,500	47.20%

State popular votes

State	Total PV	Obama	Romney	Other
Alabama	2,074,338	795,696	1,255,925	22,717
Alaska	300,495	122,640	164,676	13,179
Arizona	2,299,254	1,025,232	1,233,654	40,368
Arkansas	1,069,468	394,409	647,744	27,315
California	13,038,547	7,854,285	4,839,958	344,304

State	Total PV	Obama	Romney	Other
Colorado	2,569,522	1,323,102	1,185,243	61,177
Connecticut	1,558,960	905,083	634,892	18,985
Delaware	413,921	242,584	165,484	5,853
District of Columbia	293,764	267,070	21,381	5,313
Florida	8,474,179	4,237,756	4,163,447	72,976
Georgia	3,900,050	1,773,827	2,078,688	47,535
Hawaii	434,697	306,658	121,015	7,024
Idaho	652,274	212,787	420,911	18,576
Illinois	5,242,014	3,019,512	2,135,216	87,286
Indiana	2,624,534	1,152,887	1,420,543	51,104
Iowa	1,582,180	822,544	730,617	29,019
Kansas	1,159,971	440,726	692,634	26,611
Kentucky	1,797,212	679,370	1,087,190	30,652
Louisiana	1,994,065	809,141	1,152,262	32,662
Maine	713,180	401,306	292,276	19,598
Maryland	2,707,327	1,677,844	971,869	57,614
Massachusetts	3,167,767	1,921,290	1,188,314	58,163
Michigan	4,730,961	2,564,569	2,115,256	51,136
Minnesota	2,936,561	1,546,167	1,320,225	70,169
Mississippi	1,285,584	562,949	710,746	11,889
Missouri	2,757,323	1,223,796	1,482,440	51,087
Montana	484,048	201,839	267,928	14,281
Nebraska	794,379	302,081	475,064	17,234
Nevada	1,014,918	531,373	463,567	19,978
New Hampshire	710,972	369,561	329,918	11,493
New Jersey	3,640,292	2,125,101	1,477,568	37,623
New Mexico	783,758	415,335	335,788	32,635
New York	7,081,159	4,485,741	2,490,431	104,987
North Carolina	4,505,372	2,178,391	2,270,395	56,586
North Dakota	322,627	124,827	188,163	9,637
Ohio	5,580,840	2,827,710	2,661,433	91,697
Oklahoma	1,334,872	443,547	891,325	—
Oregon	1,789,270	970,488	754,175	64,607
Pennsylvania	5,753,670	2,990,274	2,680,434	82,962
Rhode Island	446,049	279,677	157,204	9,168
South Carolina	1,964,118	865,941	1,071,645	26,532
South Dakota	363,815	145,039	210,610	8,166
Tennessee	2,458,577	960,709	1,462,330	35,538
Texas	7,993,851	3,308,124	4,569,843	115,884
Utah	1,017,440	251,813	740,600	25,027
Vermont	299,290	199,239	92,698	7,353
Virginia	3,854,489	1,971,820	1,822,522	60,147
Washington	3,125,516	1,755,396	1,290,670	79,450
West Virginia	670,438	238,269	417,655	14,514
Wisconsin	3,068,434	1,620,985	1,407,966	39,483
Wyoming	249,061	69,286	170,962	8,813
Total	129,085,403	65,915,796	60,933,500	2,236,107

State electoral votes

State	Total EV	Obama	Romney
Alabama	9	0	9
Alaska	3	0	3
Arizona	11	0	11
Arkansas	6	0	6
California	55	55	0
Colorado	9	9	0
Connecticut	7	7	0
Delaware	3	3	0
District of Columbia	3	3	0
Florida	29	29	0
Georgia	16	0	16
Hawaii	4	4	0
Idaho	4	0	4
Illinois	20	20	0
Indiana	11	0	11
Iowa	6	6	0
Kansas	6	0	6
Kentucky	8	0	8
Louisiana	8	0	8
Maine	4	4	0
Maryland	10	10	0
Massachusetts	11	11	0
Michigan	16	16	0
Minnesota	10	10	0
Mississippi	6	0	6
Missouri	10	0	10
Montana	3	0	3
Nebraska	5	0	5
Nevada	6	6	0
New Hampshire	4	4	0
New Jersey	14	14	0
New Mexico	5	5	0
New York	29	29	0
North Carolina	15	0	15
North Dakota	3	0	3
Ohio	18	18	0
Oklahoma	7	0	7
Oregon	7	7	0
Pennsylvania	20	20	0
Rhode Island	4	4	0
South Carolina	9	0	9
South Dakota	3	0	3
Tennessee	11	0	11
Texas	38	0	38
Utah	6	0	6
Vermont	3	3	0
Virginia	13	13	0

State	Total EV	Obama	Romney
Washington	12	12	0
West Virginia	5	0	5
Wisconsin	10	10	0
Wyoming	3	0	3
Total	538	332	206

Scenarios

1% to Obama .... Obama 332, Romney 206
1% to Romney .... Obama 303, Romney 235
10K to Obama .... Obama 332, Romney 206
10K to Romney .... Obama 332, Romney 206
1964 allocation .... Obama 344, Romney 194
2020 allocation .... Obama 332, Romney 206

2016

Basics

Incumbent ....Barack Obama (D)
Prior streak ....D (2)
Prior 5 ....D (3), R (2)
Population 323,071,342
States 51
Electoral votes 538
Popular votes 136,669,276

Field

Candidate	PI	Age	State	Position	N	W	CS
Donald Trump (R)	3.1	70.38	N.Y.	Business executive	X	X	78.79
Hillary Clinton (D)	6.6	69.02	N.Y.	Former Cabinet member	X	—	72.30
Bernie Sanders (D)	5.5	75.15	Vt.	Senator	—	—	44.15
Ted Cruz (R)	7.9	45.86	Texas	Senator	—	—	28.72
Gary Johnson (LIB)	3.9	63.83	N.M.	Former governor	—	—	20.52
John Kasich (R)	6.6	64.47	Ohio	Governor	—	—	19.98
Marco Rubio (R)	7.7	45.43	Fla.	Senator	—	—	17.61
Colin Powell (R)	3.2	79.57	N.Y.	Former Cabinet member	—	—	11.84
Ben Carson (R)	4.3	65.12	Fla.	Movement leader	—	—	11.69
Ron Paul (R)	3.8	81.20	Texas	Former representative	—	—	10.62
Faith Spotted Eagle (D)	2.3	68.00	S.D.	Movement leader	—	—	10.62
Jeb Bush (R)	7.1	63.72	Fla.	Former governor	—	—	10.58
Rand Paul (R)	7.8	53.82	Ky.	Senator	—	—	10.13
Chris Christie (R)	6.7	54.15	N.J.	Governor	—	—	10.11
Carly Fiorina (R)	3.9	62.15	Va.	Business executive	—	—	10.07

Democratic nomination

Candidate	ConFB	FB%	ConLB	LB%	PriW	PriV	PriV%
Clinton	2,842	59.68%	—	—	29	17,119,048	55.53%
Sanders	1,865	39.16%	—	—	10	13,209,430	42.85%

Republican nomination

Candidate	ConFB	FB%	ConLB	LB%	PriW	PriV	PriV%
Trump	1,725	69.78%	—	—	33	13,757,263	45.57%
Cruz	484	19.58%	—	—	4	7,452,008	24.68%
Kasich	125	5.06%	—	—	1	4,197,478	13.90%
Rubio	123	4.98%	—	—	0	3,324,927	11.01%
Carson	7	0.28%	—	—	0	822,022	2.72%
Bush	3	0.12%	—	—	0	280,628	0.93%
Paul	2	0.08%	—	—	0	57,150	0.19%
Christie	0	0.00%	—	—	0	54,216	0.18%
Fiorina	0	0.00%	—	—	0	36,660	0.12%

General election

Candidate	EV	EV%	SC	PV	PV%
Trump	304	56.51%	30	62,984,828	46.09%
Clinton	227	42.19%	21	65,853,514	48.19%
Powell	3	0.56%	0	0	0.00%
Kasich	1	0.19%	0	0	0.00%
Paul	1	0.19%	0	0	0.00%
Sanders	1	0.19%	0	0	0.00%
Spotted Eagle	1	0.19%	0	0	0.00%
Johnson	0	0.00%	0	4,489,341	3.29%

State popular votes

State	Total PV	Clinton	Trump	Johnson	Other
Alabama	2,123,372	729,547	1,318,255	44,467	31,103
Alaska	318,608	116,454	163,387	18,725	20,042
Arizona	2,573,165	1,161,167	1,252,401	106,327	53,270
Arkansas	1,130,676	380,494	684,872	29,949	35,361
California	14,181,604	8,753,792	4,483,814	478,500	465,498
Colorado	2,780,247	1,338,870	1,202,484	144,121	94,772
Connecticut	1,644,920	897,572	673,215	48,676	25,457
Delaware	443,814	235,603	185,127	14,757	8,327
District of Columbia	311,268	282,830	12,723	4,906	10,809
Florida	9,420,039	4,504,975	4,617,886	207,043	90,135
Georgia	4,114,732	1,877,963	2,089,104	125,306	22,359
Hawaii	428,937	266,891	128,847	15,954	17,245
Idaho	690,255	189,765	409,055	28,331	63,104
Illinois	5,536,424	3,090,729	2,146,015	209,596	90,084
Indiana	2,734,958	1,033,126	1,557,286	133,993	10,553
Iowa	1,566,031	653,669	800,983	59,186	52,193
Kansas	1,184,402	427,005	671,018	55,406	30,973
Kentucky	1,924,149	628,854	1,202,971	53,752	38,572
Louisiana	2,029,032	780,154	1,178,638	37,978	32,262
Maine	747,927	357,735	335,593	38,105	16,494
Maryland	2,781,446	1,677,928	943,169	79,605	80,744
Massachusetts	3,325,046	1,995,196	1,090,893	138,018	100,939
Michigan	4,799,284	2,268,839	2,279,543	172,136	78,766
Minnesota	2,944,813	1,367,716	1,322,951	112,972	141,174
Mississippi	1,209,357	485,131	700,714	14,435	9,077
Missouri	2,808,605	1,071,068	1,594,511	97,359	45,667
Montana	497,147	177,709	279,240	28,037	12,161
Nebraska	844,227	284,494	495,961	38,946	24,826
Nevada	1,125,385	539,260	512,058	37,384	36,683
New Hampshire	744,296	348,526	345,790	30,777	19,203
New Jersey	3,874,046	2,148,278	1,601,933	72,477	51,358
New Mexico	798,319	385,234	319,667	74,541	18,877
New York	7,721,442	4,556,118	2,819,533	176,598	169,193
North Carolina	4,741,564	2,189,316	2,362,631	130,126	59,491
North Dakota	344,360	93,758	216,794	21,434	12,374
Ohio	5,496,487	2,394,164	2,841,005	174,498	86,820
Oklahoma	1,452,992	420,375	949,136	83,481	—
Oregon	2,001,336	1,002,106	782,403	94,231	122,596
Pennsylvania	6,165,478	2,926,441	2,970,733	146,715	121,589

State	Total PV	Clinton	Trump	Johnson	Other
Rhode Island	464,144	252,525	180,543	14,746	16,330
South Carolina	2,103,027	855,373	1,155,389	49,204	43,061
South Dakota	370,093	117,458	227,721	20,850	4,064
Tennessee	2,508,027	870,695	1,522,925	70,397	44,010
Texas	8,969,226	3,877,868	4,685,047	283,492	122,819
Utah	1,131,430	310,676	515,231	39,608	265,915
Vermont	315,067	178,573	95,369	10,078	31,047
Virginia	3,984,631	1,981,473	1,769,443	118,274	115,441
Washington	3,317,019	1,742,718	1,221,747	160,879	191,675
West Virginia	714,423	188,794	489,371	23,004	13,254
Wisconsin	2,976,150	1,382,536	1,405,284	106,674	81,656
Wyoming	255,849	55,973	174,419	13,287	12,170
Total	136,669,276	65,853,514	62,984,828	4,489,341	3,341,593

State electoral votes

State	Total EV	Trump	Clinton	Powell	Kasich	Paul	Sanders	SE
Alabama	9	9	0	0	0	0	0	0
Alaska	3	3	0	0	0	0	0	0
Arizona	11	11	0	0	0	0	0	0
Arkansas	6	6	0	0	0	0	0	0
California	55	0	55	0	0	0	0	0
Colorado	9	0	9	0	0	0	0	0
Connecticut	7	0	7	0	0	0	0	0
Delaware	3	0	3	0	0	0	0	0
District of Columbia	3	0	3	0	0	0	0	0
Florida	29	29	0	0	0	0	0	0
Georgia	16	16	0	0	0	0	0	0
Hawaii	4	0	3	0	0	0	1	0
Idaho	4	4	0	0	0	0	0	0
Illinois	20	0	20	0	0	0	0	0
Indiana	11	11	0	0	0	0	0	0
Iowa	6	6	0	0	0	0	0	0
Kansas	6	6	0	0	0	0	0	0
Kentucky	8	8	0	0	0	0	0	0
Louisiana	8	8	0	0	0	0	0	0
Maine	4	1	3	0	0	0	0	0
Maryland	10	0	10	0	0	0	0	0
Massachusetts	11	0	11	0	0	0	0	0
Michigan	16	16	0	0	0	0	0	0
Minnesota	10	0	10	0	0	0	0	0
Mississippi	6	6	0	0	0	0	0	0
Missouri	10	10	0	0	0	0	0	0
Montana	3	3	0	0	0	0	0	0
Nebraska	5	5	0	0	0	0	0	0
Nevada	6	0	6	0	0	0	0	0
New Hampshire	4	0	4	0	0	0	0	0
New Jersey	14	0	14	0	0	0	0	0
New Mexico	5	0	5	0	0	0	0	0
New York	29	0	29	0	0	0	0	0
North Carolina	15	15	0	0	0	0	0	0
North Dakota	3	3	0	0	0	0	0	0
Ohio	18	18	0	0	0	0	0	0

State	Total EV	Trump	Clinton	Powell	Kasich	Paul	Sanders	SE
Oklahoma	7	7	0	0	0	0	0	0
Oregon	7	0	7	0	0	0	0	0
Pennsylvania	20	20	0	0	0	0	0	0
Rhode Island	4	0	4	0	0	0	0	0
South Carolina	9	9	0	0	0	0	0	0
South Dakota	3	3	0	0	0	0	0	0
Tennessee	11	11	0	0	0	0	0	0
Texas	38	36	0	0	1	1	0	0
Utah	6	6	0	0	0	0	0	0
Vermont	3	0	3	0	0	0	0	0
Virginia	13	0	13	0	0	0	0	0
Washington	12	0	8	3	0	0	0	1
West Virginia	5	5	0	0	0	0	0	0
Wisconsin	10	10	0	0	0	0	0	0
Wyoming	3	3	0	0	0	0	0	0
Total	538	304	227	3	1	1	1	1

Scenarios

1% to Trump ....Trump 319, Clinton 219
1% to Clinton ....Clinton 308, Trump 230
10K to Trump...Trump 309, Clinton 229
10K to Clinton ....Trump 289, Clinton 249
1964 allocation.. Trump 305, Clinton 228, others 5
2020 allocation.. Trump 304, Clinton 227, others 7

2

CANDIDATES

A total of 302 presidential candidates met this book's qualification standards in America's 58 presidential elections. Many of these hopefuls launched multiple campaigns — James Blaine and Henry Clay were the kings with five apiece — though most candidates bowed out after a single attempt.

This chapter contains breakdowns of all 302 careers in presidential politics, providing statistics from all of the candidates' qualified runs. (Campaigns that fell short of the standards are not shown here, though they are included in all career totals in Chapter 4.)

Candidates are listed alphabetically, followed by their birth and death years. Here's what you'll find:

Year: Election in which the candidate met qualification standards.

Party: Political party or parties. See pages 18-20 for abbreviations. A hyphen indicates that a candidate ran on both tickets. A slash indicates that he began in the first party and switched to the second.

PI: Potential index.

N: Major-party nominees are designated by an X.

W: General-election winners are designated by an X.

CS: Campaign score.

ROP: Return on potential score.

Position: Position by which the candidate was best known, usually his current or most recent position.

Age: Age as of November 1 of the given year, rounded to two decimal places.

State: State in which the candidate maintained a voting address.

Additional statistics for any candidate can be found by referring back to the appropriate election or elections in Chapter 1.

A-B

John Adams (1735-1826)

Year	Party	PI	N	W	CS	ROP	Position	Age	State
1789	F	4.4	—	—	64.00	145	Former ambassador	54.01	Massachusetts
1792	F	6.4	—	—	67.23	105	Vice president	57.01	Massachusetts
1796	F	5.7	X	X	77.27	136	Vice president	61.01	Massachusetts
1800	F	7.2	X	—	73.21	102	President	65.01	Massachusetts

John Quincy Adams (1767-1848)

Year	Party	PI	N	W	CS	ROP	Position	Age	State
1820	DR	5.0	—	—	17.96	36	Cabinet member	53.31	Massachusetts
1824	DR	5.6	X	X	67.41	120	Cabinet member	57.31	Massachusetts
1828	NR	7.7	X	—	68.27	89	President	61.31	Massachusetts

Samuel Adams (1722-1803)

Year	Party	PI	N	W	CS	ROP	Position	Age	State
1796	DR	3.7	—	—	50.36	136	Governor	74.10	Massachusetts

Lamar Alexander (1940-)

Year	Party	PI	N	W	CS	ROP	Position	Age	State
1996	R	7.8	—	—	11.97	15	Former governor	56.33	Tennessee

Russell Alger (1836-1907)

Year	Party	PI	N	W	CS	ROP	Position	Age	State
1888	R	7.8	—	—	19.58	25	Former governor	52.68	Michigan

William Allen (1803-1879)

Year	Party	PI	N	W	CS	ROP	Position	Age	State
1876	D	6.9	—	—	15.83	23	Former governor	72.87	Ohio

William Boyd Allison (1829-1908)

Year	Party	PI	N	W	CS	ROP	Position	Age	State
1888	R	7.6	—	—	16.95	22	Senator	59.67	Iowa

John Anderson (1922-2017)

Year	Party	PI	N	W	CS	ROP	Position	Age	State
1980	R/NU	4.7	—	—	38.97	83	Representative	58.71	Illinois

James Armstrong (1728-1800)

Year	Party	PI	N	W	CS	ROP	Position	Age	State
1789	F	4.0	—	—	21.42	54	State official	61.00	Georgia

Chester Arthur (1829-1886)

Year	Party	PI	N	W	CS	ROP	Position	Age	State
1884	R	8.8	—	—	37.07	42	President	55.07	New York

John Ashbrook (1928-1982)

Year	Party	PI	N	W	CS	ROP	Position	Age	State
1972	R	4.2	—	—	13.02	31	Representative	44.11	Ohio

Bruce Babbitt (1938-)

Year	Party	PI	N	W	CS	ROP	Position	Age	State
1988	D	6.2	—	—	10.20	16	Former governor	50.35	Arizona

Michele Bachmann (1956-)

Year	Party	PI	N	W	CS	ROP	Position	Age	State
2012	R	4.3	—	—	10.11	24	Representative	56.57	Minnesota

Howard Baker (1925-2014)

Year	Party	PI	N	W	CS	ROP	Position	Age	State
1980	R	7.7	—	—	10.51	14	Senator	54.96	Tennessee

Alben Barkley (1877-1956)

Year	Party	PI	N	W	CS	ROP	Position	Age	State
1952	D	4.2	—	—	12.74	30	Vice president	74.94	Kentucky

Edward Bates (1793-1869)

Year	Party	PI	N	W	CS	ROP	Position	Age	State
1860	R	5.2	—	—	18.22	35	Former representative	67.16	Missouri

Gary Bauer (1946-)

Year	Party	PI	N	W	CS	ROP	Position	Age	State
2000	R	5.1	—	—	10.19	20	Movement leader	54.49	Virginia

Thomas Bayard (1828-1898)

Year	Party	PI	N	W	CS	ROP	Position	Age	State
1876	D	7.1	—	—	13.59	19	Senator	48.01	Delaware
1880	D	7.1	—	—	26.61	37	Senator	52.01	Delaware
1884	D	6.2	—	—	26.53	43	Senator	56.01	Delaware

Birch Bayh (1928-2019)

Year	Party	PI	N	W	CS	ROP	Position	Age	State
1976	D	6.9	—	—	10.32	15	Senator	48.78	Indiana

John Bell (1796-1869)

Year	Party	PI	N	W	CS	ROP	Position	Age	State
1860	CU	4.6	—	—	46.37	101	Former senator	64.70	Tennessee

Allan Benson (1871-1940)

Year	Party	PI	N	W	CS	ROP	Position	Age	State
1916	SOC	2.7	—	—	20.19	75	Journalist	44.99	New York

Lloyd Bentsen (1921-2006)

Year	Party	PI	N	W	CS	ROP	Position	Age	State
1988	D	7.6	—	—	10.62	14	Senator	67.72	Texas

John Bidwell (1819-1900)

Year	Party	PI	N	W	CS	ROP	Position	Age	State
1892	PRO	0.4	—	—	17.19	430	Movement leader	73.24	California

James Birney (1792-1857)

Year	Party	PI	N	W	CS	ROP	Position	Age	State
1844	LTY	2.6	—	—	17.35	67	Movement leader	52.74	Michigan

Joseph Blackburn (1838-1918)

Year	Party	PI	N	W	CS	ROP	Position	Age	State
1896	D	6.2	—	—	17.03	27	Senator	58.08	Kentucky

James Blaine (1830-1893)

Year	Party	PI	N	W	CS	ROP	Position	Age	State
1876	R	5.1	—	—	47.05	92	Representative	46.75	Maine
1880	R	7.3	—	—	40.02	55	Senator	50.75	Maine
1884	R	6.7	X	—	73.26	109	Former senator	54.75	Maine
1888	R	6.3	—	—	13.35	21	Former nominee	58.75	Maine
1892	R	3.7	—	—	26.05	70	Former nominee	62.75	Maine

Richard Bland (1835-1899)

Year	Party	PI	N	W	CS	ROP	Position	Age	State
1896	D	5.5	—	—	30.20	55	Former representative	61.20	Missouri

Horace Boies (1827-1923)

Year	Party	PI	N	W	CS	ROP	Position	Age	State
1892	D	6.3	—	—	19.02	30	Governor	64.90	Iowa
1896	D	6.3	—	—	15.75	25	Former governor	68.90	Iowa

William Borah (1865-1940)

Year	Party	PI	N	W	CS	ROP	Position	Age	State
1936	R	3.3	—	—	20.02	61	Senator	71.34	Idaho

Bill Bradley (1943-)

Year	Party	PI	N	W	CS	ROP	Position	Age	State
2000	D	7.1	—	—	22.10	31	Former senator	57.26	New Jersey

John Breckinridge (1821-1875)

Year	Party	PI	N	W	CS	ROP	Position	Age	State
1860	D/SD	4.7	X	—	60.76	129	Vice president	39.79	Kentucky

Benjamin Bristow (1832-1896)

Year	Party	PI	N	W	CS	ROP	Position	Age	State
1876	R	4.0	—	—	21.90	55	Cabinet member	44.37	Kentucky

Gratz Brown (1826-1885)

Year	Party	PI	N	W	CS	ROP	Position	Age	State
1872	D-LR	7.8	—	—	27.03	35	Governor	46.43	Missouri

Jerry Brown (1938-)

Year	Party	PI	N	W	CS	ROP	Position	Age	State
1976	D	6.2	—	—	21.16	34	Governor	38.57	California
1980	D	6.4	—	—	11.84	19	Governor	42.57	California
1992	D	6.8	—	—	24.83	37	Former governor	54.57	California

William Jennings Bryan (1860-1925)

Year	Party	PI	N	W	CS	ROP	Position	Age	State
1896	D-POP	4.6	X	—	70.98	154	Former representative	36.62	Nebraska
1900	D	5.6	X	—	69.53	124	Former nominee	40.62	Nebraska
1908	D	5.2	X	—	68.65	132	Former nominee	48.62	Nebraska

James Buchanan (1791-1868)

Year	Party	PI	N	W	CS	ROP	Position	Age	State
1848	D	8.2	—	—	25.17	31	Cabinet member	57.52	Pennsylvania
1852	D	7.9	—	—	35.79	45	Former Cabinet member	61.52	Pennsylvania
1856	D	5.1	X	X	79.35	156	Former Cabinet member	65.52	Pennsylvania

Pat Buchanan (1938-)

Year	Party	PI	N	W	CS	ROP	Position	Age	State
1992	R	5.2	—	—	23.85	46	Journalist	54.00	Virginia
1996	R	5.0	—	—	23.11	46	Journalist	58.00	Virginia

Aaron Burr (1756-1836)

Year	Party	PI	N	W	CS	ROP	Position	Age	State
1792	DR	4.7	—	—	19.07	41	Senator	36.73	New York
1796	DR	4.7	—	—	54.24	115	Senator	40.73	New York
1800	DR	4.9	—	—	65.31	133	Former senator	44.73	New York

Theodore Burton (1851-1929)

Year	Party	PI	N	W	CS	ROP	Position	Age	State
1916	R	5.3	—	—	16.00	30	Former senator	64.87	Ohio

George H.W. Bush (1924-2018)

Year	Party	PI	N	W	CS	ROP	Position	Age	State
1980	R	5.2	—	—	24.15	46	Former ambassador	56.39	Texas
1988	R	6.5	X	X	87.86	135	Vice president	64.39	Texas
1992	R	8.2	X	—	66.86	82	President	68.39	Texas

George W. Bush (1946-)

Year	Party	PI	N	W	CS	ROP	Position	Age	State
2000	R	7.9	X	X	77.21	98	Governor	54.32	Texas
2004	R	9.3	X	X	78.71	85	President	58.32	Texas

Jeb Bush (1953-)

Year	Party	PI	N	W	CS	ROP	Position	Age	State
2016	R	7.1	—	—	10.58	15	Former governor	63.72	Florida

Nicholas Murray Butler (1862-1947)

Year	Party	PI	N	W	CS	ROP	Position	Age	State
1920	R	5.9	—	—	14.25	24	College president	58.58	New York

Harry Byrd (1887-1966)

Year	Party	PI	N	W	CS	ROP	Position	Age	State
1944	D	5.1	—	—	14.55	29	Senator	57.39	Virginia
1960	D	6.9	—	—	19.25	28	Senator	73.39	Virginia

C-D

Simon Cameron (1799-1889)

Year	Party	PI	N	W	CS	ROP	Position	Age	State
1860	R	7.8	—	—	18.62	24	Senator	61.65	Pennsylvania

Joseph Cannon (1836-1926)

Year	Party	PI	N	W	CS	ROP	Position	Age	State
1908	R	5.3	—	—	14.71	28	Representative	72.49	Illinois

Ben Carson (1951-)

Year	Party	PI	N	W	CS	ROP	Position	Age	State
2016	R	4.3	—	—	11.69	27	Movement leader	65.12	Florida

Jimmy Carter (1924-)

Year	Party	PI	N	W	CS	ROP	Position	Age	State
1976	D	7.4	X	X	79.23	107	Former governor	52.08	Georgia
1980	D	9.0	X	—	60.93	68	President	56.08	Georgia

Lewis Cass (1782-1866)

Year	Party	PI	N	W	CS	ROP	Position	Age	State
1844	D	5.1	—	—	34.91	68	Former Cabinet member	62.06	Michigan
1848	D	6.9	X	—	71.66	104	Senator	66.06	Michigan
1852	D	6.9	—	—	42.18	61	Senator	70.06	Michigan

Salmon Chase (1808-1873)

Year	Party	PI	N	W	CS	ROP	Position	Age	State
1860	R	8.7	—	—	18.38	21	Former governor	52.80	Ohio

Shirley Chisholm (1924-2005)

Year	Party	PI	N	W	CS	ROP	Position	Age	State
1972	D	4.5	—	—	12.62	28	Representative	47.92	New York

Chris Christie (1962-)

Year	Party	PI	N	W	CS	ROP	Position	Age	State
2016	R	6.7	—	—	10.11	15	Governor	54.15	New Jersey

Frank Church (1924-1984)

Year	Party	PI	N	W	CS	ROP	Position	Age	State
1976	D	6.5	—	—	13.23	20	Senator	52.27	Idaho

Sanford Church (1815-1880)

Year	Party	PI	N	W	CS	ROP	Position	Age	State
1868	D	5.0	—	—	18.54	37	Former state official	53.54	New York

Champ Clark (1850-1921)

Year	Party	PI	N	W	CS	ROP	Position	Age	State
1912	D	3.7	—	—	42.45	115	Representative	62.65	Missouri

Wesley Clark (1944-)

Year	Party	PI	N	W	CS	ROP	Position	Age	State
2004	D	4.2	—	—	12.00	29	Former general	59.86	Arkansas

Henry Clay (1777-1852)

Year	Party	PI	N	W	CS	ROP	Position	Age	State
1824	DR	3.7	—	—	46.84	127	Representative	47.55	Kentucky
1832	NR	6.4	X	—	62.61	98	Senator	55.55	Kentucky
1840	W	6.7	—	—	42.42	63	Former nominee	63.55	Kentucky
1844	W	5.6	X	—	71.05	127	Former nominee	67.55	Kentucky
1848	W	5.1	—	—	37.63	74	Former nominee	71.55	Kentucky

Grover Cleveland (1837-1908)

Year	Party	PI	N	W	CS	ROP	Position	Age	State
1884	D	7.5	X	X	78.78	105	Governor	47.62	New York
1888	D	9.2	X	—	72.27	79	President	51.62	New York
1892	D	9.1	X	X	80.73	89	Former president	55.62	New York

Bill Clinton (1946-)

Year	Party	PI	N	W	CS	ROP	Position	Age	State
1992	D	6.5	X	X	82.15	126	Governor	46.20	Arkansas
1996	D	8.5	X	X	84.08	99	President	50.20	Arkansas

DeWitt Clinton (1769-1828)

Year	Party	PI	N	W	CS	ROP	Position	Age	State
1812	F-DR	3.7	X	—	71.10	192	Mayor	43.67	New York

George Clinton (1739-1812)

Year	Party	PI	N	W	CS	ROP	Position	Age	State
1789	DR	2.6	—	—	31.09	120	Governor	50.27	New York
1792	DR	3.2	—	—	59.98	187	Governor	53.27	New York
1796	DR	3.0	—	—	33.54	112	Former governor	57.27	New York
1808	DR	4.0	—	—	28.01	70	Vice president	69.27	New York

Hillary Clinton (1947-)

Year	Party	PI	N	W	CS	ROP	Position	Age	State
2008	D	7.0	—	—	43.42	62	Senator	61.02	New York
2016	D	6.6	X	—	72.30	110	Former Cabinet member	69.02	New York

Francis Cockrell (1834-1915)

Year	Party	PI	N	W	CS	ROP	Position	Age	State
1904	D	7.0	—	—	13.35	19	Senator	70.08	Missouri

Roscoe Conkling (1829-1888)

Year	Party	PI	N	W	CS	ROP	Position	Age	State
1876	R	8.2	—	—	20.46	25	Senator	47.01	New York

John Connally (1917-1993)

Year	Party	PI	N	W	CS	ROP	Position	Age	State
1980	R	7.4	—	—	10.38	14	Former governor	63.68	Texas

Calvin Coolidge (1872-1933)

Year	Party	PI	N	W	CS	ROP	Position	Age	State
1924	R	9.1	X	X	85.63	94	President	52.33	Massachusetts

James Cox (1870-1957)

Year	Party	PI	N	W	CS	ROP	Position	Age	State
1920	D	5.9	X	—	64.01	108	Governor	50.59	Ohio
1924	D	7.5	—	—	15.17	20	Former nominee	54.59	Ohio

Jacob Coxey (1854-1951)

Year	Party	PI	N	W	CS	ROP	Position	Age	State
1932	R/FL	2.5	—	—	10.92	44	Mayor	78.54	Ohio

Phil Crane (1930-2014)

Year	Party	PI	N	W	CS	ROP	Position	Age	State
1980	R	4.7	—	—	10.46	22	Representative	49.99	Illinois

Alan Cranston (1914-2000)

Year	Party	PI	N	W	CS	ROP	Position	Age	State
1984	D	7.0	—	—	10.17	15	Senator	70.37	California

William Crawford (1772-1834)

Year	Party	PI	N	W	CS	ROP	Position	Age	State
1824	DR	5.4	—	—	46.97	87	Cabinet member	52.69	Georgia

Ted Cruz (1970-)

Year	Party	PI	N	W	CS	ROP	Position	Age	State
2016	R	7.9	—	—	28.72	36	Senator	45.86	Texas

Albert Cummins (1850-1926)

Year	Party	PI	N	W	CS	ROP	Position	Age	State
1916	R	5.3	—	—	17.15	32	Senator	66.71	Iowa

Charles Curtis (1860-1936)

Year	Party	PI	N	W	CS	ROP	Position	Age	State
1928	R	4.1	—	—	13.53	33	Senator	68.77	Kansas

David Davis (1815-1886)

Year	Party	PI	N	W	CS	ROP	Position	Age	State
1872	D	5.1	—	—	10.97	22	Supreme Court justice	57.65	Illinois

John Davis (1873-1955)

Year	Party	PI	N	W	CS	ROP	Position	Age	State
1920	D	3.7	—	—	12.87	35	Ambassador	47.55	West Virginia
1924	D	4.4	X	—	63.46	144	Former ambassador	51.55	West Virginia

Howard Dean (1948-)

Year	Party	PI	N	W	CS	ROP	Position	Age	State
2004	D	6.0	—	—	13.32	22	Former governor	55.96	Vermont

Eugene Debs (1855-1926)

Year	Party	PI	N	W	CS	ROP	Position	Age	State
1904	SOC	2.9	—	—	19.53	67	Movement leader	48.99	Indiana
1908	SOC	2.9	—	—	19.04	66	Movement leader	52.99	Indiana
1912	SOC	1.5	—	—	29.16	194	Movement leader	56.99	Indiana
1920	SOC	0.1	—	—	20.94	2,094	Movement leader	64.99	Indiana

Chauncey Depew (1834-1928)

Year	Party	PI	N	W	CS	ROP	Position	Age	State
1888	R	4.9	—	—	19.50	40	Business executive	54.52	New York

Thomas Dewey (1902-1971)

Year	Party	PI	N	W	CS	ROP	Position	Age	State
1940	R	4.0	—	—	41.51	104	District attorney	38.61	New York
1944	R	6.3	X	—	64.76	103	Governor	42.61	New York
1948	R	6.6	X	—	69.67	106	Former nominee	46.61	New York

Bob Dole (1923-)

Year	Party	PI	N	W	CS	ROP	Position	Age	State
1988	R	7.0	—	—	21.51	31	Senator	65.28	Kansas
1996	R	6.8	X	—	67.01	99	Senator	73.28	Kansas

James Doolittle (1815-1897)

Year	Party	PI	N	W	CS	ROP	Position	Age	State
1868	D	7.9	—	—	13.27	17	Senator	53.83	Wisconsin

Stephen Douglas (1813-1861)

Year	Party	PI	N	W	CS	ROP	Position	Age	State
1852	D	6.9	—	—	15.51	22	Senator	39.52	Illinois
1856	D	7.1	—	—	18.86	27	Senator	43.52	Illinois
1860	D	7.0	X	—	57.06	82	Senator	47.52	Illinois

Michael Dukakis (1933-)

Year	Party	PI	N	W	CS	ROP	Position	Age	State
1988	D	6.7	X	—	65.32	97	Governor	54.99	Massachusetts

Pete du Pont (1935-)

Year	Party	PI	N	W	CS	ROP	Position	Age	State
1988	R	6.6	—	—	10.25	16	Former governor	53.78	Delaware

E-G

George Edmunds (1828-1919)

Year	Party	PI	N	W	CS	ROP	Position	Age	State
1880	R	7.3	—	—	13.59	19	Senator	52.75	Vermont
1884	R	7.0	—	—	19.02	27	Senator	56.75	Vermont

Edward Edwards (1863-1931)

Year	Party	PI	N	W	CS	ROP	Position	Age	State
1920	D	6.6	—	—	13.28	20	Governor	56.92	New Jersey

John Edwards (1953-)

Year	Party	PI	N	W	CS	ROP	Position	Age	State
2004	D	7.8	—	—	22.22	28	Senator	51.39	North Carolina
2008	D	8.9	—	—	11.63	13	Former senator	55.39	North Carolina

Dwight Eisenhower (1890-1969)

Year	Party	PI	N	W	CS	ROP	Position	Age	State
1952	R	5.6	X	X	89.56	160	General	62.05	New York
1956	R	8.7	X	X	91.03	105	President	66.05	New York

Oliver Ellsworth (1745-1807)

Year	Party	PI	N	W	CS	ROP	Position	Age	State
1796	F	4.8	—	—	43.29	90	Supreme Court justice	51.51	Connecticut

James English (1812-1890)

Year	Party	PI	N	W	CS	ROP	Position	Age	State
1868	D	7.0	—	—	13.99	20	Governor	56.64	Connecticut

Charles Fairbanks (1852-1918)

Year	Party	PI	N	W	CS	ROP	Position	Age	State
1908	R	8.8	—	—	13.27	15	Vice president	56.48	Indiana
1916	R	4.7	—	—	16.32	35	Former vice president	64.48	Indiana

James Farley (1888-1976)

Year	Party	PI	N	W	CS	ROP	Position	Age	State
1940	D	6.3	—	—	13.95	22	Cabinet member	52.42	New York

Stephen Field (1816-1899)

Year	Party	PI	N	W	CS	ROP	Position	Age	State
1880	D	2.3	—	—	17.03	74	Supreme Court justice	63.99	California

Millard Fillmore (1800-1874)

Year	Party	PI	N	W	CS	ROP	Position	Age	State
1852	W	9.1	—	—	45.85	50	President	52.82	New York
1856	AW	7.4	—	—	45.15	61	Former president	56.82	New York

Carly Fiorina (1954-)

Year	Party	PI	N	W	CS	ROP	Position	Age	State
2016	R	3.9	—	—	10.07	26	Business executive	62.15	Virginia

Clinton Fisk (1828-1890)

Year	Party	PI	N	W	CS	ROP	Position	Age	State
1888	PRO	3.8	—	—	17.02	45	Former general	59.90	New Jersey

John Floyd (1783-1837)

Year	Party	PI	N	W	CS	ROP	Position	Age	State
1832	D	4.2	—	—	22.71	54	Governor	49.52	Virginia

Steve Forbes (1947-)

Year	Party	PI	N	W	CS	ROP	Position	Age	State
1996	R	3.6	—	—	16.96	47	Journalist	49.29	New Jersey
2000	R	4.0	—	—	10.52	26	Journalist	53.29	New Jersey

Gerald Ford (1913-2006)

Year	Party	PI	N	W	CS	ROP	Position	Age	State
1976	R	6.6	X	—	72.98	111	President	63.30	Michigan

Henry Ford (1863-1947)

Year	Party	PI	N	W	CS	ROP	Position	Age	State
1916	R	3.8	—	—	13.29	35	Business executive	53.26	Michigan

Joseph France (1873-1939)

Year	Party	PI	N	W	CS	ROP	Position	Age	State
1932	R	5.6	—	—	19.88	36	Former senator	59.06	Maryland

John Fremont (1813-1890)

Year	Party	PI	N	W	CS	ROP	Position	Age	State
1856	R	5.3	X	—	68.16	129	Former senator	43.78	California

James Garfield (1831-1881)

Year	Party	PI	N	W	CS	ROP	Position	Age	State
1880	R	6.6	X	X	79.77	121	Representative	48.95	Ohio

John Nance Garner (1868-1967)

Year	Party	PI	N	W	CS	ROP	Position	Age	State
1932	D	3.3	—	—	16.36	50	Representative	63.94	Texas
1940	D	3.5	—	—	15.20	43	Vice president	71.94	Texas

Walter George (1878-1957)

Year	Party	PI	N	W	CS	ROP	Position	Age	State
1928	D	4.4	—	—	12.87	29	Senator	50.76	Georgia

Richard Gephardt (1941-)

Year	Party	PI	N	W	CS	ROP	Position	Age	State
1988	D	4.0	—	—	13.63	34	Representative	47.75	Missouri
2004	D	3.9	—	—	10.23	26	Representative	63.75	Missouri

Newt Gingrich (1943-)

Year	Party	PI	N	W	CS	ROP	Position	Age	State
2012	R	4.3	—	—	18.59	43	Former representative	69.37	Georgia

Rudy Giuliani (1944-)

Year	Party	PI	N	W	CS	ROP	Position	Age	State
2008	R	3.9	—	—	11.71	30	Former mayor	64.43	New York

John Glenn (1921-2016)

Year	Party	PI	N	W	CS	ROP	Position	Age	State
1984	D	6.8	—	—	12.08	18	Senator	63.29	Ohio

Barry Goldwater (1909-1998)

Year	Party	PI	N	W	CS	ROP	Position	Age	State
1964	R	6.6	X	—	60.59	92	Senator	55.83	Arizona

Al Gore (1948-)

Year	Party	PI	N	W	CS	ROP	Position	Age	State
1988	D	6.8	—	—	18.19	27	Senator	40.59	Tennessee
2000	D	8.8	X	—	74.51	85	Vice president	52.59	Tennessee

Arthur Gorman (1839-1906)

Year	Party	PI	N	W	CS	ROP	Position	Age	State
1892	D	7.4	—	—	13.19	18	Senator	53.64	Maryland

Phil Gramm (1942-)

Year	Party	PI	N	W	CS	ROP	Position	Age	State
1996	R	8.4	—	—	10.30	12	Senator	54.32	Texas

Ulysses Grant (1822-1885)

Year	Party	PI	N	W	CS	ROP	Position	Age	State
1864	R	5.6	—	—	13.35	24	General	42.51	Illinois
1868	R	6.3	X	X	85.63	136	General	46.51	Illinois
1872	R	9.0	X	X	89.28	99	President	50.51	Illinois
1880	R	8.5	—	—	42.34	50	Former president	58.51	Illinois

George Gray (1840-1925)

Year	Party	PI	N	W	CS	ROP	Position	Age	State
1908	D	6.3	—	—	14.71	23	Former senator	68.49	Delaware

Horace Greeley (1811-1872)

Year	Party	PI	N	W	CS	ROP	Position	Age	State
1872	D-LR	4.8	X	—	58.76	122	Journalist	61.74	New York

Dwight Green (1897-1958)

Year	Party	PI	N	W	CS	ROP	Position	Age	State
1948	R	6.5	—	—	13.05	20	Governor	51.81	Illinois

Walter Gresham (1832-1895)

Year	Party	PI	N	W	CS	ROP	Position	Age	State
1888	R	5.7	—	—	20.30	36	Federal judge	56.63	Indiana

James Guthrie (1792-1869)

Year	Party	PI	N	W	CS	ROP	Position	Age	State
1860	D	3.9	—	—	19.34	50	Former Cabinet member	67.91	Kentucky

H-J

John Hale (1806-1873)

Year	Party	PI	N	W	CS	ROP	Position	Age	State
1852	FS	5.4	—	—	25.71	48	Senator	46.59	New Hampshire

John Hancock (1737-1793)

Year	Party	PI	N	W	CS	ROP	Position	Age	State
1789	F	4.3	—	—	35.97	84	Governor	52.77	Massachusetts

Winfield Hancock (1824-1886)

Year	Party	PI	N	W	CS	ROP	Position	Age	State
1868	D	6.0	—	—	18.46	31	General	44.71	Pennsylvania
1876	D	6.5	—	—	18.14	28	General	52.71	Pennsylvania
1880	D	5.6	X	—	72.24	129	General	56.71	Pennsylvania

Warren Harding (1865-1923)

Year	Party	PI	N	W	CS	ROP	Position	Age	State
1920	R	6.0	X	X	88.37	147	Senator	55.00	Ohio

Tom Harkin (1939-)

Year	Party	PI	N	W	CS	ROP	Position	Age	State
1992	D	6.9	—	—	10.83	16	Senator	52.95	Iowa

Judson Harmon (1846-1927)

Year	Party	PI	N	W	CS	ROP	Position	Age	State
1912	D	5.6	—	—	20.47	37	Governor	66.74	Ohio

Averell Harriman (1891-1986)

Year	Party	PI	N	W	CS	ROP	Position	Age	State
1952	D	5.8	—	—	15.10	26	Former Cabinet member	60.96	New York
1956	D	7.4	—	—	17.64	24	Governor	64.96	New York

Fred Harris (1930-)

Year	Party	PI	N	W	CS	ROP	Position	Age	State
1976	D	6.9	—	—	10.94	16	Former senator	45.97	Oklahoma

Benjamin Harrison (1833-1901)

Year	Party	PI	N	W	CS	ROP	Position	Age	State
1888	R	7.9	X	X	79.71	101	Former senator	55.20	Indiana
1892	R	8.5	X	—	68.40	80	President	59.20	Indiana

Pat Harrison (1881-1941)

Year	Party	PI	N	W	CS	ROP	Position	Age	State
1924	D	3.4	—	—	12.40	36	Senator	43.17	Mississippi

Robert Harrison (1745-1790)

Year	Party	PI	N	W	CS	ROP	Position	Age	State
1789	F	2.3	—	—	45.73	199	State judge	44.00	Maryland

William Henry Harrison (1773-1841)

Year	Party	PI	N	W	CS	ROP	Position	Age	State
1836	W	4.9	X	—	64.80	132	Former senator	63.73	Ohio
1840	W	8.7	X	X	87.90	101	Former senator	67.73	Ohio

Gary Hart (1936-)

Year	Party	PI	N	W	CS	ROP	Position	Age	State
1984	D	6.3	—	—	37.76	60	Senator	47.93	Colorado
1988	D	6.7	—	—	11.02	16	Former senator	51.93	Colorado

John Hartranft (1830-1889)

Year	Party	PI	N	W	CS	ROP	Position	Age	State
1876	R	7.6	—	—	16.15	21	Governor	45.88	Pennsylvania

Rutherford Hayes (1822-1893)

Year	Party	PI	N	W	CS	ROP	Position	Age	State
1876	R	8.3	X	X	77.12	93	Governor	54.08	Ohio

William Randolph Hearst (1863-1951)

Year	Party	PI	N	W	CS	ROP	Position	Age	State
1904	D	5.5	—	—	24.45	44	Journalist	41.51	New York

Thomas Hendricks (1819-1885)

Year	Party	PI	N	W	CS	ROP	Position	Age	State
1872	D	8.2	—	—	43.62	53	Former senator	53.15	Indiana
1876	D	7.9	—	—	25.17	32	Governor	57.15	Indiana
1880	D	7.4	—	—	15.35	21	Former governor	61.15	Indiana
1884	D	6.4	—	—	14.39	22	Former governor	65.15	Indiana

John Henry (1750-1798)

Year	Party	PI	N	W	CS	ROP	Position	Age	State
1796	DR	4.7	—	—	21.42	46	Senator	46.00	Maryland

David Hill (1843-1910)

Year	Party	PI	N	W	CS	ROP	Position	Age	State
1892	D	8.5	—	—	19.98	24	Senator	49.17	New York

Herbert Hoover (1874-1964)

Year	Party	PI	N	W	CS	ROP	Position	Age	State
1920	R	2.6	—	—	12.56	48	Business executive	46.23	California
1928	R	4.0	X	X	90.41	226	Cabinet member	54.23	California
1932	R	7.3	X	—	61.28	84	President	58.23	California

John Hospers (1918-2011)

Year	Party	PI	N	W	CS	ROP	Position	Age	State
1972	LIB	3.3	—	—	10.62	32	Movement leader	54.40	California

Mike Huckabee (1955-)

Year	Party	PI	N	W	CS	ROP	Position	Age	State
2008	R	7.3	—	—	22.10	30	Former governor	53.19	Arkansas

Charles Evans Hughes (1862-1948)

Year	Party	PI	N	W	CS	ROP	Position	Age	State
1908	R	7.4	—	—	15.43	21	Governor	46.56	New York
1916	R	8.0	X	—	73.55	92	Supreme Court justice	54.56	New York

Cordell Hull (1871-1955)

Year	Party	PI	N	W	CS	ROP	Position	Age	State
1928	D	3.7	—	—	12.75	34	Representative	57.08	Tennessee

Hubert Humphrey (1911-1978)

Year	Party	PI	N	W	CS	ROP	Position	Age	State
1960	D	7.1	—	—	14.46	20	Senator	49.43	Minnesota
1968	D	7.8	X	—	69.19	89	Vice president	57.43	Minnesota
1972	D	6.5	—	—	25.90	40	Former nominee	61.43	Minnesota
1976	D	5.5	—	—	10.29	19	Former nominee	65.43	Minnesota

Robert Hunter (1809-1887)

Year	Party	PI	N	W	CS	ROP	Position	Age	State
1860	D	7.0	—	—	21.10	30	Senator	51.53	Virginia

Samuel Huntington (1731-1796)

Year	Party	PI	N	W	CS	ROP	Position	Age	State
1789	F	4.7	—	—	26.29	56	Governor	58.33	Connecticut

Jon Huntsman (1960-)

Year	Party	PI	N	W	CS	ROP	Position	Age	State
2012	R	6.7	—	—	10.27	15	Former governor	52.60	Utah

James Iredell (1751-1799)

Year	Party	PI	N	W	CS	ROP	Position	Age	State
1796	F	3.6	—	—	23.85	66	Supreme Court justice	45.07	North Carolina

Andrew Jackson (1767-1845)

Year	Party	PI	N	W	CS	ROP	Position	Age	State
1824	DR	5.9	X	—	69.65	118	Senator	57.63	Tennessee
1828	DR	6.9	X	X	84.82	123	Former senator	61.63	Tennessee
1832	D	7.8	X	X	87.20	112	President	65.63	Tennessee

Henry Jackson (1912-1983)

Year	Party	PI	N	W	CS	ROP	Position	Age	State
1972	D	6.3	—	—	15.37	24	Senator	60.42	Washington
1976	D	6.2	—	—	14.30	23	Senator	64.42	Washington

Jesse Jackson (1941-)

Year	Party	PI	N	W	CS	ROP	Position	Age	State
1984	D	3.3	—	—	23.30	71	Movement leader	43.07	Illinois
1988	D	3.6	—	—	33.32	93	Movement leader	47.07	Illinois

Arthur James (1883-1973)

Year	Party	PI	N	W	CS	ROP	Position	Age	State
1940	R	7.1	—	—	14.48	20	Governor	57.30	Pennsylvania

John Jay (1745-1829)

Year	Party	PI	N	W	CS	ROP	Position	Age	State
1789	F	4.1	—	—	51.15	125	Cabinet member	43.89	New York
1796	F	5.1	—	—	28.66	56	Governor	50.89	New York
1800	F	3.3	—	—	18.98	58	Governor	54.89	New York

Thomas Jefferson (1743-1826)

Year	Party	PI	N	W	CS	ROP	Position	Age	State
1792	DR	6.7	—	—	26.68	40	Cabinet member	49.55	Virginia
1796	DR	6.9	X	—	74.00	107	Former Cabinet member	53.55	Virginia
1800	DR	7.6	X	X	77.84	102	Vice president	57.55	Virginia
1804	DR	9.2	X	X	93.05	101	President	61.55	Virginia

Charles Jenkins (1805-1883)

Year	Party	PI	N	W	CS	ROP	Position	Age	State
1872	D	5.1	—	—	11.89	23	Former governor	67.82	Georgia

Andrew Johnson (1808-1875)

Year	Party	PI	N	W	CS	ROP	Position	Age	State
1860	D	6.9	—	—	13.19	19	Senator	51.84	Tennessee
1868	D	7.4	—	—	26.37	36	President	59.84	Tennessee

Gary Johnson (1953-)

Year	Party	PI	N	W	CS	ROP	Position	Age	State
2016	LIB	3.9	—	—	20.52	53	Former governor	63.83	New Mexico

Hiram Johnson (1866-1945)

Year	Party	PI	N	W	CS	ROP	Position	Age	State
1920	R	5.8	—	—	24.20	42	Senator	54.16	California
1924	R	5.4	—	—	16.26	30	Senator	58.16	California

John Johnson (1861-1909)

Year	Party	PI	N	W	CS	ROP	Position	Age	State
1908	D	6.8	—	—	13.67	20	Governor	47.26	Minnesota

Lyndon Johnson (1908-1973)

Year	Party	PI	N	W	CS	ROP	Position	Age	State
1956	D	4.5	—	—	12.89	29	Senator	48.18	Texas
1960	D	8.1	—	—	23.50	29	Senator	52.18	Texas
1964	D	9.3	X	X	93.24	100	President	56.18	Texas
1968	D	8.7	—	—	11.53	13	President	60.18	Texas

Richard Johnson (1780-1850)

Year	Party	PI	N	W	CS	ROP	Position	Age	State
1844	D	5.6	—	—	17.19	31	Former vice president	64.04	Kentucky

Samuel Johnston (1733-1816)

Year	Party	PI	N	W	CS	ROP	Position	Age	State
1796	F	6.5	—	—	21.42	33	Former senator	62.88	North Carolina

Walter Jones (1888-1963)

Year	Party	PI	N	W	CS	ROP	Position	Age	State
1956	D	1.9	—	—	10.62	56	State judge	68.04	Alabama

K-M

John Kasich (1952-)

Year	Party	PI	N	W	CS	ROP	Position	Age	State
2016	R	6.6	—	—	19.98	30	Governor	64.47	Ohio

Estes Kefauver (1903-1963)

Year	Party	PI	N	W	CS	ROP	Position	Age	State
1952	D	4.4	—	—	38.77	88	Senator	49.27	Tennessee
1956	D	5.1	—	—	21.72	43	Senator	53.27	Tennessee

Jack Kemp (1935-2009)

Year	Party	PI	N	W	CS	ROP	Position	Age	State
1988	R	5.2	—	—	11.63	22	Representative	53.30	New York

Edward Kennedy (1932-2009)

Year	Party	PI	N	W	CS	ROP	Position	Age	State
1980	D	6.8	—	—	39.18	58	Senator	48.69	Massachusetts

John Kennedy (1917-1963)

Year	Party	PI	N	W	CS	ROP	Position	Age	State
1960	D	6.2	X	X	79.58	128	Senator	43.43	Massachusetts

Robert Kennedy (1925-1968)

Year	Party	PI	N	W	CS	ROP	Position	Age	State
1968	D	6.6	—	—	19.18	29	Senator	42.95	New York

Robert Kerr (1896-1963)

Year	Party	PI	N	W	CS	ROP	Position	Age	State
1952	D	5.3	—	—	12.90	24	Senator	56.14	Oklahoma

Bob Kerrey (1943-)

Year	Party	PI	N	W	CS	ROP	Position	Age	State
1992	D	6.4	—	—	10.95	17	Senator	49.18	Nebraska

John Kerry (1943-)

Year	Party	PI	N	W	CS	ROP	Position	Age	State
2004	D	6.6	X	—	73.65	112	Senator	60.89	Massachusetts

Alan Keyes (1950-)

Year	Party	PI	N	W	CS	ROP	Position	Age	State
1996	R	3.2	—	—	11.81	37	Former ambassador	46.23	Maryland
2000	R	3.7	—	—	13.04	35	Former ambassador	50.23	Maryland

Rufus King (1755-1827)

Year	Party	PI	N	W	CS	ROP	Position	Age	State
1816	F	7.1	X	—	62.07	87	Senator	61.61	New York

Frank Knox (1874-1944)

Year	Party	PI	N	W	CS	ROP	Position	Age	State
1936	R	3.5	—	—	12.97	37	Journalist	62.83	Illinois

Philander Knox (1853-1921)

Year	Party	PI	N	W	CS	ROP	Position	Age	State
1908	R	8.2	—	—	15.51	19	Senator	55.49	Pennsylvania

Robert La Follette (1855-1925)

Year	Party	PI	N	W	CS	ROP	Position	Age	State
1912	R	6.3	—	—	15.18	24	Senator	57.38	Wisconsin
1916	R	5.2	—	—	12.89	25	Senator	61.38	Wisconsin
1924	R/P	2.2	—	—	46.37	211	Senator	69.38	Wisconsin

Alfred Landon (1887-1987)

Year	Party	PI	N	W	CS	ROP	Position	Age	State
1936	R	4.8	X	—	57.76	120	Governor	49.14	Kansas

Joseph Lane (1801-1881)

Year	Party	PI	N	W	CS	ROP	Position	Age	State
1852	D	3.1	—	—	13.59	44	Territorial delegate	50.88	Oregon

Lyndon LaRouche (1922-2019)

Year	Party	PI	N	W	CS	ROP	Position	Age	State
1996	D	3.6	—	—	13.27	37	Movement leader	74.15	Virginia

Frank Lausche (1895-1990)

Year	Party	PI	N	W	CS	ROP	Position	Age	State
1956	D	5.7	—	—	11.62	20	Governor	60.96	Ohio

William Lemke (1878-1950)

Year	Party	PI	N	W	CS	ROP	Position	Age	State
1936	U	1.8	—	—	16.26	90	Representative	58.22	North Dakota

Joseph Lieberman (1942-)

Year	Party	PI	N	W	CS	ROP	Position	Age	State
2004	D	7.2	—	—	11.04	15	Senator	62.69	Connecticut

Abraham Lincoln (1809-1865)

Year	Party	PI	N	W	CS	ROP	Position	Age	State
1860	R	6.2	X	X	78.38	126	Former representative	51.72	Illinois
1864	R	8.9	X	X	92.17	104	President	55.72	Illinois

Benjamin Lincoln (1733-1810)

Year	Party	PI	N	W	CS	ROP	Position	Age	State
1789	F	4.8	—	—	21.42	45	Former general	56.77	Massachusetts

Henry Cabot Lodge (1902-1985)

Year	Party	PI	N	W	CS	ROP	Position	Age	State
1964	R	4.8	—	—	12.05	25	Former v.p. nominee	62.33	Massachusetts

John Logan (1826-1886)

Year	Party	PI	N	W	CS	ROP	Position	Age	State
1884	R	8.1	—	—	16.15	20	Senator	58.73	Illinois

Frank Lowden (1861-1943)

Year	Party	PI	N	W	CS	ROP	Position	Age	State
1920	R	6.3	—	—	25.31	40	Governor	59.77	Illinois
1928	R	5.7	—	—	20.32	36	Former governor	67.77	Illinois

Richard Lugar (1932-2019)

Year	Party	PI	N	W	CS	ROP	Position	Age	State
1996	R	6.5	—	—	10.51	16	Senator	64.58	Indiana

Douglas MacArthur (1880-1964)

Year	Party	PI	N	W	CS	ROP	Position	Age	State
1944	R	3.9	—	—	15.89	41	General	64.77	Wisconsin

James Madison (1751-1836)

Year	Party	PI	N	W	CS	ROP	Position	Age	State
1808	DR	6.8	X	X	84.36	124	Cabinet member	57.63	Virginia
1812	DR	8.7	X	X	80.17	92	President	61.63	Virginia

Willie Person Mangum (1792-1861)

Year	Party	PI	N	W	CS	ROP	Position	Age	State
1836	W	5.4	—	—	22.34	41	Senator	44.48	North Carolina

William Marcy (1786-1857)

Year	Party	PI	N	W	CS	ROP	Position	Age	State
1852	D	5.9	—	—	17.50	30	Former Cabinet member	65.89	New York

Joseph Martin (1884-1968)

Year	Party	PI	N	W	CS	ROP	Position	Age	State
1940	R	5.1	—	—	12.63	25	Representative	55.99	Massachusetts

Claude Matthews (1845-1898)

Year	Party	PI	N	W	CS	ROP	Position	Age	State
1896	D	7.3	—	—	13.19	18	Governor	50.88	Indiana

William Gibbs McAdoo (1863-1941)

Year	Party	PI	N	W	CS	ROP	Position	Age	State
1920	D	6.3	—	—	27.41	44	Former Cabinet member	57.00	New York
1924	D	3.6	—	—	43.53	121	Former Cabinet member	61.00	California

John McCain (1936-2018)

Year	Party	PI	N	W	CS	ROP	Position	Age	State
2000	R	6.2	—	—	29.92	48	Senator	64.17	Arizona
2008	R	5.9	X	—	68.78	117	Senator	72.17	Arizona

Eugene McCarthy (1916-2005)

Year	Party	PI	N	W	CS	ROP	Position	Age	State
1968	D	6.9	—	—	33.16	48	Senator	52.59	Minnesota

George McClellan (1826-1885)

Year	Party	PI	N	W	CS	ROP	Position	Age	State
1864	D	4.7	X	—	61.66	131	General	37.91	New Jersey

Paul McCloskey (1927-)

Year	Party	PI	N	W	CS	ROP	Position	Age	State
1972	R	4.7	—	—	11.31	24	Representative	45.09	California

Joseph McDonald (1819-1891)

Year	Party	PI	N	W	CS	ROP	Position	Age	State
1884	D	7.3	—	—	15.43	21	Former senator	65.17	Indiana

George McGovern (1922-2012)

Year	Party	PI	N	W	CS	ROP	Position	Age	State
1968	D	6.0	—	—	12.79	21	Senator	46.29	South Dakota
1972	D	6.4	X	—	58.46	91	Senator	50.29	South Dakota
1984	D	6.2	—	—	11.14	18	Former nominee	62.29	South Dakota

William McKinley (1843-1901)

Year	Party	PI	N	W	CS	ROP	Position	Age	State
1892	R	8.2	—	—	26.05	32	Governor	49.76	Ohio
1896	R	8.2	X	X	81.24	99	Former governor	53.76	Ohio
1900	R	8.9	X	X	82.89	93	President	57.76	Ohio

John McLean (1785-1861)

Year	Party	PI	N	W	CS	ROP	Position	Age	State
1856	R	4.2	—	—	15.19	36	Supreme Court justice	71.64	Ohio

John R. McLean (1848-1916)

Year	Party	PI	N	W	CS	ROP	Position	Age	State
1896	D	5.0	—	—	14.63	29	Journalist	48.12	Ohio

Wilbur Mills (1909-1992)

Year	Party	PI	N	W	CS	ROP	Position	Age	State
1972	D	4.3	—	—	10.36	24	Representative	63.44	Arkansas

John Milton (1740-1804)

Year	Party	PI	N	W	CS	ROP	Position	Age	State
1789	F	3.1	—	—	26.29	85	State official	49.00	Georgia

Walter Mondale (1928-)

Year	Party	PI	N	W	CS	ROP	Position	Age	State
1984	D	7.8	X	—	58.83	75	Former vice president	56.82	Minnesota

James Monroe (1758-1831)

Year	Party	PI	N	W	CS	ROP	Position	Age	State
1816	DR	7.3	X	X	90.10	123	Cabinet member	58.51	Virginia
1820	DR	8.7	X	X	96.04	110	President	62.51	Virginia

William Morrison (1824-1909)

Year	Party	PI	N	W	CS	ROP	Position	Age	State
1880	D	6.5	—	—	16.71	26	Representative	56.13	Illinois

Levi Morton (1824-1920)

Year	Party	PI	N	W	CS	ROP	Position	Age	State
1896	R	7.8	—	—	15.03	19	Governor	72.46	New York

Oliver Morton (1823-1877)

Year	Party	PI	N	W	CS	ROP	Position	Age	State
1876	R	8.2	—	—	23.09	28	Senator	53.24	Indiana

William Murray (1869-1956)

Year	Party	PI	N	W	CS	ROP	Position	Age	State
1932	D	5.1	—	—	12.73	25	Governor	62.95	Oklahoma

Edmund Muskie (1914-1996)

Year	Party	PI	N	W	CS	ROP	Position	Age	State
1972	D	7.2	—	—	17.06	24	Senator	58.60	Maine

N-R

Ralph Nader (1934-)

Year	Party	PI	N	W	CS	ROP	Position	Age	State
2000	GRN	1.3	—	—	18.76	144	Movement leader	66.68	Connecticut

Richard Nixon (1913-1994)

Year	Party	PI	N	W	CS	ROP	Position	Age	State
1960	R	8.0	X	—	72.12	90	Vice president	47.81	California
1964	R	6.7	—	—	11.00	16	Former nominee	51.81	New York
1968	R	6.2	X	X	78.01	126	Former nominee	55.81	New York
1972	R	8.8	X	X	95.25	108	President	59.81	California

George Norris (1861-1944)

Year	Party	PI	N	W	CS	ROP	Position	Age	State
1928	R	4.3	—	—	12.58	29	Senator	67.31	Nebraska

Barack Obama (1961-)

Year	Party	PI	N	W	CS	ROP	Position	Age	State
2008	D	6.8	X	X	84.03	124	Senator	47.24	Illinois
2012	D	8.3	X	X	81.59	98	President	51.24	Illinois

Asa Packer (1805-1879)

Year	Party	PI	N	W	CS	ROP	Position	Age	State
1868	D	6.0	—	—	16.55	28	Former representative	62.84	Pennsylvania

Mitchell Palmer (1872-1936)

Year	Party	PI	N	W	CS	ROP	Position	Age	State
1920	D	4.9	—	—	27.09	55	Cabinet member	48.49	Pennsylvania

Alton Parker (1852-1926)

Year	Party	PI	N	W	CS	ROP	Position	Age	State
1904	D	4.9	X	—	66.33	135	State judge	52.47	New York

Joel Parker (1816-1888)

Year	Party	PI	N	W	CS	ROP	Position	Age	State
1868	D	6.7	—	—	13.27	20	Former governor	51.94	New Jersey

Robert Pattison (1850-1904)

Year	Party	PI	N	W	CS	ROP	Position	Age	State
1896	D	7.2	—	—	18.30	25	Former governor	45.90	Pennsylvania

Rand Paul (1963-)

Year	Party	PI	N	W	CS	ROP	Position	Age	State
2016	R	7.8	—	—	10.13	13	Senator	53.82	Kentucky

Ron Paul (1935-)

Year	Party	PI	N	W	CS	ROP	Position	Age	State
2008	R/TC	4.8	—	—	13.62	28	Representative	73.20	Texas
2012	R	4.6	—	—	18.11	39	Representative	77.20	Texas
2016	R	3.8	—	—	10.62	28	Former representative	81.20	Texas

Henry Payne (1810-1896)

Year	Party	PI	N	W	CS	ROP	Position	Age	State
1880	D	5.6	—	—	18.78	34	Former representative	69.92	Ohio

George Pendleton (1825-1889)

Year	Party	PI	N	W	CS	ROP	Position	Age	State
1868	D	6.7	—	—	36.43	54	Former representative	43.29	Ohio

Ross Perot (1930-2019)

Year	Party	PI	N	W	CS	ROP	Position	Age	State
1992	I	2.9	—	—	43.78	151	Business executive	62.35	Texas
1996	REF	2.6	—	—	36.87	142	Business executive	66.35	Texas

Rick Perry (1950-)

Year	Party	PI	N	W	CS	ROP	Position	Age	State
2012	R	7.5	—	—	10.14	14	Governor	62.66	Texas

Franklin Pierce (1804-1869)

Year	Party	PI	N	W	CS	ROP	Position	Age	State
1852	D	7.0	X	X	89.52	128	Former senator	47.94	New Hampshire
1856	D	8.1	—	—	43.05	53	President	51.94	New Hampshire

Charles Cotesworth Pinckney (1746-1825)

Year	Party	PI	N	W	CS	ROP	Position	Age	State
1796	F	3.9	—	—	18.98	49	Ambassador	50.68	South Carolina
1800	F	4.4	—	—	63.01	143	Former ambassador	54.68	South Carolina
1804	F	5.1	X	—	59.38	116	Former ambassador	58.68	South Carolina
1808	F	3.9	X	—	66.03	169	Former nominee	62.68	South Carolina

Thomas Pinckney (1750-1828)

Year	Party	PI	N	W	CS	ROP	Position	Age	State
1796	F	4.1	—	—	61.70	150	Ambassador	46.02	South Carolina

James Polk (1795-1849)

Year	Party	PI	N	W	CS	ROP	Position	Age	State
1844	D	6.7	X	X	81.33	121	Former governor	49.00	Tennessee

Colin Powell (1937-)

Year	Party	PI	N	W	CS	ROP	Position	Age	State
2016	R	3.2	—	—	11.84	37	Former Cabinet member	79.57	New York

Matthew Quay (1833-1904)

Year	Party	PI	N	W	CS	ROP	Position	Age	State
1896	R	7.5	—	—	15.35	20	Senator	63.09	Pennsylvania

Samuel Randall (1828-1890)

Year	Party	PI	N	W	CS	ROP	Position	Age	State
1884	D	6.3	—	—	17.58	28	Representative	56.06	Pennsylvania

Ronald Reagan (1911-2004)

Year	Party	PI	N	W	CS	ROP	Position	Age	State
1968	R	7.3	—	—	28.22	39	Governor	57.73	California
1976	R	6.7	—	—	47.60	71	Former governor	65.73	California
1980	R	5.7	X	X	91.16	160	Former governor	69.73	California
1984	R	8.1	X	X	95.13	117	President	73.73	California

James Reed (1861-1944)

Year	Party	PI	N	W	CS	ROP	Position	Age	State
1928	D	4.8	—	—	16.09	34	Senator	66.98	Missouri

Thomas Reed (1839-1902)

Year	Party	PI	N	W	CS	ROP	Position	Age	State
1896	R	5.2	—	—	17.27	33	Representative	57.04	Maine

James Rhodes (1909-2001)

Year	Party	PI	N	W	CS	ROP	Position	Age	State
1968	R	6.6	—	—	16.17	25	Governor	59.13	Ohio

Bill Richardson (1947-)

Year	Party	PI	N	W	CS	ROP	Position	Age	State
2008	D	5.9	—	—	10.17	17	Governor	60.96	New Mexico

Pat Robertson (1930-)

Year	Party	PI	N	W	CS	ROP	Position	Age	State
1988	R	4.5	—	—	15.41	34	Movement leader	58.61	Virginia

Nelson Rockefeller (1908-1979)

Year	Party	PI	N	W	CS	ROP	Position	Age	State
1964	R	7.6	—	—	20.93	28	Governor	56.32	New York
1968	R	7.1	—	—	21.48	30	Governor	60.32	New York

Mitt Romney (1947-)

Year	Party	PI	N	W	CS	ROP	Position	Age	State
2008	R	6.1	—	—	23.13	38	Former governor	61.64	Massachusetts
2012	R	5.9	X	—	70.93	120	Former governor	65.64	Massachusetts

Franklin Roosevelt (1882-1945)

Year	Party	PI	N	W	CS	ROP	Position	Age	State
1932	D	8.3	X	X	91.94	111	Governor	50.75	New York
1936	D	10.0	X	X	95.88	96	President	54.75	New York
1940	D	9.6	X	X	89.94	94	President	58.75	New York
1944	D	9.4	X	X	88.61	94	President	62.75	New York

Theodore Roosevelt (1858-1919)

Year	Party	PI	N	W	CS	ROP	Position	Age	State
1904	R	8.8	X	X	85.72	97	President	46.01	New York
1912	R/P	10.0	—	—	66.37	66	Former president	54.01	New York
1916	R	9.6	—	—	14.78	15	Former president	58.01	New York

Elihu Root (1845-1937)

Year	Party	PI	N	W	CS	ROP	Position	Age	State
1916	R	6.0	—	—	16.23	27	Former senator	71.71	New York

Marco Rubio (1971-)

Year	Party	PI	N	W	CS	ROP	Position	Age	State
2016	R	7.7	—	—	17.61	23	Senator	45.43	Florida

Richard Russell (1897-1971)

Year	Party	PI	N	W	CS	ROP	Position	Age	State
1948	D	4.4	—	—	22.93	52	Senator	51.00	Georgia
1952	D	5.1	—	—	23.13	45	Senator	55.00	Georgia

John Rutledge (1739-1800)

Year	Party	PI	N	W	CS	ROP	Position	Age	State
1789	F	4.5	—	—	45.73	102	Former governor	50.12	South Carolina

S-Y

Bernie Sanders (1941-)

Year	Party	PI	N	W	CS	ROP	Position	Age	State
2016	D	5.5	—	—	44.15	80	Senator	75.15	Vermont

Rick Santorum (1958-)

Year	Party	PI	N	W	CS	ROP	Position	Age	State
2012	R	7.3	—	—	22.25	30	Former senator	54.48	Pennsylvania

Winfield Scott (1786-1866)

Year	Party	PI	N	W	CS	ROP	Position	Age	State
1840	W	5.8	—	—	27.88	48	General	54.39	New Jersey
1848	W	5.0	—	—	27.96	56	General	62.39	New Jersey
1852	W	4.2	X	—	63.01	150	General	66.39	New Jersey

William Scranton (1917-2013)

Year	Party	PI	N	W	CS	ROP	Position	Age	State
1964	R	6.9	—	—	19.42	28	Governor	47.29	Pennsylvania

William Seward (1801-1872)

Year	Party	PI	N	W	CS	ROP	Position	Age	State
1860	R	8.2	—	—	39.70	48	Senator	59.46	New York

Horatio Seymour (1810-1886)

Year	Party	PI	N	W	CS	ROP	Position	Age	State
1864	D	8.0	—	—	14.23	18	Governor	54.42	New York
1868	D	7.5	X	—	67.61	90	Former governor	58.42	New York

Thomas Seymour (1807-1868)

Year	Party	PI	N	W	CS	ROP	Position	Age	State
1864	D	6.8	—	—	23.41	34	Former governor	57.09	Connecticut

John Sherman (1823-1900)

Year	Party	PI	N	W	CS	ROP	Position	Age	State
1880	R	8.1	—	—	19.82	24	Cabinet member	57.48	Ohio
1888	R	7.7	—	—	31.96	42	Senator	65.48	Ohio

Lawrence Sherman (1858-1939)

Year	Party	PI	N	W	CS	ROP	Position	Age	State
1916	R	6.1	—	—	15.63	26	Senator	57.98	Illinois

Sargent Shriver (1915-2011)

Year	Party	PI	N	W	CS	ROP	Position	Age	State
1976	D	4.2	—	—	11.14	27	Former v.p. nominee	60.98	Maryland

Paul Simon (1928-2003)

Year	Party	PI	N	W	CS	ROP	Position	Age	State
1988	D	7.1	—	—	12.66	18	Senator	59.92	Illinois

Alfred Smith (1873-1944)

Year	Party	PI	N	W	CS	ROP	Position	Age	State
1920	D	6.5	—	—	15.99	25	Governor	46.84	New York
1924	D	7.0	—	—	23.54	34	Governor	50.84	New York
1928	D	6.9	X	—	63.06	91	Governor	54.84	New York
1932	D	6.6	—	—	23.23	35	Former nominee	58.84	New York

Faith Spotted Eagle (1948-)

Year	Party	PI	N	W	CS	ROP	Position	Age	State
2016	D	2.3	—	—	10.62	46	Movement leader	68.00	South Dakota

William Sproul (1870-1928)

Year	Party	PI	N	W	CS	ROP	Position	Age	State
1920	R	6.4	—	—	15.09	24	Governor	50.13	Pennsylvania

Harold Stassen (1907-2001)

Year	Party	PI	N	W	CS	ROP	Position	Age	State
1948	R	4.5	—	—	22.01	49	Former governor	41.55	Minnesota
1952	R	3.9	—	—	13.39	34	College president	45.55	Pennsylvania

Adlai Stevenson (1900-1965)

Year	Party	PI	N	W	CS	ROP	Position	Age	State
1952	D	6.7	X	—	63.90	95	Governor	52.74	Illinois
1956	D	7.6	X	—	62.52	82	Former nominee	56.74	Illinois
1960	D	7.2	—	—	12.86	18	Former nominee	60.74	Illinois

Stuart Symington (1901-1988)

Year	Party	PI	N	W	CS	ROP	Position	Age	State
1960	D	6.9	—	—	13.00	19	Senator	59.35	Missouri

Robert Taft (1889-1953)

Year	Party	PI	N	W	CS	ROP	Position	Age	State
1940	R	5.8	—	—	32.24	56	Senator	51.15	Ohio
1948	R	5.6	—	—	22.57	40	Senator	59.15	Ohio
1952	R	4.6	—	—	32.33	70	Senator	63.15	Ohio

William Howard Taft (1857-1930)

Year	Party	PI	N	W	CS	ROP	Position	Age	State
1908	R	6.0	X	X	83.31	139	Cabinet member	51.13	Ohio
1912	R	8.2	X	—	55.09	67	President	55.13	Ohio

Zachary Taylor (1784-1850)

Year	Party	PI	N	W	CS	ROP	Position	Age	State
1848	W	4.1	X	X	78.93	193	General	63.94	Louisiana

Edward Telfair (1735-1807)

Year	Party	PI	N	W	CS	ROP	Position	Age	State
1789	DR	4.8	—	—	21.42	45	Former governor	54.00	Georgia

Norman Thomas (1884-1968)

Year	Party	PI	N	W	CS	ROP	Position	Age	State
1932	SOC	3.0	—	—	17.13	57	Movement leader	47.95	New York

Fred Thompson (1942-2015)

Year	Party	PI	N	W	CS	ROP	Position	Age	State
2008	R	7.2	—	—	10.81	15	Former senator	66.20	Tennessee

Allen Thurman (1813-1895)

Year	Party	PI	N	W	CS	ROP	Position	Age	State
1880	D	7.7	—	—	17.43	23	Senator	66.97	Ohio
1884	D	7.4	—	—	18.54	25	Former senator	70.97	Ohio

Strom Thurmond (1902-2003)

Year	Party	PI	N	W	CS	ROP	Position	Age	State
1948	SRD	2.2	—	—	34.75	158	Governor	45.91	South Carolina

Samuel Tilden (1814-1886)

Year	Party	PI	N	W	CS	ROP	Position	Age	State
1876	D	7.2	X	—	75.14	104	Governor	62.73	New York
1880	D	8.0	—	—	14.07	18	Former nominee	66.73	New York

Harry Truman (1884-1972)

Year	Party	PI	N	W	CS	ROP	Position	Age	State
1948	D	7.6	X	X	79.72	105	President	64.48	Missouri

Donald Trump (1946-)

Year	Party	PI	N	W	CS	ROP	Position	Age	State
2016	R	3.1	X	X	78.79	254	Business executive	70.38	New York

Paul Tsongas (1941-1997)

Year	Party	PI	N	W	CS	ROP	Position	Age	State
1992	D	7.0	—	—	21.82	31	Former senator	51.71	Massachusetts

Morris Udall (1922-1998)

Year	Party	PI	N	W	CS	ROP	Position	Age	State
1976	D	4.3	—	—	18.22	42	Representative	54.38	Arizona

Oscar Underwood (1862-1929)

Year	Party	PI	N	W	CS	ROP	Position	Age	State
1912	D	3.0	—	—	16.41	55	Representative	50.49	Alabama
1924	D	4.5	—	—	15.57	35	Senator	62.49	Alabama

Martin Van Buren (1782-1862)

Year	Party	PI	N	W	CS	ROP	Position	Age	State
1836	D	6.8	X	X	80.26	118	Vice president	53.91	New York
1840	D	9.1	X	—	65.49	72	President	57.91	New York
1844	D	8.7	—	—	50.00	57	Former president	61.91	New York
1848	FS	7.1	—	—	42.02	59	Former president	65.91	New York

Arthur Vandenberg (1884-1951)

Year	Party	PI	N	W	CS	ROP	Position	Age	State
1940	R	5.8	—	—	15.17	26	Senator	56.61	Michigan
1948	R	5.1	—	—	13.55	27	Senator	64.61	Michigan

George Wallace (1919-1998)

Year	Party	PI	N	W	CS	ROP	Position	Age	State
1964	D	6.4	—	—	13.23	21	Governor	45.19	Alabama
1968	D/AI	5.4	—	—	45.41	84	Former governor	49.19	Alabama
1972	D	6.5	—	—	26.62	41	Governor	53.19	Alabama
1976	D	5.6	—	—	17.84	32	Governor	57.19	Alabama

Henry Wallace (1888-1965)

Year	Party	PI	N	W	CS	ROP	Position	Age	State
1948	D/P	3.1	—	—	17.65	57	Former vice president	60.07	Iowa

Thomas Walsh (1859-1933)

Year	Party	PI	N	W	CS	ROP	Position	Age	State
1924	D	4.0	—	—	13.17	33	Senator	65.39	Montana
1928	D	3.5	—	—	10.95	31	Senator	69.39	Montana

Earl Warren (1891-1974)

Year	Party	PI	N	W	CS	ROP	Position	Age	State
1948	R	5.7	—	—	19.04	33	Governor	57.62	California
1952	R	6.2	—	—	18.38	30	Governor	61.62	California

Elihu Washburne (1816-1887)

Year	Party	PI	N	W	CS	ROP	Position	Age	State
1880	R	4.4	—	—	13.19	30	Former ambassador	64.11	Illinois

George Washington (1732-1799)

Year	Party	PI	N	W	CS	ROP	Position	Age	State
1789	F	5.6	X	X	96.18	172	Former general	57.69	Virginia
1792	F	9.7	X	X	96.18	99	President	60.69	Virginia
1796	F	9.1	—	—	21.42	24	President	64.69	Virginia

James Watson (1864-1948)

Year	Party	PI	N	W	CS	ROP	Position	Age	State
1928	R	5.1	—	—	13.57	27	Senator	64.00	Indiana

James Weaver (1833-1912)

Year	Party	PI	N	W	CS	ROP	Position	Age	State
1880	GBK	4.2	—	—	20.66	49	Representative	47.39	Iowa
1892	POP	4.1	—	—	38.80	95	Former representative	59.39	Iowa

Daniel Webster (1782-1852)

Year	Party	PI	N	W	CS	ROP	Position	Age	State
1836	W	5.0	—	—	26.29	53	Senator	54.79	Massachusetts
1848	W	7.0	—	—	16.31	23	Senator	66.79	Massachusetts
1852	W	6.0	—	—	18.52	31	Cabinet member	70.79	Massachusetts

John Weeks (1860-1926)

Year	Party	PI	N	W	CS	ROP	Position	Age	State
1916	R	6.5	—	—	16.35	25	Senator	56.56	Massachusetts

George White (1872-1953)

Year	Party	PI	N	W	CS	ROP	Position	Age	State
1932	D	6.1	—	—	12.70	21	Governor	60.20	Ohio

Hugh White (1773-1840)

Year	Party	PI	N	W	CS	ROP	Position	Age	State
1836	W	6.3	X	—	54.62	87	Senator	63.01	Tennessee

Wendell Willkie (1892-1944)

Year	Party	PI	N	W	CS	ROP	Position	Age	State
1940	R	4.7	X	—	63.60	135	Business executive	48.70	New York

Woodrow Wilson (1856-1924)

Year	Party	PI	N	W	CS	ROP	Position	Age	State
1912	D	6.6	X	X	86.26	131	Governor	55.84	New Jersey
1916	D	8.6	X	X	78.07	91	President	59.84	New Jersey

William Wirt (1772-1834)

Year	Party	PI	N	W	CS	ROP	Position	Age	State
1832	AM	3.9	—	—	35.63	91	Former Cabinet member	59.98	Maryland

Leonard Wood (1860-1927)

Year	Party	PI	N	W	CS	ROP	Position	Age	State
1920	R	4.3	—	—	31.95	74	General	60.06	New Hampshire

Levi Woodbury (1789-1851)

Year	Party	PI	N	W	CS	ROP	Position	Age	State
1848	D	7.0	—	—	24.61	35	Supreme Court justice	58.86	New Hampshire

Sam Yorty (1909-1998)

Year	Party	PI	N	W	CS	ROP	Position	Age	State
1972	D	4.3	—	—	10.30	24	Mayor	63.08	California

3

STATES

This chapter really needs little introduction. It contains state-by-state breakdowns of presidential election results. The states (naturally) are displayed in alphabetical order.

Keep in mind that, as far as this book is concerned, there are 51 states, not 50. The District of Columbia has been casting electoral votes since 1964, so it is afforded equal status in these pages.

Here's a guide to the charts for each state:

Basics

State winners (all-time): Number of times each party has won a plurality of the state's electoral votes since the state began participating in presidential elections. See pages 18-20 for abbreviations. Tie means that two or more parties tied for the plurality. Minor parties are grouped as Other.

General match (all-time): Times that the winner of the state was the same as the winner of the national election, followed by the number of times the state failed to match the nation. The matching percentage is in parentheses.

State winners (Modern Era): Winners since 1960.

General match (Modern Era): Record of matches since 1960.

Home-state candidacies: Times that a presidential candidate from the state met qualification standards. All campaigns by an individual candidate are counted separately.

Home-state nominees: Candidates from the state who won major-party nominations.

Home-state winners: Candidates from the state who won general elections.

Statewide results since 1856

Year: This chart covers the span since 1856, the beginning of head-to-head competition between Democratic and Republican nominees. If a state did not tabulate popular votes in a given election, it is not listed.

Winner: Candidate who received the most popular votes in the state, with party in parentheses.

PV%: Popular-vote percentage for the winner.

Second: Candidate who received the second-largest number of popular votes in the state, with party in parentheses.

PV%: Popular-vote percentage for the second-place finisher.

Home-state qualified candidacies

Year: Election.

Candidate: Candidate from the state who met qualification standards. Candidates are listed in chronological order, then by CS in a given year.

Party: Political party.

Position: Position by which the candidate was best known, usually his current or most recent position.

N: Major-party nominees are designated by an X.

W: General-election winners are designated by an X.

CS: Campaign score.

Additional data for each state can be found in Chapter 1, including the raw numbers of popular votes cast for each candidate in any given election, as well as the distribution of its electoral votes.

ALABAMA

Basics

State winners (all-time) .... D 28, R 14, DR 3, SD 1, Other 3
General match (all-time) 25-24 (51.02%)
State winners (Modern Era) .... D 1, R 12, Other 2
General match (Modern Era) 8-7 (53.33%)
Home-state candidacies 7
Home-state nominees 0
Home-state winners 0

NOTE: Alabama was carried by the Democratic ticket in 1960, but a majority of the state's electors voted for Harry Byrd for president.

Statewide results since 1856

Year	Winner	PV%	Second	PV%
1856	James Buchanan (D)	62.08%	Millard Fillmore (AW)	37.92%
1860	John Breckinridge (SD)	54.00%	John Bell (CU)	30.89%
1868	Ulysses Grant (R)	51.25%	Horatio Seymour (D)	48.75%
1872	Ulysses Grant (R)	53.19%	Horace Greeley (D-LR)	46.81%
1876	Samuel Tilden (D)	59.98%	Rutherford Hayes (R)	40.02%
1880	Winfield Hancock (D)	59.99%	James Garfield (R)	37.10%
1884	Grover Cleveland (D)	60.37%	James Blaine (R)	38.69%
1888	Grover Cleveland (D)	67.00%	Benjamin Harrison (R)	32.66%
1892	Grover Cleveland (D)	59.40%	James Weaver (POP)	36.55%
1896	William J. Bryan (D-POP)	66.96%	William McKinley (R)	28.61%
1900	William Jennings Bryan (D)	60.05%	William McKinley (R)	34.67%
1904	Alton Parker (D)	73.35%	Theodore Roosevelt (R)	20.66%
1908	William Jennings Bryan (D)	70.75%	William Howard Taft (R)	24.31%
1912	Woodrow Wilson (D)	69.89%	Theodore Roosevelt (P)	19.23%
1916	Woodrow Wilson (D)	75.80%	Charles Evans Hughes (R)	21.97%
1920	James Cox (D)	66.71%	Warren Harding (R)	31.94%
1924	John Davis (D)	67.81%	Calvin Coolidge (R)	27.02%
1928	Alfred Smith (D)	51.33%	Herbert Hoover (R)	48.49%
1932	Franklin Roosevelt (D)	84.76%	Herbert Hoover (R)	14.14%
1936	Franklin Roosevelt (D)	86.38%	Alfred Landon (R)	12.82%
1940	Franklin Roosevelt (D)	85.22%	Wendell Willkie (R)	14.34%
1944	Franklin Roosevelt (D)	81.28%	Thomas Dewey (R)	18.20%
1948	Strom Thurmond (SRD)	79.75%	Thomas Dewey (R)	19.04%
1952	Adlai Stevenson (D)	64.55%	Dwight Eisenhower (R)	35.02%
1956	Adlai Stevenson (D)	56.52%	Dwight Eisenhower (R)	39.39%
1960	John Kennedy (D)	56.83%	Richard Nixon (R)	41.74%
1964	Barry Goldwater (R)	69.45%	Unpledged slate (D)	30.55%
1968	George Wallace (AI)	65.86%	Hubert Humphrey (D)	18.72%
1972	Richard Nixon (R)	72.43%	George McGovern (D)	25.54%
1976	Jimmy Carter (D)	55.73%	Gerald Ford (R)	42.62%
1980	Ronald Reagan (R)	48.75%	Jimmy Carter (D)	47.45%
1984	Ronald Reagan (R)	60.54%	Walter Mondale (D)	38.28%
1988	George H.W. Bush (R)	59.17%	Michael Dukakis (D)	39.86%
1992	George H.W. Bush (R)	47.65%	Bill Clinton (D)	40.88%
1996	Bob Dole (R)	50.12%	Bill Clinton (D)	43.16%

Year	Winner	PV%	Second	PV%
2000	George W. Bush (R)	56.48%	Al Gore (D)	41.57%
2004	George W. Bush (R)	62.46%	John Kerry (D)	36.84%
2008	John McCain (R)	60.32%	Barack Obama (D)	38.74%
2012	Mitt Romney (R)	60.55%	Barack Obama (D)	38.36%
2016	Donald Trump (R)	62.08%	Hillary Clinton (D)	34.36%

Home-state qualified candidacies

Year	Candidate	Party	Position	N	W	CS
1912	Oscar Underwood	D	Representative	—	—	16.41
1924	Oscar Underwood	D	Senator	—	—	15.57
1956	Walter Jones	D	State judge	—	—	10.62
1964	George Wallace	D	Governor	—	—	13.23
1968	George Wallace	D/AI	Former governor	—	—	45.41
1972	George Wallace	D	Governor	—	—	26.62
1976	George Wallace	D	Governor	—	—	17.84

ALASKA

Basics

State winners (all-time) .... D 1, R 14
General match (all-time) 9-6 (60.00%)
State winners (Modern Era) .... D 1, R 14
General match (Modern Era) 9-6 (60.00%)
Home-state candidacies 0
Home-state nominees 0
Home-state winners 0

Statewide results since 1856

Year	Winner	PV%	Second	PV%
1960	Richard Nixon (R)	50.94%	John Kennedy (D)	49.06%
1964	Lyndon Johnson (D)	65.91%	Barry Goldwater (R)	34.09%
1968	Richard Nixon (R)	45.28%	Hubert Humphrey (D)	42.65%
1972	Richard Nixon (R)	58.13%	George McGovern (D)	34.62%
1976	Gerald Ford (R)	57.91%	Jimmy Carter (D)	35.65%
1980	Ronald Reagan (R)	54.35%	Jimmy Carter (D)	26.41%
1984	Ronald Reagan (R)	66.65%	Walter Mondale (D)	29.87%
1988	George H.W. Bush (R)	59.59%	Michael Dukakis (D)	36.27%
1992	George H.W. Bush (R)	39.46%	Bill Clinton (D)	30.29%
1996	Bob Dole (R)	50.80%	Bill Clinton (D)	33.27%
2000	George W. Bush (R)	58.62%	Al Gore (D)	27.67%
2004	George W. Bush (R)	61.07%	John Kerry (D)	35.52%
2008	John McCain (R)	59.43%	Barack Obama (D)	37.89%
2012	Mitt Romney (R)	54.80%	Barack Obama (D)	40.81%
2016	Donald Trump (R)	51.28%	Hillary Clinton (D)	36.55%

Home-state qualified candidacies

(None)

ARIZONA

Basics

State winners (all-time) .... D 8, R 19
General match (all-time) 21-6 (77.78%)
State winners (Modern Era) .... D 1, R 14
General match (Modern Era) 9-6 (60.00%)
Home-state candidacies 5
Home-state nominees 2
Home-state winners 0

Statewide results since 1856

Year	Winner	PV%	Second	PV%
1912	Woodrow Wilson (D)	43.59%	Theodore Roosevelt (P)	29.34%
1916	Woodrow Wilson (D)	57.17%	Charles Evans Hughes (R)	35.37%
1920	Warren Harding (R)	55.41%	James Cox (D)	44.23%
1924	Calvin Coolidge (R)	41.26%	John Davis (D)	35.47%
1928	Herbert Hoover (R)	57.57%	Alfred Smith (D)	42.23%
1932	Franklin Roosevelt (D)	67.03%	Herbert Hoover (R)	30.53%
1936	Franklin Roosevelt (D)	69.85%	Alfred Landon (R)	26.93%
1940	Franklin Roosevelt (D)	63.50%	Wendell Willkie (R)	36.01%
1944	Franklin Roosevelt (D)	58.80%	Thomas Dewey (R)	40.90%
1948	Harry Truman (D)	53.79%	Thomas Dewey (R)	43.82%
1952	Dwight Eisenhower (R)	58.35%	Adlai Stevenson (D)	41.65%
1956	Dwight Eisenhower (R)	61.00%	Adlai Stevenson (D)	38.90%
1960	Richard Nixon (R)	55.52%	John Kennedy (D)	44.36%
1964	Barry Goldwater (R)	50.45%	Lyndon Johnson (D)	49.45%
1968	Richard Nixon (R)	54.78%	Hubert Humphrey (D)	35.02%
1972	Richard Nixon (R)	64.67%	George McGovern (D)	31.87%
1976	Gerald Ford (R)	56.37%	Jimmy Carter (D)	39.80%
1980	Ronald Reagan (R)	60.61%	Jimmy Carter (D)	28.25%
1984	Ronald Reagan (R)	66.42%	Walter Mondale (D)	32.54%
1988	George H.W. Bush (R)	59.95%	Michael Dukakis (D)	38.74%
1992	George H.W. Bush (R)	38.47%	Bill Clinton (D)	36.52%
1996	Bill Clinton (D)	46.52%	Bob Dole (R)	44.29%
2000	George W. Bush (R)	51.02%	Al Gore (D)	44.74%
2004	George W. Bush (R)	54.87%	John Kerry (D)	44.40%
2008	John McCain (R)	53.64%	Barack Obama (D)	45.12%
2012	Mitt Romney (R)	53.66%	Barack Obama (D)	44.59%
2016	Donald Trump (R)	48.67%	Hillary Clinton (D)	45.13%

Home-state qualified candidacies

Year	Candidate	Party	Position	N	W	CS
1964	Barry Goldwater	R	Senator	X	—	60.59
1976	Morris Udall	D	Representative	—	—	18.22
1988	Bruce Babbitt	D	Former governor	—	—	10.20
2000	John McCain	R	Senator	—	—	29.92
2008	John McCain	R	Senator	X	—	68.78

ARKANSAS

Basics

State winners (all-time) .... D 32, R 10, SD 1, Other 1
General match (all-time) 26-18 (59.09%)
State winners (Modern Era) .... D 5, R 9, Other 1
General match (Modern Era) 12-3 (80.00%)
Home-state candidacies 5
Home-state nominees 2
Home-state winners 2

Statewide results since 1856

Year	Winner	PV%	Second	PV%
1856	James Buchanan (D)	67.12%	Millard Fillmore (AW)	32.88%
1860	John Breckinridge (SD)	53.06%	John Bell (CU)	37.05%
1868	Ulysses Grant (R)	53.68%	Horatio Seymour (D)	46.32%
1872	Ulysses Grant (R)	52.17%	Horace Greeley (D-LR)	47.83%
1876	Samuel Tilden (D)	59.92%	Rutherford Hayes (R)	39.87%
1880	Winfield Hancock (D)	55.82%	James Garfield (R)	38.98%
1884	Grover Cleveland (D)	57.83%	James Blaine (R)	40.71%
1888	Grover Cleveland (D)	54.80%	Benjamin Harrison (R)	38.05%
1892	Grover Cleveland (D)	59.30%	Benjamin Harrison (R)	31.78%
1896	William J. Bryan (D-POP)	73.70%	William McKinley (R)	25.11%
1900	William Jennings Bryan (D)	63.49%	William McKinley (R)	35.01%
1904	Alton Parker (D)	55.39%	Theodore Roosevelt (R)	40.20%
1908	William Jennings Bryan (D)	57.31%	William Howard Taft (R)	37.33%
1912	Woodrow Wilson (D)	55.01%	William Howard Taft (R)	20.45%
1916	Woodrow Wilson (D)	66.64%	Charles Evans Hughes (R)	28.01%
1920	James Cox (D)	58.49%	Warren Harding (R)	38.73%
1924	John Davis (D)	61.20%	Calvin Coolidge (R)	29.29%
1928	Alfred Smith (D)	60.28%	Herbert Hoover (R)	39.34%
1932	Franklin Roosevelt (D)	86.27%	Herbert Hoover (R)	12.68%
1936	Franklin Roosevelt (D)	81.80%	Alfred Landon (R)	17.86%
1940	Franklin Roosevelt (D)	78.44%	Wendell Willkie (R)	21.02%
1944	Franklin Roosevelt (D)	69.95%	Thomas Dewey (R)	29.84%
1948	Harry Truman (D)	61.72%	Thomas Dewey (R)	21.02%
1952	Adlai Stevenson (D)	55.90%	Dwight Eisenhower (R)	43.76%
1956	Adlai Stevenson (D)	52.46%	Dwight Eisenhower (R)	45.82%
1960	John Kennedy (D)	50.19%	Richard Nixon (R)	43.06%
1964	Lyndon Johnson (D)	56.06%	Barry Goldwater (R)	43.41%
1968	George Wallace (AI)	38.87%	Richard Nixon (R)	30.77%
1972	Richard Nixon (R)	68.87%	George McGovern (D)	30.69%
1976	Jimmy Carter (D)	64.96%	Gerald Ford (R)	34.90%
1980	Ronald Reagan (R)	48.13%	Jimmy Carter (D)	47.52%
1984	Ronald Reagan (R)	60.47%	Walter Mondale (D)	38.29%
1988	George H.W. Bush (R)	56.37%	Michael Dukakis (D)	42.19%
1992	Bill Clinton (D)	53.21%	George H.W. Bush (R)	35.48%
1996	Bill Clinton (D)	53.74%	Bob Dole (R)	36.80%
2000	George W. Bush (R)	51.31%	Al Gore (D)	45.86%
2004	George W. Bush (R)	54.31%	John Kerry (D)	44.55%

Year	Winner	PV%	Second	PV%
2008	John McCain (R)	58.72%	Barack Obama (D)	38.87%
2012	Mitt Romney (R)	60.57%	Barack Obama (D)	36.88%
2016	Donald Trump (R)	60.57%	Hillary Clinton (D)	33.65%

Home-state qualified candidacies

Year	Candidate	Party	Position	N	W	CS
1972	Wilbur Mills	D	Representative	—	—	10.36
1992	Bill Clinton	D	Governor	X	X	82.15
1996	Bill Clinton	D	President	X	X	84.08
2004	Wesley Clark	D	Former general	—	—	12.00
2008	Mike Huckabee	R	Former governor	—	—	22.10

CALIFORNIA

Basics

State winners (all-time) ....D 18, R 23, Other 1
General match (all-time) 34-8 (80.95%)
State winners (Modern Era) ....D 8, R 7
General match (Modern Era) 10-5 (66.67%)
Home-state candidacies 24
Home-state nominees..7
Home-state winners..4

Statewide results since 1856

Year	Winner	PV%	Second	PV%
1856	James Buchanan (D)	48.38%	Millard Fillmore (AW)	32.83%
1860	Abraham Lincoln (R)	32.32%	Stephen Douglas (D)	31.71%
1864	Abraham Lincoln (R)	58.60%	George McClellan (D)	41.40%
1868	Ulysses Grant (R)	50.24%	Horatio Seymour (D)	49.76%
1872	Ulysses Grant (R)	56.38%	Horace Greeley (D-LR)	42.51%
1876	Rutherford Hayes (R)	50.88%	Samuel Tilden (D)	49.08%
1880	Winfield Hancock (D)	48.98%	James Garfield (R)	48.89%
1884	James Blaine (R)	51.97%	Grover Cleveland (D)	45.33%
1888	Benjamin Harrison (R)	49.66%	Grover Cleveland (D)	46.84%
1892	Grover Cleveland (D)	43.83%	Benjamin Harrison (R)	43.78%
1896	William McKinley (R)	49.11%	William J. Bryan (D-POP)	41.23%
1900	William McKinley (R)	54.48%	William Jennings Bryan (D)	41.33%
1904	Theodore Roosevelt (R)	61.86%	Alton Parker (D)	26.92%
1908	William Howard Taft (R)	55.45%	William Jennings Bryan (D)	32.98%
1912	Theodore Roosevelt (P)	41.84%	Woodrow Wilson (D)	41.81%
1916	Woodrow Wilson (D)	46.63%	Charles Evans Hughes (R)	46.29%
1920	Warren Harding (R)	66.24%	James Cox (D)	24.29%
1924	Calvin Coolidge (R)	57.21%	Robert La Follette (P)	33.13%
1928	Herbert Hoover (R)	64.69%	Alfred Smith (D)	34.20%
1932	Franklin Roosevelt (D)	58.41%	Herbert Hoover (R)	37.40%
1936	Franklin Roosevelt (D)	66.95%	Alfred Landon (R)	31.70%
1940	Franklin Roosevelt (D)	57.44%	Wendell Willkie (R)	41.34%
1944	Franklin Roosevelt (D)	56.48%	Thomas Dewey (R)	42.97%
1948	Harry Truman (D)	47.57%	Thomas Dewey (R)	47.13%
1952	Dwight Eisenhower (R)	56.35%	Adlai Stevenson (D)	42.74%
1956	Dwight Eisenhower (R)	55.39%	Adlai Stevenson (D)	44.27%
1960	Richard Nixon (R)	50.10%	John Kennedy (D)	49.55%
1964	Lyndon Johnson (D)	59.11%	Barry Goldwater (R)	40.80%
1968	Richard Nixon (R)	47.82%	Hubert Humphrey (D)	44.74%
1972	Richard Nixon (R)	55.00%	George McGovern (D)	41.54%
1976	Gerald Ford (R)	49.35%	Jimmy Carter (D)	47.57%
1980	Ronald Reagan (R)	52.69%	Jimmy Carter (D)	35.91%
1984	Ronald Reagan (R)	57.52%	Walter Mondale (D)	41.27%
1988	George H.W. Bush (R)	51.13%	Michael Dukakis (D)	47.56%
1992	Bill Clinton (D)	46.01%	George H.W. Bush (R)	32.62%
1996	Bill Clinton (D)	51.10%	Bob Dole (R)	38.21%
2000	Al Gore (D)	53.45%	George W. Bush (R)	41.65%

Year	Winner	PV%	Second	PV%
2004	John Kerry (D)	54.30%	George W. Bush (R)	44.36%
2008	Barack Obama (D)	61.01%	John McCain (R)	36.96%
2012	Barack Obama (D)	60.24%	Mitt Romney (R)	37.12%
2016	Hillary Clinton (D)	61.73%	Donald Trump (R)	31.62%

Home-state qualified candidacies

Year	Candidate	Party	Position	N	W	CS
1856	John Fremont	R	Former senator	X	—	68.16
1880	Stephen Field	D	Supreme Court justice	—	—	17.03
1892	John Bidwell	PRO	Movement leader	—	—	17.19
1920	Hiram Johnson	R	Senator	—	—	24.20
1920	Herbert Hoover	R	Business executive	—	—	12.56
1924	William Gibbs McAdoo	D	Former Cabinet member	—	—	43.53
1924	Hiram Johnson	R	Senator	—	—	16.26
1928	Herbert Hoover	R	Cabinet member	X	X	90.41
1932	Herbert Hoover	R	President	X	—	61.28
1948	Earl Warren	R	Governor	—	—	19.04
1952	Earl Warren	R	Governor	—	—	18.38
1960	Richard Nixon	R	Vice president	X	—	72.12
1968	Ronald Reagan	R	Governor	—	—	28.22
1972	Richard Nixon	R	President	X	X	95.25
1972	Paul McCloskey	R	Representative	—	—	11.31
1972	John Hospers	LIB	Movement leader	—	—	10.62
1972	Sam Yorty	D	Mayor	—	—	10.30
1976	Ronald Reagan	R	Former governor	—	—	47.60
1976	Jerry Brown	D	Governor	—	—	21.16
1980	Ronald Reagan	R	Former governor	X	X	91.16
1980	Jerry Brown	D	Governor	—	—	11.84
1984	Ronald Reagan	R	President	X	X	95.13
1984	Alan Cranston	D	Senator	—	—	10.17
1992	Jerry Brown	D	Former governor	—	—	24.83

COLORADO

Basics

State winners (all-time) ....D 13, R 22, Other 1
General match (all-time) 25-11 (69.44%)
State winners (Modern Era) ....D 5, R 10
General match (Modern Era) 11-4 (73.33%)
Home-state candidacies 2
Home-state nominees 0
Home-state winners 0

Statewide results since 1856

Year	Winner	PV%	Second	PV%
1880	James Garfield (R)	51.26%	Winfield Hancock (D)	46.03%
1884	James Blaine (R)	54.25%	Grover Cleveland (D)	41.68%
1888	Benjamin Harrison (R)	55.22%	Grover Cleveland (D)	40.84%
1892	James Weaver (POP)	57.08%	Benjamin Harrison (R)	41.14%
1896	William J. Bryan (D-POP)	84.95%	William McKinley (R)	13.86%
1900	William Jennings Bryan (D)	55.55%	William McKinley (R)	41.97%
1904	Theodore Roosevelt (R)	55.26%	Alton Parker (D)	41.08%
1908	William Jennings Bryan (D)	48.00%	William Howard Taft (R)	46.88%
1912	Woodrow Wilson (D)	42.83%	Theodore Roosevelt (P)	26.98%
1916	Woodrow Wilson (D)	60.74%	Charles Evans Hughes (R)	34.75%
1920	Warren Harding (R)	59.32%	James Cox (D)	35.93%
1924	Calvin Coolidge (R)	57.02%	John Davis (D)	21.98%
1928	Herbert Hoover (R)	64.72%	Alfred Smith (D)	33.94%
1932	Franklin Roosevelt (D)	54.81%	Herbert Hoover (R)	41.43%
1936	Franklin Roosevelt (D)	60.37%	Alfred Landon (R)	37.09%
1940	Wendell Willkie (R)	50.92%	Franklin Roosevelt (D)	48.37%
1944	Thomas Dewey (R)	53.21%	Franklin Roosevelt (D)	46.40%
1948	Harry Truman (D)	51.88%	Thomas Dewey (R)	46.53%
1952	Dwight Eisenhower (R)	60.27%	Adlai Stevenson (D)	38.96%
1956	Dwight Eisenhower (R)	60.04%	Adlai Stevenson (D)	39.27%
1960	Richard Nixon (R)	54.64%	John Kennedy (D)	44.91%
1964	Lyndon Johnson (D)	61.27%	Barry Goldwater (R)	38.20%
1968	Richard Nixon (R)	50.46%	Hubert Humphrey (D)	41.32%
1972	Richard Nixon (R)	62.61%	George McGovern (D)	34.59%
1976	Gerald Ford (R)	54.03%	Jimmy Carter (D)	42.56%
1980	Ronald Reagan (R)	55.07%	Jimmy Carter (D)	31.07%
1984	Ronald Reagan (R)	63.44%	Walter Mondale (D)	35.12%
1988	George H.W. Bush (R)	53.06%	Michael Dukakis (D)	45.28%
1992	Bill Clinton (D)	40.13%	George H.W. Bush (R)	35.87%
1996	Bob Dole (R)	45.80%	Bill Clinton (D)	44.43%
2000	George W. Bush (R)	50.75%	Al Gore (D)	42.39%
2004	George W. Bush (R)	51.69%	John Kerry (D)	47.02%
2008	Barack Obama (D)	53.66%	John McCain (R)	44.71%
2012	Barack Obama (D)	51.49%	Mitt Romney (R)	46.13%
2016	Hillary Clinton (D)	48.16%	Donald Trump (R)	43.25%

Home-state qualified candidacies

Year	Candidate	Party	Position	N	W	CS
1984	Gary Hart	D	Senator	—	—	37.76
1988	Gary Hart	D	Former senator	—	—	11.02

CONNECTICUT

Basics

State winners (all-time) ....D 20, R 23, DR 2, F 8, NR 2, W 3
General match (all-time) 39-19 (67.24%)
State winners (Modern Era) ....D 10, R 5
General match (Modern Era) 10-5 (66.67%)
Home-state candidacies 6
Home-state nominees...0
Home-state winners...0

Statewide results since 1856

Year	Winner	PV%	Second	PV%
1856	John Fremont (R)	53.16%	James Buchanan (D)	43.59%
1860	Abraham Lincoln (R)	58.12%	Stephen Douglas (D)	20.62%
1864	Abraham Lincoln (R)	51.37%	George McClellan (D)	48.63%
1868	Ulysses Grant (R)	51.53%	Horatio Seymour (D)	48.47%
1872	Ulysses Grant (R)	52.41%	Horace Greeley (D-LR)	47.59%
1876	Samuel Tilden (D)	50.70%	Rutherford Hayes (R)	48.34%
1880	James Garfield (R)	50.51%	Winfield Hancock (D)	48.50%
1884	Grover Cleveland (D)	48.95%	James Blaine (R)	48.01%
1888	Grover Cleveland (D)	48.66%	Benjamin Harrison (R)	48.44%
1892	Grover Cleveland (D)	50.06%	Benjamin Harrison (R)	46.80%
1896	William McKinley (R)	63.24%	William J. Bryan (D-POP)	32.54%
1900	William McKinley (R)	56.92%	William Jennings Bryan (D)	41.07%
1904	Theodore Roosevelt (R)	58.12%	Alton Parker (D)	38.15%
1908	William Howard Taft (R)	59.41%	William Jennings Bryan (D)	35.94%
1912	Woodrow Wilson (D)	39.16%	William Howard Taft (R)	35.88%
1916	Charles Evans Hughes (R)	49.80%	Woodrow Wilson (D)	46.66%
1920	Warren Harding (R)	62.72%	James Cox (D)	33.03%
1924	Calvin Coolidge (R)	61.52%	John Davis (D)	27.52%
1928	Herbert Hoover (R)	53.63%	Alfred Smith (D)	45.58%
1932	Herbert Hoover (R)	48.54%	Franklin Roosevelt (D)	47.40%
1936	Franklin Roosevelt (D)	55.32%	Alfred Landon (R)	40.35%
1940	Franklin Roosevelt (D)	53.44%	Wendell Willkie (R)	46.30%
1944	Franklin Roosevelt (D)	52.30%	Thomas Dewey (R)	46.94%
1948	Thomas Dewey (R)	49.55%	Harry Truman (D)	47.91%
1952	Dwight Eisenhower (R)	55.70%	Adlai Stevenson (D)	43.91%
1956	Dwight Eisenhower (R)	63.72%	Adlai Stevenson (D)	36.26%
1960	John Kennedy (D)	53.73%	Richard Nixon (R)	46.27%
1964	Lyndon Johnson (D)	67.81%	Barry Goldwater (R)	32.09%
1968	Hubert Humphrey (D)	49.48%	Richard Nixon (R)	44.32%
1972	Richard Nixon (R)	58.57%	George McGovern (D)	40.13%
1976	Gerald Ford (R)	52.06%	Jimmy Carter (D)	46.90%
1980	Ronald Reagan (R)	48.16%	Jimmy Carter (D)	38.52%
1984	Ronald Reagan (R)	60.73%	Walter Mondale (D)	38.83%
1988	George H.W. Bush (R)	51.98%	Michael Dukakis (D)	46.88%
1992	Bill Clinton (D)	42.21%	George H.W. Bush (R)	35.78%
1996	Bill Clinton (D)	52.83%	Bob Dole (R)	34.69%
2000	Al Gore (D)	55.91%	George W. Bush (R)	38.44%

Year	Winner	PV%	Second	PV%
2004	John Kerry (D)	54.31%	George W. Bush (R)	43.95%
2008	Barack Obama (D)	60.59%	John McCain (R)	38.22%
2012	Barack Obama (D)	58.06%	Mitt Romney (R)	40.73%
2016	Hillary Clinton (D)	54.57%	Donald Trump (R)	40.93%

Home-state qualified candidacies

Year	Candidate	Party	Position	N	W	CS
1789	Samuel Huntington	F	Governor	—	—	26.29
1796	Oliver Ellsworth	F	Supreme Court justice	—	—	43.29
1864	Thomas Seymour	D	Former governor	—	—	23.41
1868	James English	D	Governor	—	—	13.99
2000	Ralph Nader	GRN	Movement leader	—	—	18.76
2004	Joseph Lieberman	D	Senator	—	—	11.04

DELAWARE

Basics

State winners (all-time) ....D 23, R 18, DR 2, F 8, NR 2, SD 1, W 4
General match (all-time) 36-22 (62.07%)
State winners (Modern Era) ....D 10, R 5
General match (Modern Era) 12-3 (80.00%)
Home-state candidacies 5
Home-state nominees 0
Home-state winners 0

Statewide results since 1856

Year	Winner	PV%	Second	PV%
1856	James Buchanan (D)	54.83%	Millard Fillmore (AW)	42.99%
1860	John Breckinridge (SD)	45.54%	John Bell (CU)	24.13%
1864	George McClellan (D)	51.81%	Abraham Lincoln (R)	48.19%
1868	Horatio Seymour (D)	59.00%	Ulysses Grant (R)	41.00%
1872	Ulysses Grant (R)	51.00%	Horace Greeley (D-LR)	46.77%
1876	Samuel Tilden (D)	55.45%	Rutherford Hayes (R)	44.55%
1880	Winfield Hancock (D)	51.53%	James Garfield (R)	48.03%
1884	Grover Cleveland (D)	56.55%	James Blaine (R)	43.20%
1888	Grover Cleveland (D)	55.15%	Benjamin Harrison (R)	43.51%
1892	Grover Cleveland (D)	49.90%	Benjamin Harrison (R)	48.55%
1896	William McKinley (R)	53.53%	William J. Bryan (D-POP)	42.57%
1900	William McKinley (R)	53.67%	William Jennings Bryan (D)	44.90%
1904	Theodore Roosevelt (R)	54.05%	Alton Parker (D)	44.12%
1908	William Howard Taft (R)	52.11%	William Jennings Bryan (D)	45.94%
1912	Woodrow Wilson (D)	46.48%	William Howard Taft (R)	32.86%
1916	Charles Evans Hughes (R)	50.21%	Woodrow Wilson (D)	47.78%
1920	Warren Harding (R)	55.71%	James Cox (D)	42.07%
1924	Calvin Coolidge (R)	57.70%	John Davis (D)	36.80%
1928	Herbert Hoover (R)	65.83%	Alfred Smith (D)	33.80%
1932	Herbert Hoover (R)	50.55%	Franklin Roosevelt (D)	48.11%
1936	Franklin Roosevelt (D)	54.62%	Alfred Landon (R)	42.33%
1940	Franklin Roosevelt (D)	54.70%	Wendell Willkie (R)	45.05%
1944	Franklin Roosevelt (D)	54.38%	Thomas Dewey (R)	45.27%
1948	Thomas Dewey (R)	50.04%	Harry Truman (D)	48.76%
1952	Dwight Eisenhower (R)	51.75%	Adlai Stevenson (D)	47.88%
1956	Dwight Eisenhower (R)	55.09%	Adlai Stevenson (D)	44.62%
1960	John Kennedy (D)	50.64%	Richard Nixon (R)	49.00%
1964	Lyndon Johnson (D)	60.95%	Barry Goldwater (R)	38.78%
1968	Richard Nixon (R)	45.12%	Hubert Humphrey (D)	41.61%
1972	Richard Nixon (R)	59.60%	George McGovern (D)	39.18%
1976	Jimmy Carter (D)	51.98%	Gerald Ford (R)	46.57%
1980	Ronald Reagan (R)	47.16%	Jimmy Carter (D)	44.83%
1984	Ronald Reagan (R)	59.78%	Walter Mondale (D)	39.93%
1988	George H.W. Bush (R)	55.88%	Michael Dukakis (D)	43.48%
1992	Bill Clinton (D)	43.51%	George H.W. Bush (R)	35.31%
1996	Bill Clinton (D)	51.82%	Bob Dole (R)	36.58%
2000	Al Gore (D)	54.96%	George W. Bush (R)	41.90%

Year	Winner	PV%	Second	PV%
2004	John Kerry (D)	53.35%	George W. Bush (R)	45.75%
2008	Barack Obama (D)	61.94%	John McCain (R)	36.95%
2012	Barack Obama (D)	58.61%	Mitt Romney (R)	39.98%
2016	Hillary Clinton (D)	53.09%	Donald Trump (R)	41.71%

Home-state qualified candidacies

Year	Candidate	Party	Position	N	W	CS
1876	Thomas Bayard	D	Senator	—	—	13.59
1880	Thomas Bayard	D	Senator	—	—	26.61
1884	Thomas Bayard	D	Senator	—	—	26.53
1908	George Gray	D	Former senator	—	—	14.71
1988	Pete du Pont	R	Former governor	—	—	10.25

DISTRICT OF COLUMBIA

Basics

State winners (all-time) .... D 14
General match (all-time) 6-8 (42.86%)
State winners (Modern Era) .... D 14
General match (Modern Era) 6-8 (42.86%)
Home-state candidacies 0
Home-state nominees 0
Home-state winners 0

Statewide results since 1856

Year	Winner	PV%	Second	PV%
1964	Lyndon Johnson (D)	85.50%	Barry Goldwater (R)	14.50%
1968	Hubert Humphrey (D)	81.82%	Richard Nixon (R)	18.18%
1972	George McGovern (D)	78.10%	Richard Nixon (R)	21.56%
1976	Jimmy Carter (D)	81.63%	Gerald Ford (R)	16.51%
1980	Jimmy Carter (D)	74.82%	Ronald Reagan (R)	13.44%
1984	Walter Mondale (D)	85.39%	Ronald Reagan (R)	13.73%
1988	Michael Dukakis (D)	82.65%	George H.W. Bush (R)	14.30%
1992	Bill Clinton (D)	84.64%	George H.W. Bush (R)	9.10%
1996	Bill Clinton (D)	85.19%	Bob Dole (R)	9.34%
2000	Al Gore (D)	85.16%	George W. Bush (R)	8.95%
2004	John Kerry (D)	89.18%	George W. Bush (R)	9.34%
2008	Barack Obama (D)	92.46%	John McCain (R)	6.53%
2012	Barack Obama (D)	90.91%	Mitt Romney (R)	7.28%
2016	Hillary Clinton (D)	90.86%	Donald Trump (R)	4.09%

Home-state qualified candidacies

(None)

FLORIDA

Basics

State winners (all-time) .... D 24, R 16, SD 1, W 1
General match (all-time) 31-11 (73.81%)
State winners (Modern Era) .... D 5, R 10
General match (Modern Era) 13-2 (86.67%)
Home-state candidacies 3
Home-state nominees 0
Home-state winners 0

Statewide results since 1856

Year	Winner	PV%	Second	PV%
1856	James Buchanan (D)	56.81%	Millard Fillmore (AW)	43.19%
1860	John Breckinridge (SD)	62.23%	John Bell (CU)	36.10%
1872	Ulysses Grant (R)	53.52%	Horace Greeley (D-LR)	46.48%
1876	Rutherford Hayes (R)	50.99%	Samuel Tilden (D)	49.01%
1880	Winfield Hancock (D)	54.18%	James Garfield (R)	45.83%
1884	Grover Cleveland (D)	52.96%	James Blaine (R)	46.73%
1888	Grover Cleveland (D)	59.48%	Benjamin Harrison (R)	39.89%
1892	Grover Cleveland (D)	84.78%	James Weaver (POP)	13.62%
1896	William J. Bryan (D-POP)	66.03%	William McKinley (R)	24.31%
1900	William Jennings Bryan (D)	71.08%	William McKinley (R)	18.76%
1904	Alton Parker (D)	68.82%	Theodore Roosevelt (R)	21.15%
1908	William Jennings Bryan (D)	63.02%	William Howard Taft (R)	21.58%
1912	Woodrow Wilson (D)	70.15%	Eugene Debs (SOC)	9.26%
1916	Woodrow Wilson (D)	69.34%	Charles Evans Hughes (R)	18.10%
1920	James Cox (D)	62.13%	Warren Harding (R)	30.79%
1924	John Davis (D)	56.87%	Calvin Coolidge (R)	28.06%
1928	Herbert Hoover (R)	56.83%	Alfred Smith (D)	40.12%
1932	Franklin Roosevelt (D)	74.49%	Herbert Hoover (R)	24.98%
1936	Franklin Roosevelt (D)	76.08%	Alfred Landon (R)	23.90%
1940	Franklin Roosevelt (D)	73.99%	Wendell Willkie (R)	25.98%
1944	Franklin Roosevelt (D)	70.29%	Thomas Dewey (R)	29.66%
1948	Harry Truman (D)	48.82%	Thomas Dewey (R)	33.63%
1952	Dwight Eisenhower (R)	54.99%	Adlai Stevenson (D)	44.98%
1956	Dwight Eisenhower (R)	57.19%	Adlai Stevenson (D)	42.67%
1960	Richard Nixon (R)	51.52%	John Kennedy (D)	48.49%
1964	Lyndon Johnson (D)	51.15%	Barry Goldwater (R)	48.85%
1968	Richard Nixon (R)	40.53%	Hubert Humphrey (D)	30.94%
1972	Richard Nixon (R)	71.92%	George McGovern (D)	27.80%
1976	Jimmy Carter (D)	51.93%	Gerald Ford (R)	46.64%
1980	Ronald Reagan (R)	55.52%	Jimmy Carter (D)	38.50%
1984	Ronald Reagan (R)	65.32%	Walter Mondale (D)	34.66%
1988	George H.W. Bush (R)	60.87%	Michael Dukakis (D)	38.51%
1992	George H.W. Bush (R)	40.90%	Bill Clinton (D)	39.00%
1996	Bill Clinton (D)	48.02%	Bob Dole (R)	42.32%
2000	George W. Bush (R)	48.85%	Al Gore (D)	48.84%

Year	Winner	PV%	Second	PV%
2004	George W. Bush (R)	52.10%	John Kerry (D)	47.09%
2008	Barack Obama (D)	51.03%	John McCain (R)	48.22%
2012	Barack Obama (D)	50.01%	Mitt Romney (R)	49.13%
2016	Donald Trump (R)	49.02%	Hillary Clinton (D)	47.82%

Home-state qualified candidacies

Year	Candidate	Party	Position	N	W	CS
2016	Marco Rubio	R	Senator	—	—	17.61
2016	Ben Carson	R	Movement leader	—	—	11.69
2016	Jeb Bush	R	Former governor	—	—	10.58

GEORGIA

Basics

State winners (all-time) ....D 31, R 10, DR 9, F 1, SD 1, W 3, Tie 1, Other 1
General match (all-time) 32-24-1 (56.14%)
State winners (Modern Era) ....D 4, R 10, Other 1
General match (Modern Era) 9-6 (60.00%)
Home-state candidacies 11
Home-state nominees 2
Home-state winners 1

Statewide results since 1856

Year	Winner	PV%	Second	PV%
1856	James Buchanan (D)	57.14%	Millard Fillmore (AW)	42.86%
1860	John Breckinridge (SD)	48.89%	John Bell (CU)	40.26%
1868	Horatio Seymour (D)	64.27%	Ulysses Grant (R)	35.73%
1872	Horace Greeley (D-LR)	54.97%	Ulysses Grant (R)	45.03%
1876	Samuel Tilden (D)	72.03%	Rutherford Hayes (R)	27.97%
1880	Winfield Hancock (D)	65.41%	James Garfield (R)	34.60%
1884	Grover Cleveland (D)	65.92%	James Blaine (R)	33.84%
1888	Grover Cleveland (D)	70.31%	Benjamin Harrison (R)	28.33%
1892	Grover Cleveland (D)	57.77%	Benjamin Harrison (R)	21.57%
1896	William J. Bryan (D-POP)	58.01%	William McKinley (R)	36.81%
1900	William Jennings Bryan (D)	66.86%	William McKinley (R)	28.22%
1904	Alton Parker (D)	63.72%	Theodore Roosevelt (R)	18.33%
1908	William Jennings Bryan (D)	54.53%	William Howard Taft (R)	31.40%
1912	Woodrow Wilson (D)	76.63%	Theodore Roosevelt (P)	18.10%
1916	Woodrow Wilson (D)	79.30%	Unpledged slate (P)	13.02%
1920	James Cox (D)	70.95%	Warren Harding (R)	28.74%
1924	John Davis (D)	73.97%	Calvin Coolidge (R)	18.18%
1928	Alfred Smith (D)	55.96%	Herbert Hoover (R)	43.96%
1932	Franklin Roosevelt (D)	91.60%	Herbert Hoover (R)	7.77%
1936	Franklin Roosevelt (D)	87.10%	Alfred Landon (R)	12.60%
1940	Franklin Roosevelt (D)	84.81%	Wendell Willkie (R)	14.87%
1944	Franklin Roosevelt (D)	81.74%	Thomas Dewey (R)	17.22%
1948	Harry Truman (D)	60.80%	Strom Thurmond (SRD)	20.33%
1952	Adlai Stevenson (D)	69.66%	Dwight Eisenhower (R)	30.34%
1956	Adlai Stevenson (D)	66.41%	Dwight Eisenhower (R)	33.27%
1960	John Kennedy (D)	62.54%	Richard Nixon (R)	37.43%
1964	Barry Goldwater (R)	54.12%	Lyndon Johnson (D)	45.87%
1968	George Wallace (AI)	42.84%	Richard Nixon (R)	30.40%
1972	Richard Nixon (R)	75.04%	George McGovern (D)	24.65%
1976	Jimmy Carter (D)	66.74%	Gerald Ford (R)	32.97%
1980	Jimmy Carter (D)	55.79%	Ronald Reagan (R)	40.97%
1984	Ronald Reagan (R)	60.17%	Walter Mondale (D)	39.79%
1988	George H.W. Bush (R)	59.75%	Michael Dukakis (D)	39.50%
1992	Bill Clinton (D)	43.47%	George H.W. Bush (R)	42.88%
1996	Bob Dole (R)	47.01%	Bill Clinton (D)	45.84%
2000	George W. Bush (R)	54.67%	Al Gore (D)	42.99%
2004	George W. Bush (R)	57.98%	John Kerry (D)	41.38%

Year	Winner	PV%	Second	PV%
2008	John McCain (R)	52.21%	Barack Obama (D)	46.99%
2012	Mitt Romney (R)	53.30%	Barack Obama (D)	45.48%
2016	Donald Trump (R)	50.77%	Hillary Clinton (D)	45.64%

Home-state qualified candidacies

Year	Candidate	Party	Position	N	W	CS
1789	John Milton	F	State official	—	—	26.29
1789	James Armstrong	F	State official	—	—	21.42
1789	Edward Telfair	DR	Former governor	—	—	21.42
1824	William Crawford	DR	Cabinet member	—	—	46.97
1872	Charles Jenkins	D	Former governor	—	—	11.89
1928	Walter George	D	Senator	—	—	12.87
1948	Richard Russell	D	Senator	—	—	22.93
1952	Richard Russell	D	Senator	—	—	23.13
1976	Jimmy Carter	D	Former governor	X	X	79.23
1980	Jimmy Carter	D	President	X	—	60.93
2012	Newt Gingrich	R	Former representative	—	—	18.59

HAWAII

Basics

State winners (all-time) .... D 13, R 2
General match (all-time) 9-6 (60.00%)
State winners (Modern Era) .... D 13, R 2
General match (Modern Era) 9-6 (60.00%)
Home-state candidacies 0
Home-state nominees 0
Home-state winners 0

Statewide results since 1856

Year	Winner	PV%	Second	PV%
1960	John Kennedy (D)	50.03%	Richard Nixon (R)	49.97%
1964	Lyndon Johnson (D)	78.76%	Barry Goldwater (R)	21.24%
1968	Hubert Humphrey (D)	59.83%	Richard Nixon (R)	38.70%
1972	Richard Nixon (R)	62.48%	George McGovern (D)	37.52%
1976	Jimmy Carter (D)	50.59%	Gerald Ford (R)	48.06%
1980	Jimmy Carter (D)	44.80%	Ronald Reagan (R)	42.90%
1984	Ronald Reagan (R)	55.10%	Walter Mondale (D)	43.82%
1988	Michael Dukakis (D)	54.27%	George H.W. Bush (R)	44.75%
1992	Bill Clinton (D)	48.09%	George H.W. Bush (R)	36.70%
1996	Bill Clinton (D)	56.93%	Bob Dole (R)	31.64%
2000	Al Gore (D)	55.79%	George W. Bush (R)	37.46%
2004	John Kerry (D)	54.01%	George W. Bush (R)	45.27%
2008	Barack Obama (D)	71.85%	John McCain (R)	26.58%
2012	Barack Obama (D)	70.55%	Mitt Romney (R)	27.84%
2016	Hillary Clinton (D)	62.22%	Donald Trump (R)	30.04%

Home-state qualified candidacies

(None)

IDAHO

Basics

State winners (all-time) ....D 10, R 21, Other 1
General match (all-time) 23-9 (71.88%)
State winners (Modern Era) ....D 1, R 14
General match (Modern Era) 9-6 (60.00%)
Home-state candidacies 2
Home-state nominees 0
Home-state winners 0

Statewide results since 1856

Year	Winner	PV%	Second	PV%
1892	James Weaver (POP)	54.21%	Benjamin Harrison (R)	44.31%
1896	William J. Bryan (D-POP)	78.08%	William McKinley (R)	21.34%
1900	William Jennings Bryan (D)	49.79%	William McKinley (R)	47.92%
1904	Theodore Roosevelt (R)	65.84%	Alton Parker (D)	25.46%
1908	William Howard Taft (R)	54.09%	William Jennings Bryan (D)	37.17%
1912	Woodrow Wilson (D)	32.08%	William Howard Taft (R)	31.03%
1916	Woodrow Wilson (D)	52.04%	Charles Evans Hughes (R)	41.13%
1920	Warren Harding (R)	66.03%	James Cox (D)	33.92%
1924	Calvin Coolidge (R)	47.26%	Robert La Follette (P)	36.53%
1928	Herbert Hoover (R)	64.74%	Alfred Smith (D)	34.41%
1932	Franklin Roosevelt (D)	58.70%	Herbert Hoover (R)	38.23%
1936	Franklin Roosevelt (D)	62.96%	Alfred Landon (R)	33.19%
1940	Franklin Roosevelt (D)	54.36%	Wendell Willkie (R)	45.31%
1944	Franklin Roosevelt (D)	51.56%	Thomas Dewey (R)	48.07%
1948	Harry Truman (D)	49.98%	Thomas Dewey (R)	47.26%
1952	Dwight Eisenhower (R)	65.41%	Adlai Stevenson (D)	34.42%
1956	Dwight Eisenhower (R)	61.17%	Adlai Stevenson (D)	38.78%
1960	Richard Nixon (R)	53.79%	John Kennedy (D)	46.22%
1964	Lyndon Johnson (D)	50.92%	Barry Goldwater (R)	49.08%
1968	Richard Nixon (R)	56.79%	Hubert Humphrey (D)	30.66%
1972	Richard Nixon (R)	64.24%	George McGovern (D)	26.04%
1976	Gerald Ford (R)	59.33%	Jimmy Carter (D)	36.78%
1980	Ronald Reagan (R)	66.46%	Jimmy Carter (D)	25.19%
1984	Ronald Reagan (R)	72.37%	Walter Mondale (D)	26.39%
1988	George H.W. Bush (R)	62.08%	Michael Dukakis (D)	36.01%
1992	George H.W. Bush (R)	42.03%	Bill Clinton (D)	28.42%
1996	Bob Dole (R)	52.18%	Bill Clinton (D)	33.65%
2000	George W. Bush (R)	67.17%	Al Gore (D)	27.64%
2004	George W. Bush (R)	68.38%	John Kerry (D)	30.26%
2008	John McCain (R)	61.52%	Barack Obama (D)	36.09%
2012	Mitt Romney (R)	64.53%	Barack Obama (D)	32.62%
2016	Donald Trump (R)	59.26%	Hillary Clinton (D)	27.49%

Home-state qualified candidacies

Year	Candidate	Party	Position	N	W	CS
1936	William Borah	R	Senator	—	—	20.02
1976	Frank Church	D	Senator	—	—	13.23

ILLINOIS

Basics

State winners (all-time) .... D 23, R 24, DR 3
General match (all-time) 41-9 (82.00%)
State winners (Modern Era) .... D 9, R 6
General match (Modern Era) 11-4 (73.33%)
Home-state candidacies 29
Home-state nominees 9
Home-state winners 6

Statewide results since 1856

Year	Winner	PV%	Second	PV%
1856	James Buchanan (D)	44.09%	John Fremont (R)	40.23%
1860	Abraham Lincoln (R)	50.69%	Stephen Douglas (D)	47.17%
1864	Abraham Lincoln (R)	54.42%	George McClellan (D)	45.58%
1868	Ulysses Grant (R)	55.70%	Horatio Seymour (D)	44.31%
1872	Ulysses Grant (R)	56.27%	Horace Greeley (D-LR)	43.00%
1876	Rutherford Hayes (R)	50.19%	Samuel Tilden (D)	46.65%
1880	James Garfield (R)	51.11%	Winfield Hancock (D)	44.56%
1884	James Blaine (R)	50.17%	Grover Cleveland (D)	46.44%
1888	Benjamin Harrison (R)	49.54%	Grover Cleveland (D)	46.58%
1892	Grover Cleveland (D)	48.79%	Benjamin Harrison (R)	45.71%
1896	William McKinley (R)	55.66%	William J. Bryan (D-POP)	42.69%
1900	William McKinley (R)	52.83%	William Jennings Bryan (D)	44.44%
1904	Theodore Roosevelt (R)	58.77%	Alton Parker (D)	30.43%
1908	William Howard Taft (R)	54.53%	William Jennings Bryan (D)	39.02%
1912	Woodrow Wilson (D)	35.34%	Theodore Roosevelt (P)	33.72%
1916	Charles Evans Hughes (R)	52.56%	Woodrow Wilson (D)	43.34%
1920	Warren Harding (R)	67.81%	James Cox (D)	25.51%
1924	Calvin Coolidge (R)	58.84%	John Davis (D)	23.36%
1928	Herbert Hoover (R)	56.93%	Alfred Smith (D)	42.28%
1932	Franklin Roosevelt (D)	55.23%	Herbert Hoover (R)	42.04%
1936	Franklin Roosevelt (D)	57.70%	Alfred Landon (R)	39.69%
1940	Franklin Roosevelt (D)	50.97%	Wendell Willkie (R)	48.54%
1944	Franklin Roosevelt (D)	51.52%	Thomas Dewey (R)	48.05%
1948	Harry Truman (D)	50.07%	Thomas Dewey (R)	49.22%
1952	Dwight Eisenhower (R)	54.84%	Adlai Stevenson (D)	44.94%
1956	Dwight Eisenhower (R)	59.52%	Adlai Stevenson (D)	40.29%
1960	John Kennedy (D)	49.98%	Richard Nixon (R)	49.80%
1964	Lyndon Johnson (D)	59.47%	Barry Goldwater (R)	40.53%
1968	Richard Nixon (R)	47.08%	Hubert Humphrey (D)	44.15%
1972	Richard Nixon (R)	59.03%	George McGovern (D)	40.51%
1976	Gerald Ford (R)	50.10%	Jimmy Carter (D)	48.13%
1980	Ronald Reagan (R)	49.65%	Jimmy Carter (D)	41.72%
1984	Ronald Reagan (R)	56.18%	Walter Mondale (D)	43.30%
1988	George H.W. Bush (R)	50.69%	Michael Dukakis (D)	48.61%
1992	Bill Clinton (D)	48.58%	George H.W. Bush (R)	34.34%
1996	Bill Clinton (D)	54.32%	Bob Dole (R)	36.81%
2000	Al Gore (D)	54.60%	George W. Bush (R)	42.59%

Year	Winner	PV%	Second	PV%
2004	John Kerry (D)	54.82%	George W. Bush (R)	44.48%
2008	Barack Obama (D)	61.92%	John McCain (R)	36.78%
2012	Barack Obama (D)	57.60%	Mitt Romney (R)	40.73%
2016	Hillary Clinton (D)	55.83%	Donald Trump (R)	38.76%

Home-state qualified candidacies

Year	Candidate	Party	Position	N	W	CS
1852	Stephen Douglas	D	Senator	—	—	15.51
1856	Stephen Douglas	D	Senator	—	—	18.86
1860	Abraham Lincoln	R	Former representative	X	X	78.38
1860	Stephen Douglas	D	Senator	X	—	57.06
1864	Abraham Lincoln	R	President	X	X	92.17
1864	Ulysses Grant	R	General	—	—	13.35
1868	Ulysses Grant	R	General	X	X	85.63
1872	Ulysses Grant	R	President	X	X	89.28
1872	David Davis	D	Supreme Court justice	—	—	10.97
1880	Ulysses Grant	R	Former president	—	—	42.34
1880	William Morrison	D	Representative	—	—	16.71
1880	Elihu Washburne	R	Former ambassador	—	—	13.19
1884	John Logan	R	Senator	—	—	16.15
1908	Joseph Cannon	R	Representative	—	—	14.71
1916	Lawrence Sherman	R	Senator	—	—	15.63
1920	Frank Lowden	R	Governor	—	—	25.31
1928	Frank Lowden	R	Former governor	—	—	20.32
1936	Frank Knox	R	Journalist	—	—	12.97
1948	Dwight Green	R	Governor	—	—	13.05
1952	Adlai Stevenson	D	Governor	X	—	63.90
1956	Adlai Stevenson	D	Former nominee	X	—	62.52
1960	Adlai Stevenson	D	Former nominee	—	—	12.86
1980	John Anderson	R/NU	Representative	—	—	38.97
1980	Phil Crane	R	Representative	—	—	10.46
1984	Jesse Jackson	D	Movement leader	—	—	23.30
1988	Jesse Jackson	D	Movement leader	—	—	33.32
1988	Paul Simon	D	Senator	—	—	12.66
2008	Barack Obama	D	Senator	X	X	84.03
2012	Barack Obama	D	President	X	X	81.59

INDIANA

Basics

State winners (all-time) ....D 13, R 32, DR 4, W 2
General match (all-time) 38-13 (74.51%)
State winners (Modern Era) ....D 2, R 13
General match (Modern Era) 10-5 (66.67%)
Home-state candidacies 19
Home-state nominees..2
Home-state winners...1

Statewide results since 1856

Year	Winner	PV%	Second	PV%
1856	James Buchanan (D)	50.41%	John Fremont (R)	40.09%
1860	Abraham Lincoln (R)	51.09%	Stephen Douglas (D)	42.44%
1864	Abraham Lincoln (R)	53.51%	George McClellan (D)	46.49%
1868	Ulysses Grant (R)	51.39%	Horatio Seymour (D)	48.61%
1872	Ulysses Grant (R)	53.22%	Horace Greeley (D-LR)	46.78%
1876	Samuel Tilden (D)	49.65%	Rutherford Hayes (R)	48.13%
1880	James Garfield (R)	49.32%	Winfield Hancock (D)	47.91%
1884	Grover Cleveland (D)	49.46%	James Blaine (R)	48.14%
1888	Benjamin Harrison (R)	49.05%	Grover Cleveland (D)	48.60%
1892	Grover Cleveland (D)	47.46%	Benjamin Harrison (R)	46.17%
1896	William McKinley (R)	50.82%	William J. Bryan (D-POP)	47.96%
1900	William McKinley (R)	50.61%	William Jennings Bryan (D)	46.62%
1904	Theodore Roosevelt (R)	53.99%	Alton Parker (D)	40.22%
1908	William Howard Taft (R)	48.40%	William Jennings Bryan (D)	46.91%
1912	Woodrow Wilson (D)	43.07%	Theodore Roosevelt (P)	24.75%
1916	Charles Evans Hughes (R)	47.44%	Woodrow Wilson (D)	46.47%
1920	Warren Harding (R)	55.14%	James Cox (D)	40.49%
1924	Calvin Coolidge (R)	55.25%	John Davis (D)	38.69%
1928	Herbert Hoover (R)	59.68%	Alfred Smith (D)	39.59%
1932	Franklin Roosevelt (D)	54.67%	Herbert Hoover (R)	42.94%
1936	Franklin Roosevelt (D)	56.63%	Alfred Landon (R)	41.89%
1940	Wendell Willkie (R)	50.45%	Franklin Roosevelt (D)	49.03%
1944	Thomas Dewey (R)	52.38%	Franklin Roosevelt (D)	46.73%
1948	Thomas Dewey (R)	49.58%	Harry Truman (D)	48.78%
1952	Dwight Eisenhower (R)	58.12%	Adlai Stevenson (D)	41.00%
1956	Dwight Eisenhower (R)	59.90%	Adlai Stevenson (D)	39.70%
1960	Richard Nixon (R)	55.03%	John Kennedy (D)	44.60%
1964	Lyndon Johnson (D)	55.98%	Barry Goldwater (R)	43.56%
1968	Richard Nixon (R)	50.29%	Hubert Humphrey (D)	37.99%
1972	Richard Nixon (R)	66.11%	George McGovern (D)	33.34%
1976	Gerald Ford (R)	53.32%	Jimmy Carter (D)	45.70%
1980	Ronald Reagan (R)	56.01%	Jimmy Carter (D)	37.65%
1984	Ronald Reagan (R)	61.67%	Walter Mondale (D)	37.68%
1988	George H.W. Bush (R)	59.84%	Michael Dukakis (D)	39.69%
1992	George H.W. Bush (R)	42.91%	Bill Clinton (D)	36.79%
1996	Bob Dole (R)	47.14%	Bill Clinton (D)	41.56%
2000	George W. Bush (R)	56.65%	Al Gore (D)	41.01%

Year	Winner	PV%	Second	PV%
2004	George W. Bush (R)	59.95%	John Kerry (D)	39.26%
2008	Barack Obama (D)	49.95%	John McCain (R)	48.91%
2012	Mitt Romney (R)	54.13%	Barack Obama (D)	43.93%
2016	Donald Trump (R)	56.94%	Hillary Clinton (D)	37.78%

Home-state qualified candidacies

Year	Candidate	Party	Position	N	W	CS
1872	Thomas Hendricks	D	Former senator	—	—	43.62
1876	Thomas Hendricks	D	Governor	—	—	25.17
1876	Oliver Morton	R	Senator	—	—	23.09
1880	Thomas Hendricks	D	Former governor	—	—	15.35
1884	Joseph McDonald	D	Former senator	—	—	15.43
1884	Thomas Hendricks	D	Former governor	—	—	14.39
1888	Benjamin Harrison	R	Former senator	X	X	79.71
1888	Walter Gresham	R	Federal judge	—	—	20.30
1892	Benjamin Harrison	R	President	X	—	68.40
1896	Claude Matthews	D	Governor	—	—	13.19
1904	Eugene Debs	SOC	Movement leader	—	—	19.53
1908	Eugene Debs	SOC	Movement leader	—	—	19.04
1908	Charles Fairbanks	R	Vice president	—	—	13.27
1912	Eugene Debs	SOC	Movement leader	—	—	29.16
1916	Charles Fairbanks	R	Former vice president	—	—	16.32
1920	Eugene Debs	SOC	Movement leader	—	—	20.94
1928	James Watson	R	Senator	—	—	13.57
1976	Birch Bayh	D	Senator	—	—	10.32
1996	Richard Lugar	R	Senator	—	—	10.51

IOWA

Basics

State winners (all-time) ....D 13, R 30
General match (all-time) 32-11 (74.42%)
State winners (Modern Era) ....D 7, R 8
General match (Modern Era) 11-4 (73.33%)
Home-state candidacies 8
Home-state nominees..0
Home-state winners...0

Statewide results since 1856

Year	Winner	PV%	Second	PV%
1856	John Fremont (R)	48.83%	James Buchanan (D)	40.70%
1860	Abraham Lincoln (R)	54.61%	Stephen Douglas (D)	43.22%
1864	Abraham Lincoln (R)	64.12%	George McClellan (D)	35.88%
1868	Ulysses Grant (R)	61.92%	Horatio Seymour (D)	38.08%
1872	Ulysses Grant (R)	60.81%	Horace Greeley (D-LR)	32.90%
1876	Rutherford Hayes (R)	58.39%	Samuel Tilden (D)	38.22%
1880	James Garfield (R)	56.91%	Winfield Hancock (D)	32.76%
1884	James Blaine (R)	50.08%	Grover Cleveland (D)	45.06%
1888	Benjamin Harrison (R)	52.29%	Grover Cleveland (D)	44.45%
1892	Benjamin Harrison (R)	49.60%	Grover Cleveland (D)	44.31%
1896	William McKinley (R)	55.47%	William J. Bryan (D-POP)	42.90%
1900	William McKinley (R)	58.04%	William Jennings Bryan (D)	39.46%
1904	Theodore Roosevelt (R)	63.39%	Alton Parker (D)	30.71%
1908	William Howard Taft (R)	55.62%	William Jennings Bryan (D)	40.58%
1912	Woodrow Wilson (D)	37.64%	Theodore Roosevelt (P)	32.87%
1916	Charles Evans Hughes (R)	54.06%	Woodrow Wilson (D)	42.74%
1920	Warren Harding (R)	70.92%	James Cox (D)	25.45%
1924	Calvin Coolidge (R)	55.02%	Robert La Follette (P)	28.10%
1928	Herbert Hoover (R)	61.79%	Alfred Smith (D)	37.56%
1932	Franklin Roosevelt (D)	57.69%	Herbert Hoover (R)	39.98%
1936	Franklin Roosevelt (D)	54.41%	Alfred Landon (R)	42.70%
1940	Wendell Willkie (R)	52.03%	Franklin Roosevelt (D)	47.62%
1944	Thomas Dewey (R)	51.99%	Franklin Roosevelt (D)	47.49%
1948	Harry Truman (D)	50.31%	Thomas Dewey (R)	47.58%
1952	Dwight Eisenhower (R)	63.76%	Adlai Stevenson (D)	35.59%
1956	Dwight Eisenhower (R)	59.06%	Adlai Stevenson (D)	40.65%
1960	Richard Nixon (R)	56.71%	John Kennedy (D)	43.22%
1964	Lyndon Johnson (D)	61.88%	Barry Goldwater (R)	37.92%
1968	Richard Nixon (R)	53.01%	Hubert Humphrey (D)	40.82%
1972	Richard Nixon (R)	57.61%	George McGovern (D)	40.48%
1976	Gerald Ford (R)	49.47%	Jimmy Carter (D)	48.46%
1980	Ronald Reagan (R)	51.31%	Jimmy Carter (D)	38.60%
1984	Ronald Reagan (R)	53.27%	Walter Mondale (D)	45.89%
1988	Michael Dukakis (D)	54.71%	George H.W. Bush (R)	44.50%
1992	Bill Clinton (D)	43.29%	George H.W. Bush (R)	37.27%
1996	Bill Clinton (D)	50.26%	Bob Dole (R)	39.92%
2000	Al Gore (D)	48.54%	George W. Bush (R)	48.22%

Year	Winner	PV%	Second	PV%
2004	George W. Bush (R)	49.90%	John Kerry (D)	49.23%
2008	Barack Obama (D)	53.93%	John McCain (R)	44.39%
2012	Barack Obama (D)	51.99%	Mitt Romney (R)	46.18%
2016	Donald Trump (R)	51.15%	Hillary Clinton (D)	41.74%

Home-state qualified candidacies

Year	Candidate	Party	Position	N	W	CS
1880	James Weaver	GBK	Representative	—	—	20.66
1888	William Boyd Allison	R	Senator	—	—	16.95
1892	James Weaver	POP	Former representative	—	—	38.80
1892	Horace Boies	D	Governor	—	—	19.02
1896	Horace Boies	D	Former governor	—	—	15.75
1916	Albert Cummins	R	Senator	—	—	17.15
1948	Henry Wallace	D/P	Former vice president	—	—	17.65
1992	Tom Harkin	D	Senator	—	—	10.83

KANSAS

Basics

State winners (all-time) ....D 6, R 32, Other 1
General match (all-time) 27-12 (69.23%)
State winners (Modern Era) .... D 1, R 14
General match (Modern Era) 9-6 (60.00%)
Home-state candidacies 4
Home-state nominees...2
Home-state winners..0

Statewide results since 1856

Year	Winner	PV%	Second	PV%
1864	Abraham Lincoln (R)	79.19%	George McClellan (D)	17.78%
1868	Ulysses Grant (R)	68.82%	Horatio Seymour (D)	31.17%
1872	Ulysses Grant (R)	66.47%	Horace Greeley (D-LR)	32.80%
1876	Rutherford Hayes (R)	63.10%	Samuel Tilden (D)	30.53%
1880	James Garfield (R)	60.44%	Winfield Hancock (D)	29.74%
1884	James Blaine (R)	61.52%	Grover Cleveland (D)	35.90%
1888	Benjamin Harrison (R)	55.22%	Grover Cleveland (D)	31.03%
1892	James Weaver (POP)	50.34%	Benjamin Harrison (R)	48.25%
1896	William J. Bryan (D-POP)	51.49%	William McKinley (R)	47.45%
1900	William McKinley (R)	52.56%	William Jennings Bryan (D)	45.96%
1904	Theodore Roosevelt (R)	64.87%	Alton Parker (D)	26.19%
1908	William Howard Taft (R)	52.47%	William Jennings Bryan (D)	42.87%
1912	Woodrow Wilson (D)	39.30%	Theodore Roosevelt (P)	32.88%
1916	Woodrow Wilson (D)	49.95%	Charles Evans Hughes (R)	44.09%
1920	Warren Harding (R)	64.76%	James Cox (D)	32.52%
1924	Calvin Coolidge (R)	61.54%	John Davis (D)	23.60%
1928	Herbert Hoover (R)	72.02%	Alfred Smith (D)	27.06%
1932	Franklin Roosevelt (D)	53.56%	Herbert Hoover (R)	44.13%
1936	Franklin Roosevelt (D)	53.67%	Alfred Landon (R)	45.95%
1940	Wendell Willkie (R)	56.86%	Franklin Roosevelt (D)	42.40%
1944	Thomas Dewey (R)	60.25%	Franklin Roosevelt (D)	39.18%
1948	Thomas Dewey (R)	53.63%	Harry Truman (D)	44.61%
1952	Dwight Eisenhower (R)	68.77%	Adlai Stevenson (D)	30.50%
1956	Dwight Eisenhower (R)	65.44%	Adlai Stevenson (D)	34.21%
1960	Richard Nixon (R)	60.45%	John Kennedy (D)	39.11%
1964	Lyndon Johnson (D)	54.09%	Barry Goldwater (R)	45.06%
1968	Richard Nixon (R)	54.85%	Hubert Humphrey (D)	34.72%
1972	Richard Nixon (R)	67.66%	George McGovern (D)	29.50%
1976	Gerald Ford (R)	52.49%	Jimmy Carter (D)	44.94%
1980	Ronald Reagan (R)	57.85%	Jimmy Carter (D)	33.29%
1984	Ronald Reagan (R)	66.27%	Walter Mondale (D)	32.60%
1988	George H.W. Bush (R)	55.79%	Michael Dukakis (D)	42.56%
1992	George H.W. Bush (R)	38.88%	Bill Clinton (D)	33.74%
1996	Bob Dole (R)	54.29%	Bill Clinton (D)	36.09%
2000	George W. Bush (R)	58.04%	Al Gore (D)	37.24%

Year	Winner	PV%	Second	PV%
2004	George W. Bush (R)	62.00%	John Kerry (D)	36.62%
2008	John McCain (R)	56.61%	Barack Obama (D)	41.65%
2012	Mitt Romney (R)	59.71%	Barack Obama (D)	38.00%
2016	Donald Trump (R)	56.66%	Hillary Clinton (D)	36.05%

Home-state qualified candidacies

Year	Candidate	Party	Position	N	W	CS
1928	Charles Curtis	R	Senator	—	—	13.53
1936	Alfred Landon	R	Governor	X	—	57.76
1988	Bob Dole	R	Senator	—	—	21.51
1996	Bob Dole	R	Senator	X	—	67.01

KENTUCKY

Basics

State winners (all-time) .... D 25, R 15, DR 9, NR 1, W 5, Tie 1, Other 1
General match (all-time) 35-21-1 (61.40%)
State winners (Modern Era) .... D 4, R 11
General match (Modern Era) 12-3 (80.00%)
Home-state candidacies 12
Home-state nominees... 3
Home-state winners... 0

Statewide results since 1856

Year	Winner	PV%	Second	PV%
1856	James Buchanan (D)	52.54%	Millard Fillmore (AW)	47.46%
1860	John Bell (CU)	45.18%	John Breckinridge (SD)	36.35%
1864	George McClellan (D)	69.83%	Abraham Lincoln (R)	30.17%
1868	Horatio Seymour (D)	74.55%	Ulysses Grant (R)	25.45%
1872	Horace Greeley (D-LR)	52.31%	Ulysses Grant (R)	46.45%
1876	Samuel Tilden (D)	61.51%	Rutherford Hayes (R)	37.42%
1880	Winfield Hancock (D)	55.86%	James Garfield (R)	39.74%
1884	Grover Cleveland (D)	55.30%	James Blaine (R)	42.97%
1888	Grover Cleveland (D)	53.30%	Benjamin Harrison (R)	44.99%
1892	Grover Cleveland (D)	51.48%	Benjamin Harrison (R)	39.74%
1896	William McKinley (R)	48.93%	William J. Bryan (D-POP)	48.86%
1900	William Jennings Bryan (D)	50.24%	William McKinley (R)	48.51%
1904	Alton Parker (D)	49.82%	Theodore Roosevelt (R)	47.13%
1908	William Jennings Bryan (D)	49.74%	William Howard Taft (R)	48.03%
1912	Woodrow Wilson (D)	48.40%	William Howard Taft (R)	25.46%
1916	Woodrow Wilson (D)	51.91%	Charles Evans Hughes (R)	46.50%
1920	James Cox (D)	49.69%	Warren Harding (R)	49.26%
1924	Calvin Coolidge (R)	48.89%	John Davis (D)	46.03%
1928	Herbert Hoover (R)	59.34%	Alfred Smith (D)	40.52%
1932	Franklin Roosevelt (D)	59.06%	Herbert Hoover (R)	40.15%
1936	Franklin Roosevelt (D)	58.51%	Alfred Landon (R)	39.92%
1940	Franklin Roosevelt (D)	57.45%	Wendell Willkie (R)	42.30%
1944	Franklin Roosevelt (D)	54.45%	Thomas Dewey (R)	45.22%
1948	Harry Truman (D)	56.74%	Thomas Dewey (R)	41.48%
1952	Adlai Stevenson (D)	49.92%	Dwight Eisenhower (R)	49.84%
1956	Dwight Eisenhower (R)	54.30%	Adlai Stevenson (D)	45.21%
1960	Richard Nixon (R)	53.59%	John Kennedy (D)	46.41%
1964	Lyndon Johnson (D)	64.02%	Barry Goldwater (R)	35.65%
1968	Richard Nixon (R)	43.79%	Hubert Humphrey (D)	37.65%
1972	Richard Nixon (R)	63.37%	George McGovern (D)	34.77%
1976	Jimmy Carter (D)	52.75%	Gerald Ford (R)	45.57%
1980	Ronald Reagan (R)	49.07%	Jimmy Carter (D)	47.61%
1984	Ronald Reagan (R)	60.01%	Walter Mondale (D)	39.40%
1988	George H.W. Bush (R)	55.52%	Michael Dukakis (D)	43.88%
1992	Bill Clinton (D)	44.55%	George H.W. Bush (R)	41.34%
1996	Bill Clinton (D)	45.84%	Bob Dole (R)	44.88%
2000	George W. Bush (R)	56.50%	Al Gore (D)	41.37%

Year	Winner	PV%	Second	PV%
2004	George W. Bush (R)	59.55%	John Kerry (D)	39.69%
2008	John McCain (R)	57.40%	Barack Obama (D)	41.17%
2012	Mitt Romney (R)	60.49%	Barack Obama (D)	37.80%
2016	Donald Trump (R)	62.52%	Hillary Clinton (D)	32.68%

Home-state qualified candidacies

Year	Candidate	Party	Position	N	W	CS
1824	Henry Clay	DR	Representative	—	—	46.84
1832	Henry Clay	NR	Senator	X	—	62.61
1840	Henry Clay	W	Former nominee	—	—	42.42
1844	Henry Clay	W	Former nominee	X	—	71.05
1844	Richard Johnson	D	Former vice president	—	—	17.19
1848	Henry Clay	W	Former nominee	—	—	37.63
1860	John Breckinridge	D/SD	Vice president	X	—	60.76
1860	James Guthrie	D	Former Cabinet member	—	—	19.34
1876	Benjamin Bristow	R	Cabinet member	—	—	21.90
1896	Joseph Blackburn	D	Senator	—	—	17.03
1952	Alben Barkley	D	Vice president	—	—	12.74
2016	Rand Paul	R	Senator	—	—	10.13

LOUISIANA

Basics

State winners (all-time) .... D 28, R 12, DR 5, SD 1, W 2, Other 2
General match (all-time) 32-18 (64.00%)
State winners (Modern Era) .... D 4, R 10, Other 1
General match (Modern Era) 11-4 (73.33%)
Home-state candidacies 1
Home-state nominees 1
Home-state winners 1

Statewide results since 1856

Year	Winner	PV%	Second	PV%
1856	James Buchanan (D)	51.70%	Millard Fillmore (AW)	48.30%
1860	John Breckinridge (SD)	44.90%	John Bell (CU)	40.00%
1868	Horatio Seymour (D)	70.69%	Ulysses Grant (R)	29.31%
1872	Ulysses Grant (R)	55.69%	Horace Greeley (D-LR)	44.31%
1876	Rutherford Hayes (R)	51.65%	Samuel Tilden (D)	48.35%
1880	Winfield Hancock (D)	62.27%	James Garfield (R)	37.31%
1884	Grover Cleveland (D)	57.22%	James Blaine (R)	42.37%
1888	Grover Cleveland (D)	73.37%	Benjamin Harrison (R)	26.46%
1892	Grover Cleveland (D)	74.33%	Benjamin Harrison (R)	23.59%
1896	William J. Bryan (D-POP)	76.38%	William McKinley (R)	21.81%
1900	William Jennings Bryan (D)	79.03%	William McKinley (R)	20.96%
1904	Alton Parker (D)	88.50%	Theodore Roosevelt (R)	9.66%
1908	William Jennings Bryan (D)	84.63%	William Howard Taft (R)	11.93%
1912	Woodrow Wilson (D)	76.81%	Theodore Roosevelt (P)	11.71%
1916	Woodrow Wilson (D)	85.91%	Charles Evans Hughes (R)	6.96%
1920	James Cox (D)	69.24%	Warren Harding (R)	30.49%
1924	John Davis (D)	76.44%	Calvin Coolidge (R)	20.23%
1928	Alfred Smith (D)	76.29%	Herbert Hoover (R)	23.70%
1932	Franklin Roosevelt (D)	92.79%	Herbert Hoover (R)	7.01%
1936	Franklin Roosevelt (D)	88.82%	Alfred Landon (R)	11.16%
1940	Franklin Roosevelt (D)	85.88%	Wendell Willkie (R)	14.09%
1944	Franklin Roosevelt (D)	80.59%	Thomas Dewey (R)	19.39%
1948	Strom Thurmond (SRD)	49.07%	Harry Truman (D)	32.75%
1952	Adlai Stevenson (D)	52.92%	Dwight Eisenhower (R)	47.08%
1956	Dwight Eisenhower (R)	53.28%	Adlai Stevenson (D)	39.51%
1960	John Kennedy (D)	50.42%	Richard Nixon (R)	28.59%
1964	Barry Goldwater (R)	56.82%	Lyndon Johnson (D)	43.19%
1968	George Wallace (AI)	48.32%	Hubert Humphrey (D)	28.21%
1972	Richard Nixon (R)	65.32%	George McGovern (D)	28.35%
1976	Jimmy Carter (D)	51.73%	Gerald Ford (R)	45.95%
1980	Ronald Reagan (R)	51.20%	Jimmy Carter (D)	45.75%
1984	Ronald Reagan (R)	60.77%	Walter Mondale (D)	38.18%
1988	George H.W. Bush (R)	54.28%	Michael Dukakis (D)	44.07%
1992	Bill Clinton (D)	45.59%	George H.W. Bush (R)	40.97%
1996	Bill Clinton (D)	52.01%	Bob Dole (R)	39.94%
2000	George W. Bush (R)	52.55%	Al Gore (D)	44.88%
2004	George W. Bush (R)	56.72%	John Kerry (D)	42.22%

Year	Winner	PV%	Second	PV%
2008	John McCain (R)	58.56%	Barack Obama (D)	39.93%
2012	Mitt Romney (R)	57.79%	Barack Obama (D)	40.58%
2016	Donald Trump (R)	58.09%	Hillary Clinton (D)	38.45%

Home-state qualified candidacies

Year	Candidate	Party	Position	N	W	CS
1848	Zachary Taylor	W	General	X	X	78.93

MAINE

Basics

State winners (all-time) ....D 15, R 31, DR 2, NR 1, W 1
General match (all-time) 33-17 (66.00%)
State winners (Modern Era) ....D 9, R 6
General match (Modern Era) 9-6 (60.00%)
Home-state candidacies 7
Home-state nominees 1
Home-state winners 0

Statewide results since 1856

Year	Winner	PV%	Second	PV%
1856	John Fremont (R)	61.34%	James Buchanan (D)	35.68%
1860	Abraham Lincoln (R)	62.24%	Stephen Douglas (D)	29.42%
1864	Abraham Lincoln (R)	59.17%	George McClellan (D)	40.83%
1868	Ulysses Grant (R)	62.41%	Horatio Seymour (D)	37.59%
1872	Ulysses Grant (R)	67.86%	Horace Greeley (D-LR)	32.14%
1876	Rutherford Hayes (R)	56.65%	Samuel Tilden (D)	42.65%
1880	James Garfield (R)	51.46%	Winfield Hancock (D)	45.32%
1884	James Blaine (R)	55.34%	Grover Cleveland (D)	39.97%
1888	Benjamin Harrison (R)	57.49%	Grover Cleveland (D)	39.35%
1892	Benjamin Harrison (R)	54.20%	Grover Cleveland (D)	41.40%
1896	William McKinley (R)	67.90%	William J. Bryan (D-POP)	29.21%
1900	William McKinley (R)	61.67%	William Jennings Bryan (D)	35.12%
1904	Theodore Roosevelt (R)	67.10%	Alton Parker (D)	28.79%
1908	William Howard Taft (R)	63.00%	William Jennings Bryan (D)	33.29%
1912	Woodrow Wilson (D)	39.43%	Theodore Roosevelt (P)	37.41%
1916	Charles Evans Hughes (R)	50.99%	Woodrow Wilson (D)	46.98%
1920	Warren Harding (R)	68.92%	James Cox (D)	29.80%
1924	Calvin Coolidge (R)	72.03%	John Davis (D)	21.83%
1928	Herbert Hoover (R)	68.63%	Alfred Smith (D)	30.96%
1932	Herbert Hoover (R)	55.83%	Franklin Roosevelt (D)	43.19%
1936	Alfred Landon (R)	55.49%	Franklin Roosevelt (D)	41.52%
1940	Wendell Willkie (R)	51.10%	Franklin Roosevelt (D)	48.77%
1944	Thomas Dewey (R)	52.44%	Franklin Roosevelt (D)	47.45%
1948	Thomas Dewey (R)	56.74%	Harry Truman (D)	42.27%
1952	Dwight Eisenhower (R)	66.05%	Adlai Stevenson (D)	33.77%
1956	Dwight Eisenhower (R)	70.87%	Adlai Stevenson (D)	29.14%
1960	Richard Nixon (R)	57.05%	John Kennedy (D)	42.95%
1964	Lyndon Johnson (D)	68.84%	Barry Goldwater (R)	31.16%
1968	Hubert Humphrey (D)	55.31%	Richard Nixon (R)	43.07%
1972	Richard Nixon (R)	61.50%	George McGovern (D)	38.51%
1976	Gerald Ford (R)	48.91%	Jimmy Carter (D)	48.07%
1980	Ronald Reagan (R)	45.61%	Jimmy Carter (D)	42.25%
1984	Ronald Reagan (R)	60.83%	Walter Mondale (D)	38.78%
1988	George H.W. Bush (R)	55.34%	Michael Dukakis (D)	43.88%
1992	Bill Clinton (D)	38.77%	Ross Perot (I)	30.44%
1996	Bill Clinton (D)	51.62%	Bob Dole (R)	30.76%
2000	Al Gore (D)	49.09%	George W. Bush (R)	43.97%

Year	Winner	PV%	Second	PV%
2004	John Kerry (D)	53.57%	George W. Bush (R)	44.58%
2008	Barack Obama (D)	57.71%	John McCain (R)	40.38%
2012	Barack Obama (D)	56.27%	Mitt Romney (R)	40.98%
2016	Hillary Clinton (D)	47.83%	Donald Trump (R)	44.87%

Home-state qualified candidacies

Year	Candidate	Party	Position	N	W	CS
1876	James Blaine	R	Representative	—	—	47.05
1880	James Blaine	R	Senator	—	—	40.02
1884	James Blaine	R	Former senator	X	—	73.26
1888	James Blaine	R	Former nominee	—	—	13.35
1892	James Blaine	R	Former nominee	—	—	26.05
1896	Thomas Reed	R	Representative	—	—	17.27
1972	Edmund Muskie	D	Senator	—	—	17.06

MARYLAND

Basics

State winners (all-time) .... D 28, R 12, DR 6, F 3, NR 2, SD 1, W 4, Tie 1, Other 1
General match (all-time) 37-20-1 (63.79%)
State winners (Modern Era) .... D 12, R 3
General match (Modern Era) 10-5 (66.67%)
Home-state candidacies 8
Home-state nominees 0
Home-state winners 0

Statewide results since 1856

Year	Winner	PV%	Second	PV%
1856	Millard Fillmore (AW)	54.63%	James Buchanan (D)	45.04%
1860	John Breckinridge (SD)	45.93%	John Bell (CU)	45.15%
1864	Abraham Lincoln (R)	55.09%	George McClellan (D)	44.91%
1868	Horatio Seymour (D)	67.20%	Ulysses Grant (R)	32.80%
1872	Horace Greeley (D-LR)	50.35%	Ulysses Grant (R)	49.66%
1876	Samuel Tilden (D)	56.05%	Rutherford Hayes (R)	43.96%
1880	Winfield Hancock (D)	54.15%	James Garfield (R)	45.37%
1884	Grover Cleveland (D)	52.16%	James Blaine (R)	46.14%
1888	Grover Cleveland (D)	50.34%	Benjamin Harrison (R)	47.40%
1892	Grover Cleveland (D)	53.39%	Benjamin Harrison (R)	43.48%
1896	William McKinley (R)	54.73%	William J. Bryan (D-POP)	41.62%
1900	William McKinley (R)	51.50%	William Jennings Bryan (D)	46.23%
1904	Theodore Roosevelt (R)	48.83%	Alton Parker (D)	48.81%
1908	William Howard Taft (R)	48.85%	William Jennings Bryan (D)	48.59%
1912	Woodrow Wilson (D)	48.57%	Theodore Roosevelt (P)	24.91%
1916	Woodrow Wilson (D)	52.80%	Charles Evans Hughes (R)	44.78%
1920	Warren Harding (R)	55.11%	James Cox (D)	42.16%
1924	Calvin Coolidge (R)	45.29%	John Davis (D)	41.29%
1928	Herbert Hoover (R)	57.06%	Alfred Smith (D)	42.33%
1932	Franklin Roosevelt (D)	61.50%	Herbert Hoover (R)	36.04%
1936	Franklin Roosevelt (D)	62.35%	Alfred Landon (R)	37.04%
1940	Franklin Roosevelt (D)	58.26%	Wendell Willkie (R)	40.83%
1944	Franklin Roosevelt (D)	51.85%	Thomas Dewey (R)	48.15%
1948	Thomas Dewey (R)	49.40%	Harry Truman (D)	48.01%
1952	Dwight Eisenhower (R)	55.36%	Adlai Stevenson (D)	43.83%
1956	Dwight Eisenhower (R)	60.00%	Adlai Stevenson (D)	39.94%
1960	John Kennedy (D)	53.61%	Richard Nixon (R)	46.39%
1964	Lyndon Johnson (D)	65.47%	Barry Goldwater (R)	34.53%
1968	Hubert Humphrey (D)	43.59%	Richard Nixon (R)	41.94%
1972	Richard Nixon (R)	61.26%	George McGovern (D)	37.36%
1976	Jimmy Carter (D)	52.76%	Gerald Ford (R)	46.72%
1980	Jimmy Carter (D)	47.14%	Ronald Reagan (R)	44.18%
1984	Ronald Reagan (R)	52.51%	Walter Mondale (D)	47.02%
1988	George H.W. Bush (R)	51.11%	Michael Dukakis (D)	48.20%
1992	Bill Clinton (D)	49.80%	George H.W. Bush (R)	35.62%
1996	Bill Clinton (D)	54.26%	Bob Dole (R)	38.27%
2000	Al Gore (D)	56.57%	George W. Bush (R)	40.18%

Year	Winner	PV%	Second	PV%
2004	John Kerry (D)	55.91%	George W. Bush (R)	42.93%
2008	Barack Obama (D)	61.92%	John McCain (R)	36.48%
2012	Barack Obama (D)	61.97%	Mitt Romney (R)	35.90%
2016	Hillary Clinton (D)	60.33%	Donald Trump (R)	33.91%

Home-state qualified candidacies

Year	Candidate	Party	Position	N	W	CS
1789	Robert Harrison	F	State judge	—	—	45.73
1796	John Henry	DR	Senator	—	—	21.42
1832	William Wirt	AM	Former Cabinet member	—	—	35.63
1892	Arthur Gorman	D	Senator	—	—	13.19
1932	Joseph France	R	Former senator	—	—	19.88
1976	Sargent Shriver	D	Former v.p. nominee	—	—	11.14
1996	Alan Keyes	R	Former ambassador	—	—	11.81
2000	Alan Keyes	R	Former ambassador	—	—	13.04

MASSACHUSETTS

Basics

State winners (all-time) ....D 20, R 21, DR 3, F 7, NR 2, W 5
General match (all-time) 38-20 (65.52%)
State winners (Modern Era) ....D 13, R 2
General match (Modern Era) 9-6 (60.00%)
Home-state candidacies 24
Home-state nominees 9
Home-state winners 4

Statewide results since 1856

Year	Winner	PV%	Second	PV%
1856	John Fremont (R)	63.61%	James Buchanan (D)	23.08%
1860	Abraham Lincoln (R)	62.80%	Stephen Douglas (D)	20.23%
1864	Abraham Lincoln (R)	72.22%	George McClellan (D)	27.78%
1868	Ulysses Grant (R)	69.76%	Horatio Seymour (D)	30.23%
1872	Ulysses Grant (R)	69.27%	Horace Greeley (D-LR)	30.73%
1876	Rutherford Hayes (R)	57.80%	Samuel Tilden (D)	41.90%
1880	James Garfield (R)	58.48%	Winfield Hancock (D)	39.63%
1884	James Blaine (R)	48.36%	Grover Cleveland (D)	40.33%
1888	Benjamin Harrison (R)	53.42%	Grover Cleveland (D)	44.04%
1892	Benjamin Harrison (R)	51.87%	Grover Cleveland (D)	45.22%
1896	William McKinley (R)	69.52%	William J. Bryan (D-POP)	26.27%
1900	William McKinley (R)	57.59%	William Jennings Bryan (D)	37.85%
1904	Theodore Roosevelt (R)	57.92%	Alton Parker (D)	37.24%
1908	William Howard Taft (R)	58.21%	William Jennings Bryan (D)	34.04%
1912	Woodrow Wilson (D)	35.53%	William Howard Taft (R)	31.95%
1916	Charles Evans Hughes (R)	50.54%	Woodrow Wilson (D)	46.61%
1920	Warren Harding (R)	68.55%	James Cox (D)	27.84%
1924	Calvin Coolidge (R)	62.26%	John Davis (D)	24.86%
1928	Alfred Smith (D)	50.24%	Herbert Hoover (R)	49.15%
1932	Franklin Roosevelt (D)	50.64%	Herbert Hoover (R)	46.64%
1936	Franklin Roosevelt (D)	51.23%	Alfred Landon (R)	41.76%
1940	Franklin Roosevelt (D)	53.11%	Wendell Willkie (R)	46.36%
1944	Franklin Roosevelt (D)	52.80%	Thomas Dewey (R)	46.99%
1948	Harry Truman (D)	54.66%	Thomas Dewey (R)	43.16%
1952	Dwight Eisenhower (R)	54.22%	Adlai Stevenson (D)	45.46%
1956	Dwight Eisenhower (R)	59.32%	Adlai Stevenson (D)	40.37%
1960	John Kennedy (D)	60.22%	Richard Nixon (R)	39.55%
1964	Lyndon Johnson (D)	76.19%	Barry Goldwater (R)	23.45%
1968	Hubert Humphrey (D)	63.01%	Richard Nixon (R)	32.89%
1972	George McGovern (D)	54.20%	Richard Nixon (R)	45.23%
1976	Jimmy Carter (D)	56.11%	Gerald Ford (R)	40.44%
1980	Ronald Reagan (R)	41.92%	Jimmy Carter (D)	41.77%
1984	Ronald Reagan (R)	51.22%	Walter Mondale (D)	48.43%
1988	Michael Dukakis (D)	53.23%	George H.W. Bush (R)	45.38%
1992	Bill Clinton (D)	47.54%	George H.W. Bush (R)	29.02%
1996	Bill Clinton (D)	61.47%	Bob Dole (R)	28.09%
2000	Al Gore (D)	59.80%	George W. Bush (R)	32.50%

Year	Winner	PV%	Second	PV%
2004	John Kerry (D)	61.94%	George W. Bush (R)	36.78%
2008	Barack Obama (D)	61.80%	John McCain (R)	35.99%
2012	Barack Obama (D)	60.65%	Mitt Romney (R)	37.51%
2016	Hillary Clinton (D)	60.01%	Donald Trump (R)	32.81%

Home-state qualified candidacies

Year	Candidate	Party	Position	N	W	CS
1789	John Adams	F	Former ambassador	—	—	64.00
1789	John Hancock	F	Governor	—	—	35.97
1789	Benjamin Lincoln	F	Former general	—	—	21.42
1792	John Adams	F	Vice president	—	—	67.23
1796	John Adams	F	Vice president	X	X	77.27
1796	Samuel Adams	DR	Governor	—	—	50.36
1800	John Adams	F	President	X	—	73.21
1820	John Quincy Adams	DR	Cabinet member	—	—	17.96
1824	John Quincy Adams	DR	Cabinet member	X	X	67.41
1828	John Quincy Adams	NR	President	X	—	68.27
1836	Daniel Webster	W	Senator	—	—	26.29
1848	Daniel Webster	W	Senator	—	—	16.31
1852	Daniel Webster	W	Cabinet member	—	—	18.52
1916	John Weeks	R	Senator	—	—	16.35
1924	Calvin Coolidge	R	President	X	X	85.63
1940	Joseph Martin	R	Representative	—	—	12.63
1960	John Kennedy	D	Senator	X	X	79.58
1964	Henry Cabot Lodge	R	Former v.p. nominee	—	—	12.05
1980	Edward Kennedy	D	Senator	—	—	39.18
1988	Michael Dukakis	D	Governor	X	—	65.32
1992	Paul Tsongas	D	Former senator	—	—	21.82
2004	John Kerry	D	Senator	X	—	73.65
2008	Mitt Romney	R	Former governor	—	—	23.13
2012	Mitt Romney	R	Former governor	X	—	70.93

MICHIGAN

Basics

State winners (all-time) .... D 16, R 28, W 1, Other 1
General match (all-time) 34-12 (73.91%)
State winners (Modern Era) .... D 9, R 6
General match (Modern Era) 11-4 (73.33%)
Home-state candidacies 9
Home-state nominees 2
Home-state winners 0

Statewide results since 1856

Year	Winner	PV%	Second	PV%
1856	John Fremont (R)	57.15%	James Buchanan (D)	41.52%
1860	Abraham Lincoln (R)	57.17%	Stephen Douglas (D)	42.04%
1864	Abraham Lincoln (R)	55.34%	George McClellan (D)	44.66%
1868	Ulysses Grant (R)	56.98%	Horatio Seymour (D)	43.02%
1872	Ulysses Grant (R)	62.63%	Horace Greeley (D-LR)	35.50%
1876	Rutherford Hayes (R)	52.41%	Samuel Tilden (D)	44.49%
1880	James Garfield (R)	52.49%	Winfield Hancock (D)	37.27%
1884	James Blaine (R)	48.03%	Grover Cleveland (D)	47.20%
1888	Benjamin Harrison (R)	49.73%	Grover Cleveland (D)	44.91%
1892	Benjamin Harrison (R)	47.70%	Grover Cleveland (D)	43.35%
1896	William McKinley (R)	53.77%	William J. Bryan (D-POP)	43.47%
1900	William McKinley (R)	58.11%	William Jennings Bryan (D)	38.88%
1904	Theodore Roosevelt (R)	69.53%	Alton Parker (D)	25.78%
1908	William Howard Taft (R)	61.94%	William Jennings Bryan (D)	32.45%
1912	Theodore Roosevelt (P)	38.92%	William Howard Taft (R)	27.64%
1916	Charles Evans Hughes (R)	52.24%	Woodrow Wilson (D)	43.90%
1920	Warren Harding (R)	72.76%	James Cox (D)	22.27%
1924	Calvin Coolidge (R)	75.37%	John Davis (D)	13.13%
1928	Herbert Hoover (R)	70.36%	Alfred Smith (D)	28.92%
1932	Franklin Roosevelt (D)	52.36%	Herbert Hoover (R)	44.44%
1936	Franklin Roosevelt (D)	56.33%	Alfred Landon (R)	38.76%
1940	Wendell Willkie (R)	49.85%	Franklin Roosevelt (D)	49.52%
1944	Franklin Roosevelt (D)	50.19%	Thomas Dewey (R)	49.18%
1948	Thomas Dewey (R)	49.23%	Harry Truman (D)	47.57%
1952	Dwight Eisenhower (R)	55.44%	Adlai Stevenson (D)	43.97%
1956	Dwight Eisenhower (R)	55.63%	Adlai Stevenson (D)	44.15%
1960	John Kennedy (D)	50.85%	Richard Nixon (R)	48.84%
1964	Lyndon Johnson (D)	66.71%	Barry Goldwater (R)	33.10%
1968	Hubert Humphrey (D)	48.18%	Richard Nixon (R)	41.46%
1972	Richard Nixon (R)	56.21%	George McGovern (D)	41.82%
1976	Gerald Ford (R)	51.83%	Jimmy Carter (D)	46.44%
1980	Ronald Reagan (R)	48.99%	Jimmy Carter (D)	42.50%
1984	Ronald Reagan (R)	59.23%	Walter Mondale (D)	40.24%
1988	George H.W. Bush (R)	53.57%	Michael Dukakis (D)	45.67%
1992	Bill Clinton (D)	43.77%	George H.W. Bush (R)	36.38%
1996	Bill Clinton (D)	51.70%	Bob Dole (R)	38.49%
2000	Al Gore (D)	51.28%	George W. Bush (R)	46.15%

Year	Winner	PV%	Second	PV%
2004	John Kerry (D)	51.23%	George W. Bush (R)	47.81%
2008	Barack Obama (D)	57.43%	John McCain (R)	40.96%
2012	Barack Obama (D)	54.21%	Mitt Romney (R)	44.71%
2016	Donald Trump (R)	47.50%	Hillary Clinton (D)	47.28%

Home-state qualified candidacies

Year	Candidate	Party	Position	N	W	CS
1844	Lewis Cass	D	Former Cabinet member	—	—	34.91
1844	James Birney	LTY	Movement leader	—	—	17.35
1848	Lewis Cass	D	Senator	X	—	71.66
1852	Lewis Cass	D	Senator	—	—	42.18
1888	Russell Alger	R	Former governor	—	—	19.58
1916	Henry Ford	R	Business executive	—	—	13.29
1940	Arthur Vandenberg	R	Senator	—	—	15.17
1948	Arthur Vandenberg	R	Senator	—	—	13.55
1976	Gerald Ford	R	President	X	—	72.98

MINNESOTA

Basics

State winners (all-time) ....D 19, R 20, Other 1
General match (all-time) 29-11 (72.50%)
State winners (Modern Era) .... D 14, R 1
General match (Modern Era) 8-7 (53.33%)
Home-state candidacies 9
Home-state nominees 2
Home-state winners 0

Statewide results since 1856

Year	Winner	PV%	Second	PV%
1860	Abraham Lincoln (R)	63.41%	Stephen Douglas (D)	34.25%
1864	Abraham Lincoln (R)	58.99%	George McClellan (D)	40.95%
1868	Ulysses Grant (R)	60.80%	Horatio Seymour (D)	39.20%
1872	Ulysses Grant (R)	61.35%	Horace Greeley (D-LR)	38.46%
1876	Rutherford Hayes (R)	58.80%	Samuel Tilden (D)	39.33%
1880	James Garfield (R)	62.29%	Winfield Hancock (D)	35.35%
1884	James Blaine (R)	58.78%	Grover Cleveland (D)	36.87%
1888	Benjamin Harrison (R)	54.15%	Grover Cleveland (D)	39.66%
1892	Benjamin Harrison (R)	45.93%	Grover Cleveland (D)	37.78%
1896	William McKinley (R)	56.62%	William J. Bryan (D-POP)	40.89%
1900	William McKinley (R)	60.21%	William Jennings Bryan (D)	35.69%
1904	Theodore Roosevelt (R)	73.98%	Alton Parker (D)	18.84%
1908	William Howard Taft (R)	59.11%	William Jennings Bryan (D)	33.02%
1912	Theodore Roosevelt (P)	37.66%	Woodrow Wilson (D)	31.84%
1916	Charles Evans Hughes (R)	46.35%	Woodrow Wilson (D)	46.25%
1920	Warren Harding (R)	70.59%	James Cox (D)	19.43%
1924	Calvin Coolidge (R)	51.18%	Robert La Follette (P)	41.26%
1928	Herbert Hoover (R)	57.78%	Alfred Smith (D)	40.83%
1932	Franklin Roosevelt (D)	59.91%	Herbert Hoover (R)	36.29%
1936	Franklin Roosevelt (D)	61.84%	Alfred Landon (R)	31.02%
1940	Franklin Roosevelt (D)	51.49%	Wendell Willkie (R)	47.66%
1944	Franklin Roosevelt (D)	52.41%	Thomas Dewey (R)	46.86%
1948	Harry Truman (D)	57.17%	Thomas Dewey (R)	39.90%
1952	Dwight Eisenhower (R)	55.33%	Adlai Stevenson (D)	44.11%
1956	Dwight Eisenhower (R)	53.68%	Adlai Stevenson (D)	46.08%
1960	John Kennedy (D)	50.58%	Richard Nixon (R)	49.16%
1964	Lyndon Johnson (D)	63.76%	Barry Goldwater (R)	36.00%
1968	Hubert Humphrey (D)	54.00%	Richard Nixon (R)	41.46%
1972	Richard Nixon (R)	51.58%	George McGovern (D)	46.07%
1976	Jimmy Carter (D)	54.90%	Gerald Ford (R)	42.02%
1980	Jimmy Carter (D)	46.50%	Ronald Reagan (R)	42.56%
1984	Walter Mondale (D)	49.72%	Ronald Reagan (R)	49.54%
1988	Michael Dukakis (D)	52.91%	George H.W. Bush (R)	45.90%
1992	Bill Clinton (D)	43.49%	George H.W. Bush (R)	31.85%
1996	Bill Clinton (D)	51.10%	Bob Dole (R)	34.96%
2000	Al Gore (D)	47.91%	George W. Bush (R)	45.50%
2004	John Kerry (D)	51.09%	George W. Bush (R)	47.61%

Year	Winner	PV%	Second		PV%
2008	Barack Obama (D)	54.06%	John McCain (R)		43.82%
2012	Barack Obama (D)	52.65%	Mitt Romney (R)		44.96%
2016	Hillary Clinton (D)	46.45%	Donald Trump (R)		44.93%

Home-state qualified candidacies

Year	Candidate	Party	Position	N	W	CS
1908	John Johnson	D	Governor	—	—	13.67
1948	Harold Stassen	R	Former governor	—	—	22.01
1960	Hubert Humphrey	D	Senator	—	—	14.46
1968	Hubert Humphrey	D	Vice president	X	—	69.19
1968	Eugene McCarthy	D	Senator	—	—	33.16
1972	Hubert Humphrey	D	Former nominee	—	—	25.90
1976	Hubert Humphrey	D	Former nominee	—	—	10.29
1984	Walter Mondale	D	Former vice president	X	—	58.83
2012	Michele Bachmann	R	Representative	—	—	10.11

MISSISSIPPI

Basics

State winners (all-time) ....D 27, R 13, DR 3, SD 1, W 1, Other 3
General match (all-time) 25-23 (52.08%)
State winners (Modern Era) ....D 1, R 12, Other 2
General match (Modern Era) 8-7 (53.33%)
Home-state candidacies 1
Home-state nominees 0
Home-state winners 0

Statewide results since 1856

Year	Winner	PV%	Second	PV%
1856	James Buchanan (D)	59.44%	Millard Fillmore (AW)	40.56%
1860	John Breckinridge (SD)	59.00%	John Bell (CU)	36.25%
1872	Ulysses Grant (R)	63.48%	Horace Greeley (D-LR)	36.52%
1876	Samuel Tilden (D)	68.08%	Rutherford Hayes (R)	31.92%
1880	Winfield Hancock (D)	64.71%	James Garfield (R)	29.76%
1884	Grover Cleveland (D)	64.34%	James Blaine (R)	35.66%
1888	Grover Cleveland (D)	73.80%	Benjamin Harrison (R)	25.99%
1892	Grover Cleveland (D)	76.22%	James Weaver (POP)	19.27%
1896	William J. Bryan (D-POP)	91.04%	William McKinley (R)	6.93%
1900	William Jennings Bryan (D)	87.56%	William McKinley (R)	9.66%
1904	Alton Parker (D)	91.08%	Theodore Roosevelt (R)	5.59%
1908	William Jennings Bryan (D)	90.11%	William Howard Taft (R)	6.52%
1912	Woodrow Wilson (D)	88.90%	Theodore Roosevelt (P)	5.50%
1916	Woodrow Wilson (D)	92.78%	Charles Evans Hughes (R)	4.91%
1920	James Cox (D)	83.95%	Warren Harding (R)	14.06%
1924	John Davis (D)	89.36%	Calvin Coolidge (R)	7.55%
1928	Alfred Smith (D)	82.17%	Herbert Hoover (R)	17.83%
1932	Franklin Roosevelt (D)	95.98%	Herbert Hoover (R)	3.55%
1936	Franklin Roosevelt (D)	97.03%	Alfred Landon (R)	2.76%
1940	Franklin Roosevelt (D)	95.70%	Wendell Willkie (R)	4.19%
1944	Franklin Roosevelt (D)	93.56%	Thomas Dewey (R)	6.44%
1948	Strom Thurmond (SRD)	87.17%	Harry Truman (D)	10.09%
1952	Adlai Stevenson (D)	60.44%	Dwight Eisenhower (R)	39.56%
1956	Adlai Stevenson (D)	58.22%	Dwight Eisenhower (R)	24.46%
1960	Unpledged slate (D)	38.99%	John Kennedy (D)	36.34%
1964	Barry Goldwater (R)	87.14%	Lyndon Johnson (D)	12.86%
1968	George Wallace (AI)	63.46%	Hubert Humphrey (D)	23.02%
1972	Richard Nixon (R)	78.20%	George McGovern (D)	19.63%
1976	Jimmy Carter (D)	49.56%	Gerald Ford (R)	47.68%
1980	Ronald Reagan (R)	49.42%	Jimmy Carter (D)	48.09%
1984	Ronald Reagan (R)	61.88%	Walter Mondale (D)	37.42%
1988	George H.W. Bush (R)	59.89%	Michael Dukakis (D)	39.07%
1992	George H.W. Bush (R)	49.68%	Bill Clinton (D)	40.77%
1996	Bob Dole (R)	49.21%	Bill Clinton (D)	44.08%
2000	George W. Bush (R)	57.62%	Al Gore (D)	40.70%

Year	Winner	PV%	Second	PV%
2004	George W. Bush (R)	59.45%	John Kerry (D)	39.76%
2008	John McCain (R)	56.18%	Barack Obama (D)	43.00%
2012	Mitt Romney (R)	55.29%	Barack Obama (D)	43.79%
2016	Donald Trump (R)	57.94%	Hillary Clinton (D)	40.12%

Home-state qualified candidacies

Year	Candidate	Party	Position	N	W	CS
1924	Pat Harrison	D	Senator	—	—	12.40

MISSOURI

Basics

State winners (all-time) .... D 29, R 18, DR 3
General match (all-time) 37-13 (74.00%)
State winners (Modern Era) .... D 5, R 10
General match (Modern Era) 13-2 (86.67%)
Home-state candidacies 10
Home-state nominees 1
Home-state winners 1

Statewide results since 1856

Year	Winner	PV%	Second	PV%
1856	James Buchanan (D)	54.43%	Millard Fillmore (AW)	45.57%
1860	Stephen Douglas (D)	35.52%	John Bell (CU)	35.26%
1864	Abraham Lincoln (R)	69.72%	George McClellan (D)	30.28%
1868	Ulysses Grant (R)	56.96%	Horatio Seymour (D)	43.04%
1872	Horace Greeley (D-LR)	55.46%	Ulysses Grant (R)	43.65%
1876	Samuel Tilden (D)	57.64%	Rutherford Hayes (R)	41.36%
1880	Winfield Hancock (D)	52.51%	James Garfield (R)	38.67%
1884	Grover Cleveland (D)	53.49%	James Blaine (R)	46.02%
1888	Grover Cleveland (D)	50.24%	Benjamin Harrison (R)	45.32%
1892	Grover Cleveland (D)	49.56%	Benjamin Harrison (R)	42.03%
1896	William J. Bryan (D-POP)	53.95%	William McKinley (R)	45.24%
1900	William Jennings Bryan (D)	51.48%	William McKinley (R)	45.94%
1904	Theodore Roosevelt (R)	49.93%	Alton Parker (D)	46.02%
1908	William Howard Taft (R)	48.50%	William Jennings Bryan (D)	48.42%
1912	Woodrow Wilson (D)	47.35%	William Howard Taft (R)	29.75%
1916	Woodrow Wilson (D)	50.59%	Charles Evans Hughes (R)	46.94%
1920	Warren Harding (R)	54.59%	James Cox (D)	43.14%
1924	Calvin Coolidge (R)	49.50%	John Davis (D)	43.89%
1928	Herbert Hoover (R)	55.57%	Alfred Smith (D)	44.15%
1932	Franklin Roosevelt (D)	63.69%	Herbert Hoover (R)	35.08%
1936	Franklin Roosevelt (D)	60.76%	Alfred Landon (R)	38.17%
1940	Franklin Roosevelt (D)	52.27%	Wendell Willkie (R)	47.50%
1944	Franklin Roosevelt (D)	51.37%	Thomas Dewey (R)	48.43%
1948	Harry Truman (D)	58.11%	Thomas Dewey (R)	41.49%
1952	Dwight Eisenhower (R)	50.71%	Adlai Stevenson (D)	49.14%
1956	Adlai Stevenson (D)	50.11%	Dwight Eisenhower (R)	49.89%
1960	John Kennedy (D)	50.26%	Richard Nixon (R)	49.74%
1964	Lyndon Johnson (D)	64.05%	Barry Goldwater (R)	35.95%
1968	Richard Nixon (R)	44.87%	Hubert Humphrey (D)	43.74%
1972	Richard Nixon (R)	62.18%	George McGovern (D)	37.57%
1976	Jimmy Carter (D)	51.11%	Gerald Ford (R)	47.47%
1980	Ronald Reagan (R)	51.16%	Jimmy Carter (D)	44.35%
1984	Ronald Reagan (R)	60.02%	Walter Mondale (D)	39.98%
1988	George H.W. Bush (R)	51.82%	Michael Dukakis (D)	47.84%
1992	Bill Clinton (D)	44.07%	George H.W. Bush (R)	33.92%
1996	Bill Clinton (D)	47.54%	Bob Dole (R)	41.24%
2000	George W. Bush (R)	50.42%	Al Gore (D)	47.08%

Year	Winner	PV%	Second	PV%
2004	George W. Bush (R)	53.30%	John Kerry (D)	46.10%
2008	John McCain (R)	49.43%	Barack Obama (D)	49.29%
2012	Mitt Romney (R)	53.76%	Barack Obama (D)	44.38%
2016	Donald Trump (R)	56.77%	Hillary Clinton (D)	38.14%

Home-state qualified candidacies

Year	Candidate	Party	Position	N	W	CS
1860	Edward Bates	R	Former representative	—	—	18.22
1872	Gratz Brown	D-LR	Governor	—	—	27.03
1896	Richard Bland	D	Former representative	—	—	30.20
1904	Francis Cockrell	D	Senator	—	—	13.35
1912	Champ Clark	D	Representative	—	—	42.45
1928	James Reed	D	Senator	—	—	16.09
1948	Harry Truman	D	President	X	X	79.72
1960	Stuart Symington	D	Senator	—	—	13.00
1988	Richard Gephardt	D	Representative	—	—	13.63
2004	Richard Gephardt	D	Representative	—	—	10.23

MONTANA

Basics

State winners (all-time) .... D 11, R 21
General match (all-time) 24-8 (75.00%)
State winners (Modern Era) .... D 2, R 13
General match (Modern Era) 10-5 (66.67%)
Home-state candidacies 2
Home-state nominees 0
Home-state winners 0

Statewide results since 1856

Year	Winner	PV%	Second	PV%
1892	Benjamin Harrison (R)	42.44%	Grover Cleveland (D)	39.79%
1896	William J. Bryan (D-POP)	79.93%	William McKinley (R)	19.71%
1900	William Jennings Bryan (D)	58.43%	William McKinley (R)	39.79%
1904	Theodore Roosevelt (R)	53.48%	Alton Parker (D)	34.32%
1908	William Howard Taft (R)	46.90%	William Jennings Bryan (D)	42.63%
1912	Woodrow Wilson (D)	35.05%	Theodore Roosevelt (P)	28.30%
1916	Woodrow Wilson (D)	56.80%	Charles Evans Hughes (R)	37.60%
1920	Warren Harding (R)	61.13%	James Cox (D)	32.05%
1924	Calvin Coolidge (R)	42.57%	Robert La Follette (P)	37.82%
1928	Herbert Hoover (R)	58.37%	Alfred Smith (D)	40.48%
1932	Franklin Roosevelt (D)	58.80%	Herbert Hoover (R)	36.07%
1936	Franklin Roosevelt (D)	69.28%	Alfred Landon (R)	27.59%
1940	Franklin Roosevelt (D)	58.78%	Wendell Willkie (R)	40.17%
1944	Franklin Roosevelt (D)	54.28%	Thomas Dewey (R)	44.93%
1948	Harry Truman (D)	53.09%	Thomas Dewey (R)	43.15%
1952	Dwight Eisenhower (R)	59.39%	Adlai Stevenson (D)	40.08%
1956	Dwight Eisenhower (R)	57.14%	Adlai Stevenson (D)	42.87%
1960	Richard Nixon (R)	51.10%	John Kennedy (D)	48.60%
1964	Lyndon Johnson (D)	58.95%	Barry Goldwater (R)	40.57%
1968	Richard Nixon (R)	50.60%	Hubert Humphrey (D)	41.59%
1972	Richard Nixon (R)	57.93%	George McGovern (D)	37.85%
1976	Gerald Ford (R)	52.84%	Jimmy Carter (D)	45.40%
1980	Ronald Reagan (R)	56.83%	Jimmy Carter (D)	32.43%
1984	Ronald Reagan (R)	60.47%	Walter Mondale (D)	38.18%
1988	George H.W. Bush (R)	52.07%	Michael Dukakis (D)	46.20%
1992	Bill Clinton (D)	37.63%	George H.W. Bush (R)	35.12%
1996	Bob Dole (R)	44.11%	Bill Clinton (D)	41.23%
2000	George W. Bush (R)	58.44%	Al Gore (D)	33.36%
2004	George W. Bush (R)	59.07%	John Kerry (D)	38.56%
2008	John McCain (R)	49.51%	Barack Obama (D)	47.25%
2012	Mitt Romney (R)	55.35%	Barack Obama (D)	41.70%
2016	Donald Trump (R)	56.17%	Hillary Clinton (D)	35.75%

Home-state qualified candidacies

Year	Candidate	Party	Position	N	W	CS
1924	Thomas Walsh	D	Senator	—	—	13.17
1928	Thomas Walsh	D	Senator	—	—	10.95

NEBRASKA

Basics

State winners (all-time) .... D 7, R 31
General match (all-time) 25-13 (65.79%)
State winners (Modern Era) .... D 1, R 14
General match (Modern Era) 9-6 (60.00%)
Home-state candidacies 5
Home-state nominees 3
Home-state winners 0

Statewide results since 1856

Year	Winner	PV%	Second	PV%
1868	Ulysses Grant (R)	63.91%	Horatio Seymour (D)	36.09%
1872	Ulysses Grant (R)	70.68%	Horace Greeley (D-LR)	29.32%
1876	Rutherford Hayes (R)	64.79%	Samuel Tilden (D)	35.21%
1880	James Garfield (R)	62.94%	Winfield Hancock (D)	32.65%
1884	James Blaine (R)	57.31%	Grover Cleveland (D)	40.53%
1888	Benjamin Harrison (R)	53.51%	Grover Cleveland (D)	39.75%
1892	Benjamin Harrison (R)	43.56%	James Weaver (POP)	41.52%
1896	William J. Bryan (D-POP)	51.53%	William McKinley (R)	46.18%
1900	William McKinley (R)	50.46%	William Jennings Bryan (D)	47.22%
1904	Theodore Roosevelt (R)	61.38%	Alton Parker (D)	23.44%
1908	William Jennings Bryan (D)	49.14%	William Howard Taft (R)	47.60%
1912	Woodrow Wilson (D)	43.69%	Theodore Roosevelt (P)	29.13%
1916	Woodrow Wilson (D)	55.28%	Charles Evans Hughes (R)	40.99%
1920	Warren Harding (R)	64.66%	James Cox (D)	31.25%
1924	Calvin Coolidge (R)	47.24%	John Davis (D)	29.62%
1928	Herbert Hoover (R)	63.19%	Alfred Smith (D)	36.18%
1932	Franklin Roosevelt (D)	62.98%	Herbert Hoover (R)	35.29%
1936	Franklin Roosevelt (D)	57.14%	Alfred Landon (R)	40.74%
1940	Wendell Willkie (R)	57.19%	Franklin Roosevelt (D)	42.81%
1944	Thomas Dewey (R)	58.58%	Franklin Roosevelt (D)	41.42%
1948	Thomas Dewey (R)	54.15%	Harry Truman (D)	45.85%
1952	Dwight Eisenhower (R)	69.15%	Adlai Stevenson (D)	30.85%
1956	Dwight Eisenhower (R)	65.51%	Adlai Stevenson (D)	34.49%
1960	Richard Nixon (R)	62.07%	John Kennedy (D)	37.93%
1964	Lyndon Johnson (D)	52.61%	Barry Goldwater (R)	47.39%
1968	Richard Nixon (R)	59.82%	Hubert Humphrey (D)	31.81%
1972	Richard Nixon (R)	70.50%	George McGovern (D)	29.50%
1976	Gerald Ford (R)	59.19%	Jimmy Carter (D)	38.46%
1980	Ronald Reagan (R)	65.53%	Jimmy Carter (D)	26.04%
1984	Ronald Reagan (R)	70.55%	Walter Mondale (D)	28.81%
1988	George H.W. Bush (R)	60.16%	Michael Dukakis (D)	39.19%
1992	George H.W. Bush (R)	46.60%	Bill Clinton (D)	29.40%
1996	Bob Dole (R)	53.66%	Bill Clinton (D)	34.95%
2000	George W. Bush (R)	62.25%	Al Gore (D)	33.25%
2004	George W. Bush (R)	65.90%	John Kerry (D)	32.68%

Year	Winner	PV%	Second	PV%
2008	John McCain (R)	56.53%	Barack Obama (D)	41.60%
2012	Mitt Romney (R)	59.80%	Barack Obama (D)	38.03%
2016	Donald Trump (R)	58.75%	Hillary Clinton (D)	33.70%

Home-state qualified candidacies

Year	Candidate	Party	Position	N	W	CS
1896	William Jennings Bryan	D-POP	Former representative	X	—	70.98
1900	William Jennings Bryan	D	Former nominee	X	—	69.53
1908	William Jennings Bryan	D	Former nominee	X	—	68.65
1928	George Norris	R	Senator	—	—	12.58
1992	Bob Kerrey	D	Senator	—	—	10.95

NEVADA

Basics

State winners (all-time) ....D 18, R 20, Other 1
General match (all-time) 31-8 (79.49%)
State winners (Modern Era) ....D 7, R 8
General match (Modern Era) 13-2 (86.67%)
Home-state candidacies 0
Home-state nominees 0
Home-state winners 0

Statewide results since 1856

Year	Winner	PV%	Second	PV%
1864	Abraham Lincoln (R)	59.84%	George McClellan (D)	40.16%
1868	Ulysses Grant (R)	55.39%	Horatio Seymour (D)	44.62%
1872	Ulysses Grant (R)	57.43%	Horace Greeley (D-LR)	42.57%
1876	Rutherford Hayes (R)	52.73%	Samuel Tilden (D)	47.27%
1880	Winfield Hancock (D)	52.40%	James Garfield (R)	47.60%
1884	James Blaine (R)	56.16%	Grover Cleveland (D)	43.64%
1888	Benjamin Harrison (R)	57.50%	Grover Cleveland (D)	42.18%
1892	James Weaver (POP)	66.75%	Benjamin Harrison (R)	25.97%
1896	William J. Bryan (D-POP)	75.65%	William McKinley (R)	18.79%
1900	William Jennings Bryan (D)	62.25%	William McKinley (R)	37.75%
1904	Theodore Roosevelt (R)	56.66%	Alton Parker (D)	32.87%
1908	William Jennings Bryan (D)	45.72%	William Howard Taft (R)	43.93%
1912	Woodrow Wilson (D)	39.70%	Theodore Roosevelt (P)	27.94%
1916	Woodrow Wilson (D)	53.36%	Charles Evans Hughes (R)	36.40%
1920	Warren Harding (R)	56.92%	James Cox (D)	36.23%
1924	Calvin Coolidge (R)	41.76%	Robert La Follette (P)	36.29%
1928	Herbert Hoover (R)	56.54%	Alfred Smith (D)	43.47%
1932	Franklin Roosevelt (D)	69.41%	Herbert Hoover (R)	30.59%
1936	Franklin Roosevelt (D)	72.81%	Alfred Landon (R)	27.19%
1940	Franklin Roosevelt (D)	60.08%	Wendell Willkie (R)	39.92%
1944	Franklin Roosevelt (D)	54.62%	Thomas Dewey (R)	45.38%
1948	Harry Truman (D)	50.37%	Thomas Dewey (R)	47.26%
1952	Dwight Eisenhower (R)	61.45%	Adlai Stevenson (D)	38.56%
1956	Dwight Eisenhower (R)	57.97%	Adlai Stevenson (D)	42.03%
1960	John Kennedy (D)	51.16%	Richard Nixon (R)	48.84%
1964	Lyndon Johnson (D)	58.58%	Barry Goldwater (R)	41.42%
1968	Richard Nixon (R)	47.46%	Hubert Humphrey (D)	39.29%
1972	Richard Nixon (R)	63.68%	George McGovern (D)	36.32%
1976	Gerald Ford (R)	50.17%	Jimmy Carter (D)	45.81%
1980	Ronald Reagan (R)	62.54%	Jimmy Carter (D)	26.89%
1984	Ronald Reagan (R)	65.85%	Walter Mondale (D)	31.97%
1988	George H.W. Bush (R)	58.86%	Michael Dukakis (D)	37.92%
1992	Bill Clinton (D)	37.36%	George H.W. Bush (R)	34.73%
1996	Bill Clinton (D)	43.93%	Bob Dole (R)	42.92%
2000	George W. Bush (R)	49.52%	Al Gore (D)	45.98%

Year	Winner	PV%	Second	PV%
2004	George W. Bush (R)	50.47%	John Kerry (D)	47.88%
2008	Barack Obama (D)	55.15%	John McCain (R)	42.65%
2012	Barack Obama (D)	52.36%	Mitt Romney (R)	45.68%
2016	Hillary Clinton (D)	47.92%	Donald Trump (R)	45.50%

Home-state qualified candidacies

(None)

NEW HAMPSHIRE

Basics

State winners (all-time) .... D 18, R 29, DR 4, F 6, NR 1
General match (all-time) 43-15 (74.14%)
State winners (Modern Era) .... D 7, R 8
General match (Modern Era) 11-4 (73.33%)
Home-state candidacies 5
Home-state nominees 1
Home-state winners 1

Statewide results since 1856

Year	Winner	PV%	Second	PV%
1856	John Fremont (R)	53.71%	James Buchanan (D)	45.71%
1860	Abraham Lincoln (R)	56.90%	Stephen Douglas (D)	39.26%
1864	Abraham Lincoln (R)	52.56%	George McClellan (D)	47.44%
1868	Ulysses Grant (R)	55.22%	Horatio Seymour (D)	44.76%
1872	Ulysses Grant (R)	53.94%	Horace Greeley (D-LR)	45.61%
1876	Rutherford Hayes (R)	51.83%	Samuel Tilden (D)	48.05%
1880	James Garfield (R)	51.94%	Winfield Hancock (D)	47.24%
1884	James Blaine (R)	51.14%	Grover Cleveland (D)	46.34%
1888	Benjamin Harrison (R)	50.38%	Grover Cleveland (D)	47.79%
1892	Benjamin Harrison (R)	51.11%	Grover Cleveland (D)	47.11%
1896	William McKinley (R)	68.66%	William J. Bryan (D-POP)	25.42%
1900	William McKinley (R)	59.33%	William Jennings Bryan (D)	38.42%
1904	Theodore Roosevelt (R)	60.07%	Alton Parker (D)	37.79%
1908	William Howard Taft (R)	59.32%	William Jennings Bryan (D)	37.56%
1912	Woodrow Wilson (D)	39.48%	William Howard Taft (R)	37.43%
1916	Woodrow Wilson (D)	49.12%	Charles Evans Hughes (R)	49.06%
1920	Warren Harding (R)	59.84%	James Cox (D)	39.39%
1924	Calvin Coolidge (R)	59.83%	John Davis (D)	34.72%
1928	Herbert Hoover (R)	58.65%	Alfred Smith (D)	41.02%
1932	Herbert Hoover (R)	50.42%	Franklin Roosevelt (D)	48.99%
1936	Franklin Roosevelt (D)	49.73%	Alfred Landon (R)	47.98%
1940	Franklin Roosevelt (D)	53.22%	Wendell Willkie (R)	46.78%
1944	Franklin Roosevelt (D)	52.11%	Thomas Dewey (R)	47.87%
1948	Thomas Dewey (R)	52.41%	Harry Truman (D)	46.66%
1952	Dwight Eisenhower (R)	60.92%	Adlai Stevenson (D)	39.08%
1956	Dwight Eisenhower (R)	66.11%	Adlai Stevenson (D)	33.85%
1960	Richard Nixon (R)	53.42%	John Kennedy (D)	46.58%
1964	Lyndon Johnson (D)	63.89%	Barry Goldwater (R)	36.11%
1968	Richard Nixon (R)	52.10%	Hubert Humphrey (D)	43.93%
1972	Richard Nixon (R)	63.98%	George McGovern (D)	34.86%
1976	Gerald Ford (R)	54.75%	Jimmy Carter (D)	43.47%
1980	Ronald Reagan (R)	57.74%	Jimmy Carter (D)	28.35%
1984	Ronald Reagan (R)	68.64%	Walter Mondale (D)	30.95%
1988	George H.W. Bush (R)	62.42%	Michael Dukakis (D)	36.29%
1992	Bill Clinton (D)	38.86%	George H.W. Bush (R)	37.64%
1996	Bill Clinton (D)	49.32%	Bob Dole (R)	39.37%
2000	George W. Bush (R)	48.07%	Al Gore (D)	46.80%

Year	Winner	PV%	Second	PV%
2004	John Kerry (D)	50.24%	George W. Bush (R)	48.87%
2008	Barack Obama (D)	54.13%	John McCain (R)	44.52%
2012	Barack Obama (D)	51.98%	Mitt Romney (R)	46.40%
2016	Hillary Clinton (D)	46.83%	Donald Trump (R)	46.46%

Home-state qualified candidacies

Year	Candidate	Party	Position	N	W	CS
1848	Levi Woodbury	D	Supreme Court justice	—	—	24.61
1852	Franklin Pierce	D	Former senator	X	X	89.52
1852	John Hale	FS	Senator	—	—	25.71
1856	Franklin Pierce	D	President	—	—	43.05
1920	Leonard Wood	R	General	—	—	31.95

NEW JERSEY

Basics

State winners (all-time) ....D 24, R 19, DR 5, F 5, NR 1, W 4
General match (all-time) 41-17 (70.69%)
State winners (Modern Era) ....D 9, R 6
General match (Modern Era) 11-4 (73.33%)
Home-state candidacies 13
Home-state nominees 4
Home-state winners 2

Statewide results since 1856

Year	Winner	PV%	Second	PV%
1856	James Buchanan (D)	47.23%	John Fremont (R)	28.51%
1860	Stephen Douglas (D)	51.87%	Abraham Lincoln (R)	48.13%
1864	George McClellan (D)	52.84%	Abraham Lincoln (R)	47.17%
1868	Horatio Seymour (D)	50.88%	Ulysses Grant (R)	49.12%
1872	Ulysses Grant (R)	54.41%	Horace Greeley (D-LR)	45.59%
1876	Samuel Tilden (D)	52.66%	Rutherford Hayes (R)	47.01%
1880	Winfield Hancock (D)	49.84%	James Garfield (R)	49.02%
1884	Grover Cleveland (D)	48.97%	James Blaine (R)	47.32%
1888	Grover Cleveland (D)	49.87%	Benjamin Harrison (R)	47.52%
1892	Grover Cleveland (D)	50.67%	Benjamin Harrison (R)	46.24%
1896	William McKinley (R)	59.67%	William J. Bryan (D-POP)	36.03%
1900	William McKinley (R)	55.28%	William Jennings Bryan (D)	41.09%
1904	Theodore Roosevelt (R)	56.68%	Alton Parker (D)	38.05%
1908	William Howard Taft (R)	56.80%	William Jennings Bryan (D)	39.08%
1912	Woodrow Wilson (D)	41.19%	Theodore Roosevelt (P)	33.59%
1916	Charles Evans Hughes (R)	54.40%	Woodrow Wilson (D)	42.68%
1920	Warren Harding (R)	67.60%	James Cox (D)	28.43%
1924	Calvin Coolidge (R)	62.16%	John Davis (D)	27.39%
1928	Herbert Hoover (R)	59.77%	Alfred Smith (D)	39.79%
1932	Franklin Roosevelt (D)	49.49%	Herbert Hoover (R)	47.59%
1936	Franklin Roosevelt (D)	59.54%	Alfred Landon (R)	39.57%
1940	Franklin Roosevelt (D)	51.55%	Wendell Willkie (R)	47.93%
1944	Franklin Roosevelt (D)	50.31%	Thomas Dewey (R)	48.95%
1948	Thomas Dewey (R)	50.33%	Harry Truman (D)	45.93%
1952	Dwight Eisenhower (R)	56.80%	Adlai Stevenson (D)	42.01%
1956	Dwight Eisenhower (R)	64.68%	Adlai Stevenson (D)	34.23%
1960	John Kennedy (D)	49.96%	Richard Nixon (R)	49.16%
1964	Lyndon Johnson (D)	65.61%	Barry Goldwater (R)	33.86%
1968	Richard Nixon (R)	46.10%	Hubert Humphrey (D)	43.97%
1972	Richard Nixon (R)	61.57%	George McGovern (D)	36.77%
1976	Gerald Ford (R)	50.08%	Jimmy Carter (D)	47.92%
1980	Ronald Reagan (R)	51.97%	Jimmy Carter (D)	38.56%
1984	Ronald Reagan (R)	60.09%	Walter Mondale (D)	39.20%
1988	George H.W. Bush (R)	56.24%	Michael Dukakis (D)	42.60%
1992	Bill Clinton (D)	42.95%	George H.W. Bush (R)	40.58%
1996	Bill Clinton (D)	53.72%	Bob Dole (R)	35.86%
2000	Al Gore (D)	56.13%	George W. Bush (R)	40.29%

Year	Winner	PV%	Second	PV%
2004	John Kerry (D)	52.92%	George W. Bush (R)	46.24%
2008	Barack Obama (D)	57.27%	John McCain (R)	41.70%
2012	Barack Obama (D)	58.38%	Mitt Romney (R)	40.59%
2016	Hillary Clinton (D)	55.45%	Donald Trump (R)	41.35%

Home-state qualified candidacies

Year	Candidate	Party	Position	N	W	CS
1840	Winfield Scott	W	General	—	—	27.88
1848	Winfield Scott	W	General	—	—	27.96
1852	Winfield Scott	W	General	X	—	63.01
1864	George McClellan	D	General	X	—	61.66
1868	Joel Parker	D	Former governor	—	—	13.27
1888	Clinton Fisk	PRO	Former general	—	—	17.02
1912	Woodrow Wilson	D	Governor	X	X	86.26
1916	Woodrow Wilson	D	President	X	X	78.07
1920	Edward Edwards	D	Governor	—	—	13.28
1996	Steve Forbes	R	Journalist	—	—	16.96
2000	Bill Bradley	D	Former senator	—	—	22.10
2000	Steve Forbes	R	Journalist	—	—	10.52
2016	Chris Christie	R	Governor	—	—	10.11

NEW MEXICO

Basics

State winners (all-time) ....D 15, R 12
General match (all-time) 24-3 (88.89%)
State winners (Modern Era) ....D 8, R 7
General match (Modern Era) 12-3 (80.00%)
Home-state candidacies 2
Home-state nominees 0
Home-state winners 0

Statewide results since 1856

Year	Winner	PV%	Second	PV%
1912	Woodrow Wilson (D)	41.87%	William Howard Taft (R)	35.17%
1916	Woodrow Wilson (D)	50.38%	Charles Evans Hughes (R)	46.50%
1920	Warren Harding (R)	54.68%	James Cox (D)	44.27%
1924	Calvin Coolidge (R)	48.52%	John Davis (D)	43.02%
1928	Herbert Hoover (R)	59.04%	Alfred Smith (D)	40.83%
1932	Franklin Roosevelt (D)	62.72%	Herbert Hoover (R)	35.76%
1936	Franklin Roosevelt (D)	62.69%	Alfred Landon (R)	36.50%
1940	Franklin Roosevelt (D)	56.59%	Wendell Willkie (R)	43.28%
1944	Franklin Roosevelt (D)	53.47%	Thomas Dewey (R)	46.44%
1948	Harry Truman (D)	56.38%	Thomas Dewey (R)	42.93%
1952	Dwight Eisenhower (R)	55.39%	Adlai Stevenson (D)	44.28%
1956	Dwight Eisenhower (R)	57.81%	Adlai Stevenson (D)	41.78%
1960	John Kennedy (D)	50.15%	Richard Nixon (R)	49.42%
1964	Lyndon Johnson (D)	59.04%	Barry Goldwater (R)	40.42%
1968	Richard Nixon (R)	51.84%	Hubert Humphrey (D)	39.74%
1972	Richard Nixon (R)	61.00%	George McGovern (D)	36.53%
1976	Gerald Ford (R)	50.53%	Jimmy Carter (D)	48.07%
1980	Ronald Reagan (R)	54.88%	Jimmy Carter (D)	36.73%
1984	Ronald Reagan (R)	59.70%	Walter Mondale (D)	39.23%
1988	George H.W. Bush (R)	51.86%	Michael Dukakis (D)	46.90%
1992	Bill Clinton (D)	45.90%	George H.W. Bush (R)	37.34%
1996	Bill Clinton (D)	49.18%	Bob Dole (R)	41.86%
2000	Al Gore (D)	47.91%	George W. Bush (R)	47.85%
2004	George W. Bush (R)	49.84%	John Kerry (D)	49.05%
2008	Barack Obama (D)	56.91%	John McCain (R)	41.78%
2012	Barack Obama (D)	52.99%	Mitt Romney (R)	42.84%
2016	Hillary Clinton (D)	48.26%	Donald Trump (R)	40.04%

Home-state qualified candidacies

Year	Candidate	Party	Position	N	W	CS
2008	Bill Richardson	D	Governor	—	—	10.17
2016	Gary Johnson	LIB	Former governor	—	—	20.52

NEW YORK

Basics

State winners (all-time) ....D 25, R 20, DR 7, F 2, W 2, Tie 1
General match (all-time) 45-11-1 (78.95%)
State winners (Modern Era) ....D 12, R 3
General match (Modern Era) 10-5 (66.67%)
Home-state candidacies 75
Home-state nominees 26
Home-state winners 12

Statewide results since 1856

Year	Winner	PV%	Second	PV%
1856	John Fremont (R)	46.27%	James Buchanan (D)	32.84%
1860	Abraham Lincoln (R)	53.71%	Stephen Douglas (D)	46.29%
1864	Abraham Lincoln (R)	50.46%	George McClellan (D)	49.54%
1868	Horatio Seymour (D)	50.59%	Ulysses Grant (R)	49.41%
1872	Ulysses Grant (R)	53.12%	Horace Greeley (D-LR)	46.68%
1876	Samuel Tilden (D)	51.40%	Rutherford Hayes (R)	48.17%
1880	James Garfield (R)	50.32%	Winfield Hancock (D)	48.42%
1884	Grover Cleveland (D)	48.25%	James Blaine (R)	48.16%
1888	Benjamin Harrison (R)	49.20%	Grover Cleveland (D)	48.11%
1892	Grover Cleveland (D)	48.99%	Benjamin Harrison (R)	45.58%
1896	William McKinley (R)	57.58%	William J. Bryan (D-POP)	38.72%
1900	William McKinley (R)	53.10%	William Jennings Bryan (D)	43.83%
1904	Theodore Roosevelt (R)	53.13%	Alton Parker (D)	42.28%
1908	William Howard Taft (R)	53.11%	William Jennings Bryan (D)	40.74%
1912	Woodrow Wilson (D)	41.28%	William Howard Taft (R)	28.68%
1916	Charles Evans Hughes (R)	51.53%	Woodrow Wilson (D)	44.51%
1920	Warren Harding (R)	64.56%	James Cox (D)	26.95%
1924	Calvin Coolidge (R)	55.76%	John Davis (D)	29.13%
1928	Herbert Hoover (R)	49.79%	Alfred Smith (D)	47.44%
1932	Franklin Roosevelt (D)	54.07%	Herbert Hoover (R)	41.33%
1936	Franklin Roosevelt (D)	58.85%	Alfred Landon (R)	38.97%
1940	Franklin Roosevelt (D)	51.61%	Wendell Willkie (R)	48.04%
1944	Franklin Roosevelt (D)	52.31%	Thomas Dewey (R)	47.30%
1948	Thomas Dewey (R)	45.99%	Harry Truman (D)	45.01%
1952	Dwight Eisenhower (R)	55.45%	Adlai Stevenson (D)	43.55%
1956	Dwight Eisenhower (R)	61.24%	Adlai Stevenson (D)	38.73%
1960	John Kennedy (D)	52.53%	Richard Nixon (R)	47.27%
1964	Lyndon Johnson (D)	68.56%	Barry Goldwater (R)	31.31%
1968	Hubert Humphrey (D)	49.74%	Richard Nixon (R)	44.29%
1972	Richard Nixon (R)	58.51%	George McGovern (D)	41.18%
1976	Jimmy Carter (D)	51.87%	Gerald Ford (R)	47.46%
1980	Ronald Reagan (R)	46.66%	Jimmy Carter (D)	43.99%
1984	Ronald Reagan (R)	53.84%	Walter Mondale (D)	45.83%
1988	Michael Dukakis (D)	51.62%	George H.W. Bush (R)	47.52%
1992	Bill Clinton (D)	49.73%	George H.W. Bush (R)	33.88%
1996	Bill Clinton (D)	59.47%	Bob Dole (R)	30.61%
2000	Al Gore (D)	60.21%	George W. Bush (R)	35.23%

Year	Winner	PV%	Second	PV%
2004	John Kerry (D)	58.37%	George W. Bush (R)	40.08%
2008	Barack Obama (D)	62.88%	John McCain (R)	36.03%
2012	Barack Obama (D)	63.35%	Mitt Romney (R)	35.17%
2016	Hillary Clinton (D)	59.01%	Donald Trump (R)	36.52%

Home-state qualified candidacies

Year	Candidate	Party	Position	N	W	CS
1789	John Jay	F	Cabinet member	—	—	51.15
1789	George Clinton	DR	Governor	—	—	31.09
1792	George Clinton	DR	Governor	—	—	59.98
1792	Aaron Burr	DR	Senator	—	—	19.07
1796	Aaron Burr	DR	Senator	—	—	54.24
1796	George Clinton	DR	Former governor	—	—	33.54
1796	John Jay	F	Governor	—	—	28.66
1800	Aaron Burr	DR	Former senator	—	—	65.31
1800	John Jay	F	Governor	—	—	18.98
1808	George Clinton	DR	Vice president	—	—	28.01
1812	DeWitt Clinton	F-DR	Mayor	X	—	71.10
1816	Rufus King	F	Senator	X	—	62.07
1836	Martin Van Buren	D	Vice president	X	X	80.26
1840	Martin Van Buren	D	President	X	—	65.49
1844	Martin Van Buren	D	Former president	—	—	50.00
1848	Martin Van Buren	FS	Former president	—	—	42.02
1852	Millard Fillmore	W	President	—	—	45.85
1852	William Marcy	D	Former Cabinet member	—	—	17.50
1856	Millard Fillmore	AW	Former president	—	—	45.15
1860	William Seward	R	Senator	—	—	39.70
1864	Horatio Seymour	D	Governor	—	—	14.23
1868	Horatio Seymour	D	Former governor	X	—	67.61
1868	Sanford Church	D	Former state official	—	—	18.54
1872	Horace Greeley	D-LR	Journalist	X	—	58.76
1876	Samuel Tilden	D	Governor	X	—	75.14
1876	Roscoe Conkling	R	Senator	—	—	20.46
1880	Samuel Tilden	D	Former nominee	—	—	14.07
1884	Grover Cleveland	D	Governor	X	X	78.78
1884	Chester Arthur	R	President	—	—	37.07
1888	Grover Cleveland	D	President	X	—	72.27
1888	Chauncey Depew	R	Business executive	—	—	19.50
1892	Grover Cleveland	D	Former president	X	X	80.73
1892	David Hill	D	Senator	—	—	19.98
1896	Levi Morton	R	Governor	—	—	15.03
1904	Theodore Roosevelt	R	President	X	X	85.72
1904	Alton Parker	D	State judge	X	—	66.33
1904	William Randolph Hearst	D	Journalist	—	—	24.45
1908	Charles Evans Hughes	R	Governor	—	—	15.43
1912	Theodore Roosevelt	R/P	Former president	—	—	66.37
1916	Charles Evans Hughes	R	Supreme Court justice	X	—	73.55
1916	Allan Benson	SOC	Journalist	—	—	20.19
1916	Elihu Root	R	Former senator	—	—	16.23
1916	Theodore Roosevelt	R	Former president	—	—	14.78
1920	William Gibbs McAdoo	D	Former Cabinet member	—	—	27.41
1920	Alfred Smith	D	Governor	—	—	15.99

Year	Candidate	Party	Position	N	W	CS
1920	Nicholas Murray Butler	R	College president	—	—	14.25
1924	Alfred Smith	D	Governor	—	—	23.54
1928	Alfred Smith	D	Governor	X	—	63.06
1932	Franklin Roosevelt	D	Governor	X	X	91.94
1932	Alfred Smith	D	Former nominee	—	—	23.23
1932	Norman Thomas	SOC	Movement leader	—	—	17.13
1936	Franklin Roosevelt	D	President	X	X	95.88
1940	Franklin Roosevelt	D	President	X	X	89.94
1940	Wendell Willkie	R	Business executive	X	—	63.60
1940	Thomas Dewey	R	District attorney	—	—	41.51
1940	James Farley	D	Cabinet member	—	—	13.95
1944	Franklin Roosevelt	D	President	X	X	88.61
1944	Thomas Dewey	R	Governor	X	—	64.76
1948	Thomas Dewey	R	Former nominee	X	—	69.67
1952	Dwight Eisenhower	R	General	X	X	89.56
1952	Averell Harriman	D	Former Cabinet member	—	—	15.10
1956	Dwight Eisenhower	R	President	X	X	91.03
1956	Averell Harriman	D	Governor	—	—	17.64
1964	Nelson Rockefeller	R	Governor	—	—	20.93
1964	Richard Nixon	R	Former nominee	—	—	11.00
1968	Richard Nixon	R	Former nominee	X	X	78.01
1968	Nelson Rockefeller	R	Governor	—	—	21.48
1968	Robert Kennedy	D	Senator	—	—	19.18
1972	Shirley Chisholm	D	Representative	—	—	12.62
1988	Jack Kemp	R	Representative	—	—	11.63
2008	Hillary Clinton	D	Senator	—	—	43.42
2008	Rudy Giuliani	R	Former mayor	—	—	11.71
2016	Donald Trump	R	Business executive	X	X	78.79
2016	Hillary Clinton	D	Former Cabinet member	X	—	72.30
2016	Colin Powell	R	Former Cabinet member	—	—	11.84

NORTH CAROLINA

Basics

State winners (all-time) ....D 28, R 14, DR 9, SD 1, W 3, Tie 1
General match (all-time) 37-18-1 (66.07%)
State winners (Modern Era) .... D 4, R 11
General match (Modern Era) 12-3 (80.00%)
Home-state candidacies 5
Home-state nominees 0
Home-state winners 0

Statewide results since 1856

Year	Winner	PV%	Second	PV%
1856	James Buchanan (D)	56.78%	Millard Fillmore (AW)	43.22%
1860	John Breckinridge (SD)	50.51%	John Bell (CU)	46.66%
1868	Ulysses Grant (R)	53.41%	Horatio Seymour (D)	46.59%
1872	Ulysses Grant (R)	57.38%	Horace Greeley (D-LR)	42.46%
1876	Samuel Tilden (D)	53.62%	Rutherford Hayes (R)	46.38%
1880	Winfield Hancock (D)	51.55%	James Garfield (R)	47.98%
1884	Grover Cleveland (D)	53.25%	James Blaine (R)	46.59%
1888	Grover Cleveland (D)	51.88%	Benjamin Harrison (R)	47.14%
1892	Grover Cleveland (D)	47.44%	Benjamin Harrison (R)	35.80%
1896	William J. Bryan (D-POP)	52.64%	William McKinley (R)	46.82%
1900	William Jennings Bryan (D)	53.92%	William McKinley (R)	45.47%
1904	Alton Parker (D)	59.71%	Theodore Roosevelt (R)	39.67%
1908	William Jennings Bryan (D)	54.22%	William Howard Taft (R)	45.49%
1912	Woodrow Wilson (D)	59.24%	Theodore Roosevelt (P)	28.36%
1916	Woodrow Wilson (D)	58.10%	Charles Evans Hughes (R)	41.71%
1920	James Cox (D)	56.69%	Warren Harding (R)	43.22%
1924	John Davis (D)	59.01%	Calvin Coolidge (R)	39.61%
1928	Herbert Hoover (R)	54.94%	Alfred Smith (D)	45.06%
1932	Franklin Roosevelt (D)	69.93%	Herbert Hoover (R)	29.28%
1936	Franklin Roosevelt (D)	73.40%	Alfred Landon (R)	26.60%
1940	Franklin Roosevelt (D)	74.03%	Wendell Willkie (R)	25.97%
1944	Franklin Roosevelt (D)	66.71%	Thomas Dewey (R)	33.29%
1948	Harry Truman (D)	58.02%	Thomas Dewey (R)	32.68%
1952	Adlai Stevenson (D)	53.91%	Dwight Eisenhower (R)	46.09%
1956	Adlai Stevenson (D)	50.66%	Dwight Eisenhower (R)	49.34%
1960	John Kennedy (D)	52.11%	Richard Nixon (R)	47.89%
1964	Lyndon Johnson (D)	56.15%	Barry Goldwater (R)	43.85%
1968	Richard Nixon (R)	39.51%	George Wallace (AI)	31.26%
1972	Richard Nixon (R)	69.46%	George McGovern (D)	28.89%
1976	Jimmy Carter (D)	55.24%	Gerald Ford (R)	44.19%
1980	Ronald Reagan (R)	49.31%	Jimmy Carter (D)	47.18%
1984	Ronald Reagan (R)	61.90%	Walter Mondale (D)	37.89%
1988	George H.W. Bush (R)	57.97%	Michael Dukakis (D)	41.71%
1992	George H.W. Bush (R)	43.44%	Bill Clinton (D)	42.65%
1996	Bob Dole (R)	48.73%	Bill Clinton (D)	44.04%
2000	George W. Bush (R)	56.03%	Al Gore (D)	43.20%
2004	George W. Bush (R)	56.02%	John Kerry (D)	43.58%

Year	Winner	PV%	Second	PV%
2008	Barack Obama (D)	49.70%	John McCain (R)	49.38%
2012	Mitt Romney (R)	50.39%	Barack Obama (D)	48.35%
2016	Donald Trump (R)	49.83%	Hillary Clinton (D)	46.17%

Home-state qualified candidacies

Year	Candidate	Party	Position	N	W	CS
1796	James Iredell	F	Supreme Court justice	—	—	23.85
1796	Samuel Johnston	F	Former senator	—	—	21.42
1836	Willie Person Mangum	W	Senator	—	—	22.34
2004	John Edwards	D	Senator	—	—	22.22
2008	John Edwards	D	Former senator	—	—	11.63

NORTH DAKOTA

Basics

State winners (all-time) ....D 5, R 26, Tie 1
General match (all-time) 22-9-1 (68.75%)
State winners (Modern Era) ....D 1, R 14
General match (Modern Era) 9-6 (60.00%)
Home-state candidacies 1
Home-state nominees 0
Home-state winners 0

Statewide results since 1856

Year	Winner	PV%	Second	PV%
1892	James Weaver (POP)	49.01%	Benjamin Harrison (R)	48.51%
1896	William McKinley (R)	55.57%	William J. Bryan (D-POP)	43.65%
1900	William McKinley (R)	62.13%	William Jennings Bryan (D)	35.52%
1904	Theodore Roosevelt (R)	74.94%	Alton Parker (D)	20.34%
1908	William Howard Taft (R)	61.02%	William Jennings Bryan (D)	34.79%
1912	Woodrow Wilson (D)	34.17%	Theodore Roosevelt (P)	29.75%
1916	Woodrow Wilson (D)	47.84%	Charles Evans Hughes (R)	46.34%
1920	Warren Harding (R)	77.79%	James Cox (D)	18.19%
1924	Calvin Coolidge (R)	47.69%	Robert La Follette (P)	45.17%
1928	Herbert Hoover (R)	54.79%	Alfred Smith (D)	44.47%
1932	Franklin Roosevelt (D)	69.59%	Herbert Hoover (R)	28.00%
1936	Franklin Roosevelt (D)	59.61%	Alfred Landon (R)	26.58%
1940	Wendell Willkie (R)	55.06%	Franklin Roosevelt (D)	44.18%
1944	Thomas Dewey (R)	53.84%	Franklin Roosevelt (D)	45.48%
1948	Thomas Dewey (R)	52.17%	Harry Truman (D)	43.41%
1952	Dwight Eisenhower (R)	70.97%	Adlai Stevenson (D)	28.39%
1956	Dwight Eisenhower (R)	61.72%	Adlai Stevenson (D)	38.09%
1960	Richard Nixon (R)	55.42%	John Kennedy (D)	44.52%
1964	Lyndon Johnson (D)	57.97%	Barry Goldwater (R)	41.88%
1968	Richard Nixon (R)	55.94%	Hubert Humphrey (D)	38.23%
1972	Richard Nixon (R)	62.07%	George McGovern (D)	35.79%
1976	Gerald Ford (R)	51.64%	Jimmy Carter (D)	45.79%
1980	Ronald Reagan (R)	64.23%	Jimmy Carter (D)	26.26%
1984	Ronald Reagan (R)	64.84%	Walter Mondale (D)	33.80%
1988	George H.W. Bush (R)	56.03%	Michael Dukakis (D)	42.97%
1992	George H.W. Bush (R)	44.22%	Bill Clinton (D)	32.18%
1996	Bob Dole (R)	46.94%	Bill Clinton (D)	40.13%
2000	George W. Bush (R)	60.66%	Al Gore (D)	33.06%
2004	George W. Bush (R)	62.86%	John Kerry (D)	35.50%
2008	John McCain (R)	53.25%	Barack Obama (D)	44.62%
2012	Mitt Romney (R)	58.32%	Barack Obama (D)	38.69%
2016	Donald Trump (R)	62.96%	Hillary Clinton (D)	27.23%

Home-state qualified candidacies

Year	Candidate	Party	Position	N	W	CS
1936	William Lemke	U	Representative	—	—	16.26

OHIO

Basics

State winners (all-time) ....D 15, R 29, DR 7, W 3
General match (all-time) 45-9 (83.33%)
State winners (Modern Era) ....D 6, R 9
General match (Modern Era) 14-1 (93.33%)
Home-state candidacies 34
Home-state nominees 10
Home-state winners 7

Statewide results since 1856

Year	Winner	PV%	Second	PV%
1856	John Fremont (R)	48.49%	James Buchanan (D)	44.20%
1860	Abraham Lincoln (R)	52.32%	Stephen Douglas (D)	42.32%
1864	Abraham Lincoln (R)	56.37%	George McClellan (D)	43.63%
1868	Ulysses Grant (R)	54.02%	Horatio Seymour (D)	45.99%
1872	Ulysses Grant (R)	53.24%	Horace Greeley (D-LR)	46.15%
1876	Rutherford Hayes (R)	50.21%	Samuel Tilden (D)	49.07%
1880	James Garfield (R)	51.73%	Winfield Hancock (D)	47.02%
1884	James Blaine (R)	50.99%	Grover Cleveland (D)	46.94%
1888	Benjamin Harrison (R)	49.57%	Grover Cleveland (D)	47.11%
1892	Benjamin Harrison (R)	47.66%	Grover Cleveland (D)	47.53%
1896	William McKinley (R)	51.86%	William J. Bryan (D-POP)	46.82%
1900	William McKinley (R)	52.30%	William Jennings Bryan (D)	45.66%
1904	Theodore Roosevelt (R)	59.75%	Alton Parker (D)	34.32%
1908	William Howard Taft (R)	51.03%	William Jennings Bryan (D)	44.82%
1912	Woodrow Wilson (D)	40.96%	William Howard Taft (R)	26.82%
1916	Woodrow Wilson (D)	51.86%	Charles Evans Hughes (R)	44.18%
1920	Warren Harding (R)	58.47%	James Cox (D)	38.58%
1924	Calvin Coolidge (R)	58.33%	John Davis (D)	23.70%
1928	Herbert Hoover (R)	64.89%	Alfred Smith (D)	34.45%
1932	Franklin Roosevelt (D)	49.88%	Herbert Hoover (R)	47.03%
1936	Franklin Roosevelt (D)	57.99%	Alfred Landon (R)	37.44%
1940	Franklin Roosevelt (D)	52.20%	Wendell Willkie (R)	47.80%
1944	Thomas Dewey (R)	50.18%	Franklin Roosevelt (D)	49.82%
1948	Harry Truman (D)	49.48%	Thomas Dewey (R)	49.24%
1952	Dwight Eisenhower (R)	56.76%	Adlai Stevenson (D)	43.24%
1956	Dwight Eisenhower (R)	61.11%	Adlai Stevenson (D)	38.89%
1960	Richard Nixon (R)	53.28%	John Kennedy (D)	46.72%
1964	Lyndon Johnson (D)	62.94%	Barry Goldwater (R)	37.06%
1968	Richard Nixon (R)	45.23%	Hubert Humphrey (D)	42.95%
1972	Richard Nixon (R)	59.63%	George McGovern (D)	38.07%
1976	Jimmy Carter (D)	48.92%	Gerald Ford (R)	48.65%
1980	Ronald Reagan (R)	51.51%	Jimmy Carter (D)	40.91%
1984	Ronald Reagan (R)	58.90%	Walter Mondale (D)	40.14%
1988	George H.W. Bush (R)	55.00%	Michael Dukakis (D)	44.15%
1992	Bill Clinton (D)	40.18%	George H.W. Bush (R)	38.35%
1996	Bill Clinton (D)	47.38%	Bob Dole (R)	41.02%
2000	George W. Bush (R)	49.97%	Al Gore (D)	46.46%

Year	Winner	PV%	Second	PV%
2004	George W. Bush (R)	50.81%	John Kerry (D)	48.71%
2008	Barack Obama (D)	51.50%	John McCain (R)	46.91%
2012	Barack Obama (D)	50.67%	Mitt Romney (R)	47.69%
2016	Donald Trump (R)	51.69%	Hillary Clinton (D)	43.56%

Home-state qualified candidacies

Year	Candidate	Party	Position	N	W	CS
1836	William Henry Harrison	W	Former senator	X	—	64.80
1840	William Henry Harrison	W	Former senator	X	X	87.90
1856	John McLean	R	Supreme Court justice	—	—	15.19
1860	Salmon Chase	R	Former governor	—	—	18.38
1868	George Pendleton	D	Former representative	—	—	36.43
1876	Rutherford Hayes	R	Governor	X	X	77.12
1876	William Allen	D	Former governor	—	—	15.83
1880	James Garfield	R	Representative	X	X	79.77
1880	John Sherman	R	Cabinet member	—	—	19.82
1880	Henry Payne	D	Former representative	—	—	18.78
1880	Allen Thurman	D	Senator	—	—	17.43
1884	Allen Thurman	D	Former senator	—	—	18.54
1888	John Sherman	R	Senator	—	—	31.96
1892	William McKinley	R	Governor	—	—	26.05
1896	William McKinley	R	Former governor	X	X	81.24
1896	John R. McLean	D	Journalist	—	—	14.63
1900	William McKinley	R	President	X	X	82.89
1908	William Howard Taft	R	Cabinet member	X	X	83.31
1912	William Howard Taft	R	President	X	—	55.09
1912	Judson Harmon	D	Governor	—	—	20.47
1916	Theodore Burton	R	Former senator	—	—	16.00
1920	Warren Harding	R	Senator	X	X	88.37
1920	James Cox	D	Governor	X	—	64.01
1924	James Cox	D	Former nominee	—	—	15.17
1932	George White	D	Governor	—	—	12.70
1932	Jacob Coxey	R/FL	Mayor	—	—	10.92
1940	Robert Taft	R	Senator	—	—	32.24
1948	Robert Taft	R	Senator	—	—	22.57
1952	Robert Taft	R	Senator	—	—	32.33
1956	Frank Lausche	D	Governor	—	—	11.62
1968	James Rhodes	R	Governor	—	—	16.17
1972	John Ashbrook	R	Representative	—	—	13.02
1984	John Glenn	D	Senator	—	—	12.08
2016	John Kasich	R	Governor	—	—	19.98

OKLAHOMA

Basics

State winners (all-time) .... D 10, R 18
General match (all-time) 20-8 (71.43%)
State winners (Modern Era) .... D 1, R 14
General match (Modern Era) 9-6 (60.00%)
Home-state candidacies 3
Home-state nominees 0
Home-state winners 0

Statewide results since 1856

Year	Winner	PV%	Second	PV%
1908	William Jennings Bryan (D)	48.13%	William Howard Taft (R)	43.45%
1912	Woodrow Wilson (D)	46.96%	William Howard Taft (R)	35.76%
1916	Woodrow Wilson (D)	50.67%	Charles Evans Hughes (R)	33.26%
1920	Warren Harding (R)	50.21%	James Cox (D)	44.50%
1924	John Davis (D)	48.45%	Calvin Coolidge (R)	42.76%
1928	Herbert Hoover (R)	63.72%	Alfred Smith (D)	35.44%
1932	Franklin Roosevelt (D)	73.30%	Herbert Hoover (R)	26.70%
1936	Franklin Roosevelt (D)	66.83%	Alfred Landon (R)	32.69%
1940	Franklin Roosevelt (D)	57.41%	Wendell Willkie (R)	42.23%
1944	Franklin Roosevelt (D)	55.57%	Thomas Dewey (R)	44.20%
1948	Harry Truman (D)	62.75%	Thomas Dewey (R)	37.25%
1952	Dwight Eisenhower (R)	54.59%	Adlai Stevenson (D)	45.41%
1956	Dwight Eisenhower (R)	55.13%	Adlai Stevenson (D)	44.87%
1960	Richard Nixon (R)	59.02%	John Kennedy (D)	40.98%
1964	Lyndon Johnson (D)	55.75%	Barry Goldwater (R)	44.25%
1968	Richard Nixon (R)	47.68%	Hubert Humphrey (D)	31.99%
1972	Richard Nixon (R)	73.70%	George McGovern (D)	24.00%
1976	Gerald Ford (R)	49.96%	Jimmy Carter (D)	48.75%
1980	Ronald Reagan (R)	60.50%	Jimmy Carter (D)	34.97%
1984	Ronald Reagan (R)	68.61%	Walter Mondale (D)	30.67%
1988	George H.W. Bush (R)	57.93%	Michael Dukakis (D)	41.28%
1992	George H.W. Bush (R)	42.65%	Bill Clinton (D)	34.03%
1996	Bob Dole (R)	48.26%	Bill Clinton (D)	40.45%
2000	George W. Bush (R)	60.31%	Al Gore (D)	38.43%
2004	George W. Bush (R)	65.57%	John Kerry (D)	34.43%
2008	John McCain (R)	65.65%	Barack Obama (D)	34.36%
2012	Mitt Romney (R)	66.77%	Barack Obama (D)	33.23%
2016	Donald Trump (R)	65.32%	Hillary Clinton (D)	28.93%

Home-state qualified candidacies

Year	Candidate	Party	Position	N	W	CS
1932	William Murray	D	Governor	—	—	12.73
1952	Robert Kerr	D	Senator	—	—	12.90
1976	Fred Harris	D	Former senator	—	—	10.94

OREGON

Basics

State winners (all-time) ....D 15, R 25
General match (all-time) 29-11 (72.50%)
State winners (Modern Era) ....D 9, R 6
General match (Modern Era) 9-6 (60.00%)
Home-state candidacies 1
Home-state nominees 0
Home-state winners 0

Statewide results since 1856

Year	Winner	PV%	Second	PV%
1860	Abraham Lincoln (R)	36.11%	John Breckinridge (SD)	34.39%
1864	Abraham Lincoln (R)	53.89%	George McClellan (D)	46.09%
1868	Horatio Seymour (D)	50.37%	Ulysses Grant (R)	49.63%
1872	Ulysses Grant (R)	58.78%	Horace Greeley (D-LR)	38.50%
1876	Rutherford Hayes (R)	50.91%	Samuel Tilden (D)	47.39%
1880	James Garfield (R)	50.49%	Winfield Hancock (D)	48.86%
1884	James Blaine (R)	50.96%	Grover Cleveland (D)	46.69%
1888	Benjamin Harrison (R)	53.79%	Grover Cleveland (D)	42.85%
1892	Benjamin Harrison (R)	44.66%	James Weaver (POP)	34.29%
1896	William McKinley (R)	50.03%	William J. Bryan (D-POP)	48.02%
1900	William McKinley (R)	55.25%	William Jennings Bryan (D)	39.64%
1904	Theodore Roosevelt (R)	67.27%	Alton Parker (D)	19.33%
1908	William Howard Taft (R)	56.50%	William Jennings Bryan (D)	34.19%
1912	Woodrow Wilson (D)	34.34%	Theodore Roosevelt (P)	27.44%
1916	Charles Evans Hughes (R)	48.47%	Woodrow Wilson (D)	45.90%
1920	Warren Harding (R)	60.20%	James Cox (D)	33.55%
1924	Calvin Coolidge (R)	51.01%	Robert La Follette (P)	24.47%
1928	Herbert Hoover (R)	64.18%	Alfred Smith (D)	34.14%
1932	Franklin Roosevelt (D)	58.00%	Herbert Hoover (R)	36.89%
1936	Franklin Roosevelt (D)	64.43%	Alfred Landon (R)	29.64%
1940	Franklin Roosevelt (D)	53.70%	Wendell Willkie (R)	45.62%
1944	Franklin Roosevelt (D)	51.78%	Thomas Dewey (R)	46.94%
1948	Thomas Dewey (R)	49.78%	Harry Truman (D)	46.40%
1952	Dwight Eisenhower (R)	60.54%	Adlai Stevenson (D)	38.93%
1956	Dwight Eisenhower (R)	55.21%	Adlai Stevenson (D)	44.72%
1960	Richard Nixon (R)	52.56%	John Kennedy (D)	47.32%
1964	Lyndon Johnson (D)	63.72%	Barry Goldwater (R)	35.96%
1968	Richard Nixon (R)	49.83%	Hubert Humphrey (D)	43.78%
1972	Richard Nixon (R)	52.45%	George McGovern (D)	42.33%
1976	Gerald Ford (R)	47.78%	Jimmy Carter (D)	47.62%
1980	Ronald Reagan (R)	48.33%	Jimmy Carter (D)	38.67%
1984	Ronald Reagan (R)	55.91%	Walter Mondale (D)	43.74%
1988	Michael Dukakis (D)	51.28%	George H.W. Bush (R)	46.61%
1992	Bill Clinton (D)	42.48%	George H.W. Bush (R)	32.53%
1996	Bill Clinton (D)	47.15%	Bob Dole (R)	39.06%
2000	Al Gore (D)	46.96%	George W. Bush (R)	46.52%
2004	John Kerry (D)	51.35%	George W. Bush (R)	47.19%

Year	Winner	PV%	Second	PV%
2008	Barack Obama (D)	56.75%	John McCain (R)	40.40%
2012	Barack Obama (D)	54.24%	Mitt Romney (R)	42.15%
2016	Hillary Clinton (D)	50.07%	Donald Trump (R)	39.09%

Home-state qualified candidacies

Year	Candidate	Party	Position	N	W	CS
1852	Joseph Lane	D	Territorial delegate	—	—	13.59

PENNSYLVANIA

Basics

State winners (all-time) ....D 18, R 26, DR 9, F 2, W 2, Other 1
General match (all-time) 47-11 (81.03%)
State winners (Modern Era) ....D 10, R 5
General match (Modern Era) 12-3 (80.00%)
Home-state candidacies 19
Home-state nominees...2
Home-state winners..1

Statewide results since 1856

Year	Winner	PV%	Second	PV%
1856	James Buchanan (D)	50.07%	John Fremont (R)	32.10%
1860	Abraham Lincoln (R)	56.26%	John Breckinridge (SD)	37.54%
1864	Abraham Lincoln (R)	51.75%	George McClellan (D)	48.25%
1868	Ulysses Grant (R)	52.20%	Horatio Seymour (D)	47.80%
1872	Ulysses Grant (R)	62.25%	Horace Greeley (D-LR)	37.75%
1876	Rutherford Hayes (R)	50.62%	Samuel Tilden (D)	48.25%
1880	James Garfield (R)	50.84%	Winfield Hancock (D)	46.58%
1884	James Blaine (R)	52.73%	Grover Cleveland (D)	43.68%
1888	Benjamin Harrison (R)	52.74%	Grover Cleveland (D)	44.77%
1892	Benjamin Harrison (R)	51.45%	Grover Cleveland (D)	45.09%
1896	William McKinley (R)	60.98%	William J. Bryan (D-POP)	35.76%
1900	William McKinley (R)	60.75%	William Jennings Bryan (D)	36.16%
1904	Theodore Roosevelt (R)	68.00%	Alton Parker (D)	27.33%
1908	William Howard Taft (R)	58.84%	William Jennings Bryan (D)	35.41%
1912	Theodore Roosevelt (P)	36.54%	Woodrow Wilson (D)	32.49%
1916	Charles Evans Hughes (R)	54.26%	Woodrow Wilson (D)	40.22%
1920	Warren Harding (R)	65.81%	James Cox (D)	27.18%
1924	Calvin Coolidge (R)	65.34%	John Davis (D)	19.08%
1928	Herbert Hoover (R)	65.24%	Alfred Smith (D)	33.89%
1932	Herbert Hoover (R)	50.84%	Franklin Roosevelt (D)	45.33%
1936	Franklin Roosevelt (D)	56.88%	Alfred Landon (R)	40.85%
1940	Franklin Roosevelt (D)	53.23%	Wendell Willkie (R)	46.33%
1944	Franklin Roosevelt (D)	51.14%	Thomas Dewey (R)	48.36%
1948	Thomas Dewey (R)	50.92%	Harry Truman (D)	46.92%
1952	Dwight Eisenhower (R)	52.74%	Adlai Stevenson (D)	46.85%
1956	Dwight Eisenhower (R)	56.49%	Adlai Stevenson (D)	43.30%
1960	John Kennedy (D)	51.06%	Richard Nixon (R)	48.74%
1964	Lyndon Johnson (D)	64.92%	Barry Goldwater (R)	34.70%
1968	Hubert Humphrey (D)	47.59%	Richard Nixon (R)	44.02%
1972	Richard Nixon (R)	59.11%	George McGovern (D)	39.13%
1976	Jimmy Carter (D)	50.40%	Gerald Ford (R)	47.73%
1980	Ronald Reagan (R)	49.59%	Jimmy Carter (D)	42.48%
1984	Ronald Reagan (R)	53.34%	Walter Mondale (D)	45.99%
1988	George H.W. Bush (R)	50.71%	Michael Dukakis (D)	48.39%
1992	Bill Clinton (D)	45.15%	George H.W. Bush (R)	36.13%
1996	Bill Clinton (D)	49.17%	Bob Dole (R)	39.97%
2000	Al Gore (D)	50.60%	George W. Bush (R)	46.43%

Year	Winner	PV%	Second	PV%
2004	John Kerry (D)	50.92%	George W. Bush (R)	48.42%
2008	Barack Obama (D)	54.49%	John McCain (R)	44.17%
2012	Barack Obama (D)	51.97%	Mitt Romney (R)	46.59%
2016	Donald Trump (R)	48.18%	Hillary Clinton (D)	47.47%

Home-state qualified candidacies

Year	Candidate	Party	Position	N	W	CS
1848	James Buchanan	D	Cabinet member	—	—	25.17
1852	James Buchanan	D	Former Cabinet member	—	—	35.79
1856	James Buchanan	D	Former Cabinet member	X	X	79.35
1860	Simon Cameron	R	Senator	—	—	18.62
1868	Winfield Hancock	D	General	—	—	18.46
1868	Asa Packer	D	Former representative	—	—	16.55
1876	Winfield Hancock	D	General	—	—	18.14
1876	John Hartranft	R	Governor	—	—	16.15
1880	Winfield Hancock	D	General	X	—	72.24
1884	Samuel Randall	D	Representative	—	—	17.58
1896	Robert Pattison	D	Former governor	—	—	18.30
1896	Matthew Quay	R	Senator	—	—	15.35
1908	Philander Knox	R	Senator	—	—	15.51
1920	Mitchell Palmer	D	Cabinet member	—	—	27.09
1920	William Sproul	R	Governor	—	—	15.09
1940	Arthur James	R	Governor	—	—	14.48
1952	Harold Stassen	R	College president	—	—	13.39
1964	William Scranton	R	Governor	—	—	19.42
2012	Rick Santorum	R	Former senator	—	—	22.25

RHODE ISLAND

Basics

State winners (all-time) ....D 22, R 21, DR 4, F 5, NR 2, W 3
General match (all-time) 40-17 (70.18%)
State winners (Modern Era) ....D 13, R 2
General match (Modern Era) 9-6 (60.00%)
Home-state candidacies 0
Home-state nominees 0
Home-state winners 0

Statewide results since 1856

Year	Winner	PV%	Second	PV%
1856	John Fremont (R)	57.85%	James Buchanan (D)	33.70%
1860	Abraham Lincoln (R)	61.37%	Stephen Douglas (D)	38.63%
1864	Abraham Lincoln (R)	62.21%	George McClellan (D)	37.79%
1868	Ulysses Grant (R)	66.72%	Horatio Seymour (D)	33.28%
1872	Ulysses Grant (R)	71.94%	Horace Greeley (D-LR)	28.06%
1876	Rutherford Hayes (R)	59.58%	Samuel Tilden (D)	40.42%
1880	James Garfield (R)	62.24%	Winfield Hancock (D)	36.87%
1884	James Blaine (R)	58.07%	Grover Cleveland (D)	37.81%
1888	Benjamin Harrison (R)	53.88%	Grover Cleveland (D)	42.99%
1892	Benjamin Harrison (R)	50.71%	Grover Cleveland (D)	45.75%
1896	William McKinley (R)	68.33%	William J. Bryan (D-POP)	26.39%
1900	William McKinley (R)	59.74%	William Jennings Bryan (D)	35.04%
1904	Theodore Roosevelt (R)	60.60%	Alton Parker (D)	36.18%
1908	William Howard Taft (R)	60.76%	William Jennings Bryan (D)	34.16%
1912	Woodrow Wilson (D)	39.04%	William Howard Taft (R)	35.57%
1916	Charles Evans Hughes (R)	51.08%	Woodrow Wilson (D)	46.00%
1920	Warren Harding (R)	63.97%	James Cox (D)	32.78%
1924	Calvin Coolidge (R)	59.63%	John Davis (D)	36.46%
1928	Alfred Smith (D)	50.16%	Herbert Hoover (R)	49.55%
1932	Franklin Roosevelt (D)	55.08%	Herbert Hoover (R)	43.31%
1936	Franklin Roosevelt (D)	52.97%	Alfred Landon (R)	40.30%
1940	Franklin Roosevelt (D)	56.73%	Wendell Willkie (R)	43.17%
1944	Franklin Roosevelt (D)	58.59%	Thomas Dewey (R)	41.26%
1948	Harry Truman (D)	57.59%	Thomas Dewey (R)	41.44%
1952	Dwight Eisenhower (R)	50.89%	Adlai Stevenson (D)	49.05%
1956	Dwight Eisenhower (R)	58.26%	Adlai Stevenson (D)	41.74%
1960	John Kennedy (D)	63.63%	Richard Nixon (R)	36.37%
1964	Lyndon Johnson (D)	80.87%	Barry Goldwater (R)	19.13%
1968	Hubert Humphrey (D)	64.03%	Richard Nixon (R)	31.78%
1972	Richard Nixon (R)	53.00%	George McGovern (D)	46.81%
1976	Jimmy Carter (D)	55.36%	Gerald Ford (R)	44.08%
1980	Jimmy Carter (D)	47.67%	Ronald Reagan (R)	37.20%
1984	Ronald Reagan (R)	51.67%	Walter Mondale (D)	48.02%
1988	Michael Dukakis (D)	55.64%	George H.W. Bush (R)	43.93%
1992	Bill Clinton (D)	47.04%	George H.W. Bush (R)	29.02%
1996	Bill Clinton (D)	59.71%	Bob Dole (R)	26.82%
2000	Al Gore (D)	60.99%	George W. Bush (R)	31.91%

Year	Winner	PV%	Second	PV%
2004	John Kerry (D)	59.42%	George W. Bush (R)	38.67%
2008	Barack Obama (D)	62.86%	John McCain (R)	35.06%
2012	Barack Obama (D)	62.70%	Mitt Romney (R)	35.24%
2016	Hillary Clinton (D)	54.41%	Donald Trump (R)	38.90%

Home-state qualified candidacies

(None)

SOUTH CAROLINA

Basics

State winners (all-time) ....D 26, R 16, DR 8, F 2, SD 1, W 1, Tie 1, Other 2
General match (all-time) 33-23-1 (57.90%)
State winners (Modern Era) .... D 2, R 13
General match (Modern Era) 10-5 (66.67%)
Home-state candidacies 7
Home-state nominees 2
Home-state winners 0

Statewide results since 1856

Year	Winner	PV%	Second	PV%
1868	Ulysses Grant (R)	57.93%	Horatio Seymour (D)	42.07%
1872	Ulysses Grant (R)	75.73%	Horace Greeley (D-LR)	23.78%
1876	Rutherford Hayes (R)	50.24%	Samuel Tilden (D)	49.76%
1880	Winfield Hancock (D)	65.51%	James Garfield (R)	34.13%
1884	Grover Cleveland (D)	75.25%	James Blaine (R)	23.41%
1888	Grover Cleveland (D)	82.28%	Benjamin Harrison (R)	17.17%
1892	Grover Cleveland (D)	77.56%	Benjamin Harrison (R)	18.93%
1896	William J. Bryan (D-POP)	85.30%	William McKinley (R)	13.51%
1900	William Jennings Bryan (D)	93.05%	William McKinley (R)	6.95%
1904	Alton Parker (D)	95.40%	Theodore Roosevelt (R)	4.60%
1908	William Jennings Bryan (D)	93.84%	William Howard Taft (R)	5.94%
1912	Woodrow Wilson (D)	95.94%	Theodore Roosevelt (P)	2.57%
1916	Woodrow Wilson (D)	96.71%	Charles Evans Hughes (R)	2.42%
1920	James Cox (D)	96.05%	Warren Harding (R)	3.91%
1924	John Davis (D)	96.56%	Calvin Coolidge (R)	2.21%
1928	Alfred Smith (D)	91.39%	Herbert Hoover (R)	8.54%
1932	Franklin Roosevelt (D)	98.03%	Herbert Hoover (R)	1.90%
1936	Franklin Roosevelt (D)	98.57%	Alfred Landon (R)	1.43%
1940	Franklin Roosevelt (D)	95.63%	Wendell Willkie (R)	4.37%
1944	Franklin Roosevelt (D)	87.64%	Unpledged slate (D)	7.54%
1948	Strom Thurmond (SRD)	71.97%	Harry Truman (D)	24.14%
1952	Adlai Stevenson (D)	50.72%	Unpledged slate (R)	46.41%
1956	Adlai Stevenson (D)	45.37%	Unpledged slate (D)	29.45%
1960	John Kennedy (D)	51.24%	Richard Nixon (R)	48.76%
1964	Barry Goldwater (R)	58.89%	Lyndon Johnson (D)	41.11%
1968	Richard Nixon (R)	38.09%	George Wallace (AI)	32.30%
1972	Richard Nixon (R)	70.78%	George McGovern (D)	27.72%
1976	Jimmy Carter (D)	56.17%	Gerald Ford (R)	43.13%
1980	Ronald Reagan (R)	49.42%	Jimmy Carter (D)	48.14%
1984	Ronald Reagan (R)	63.55%	Walter Mondale (D)	35.57%
1988	George H.W. Bush (R)	61.51%	Michael Dukakis (D)	37.58%
1992	George H.W. Bush (R)	48.02%	Bill Clinton (D)	39.88%
1996	Bob Dole (R)	49.79%	Bill Clinton (D)	43.96%
2000	George W. Bush (R)	56.84%	Al Gore (D)	40.90%
2004	George W. Bush (R)	57.98%	John Kerry (D)	40.90%

Year	Winner	PV%	Second	PV%
2008	John McCain (R)	53.87%	Barack Obama (D)	44.90%
2012	Mitt Romney (R)	54.56%	Barack Obama (D)	44.09%
2016	Donald Trump (R)	54.94%	Hillary Clinton (D)	40.67%

Home-state qualified candidacies

Year	Candidate	Party	Position	N	W	CS
1789	John Rutledge	F	Former governor	—	—	45.73
1796	Thomas Pinckney	F	Ambassador	—	—	61.70
1796	Charles C. Pinckney	F	Ambassador	—	—	18.98
1800	Charles C. Pinckney	F	Former ambassador	—	—	63.01
1804	Charles C. Pinckney	F	Former ambassador	X	—	59.38
1808	Charles C. Pinckney	F	Former nominee	X	—	66.03
1948	Strom Thurmond	SRD	Governor	—	—	34.75

SOUTH DAKOTA

Basics

State winners (all-time) .... D 4, R 27, Other 1
General match (all-time) 19-13 (59.38%)
State winners (Modern Era) .... D 1, R 14
General match (Modern Era) 9-6 (60.00%)
Home-state candidacies 4
Home-state nominees 1
Home-state winners 0

Statewide results since 1856

Year	Winner	PV%	Second	PV%
1892	Benjamin Harrison (R)	49.48%	James Weaver (POP)	37.64%
1896	William J. Bryan (D-POP)	49.71%	William McKinley (R)	49.48%
1900	William McKinley (R)	56.75%	William Jennings Bryan (D)	41.11%
1904	Theodore Roosevelt (R)	71.09%	Alton Parker (D)	21.67%
1908	William Howard Taft (R)	58.84%	William Jennings Bryan (D)	35.08%
1912	Theodore Roosevelt (P)	50.56%	Woodrow Wilson (D)	42.07%
1916	Charles Evans Hughes (R)	49.80%	Woodrow Wilson (D)	45.91%
1920	Warren Harding (R)	60.74%	James Cox (D)	19.72%
1924	Calvin Coolidge (R)	49.69%	Robert La Follette (P)	36.96%
1928	Herbert Hoover (R)	60.19%	Alfred Smith (D)	39.21%
1932	Franklin Roosevelt (D)	63.62%	Herbert Hoover (R)	34.40%
1936	Franklin Roosevelt (D)	54.02%	Alfred Landon (R)	42.50%
1940	Wendell Willkie (R)	57.41%	Franklin Roosevelt (D)	42.59%
1944	Thomas Dewey (R)	58.33%	Franklin Roosevelt (D)	41.67%
1948	Thomas Dewey (R)	51.84%	Harry Truman (D)	47.04%
1952	Dwight Eisenhower (R)	69.27%	Adlai Stevenson (D)	30.73%
1956	Dwight Eisenhower (R)	58.39%	Adlai Stevenson (D)	41.62%
1960	Richard Nixon (R)	58.21%	John Kennedy (D)	41.79%
1964	Lyndon Johnson (D)	55.61%	Barry Goldwater (R)	44.39%
1968	Richard Nixon (R)	53.27%	Hubert Humphrey (D)	41.96%
1972	Richard Nixon (R)	54.15%	George McGovern (D)	45.52%
1976	Gerald Ford (R)	50.39%	Jimmy Carter (D)	48.91%
1980	Ronald Reagan (R)	60.53%	Jimmy Carter (D)	31.69%
1984	Ronald Reagan (R)	63.00%	Walter Mondale (D)	36.53%
1988	George H.W. Bush (R)	52.85%	Michael Dukakis (D)	46.51%
1992	George H.W. Bush (R)	40.66%	Bill Clinton (D)	37.14%
1996	Bob Dole (R)	46.49%	Bill Clinton (D)	43.03%
2000	George W. Bush (R)	60.30%	Al Gore (D)	37.56%
2004	George W. Bush (R)	59.91%	John Kerry (D)	38.44%
2008	John McCain (R)	53.16%	Barack Obama (D)	44.75%
2012	Mitt Romney (R)	57.89%	Barack Obama (D)	39.87%
2016	Donald Trump (R)	61.53%	Hillary Clinton (D)	31.74%

Home-state qualified candidacies

Year	Candidate	Party	Position	N	W	CS
1968	George McGovern	D	Senator	—	—	12.79
1972	George McGovern	D	Senator	X	—	58.46
1984	George McGovern	D	Former nominee	—	—	11.14
2016	Faith Spotted Eagle	D	Movement leader	—	—	10.62

TENNESSEE

Basics

State winners (all-time) ....D 24, R 16, DR 9, W 5, Other 1
General match (all-time) 37-18 (67.27%)
State winners (Modern Era) ....D 4, R 11
General match (Modern Era) 12-3 (80.00%)
Home-state candidacies 16
Home-state nominees 6
Home-state winners 3

Statewide results since 1856

Year	Winner	PV%	Second	PV%
1856	James Buchanan (D)	52.18%	Millard Fillmore (AW)	47.82%
1860	John Bell (CU)	47.72%	John Breckinridge (SD)	44.56%
1868	Ulysses Grant (R)	68.43%	Horatio Seymour (D)	31.57%
1872	Horace Greeley (D-LR)	52.16%	Ulysses Grant (R)	47.84%
1876	Samuel Tilden (D)	59.79%	Rutherford Hayes (R)	40.21%
1880	Winfield Hancock (D)	53.26%	James Garfield (R)	44.26%
1884	Grover Cleveland (D)	51.45%	James Blaine (R)	47.74%
1888	Grover Cleveland (D)	52.18%	Benjamin Harrison (R)	45.85%
1892	Grover Cleveland (D)	51.36%	Benjamin Harrison (R)	37.83%
1896	William J. Bryan (D-POP)	52.09%	William McKinley (R)	46.33%
1900	William Jennings Bryan (D)	53.03%	William McKinley (R)	44.95%
1904	Alton Parker (D)	54.23%	Theodore Roosevelt (R)	43.40%
1908	William Jennings Bryan (D)	52.73%	William Howard Taft (R)	45.87%
1912	Woodrow Wilson (D)	52.80%	William Howard Taft (R)	24.00%
1916	Woodrow Wilson (D)	56.31%	Charles Evans Hughes (R)	42.70%
1920	Warren Harding (R)	51.22%	James Cox (D)	48.26%
1924	John Davis (D)	52.93%	Calvin Coolidge (R)	43.46%
1928	Herbert Hoover (R)	55.32%	Alfred Smith (D)	44.49%
1932	Franklin Roosevelt (D)	66.49%	Herbert Hoover (R)	32.48%
1936	Franklin Roosevelt (D)	68.78%	Alfred Landon (R)	30.81%
1940	Franklin Roosevelt (D)	67.25%	Wendell Willkie (R)	32.35%
1944	Franklin Roosevelt (D)	60.45%	Thomas Dewey (R)	39.22%
1948	Harry Truman (D)	49.14%	Thomas Dewey (R)	36.87%
1952	Dwight Eisenhower (R)	49.99%	Adlai Stevenson (D)	49.71%
1956	Dwight Eisenhower (R)	49.21%	Adlai Stevenson (D)	48.60%
1960	Richard Nixon (R)	52.92%	John Kennedy (D)	45.78%
1964	Lyndon Johnson (D)	55.51%	Barry Goldwater (R)	44.49%
1968	Richard Nixon (R)	37.85%	George Wallace (AI)	34.02%
1972	Richard Nixon (R)	67.70%	George McGovern (D)	29.75%
1976	Jimmy Carter (D)	55.94%	Gerald Ford (R)	42.94%
1980	Ronald Reagan (R)	48.70%	Jimmy Carter (D)	48.41%
1984	Ronald Reagan (R)	57.84%	Walter Mondale (D)	41.57%
1988	George H.W. Bush (R)	57.89%	Michael Dukakis (D)	41.55%
1992	Bill Clinton (D)	47.09%	George H.W. Bush (R)	42.43%
1996	Bill Clinton (D)	48.00%	Bob Dole (R)	45.59%
2000	George W. Bush (R)	51.15%	Al Gore (D)	47.29%
2004	George W. Bush (R)	56.80%	John Kerry (D)	42.53%

Year	Winner	PV%	Second	PV%
2008	John McCain (R)	56.90%	Barack Obama (D)	41.83%
2012	Mitt Romney (R)	59.48%	Barack Obama (D)	39.08%
2016	Donald Trump (R)	60.72%	Hillary Clinton (D)	34.72%

Home-state qualified candidacies

Year	Candidate	Party	Position	N	W	CS
1824	Andrew Jackson	DR	Senator	X	—	69.65
1828	Andrew Jackson	DR	Former senator	X	X	84.82
1832	Andrew Jackson	D	President	X	X	87.20
1836	Hugh White	W	Senator	X	—	54.62
1844	James Polk	D	Former governor	X	X	81.33
1860	John Bell	CU	Former senator	—	—	46.37
1860	Andrew Johnson	D	Senator	—	—	13.19
1868	Andrew Johnson	D	President	—	—	26.37
1928	Cordell Hull	D	Representative	—	—	12.75
1952	Estes Kefauver	D	Senator	—	—	38.77
1956	Estes Kefauver	D	Senator	—	—	21.72
1980	Howard Baker	R	Senator	—	—	10.51
1988	Al Gore	D	Senator	—	—	18.19
1996	Lamar Alexander	R	Former governor	—	—	11.97
2000	Al Gore	D	Vice president	X	—	74.51
2008	Fred Thompson	R	Former senator	—	—	10.81

TEXAS

Basics

State winners (all-time) ....D 26, R 14, SD 1
General match (all-time) 24-17 (58.54%)
State winners (Modern Era) .... D 4, R 11
General match (Modern Era) 10-5 (66.67%)
Home-state candidacies 21
Home-state nominees...5
Home-state winners...4

Statewide results since 1856

Year	Winner	PV%	Second	PV%
1856	James Buchanan (D)	66.65%	Millard Fillmore (AW)	33.35%
1860	John Breckinridge (SD)	75.50%	John Bell (CU)	24.47%
1872	Horace Greeley (D-LR)	58.49%	Ulysses Grant (R)	41.41%
1876	Samuel Tilden (D)	70.25%	Rutherford Hayes (R)	29.73%
1880	Winfield Hancock (D)	64.81%	James Garfield (R)	23.78%
1884	Grover Cleveland (D)	69.34%	James Blaine (R)	28.59%
1888	Grover Cleveland (D)	65.01%	Benjamin Harrison (R)	25.86%
1892	Grover Cleveland (D)	56.61%	James Weaver (POP)	23.60%
1896	William J. Bryan (D-POP)	51.90%	William McKinley (R)	31.67%
1900	William Jennings Bryan (D)	63.15%	William McKinley (R)	30.91%
1904	Alton Parker (D)	71.53%	Theodore Roosevelt (R)	21.96%
1908	William Jennings Bryan (D)	73.97%	William Howard Taft (R)	22.40%
1912	Woodrow Wilson (D)	72.74%	William Howard Taft (R)	9.41%
1916	Woodrow Wilson (D)	76.92%	Charles Evans Hughes (R)	17.45%
1920	James Cox (D)	59.23%	Warren Harding (R)	23.59%
1924	John Davis (D)	73.57%	Calvin Coolidge (R)	19.91%
1928	Herbert Hoover (R)	51.77%	Alfred Smith (D)	48.10%
1932	Franklin Roosevelt (D)	88.06%	Herbert Hoover (R)	11.35%
1936	Franklin Roosevelt (D)	87.08%	Alfred Landon (R)	12.32%
1940	Franklin Roosevelt (D)	80.69%	Wendell Willkie (R)	19.13%
1944	Franklin Roosevelt (D)	71.42%	Thomas Dewey (R)	16.64%
1948	Harry Truman (D)	65.44%	Thomas Dewey (R)	24.60%
1952	Dwight Eisenhower (R)	53.13%	Adlai Stevenson (D)	46.69%
1956	Dwight Eisenhower (R)	55.27%	Adlai Stevenson (D)	43.98%
1960	John Kennedy (D)	50.52%	Richard Nixon (R)	48.52%
1964	Lyndon Johnson (D)	63.32%	Barry Goldwater (R)	36.49%
1968	Hubert Humphrey (D)	41.14%	Richard Nixon (R)	39.88%
1972	Richard Nixon (R)	66.23%	George McGovern (D)	33.25%
1976	Jimmy Carter (D)	51.14%	Gerald Ford (R)	47.97%
1980	Ronald Reagan (R)	55.28%	Jimmy Carter (D)	41.42%
1984	Ronald Reagan (R)	63.61%	Walter Mondale (D)	36.11%
1988	George H.W. Bush (R)	55.95%	Michael Dukakis (D)	43.35%
1992	George H.W. Bush (R)	40.56%	Bill Clinton (D)	37.08%
1996	Bob Dole (R)	48.76%	Bill Clinton (D)	43.83%
2000	George W. Bush (R)	59.30%	Al Gore (D)	37.98%

Year	Winner	PV%	Second	PV%
2004	George W. Bush (R)	61.09%	John Kerry (D)	38.22%
2008	John McCain (R)	55.45%	Barack Obama (D)	43.68%
2012	Mitt Romney (R)	57.17%	Barack Obama (D)	41.38%
2016	Donald Trump (R)	52.24%	Hillary Clinton (D)	43.24%

Home-state qualified candidacies

Year	Candidate	Party	Position	N	W	CS
1932	John Nance Garner	D	Representative	—	—	16.36
1940	John Nance Garner	D	Vice president	—	—	15.20
1956	Lyndon Johnson	D	Senator	—	—	12.89
1960	Lyndon Johnson	D	Senator	—	—	23.50
1964	Lyndon Johnson	D	President	X	X	93.24
1968	Lyndon Johnson	D	President	—	—	11.53
1980	George H.W. Bush	R	Former ambassador	—	—	24.15
1980	John Connally	R	Former governor	—	—	10.38
1988	George H.W. Bush	R	Vice president	X	X	87.86
1988	Lloyd Bentsen	D	Senator	—	—	10.62
1992	George H.W. Bush	R	President	X	—	66.86
1992	Ross Perot	I	Business executive	—	—	43.78
1996	Ross Perot	REF	Business executive	—	—	36.87
1996	Phil Gramm	R	Senator	—	—	10.30
2000	George W. Bush	R	Governor	X	X	77.21
2004	George W. Bush	R	President	X	X	78.71
2008	Ron Paul	R/TC	Representative	—	—	13.62
2012	Ron Paul	R	Representative	—	—	18.11
2012	Rick Perry	R	Governor	—	—	10.14
2016	Ted Cruz	R	Senator	—	—	28.72
2016	Ron Paul	R	Former representative	—	—	10.62

UTAH

Basics

State winners (all-time) .... D 8, R 23
General match (all-time) 23-8 (74.19%)
State winners (Modern Era) .... D 1, R 14
General match (Modern Era) 9-6 (60.00%)
Home-state candidacies 1
Home-state nominees 0
Home-state winners 0

Statewide results since 1856

Year	Winner	PV%	Second	PV%
1896	William J. Bryan (D-POP)	82.73%	William McKinley (R)	17.27%
1900	William McKinley (R)	50.60%	William Jennings Bryan (D)	48.30%
1904	Theodore Roosevelt (R)	61.45%	Alton Parker (D)	32.88%
1908	William Howard Taft (R)	56.24%	William Jennings Bryan (D)	39.18%
1912	William Howard Taft (R)	37.42%	Woodrow Wilson (D)	32.58%
1916	Woodrow Wilson (D)	58.78%	Charles Evans Hughes (R)	37.82%
1920	Warren Harding (R)	55.93%	James Cox (D)	38.84%
1924	Calvin Coolidge (R)	49.26%	John Davis (D)	29.94%
1928	Herbert Hoover (R)	53.58%	Alfred Smith (D)	45.86%
1932	Franklin Roosevelt (D)	56.52%	Herbert Hoover (R)	41.05%
1936	Franklin Roosevelt (D)	69.34%	Alfred Landon (R)	29.79%
1940	Franklin Roosevelt (D)	62.25%	Wendell Willkie (R)	37.59%
1944	Franklin Roosevelt (D)	60.44%	Thomas Dewey (R)	39.42%
1948	Harry Truman (D)	53.98%	Thomas Dewey (R)	45.02%
1952	Dwight Eisenhower (R)	58.93%	Adlai Stevenson (D)	41.08%
1956	Dwight Eisenhower (R)	64.56%	Adlai Stevenson (D)	35.44%
1960	Richard Nixon (R)	54.81%	John Kennedy (D)	45.17%
1964	Lyndon Johnson (D)	54.71%	Barry Goldwater (R)	45.29%
1968	Richard Nixon (R)	56.50%	Hubert Humphrey (D)	37.08%
1972	Richard Nixon (R)	67.64%	George McGovern (D)	26.39%
1976	Gerald Ford (R)	62.44%	Jimmy Carter (D)	33.65%
1980	Ronald Reagan (R)	72.77%	Jimmy Carter (D)	20.57%
1984	Ronald Reagan (R)	74.50%	Walter Mondale (D)	24.68%
1988	George H.W. Bush (R)	66.22%	Michael Dukakis (D)	32.05%
1992	George H.W. Bush (R)	43.37%	Ross Perot (I)	27.34%
1996	Bob Dole (R)	54.37%	Bill Clinton (D)	33.30%
2000	George W. Bush (R)	66.83%	Al Gore (D)	26.35%
2004	George W. Bush (R)	71.54%	John Kerry (D)	26.00%
2008	John McCain (R)	62.58%	Barack Obama (D)	34.41%
2012	Mitt Romney (R)	72.79%	Barack Obama (D)	24.75%
2016	Donald Trump (R)	45.54%	Hillary Clinton (D)	27.46%

Home-state qualified candidacies

Year	Candidate	Party	Position	N	W	CS
2012	Jon Huntsman	R	Former governor	—	—	10.27

VERMONT

Basics

State winners (all-time) .... D 8, R 33, DR 6, F 3, NR 1, W 5, Other 1
General match (all-time) 36-21 (63.16%)
State winners (Modern Era) .... D 8, R 7
General match (Modern Era) 10-5 (66.67%)
Home-state candidacies 4
Home-state nominees 0
Home-state winners 0

Statewide results since 1856

Year	Winner	PV%	Second	PV%
1856	John Fremont (R)	78.07%	James Buchanan (D)	20.86%
1860	Abraham Lincoln (R)	75.73%	Stephen Douglas (D)	19.37%
1864	Abraham Lincoln (R)	76.10%	George McClellan (D)	23.90%
1868	Ulysses Grant (R)	78.57%	Horatio Seymour (D)	21.43%
1872	Ulysses Grant (R)	78.33%	Horace Greeley (D-LR)	20.63%
1876	Rutherford Hayes (R)	68.40%	Samuel Tilden (D)	31.42%
1880	James Garfield (R)	70.00%	Winfield Hancock (D)	28.14%
1884	James Blaine (R)	66.51%	Grover Cleveland (D)	29.17%
1888	Benjamin Harrison (R)	71.20%	Grover Cleveland (D)	26.45%
1892	Benjamin Harrison (R)	68.10%	Grover Cleveland (D)	29.26%
1896	William McKinley (R)	80.10%	William J. Bryan (D-POP)	15.95%
1900	William McKinley (R)	75.73%	William Jennings Bryan (D)	22.86%
1904	Theodore Roosevelt (R)	77.97%	Alton Parker (D)	18.84%
1908	William Howard Taft (R)	75.08%	William Jennings Bryan (D)	21.82%
1912	William Howard Taft (R)	37.10%	Theodore Roosevelt (P)	35.24%
1916	Charles Evans Hughes (R)	62.43%	Woodrow Wilson (D)	35.22%
1920	Warren Harding (R)	75.82%	James Cox (D)	23.25%
1924	Calvin Coolidge (R)	78.22%	John Davis (D)	15.67%
1928	Herbert Hoover (R)	66.87%	Alfred Smith (D)	32.87%
1932	Herbert Hoover (R)	57.66%	Franklin Roosevelt (D)	41.08%
1936	Alfred Landon (R)	56.39%	Franklin Roosevelt (D)	43.24%
1940	Wendell Willkie (R)	54.78%	Franklin Roosevelt (D)	44.92%
1944	Thomas Dewey (R)	57.06%	Franklin Roosevelt (D)	42.93%
1948	Thomas Dewey (R)	61.54%	Harry Truman (D)	36.92%
1952	Dwight Eisenhower (R)	71.45%	Adlai Stevenson (D)	28.23%
1956	Dwight Eisenhower (R)	72.16%	Adlai Stevenson (D)	27.81%
1960	Richard Nixon (R)	58.65%	John Kennedy (D)	41.35%
1964	Lyndon Johnson (D)	66.30%	Barry Goldwater (R)	33.69%
1968	Richard Nixon (R)	52.75%	Hubert Humphrey (D)	43.53%
1972	Richard Nixon (R)	62.66%	George McGovern (D)	36.47%
1976	Gerald Ford (R)	54.37%	Jimmy Carter (D)	43.12%
1980	Ronald Reagan (R)	44.36%	Jimmy Carter (D)	38.42%
1984	Ronald Reagan (R)	57.92%	Walter Mondale (D)	40.81%
1988	George H.W. Bush (R)	51.10%	Michael Dukakis (D)	47.58%
1992	Bill Clinton (D)	46.11%	George H.W. Bush (R)	30.42%
1996	Bill Clinton (D)	53.35%	Bob Dole (R)	31.09%
2000	Al Gore (D)	50.64%	George W. Bush (R)	40.70%

Year	Winner	PV%	Second	PV%
2004	John Kerry (D)	58.94%	George W. Bush (R)	38.80%
2008	Barack Obama (D)	67.46%	John McCain (R)	30.45%
2012	Barack Obama (D)	66.57%	Mitt Romney (R)	30.97%
2016	Hillary Clinton (D)	56.68%	Donald Trump (R)	30.27%

Home-state qualified candidacies

Year	Candidate	Party	Position	N	W	CS
1880	George Edmunds	R	Senator	—	—	13.59
1884	George Edmunds	R	Senator	—	—	19.02
2004	Howard Dean	D	Former governor	—	—	13.32
2016	Bernie Sanders	D	Senator	—	—	44.15

VIRGINIA

Basics

State winners (all-time) .... D 29, R 15, DR 9, F 1, Tie 1, Other 1
General match (all-time) 36-19-1 (64.29%)
State winners (Modern Era) .... D 4, R 11
General match (Modern Era) 10-5 (66.67%)
Home-state candidacies 21
Home-state nominees 9
Home-state winners 8

Statewide results since 1856

Year	Winner	PV%	Second	PV%
1856	James Buchanan (D)	59.96%	Millard Fillmore (AW)	40.04%
1860	John Bell (CU)	44.63%	John Breckinridge (SD)	44.54%
1872	Ulysses Grant (R)	50.47%	Horace Greeley (D-LR)	49.49%
1876	Samuel Tilden (D)	59.58%	Rutherford Hayes (R)	40.42%
1880	Winfield Hancock (D)	60.49%	James Garfield (R)	39.33%
1884	Grover Cleveland (D)	51.05%	James Blaine (R)	48.90%
1888	Grover Cleveland (D)	49.99%	Benjamin Harrison (R)	49.46%
1892	Grover Cleveland (D)	56.17%	Benjamin Harrison (R)	38.70%
1896	William J. Bryan (D-POP)	52.50%	William McKinley (R)	45.94%
1900	William Jennings Bryan (D)	55.29%	William McKinley (R)	43.82%
1904	Alton Parker (D)	61.84%	Theodore Roosevelt (R)	36.95%
1908	William Jennings Bryan (D)	60.52%	William Howard Taft (R)	38.36%
1912	Woodrow Wilson (D)	65.95%	William Howard Taft (R)	17.00%
1916	Woodrow Wilson (D)	66.77%	Charles Evans Hughes (R)	32.05%
1920	James Cox (D)	61.33%	Warren Harding (R)	37.86%
1924	John Davis (D)	62.48%	Calvin Coolidge (R)	32.79%
1928	Herbert Hoover (R)	53.91%	Alfred Smith (D)	45.90%
1932	Franklin Roosevelt (D)	68.46%	Herbert Hoover (R)	30.09%
1936	Franklin Roosevelt (D)	70.23%	Alfred Landon (R)	29.39%
1940	Franklin Roosevelt (D)	68.08%	Wendell Willkie (R)	31.55%
1944	Franklin Roosevelt (D)	62.36%	Thomas Dewey (R)	37.39%
1948	Harry Truman (D)	47.89%	Thomas Dewey (R)	41.04%
1952	Dwight Eisenhower (R)	56.33%	Adlai Stevenson (D)	43.36%
1956	Dwight Eisenhower (R)	55.37%	Adlai Stevenson (D)	38.36%
1960	Richard Nixon (R)	52.44%	John Kennedy (D)	46.97%
1964	Lyndon Johnson (D)	53.54%	Barry Goldwater (R)	46.18%
1968	Richard Nixon (R)	43.36%	Hubert Humphrey (D)	32.49%
1972	Richard Nixon (R)	67.84%	George McGovern (D)	30.12%
1976	Gerald Ford (R)	49.29%	Jimmy Carter (D)	47.96%
1980	Ronald Reagan (R)	53.03%	Jimmy Carter (D)	40.31%
1984	Ronald Reagan (R)	62.29%	Walter Mondale (D)	37.09%
1988	George H.W. Bush (R)	59.74%	Michael Dukakis (D)	39.23%
1992	George H.W. Bush (R)	44.97%	Bill Clinton (D)	40.59%
1996	Bob Dole (R)	47.11%	Bill Clinton (D)	45.15%
2000	George W. Bush (R)	52.47%	Al Gore (D)	44.44%

Year	Winner	PV%	Second	PV%
2004	George W. Bush (R)	53.68%	John Kerry (D)	45.48%
2008	Barack Obama (D)	52.63%	John McCain (R)	46.33%
2012	Barack Obama (D)	51.16%	Mitt Romney (R)	47.28%
2016	Hillary Clinton (D)	49.73%	Donald Trump (R)	44.41%

Home-state qualified candidacies

Year	Candidate	Party	Position	N	W	CS
1789	George Washington	F	Former general	X	X	96.18
1792	George Washington	F	President	X	X	96.18
1792	Thomas Jefferson	DR	Cabinet member	—	—	26.68
1796	Thomas Jefferson	DR	Former Cabinet member	X	—	74.00
1796	George Washington	F	President	—	—	21.42
1800	Thomas Jefferson	DR	Vice president	X	X	77.84
1804	Thomas Jefferson	DR	President	X	X	93.05
1808	James Madison	DR	Cabinet member	X	X	84.36
1812	James Madison	DR	President	X	X	80.17
1816	James Monroe	DR	Cabinet member	X	X	90.10
1820	James Monroe	DR	President	X	X	96.04
1832	John Floyd	D	Governor	—	—	22.71
1860	Robert Hunter	D	Senator	—	—	21.10
1944	Harry Byrd	D	Senator	—	—	14.55
1960	Harry Byrd	D	Senator	—	—	19.25
1988	Pat Robertson	R	Movement leader	—	—	15.41
1992	Pat Buchanan	R	Journalist	—	—	23.85
1996	Pat Buchanan	R	Journalist	—	—	23.11
1996	Lyndon LaRouche	D	Movement leader	—	—	13.27
2000	Gary Bauer	R	Movement leader	—	—	10.19
2016	Carly Fiorina	R	Business executive	—	—	10.07

WASHINGTON

Basics

State winners (all-time) ....D 17, R 14, Other 1
General match (all-time) 22-10 (68.75%)
State winners (Modern Era) .... D 10, R 5
General match (Modern Era) 8-7 (53.33%)
Home-state candidacies 2
Home-state nominees 0
Home-state winners 0

Statewide results since 1856

Year	Winner	PV%	Second	PV%
1892	Benjamin Harrison (R)	41.45%	Grover Cleveland (D)	33.88%
1896	William J. Bryan (D-POP)	55.28%	William McKinley (R)	41.90%
1900	William McKinley (R)	53.44%	William Jennings Bryan (D)	41.70%
1904	Theodore Roosevelt (R)	69.96%	Alton Parker (D)	19.36%
1908	William Howard Taft (R)	57.78%	William Jennings Bryan (D)	31.80%
1912	Theodore Roosevelt (P)	35.22%	Woodrow Wilson (D)	26.90%
1916	Woodrow Wilson (D)	48.13%	Charles Evans Hughes (R)	43.89%
1920	Warren Harding (R)	55.96%	James Cox (D)	21.14%
1924	Calvin Coolidge (R)	52.24%	Robert La Follette (P)	35.76%
1928	Herbert Hoover (R)	67.06%	Alfred Smith (D)	31.30%
1932	Franklin Roosevelt (D)	57.46%	Herbert Hoover (R)	33.94%
1936	Franklin Roosevelt (D)	66.38%	Alfred Landon (R)	29.88%
1940	Franklin Roosevelt (D)	58.22%	Wendell Willkie (R)	40.58%
1944	Franklin Roosevelt (D)	56.84%	Thomas Dewey (R)	42.24%
1948	Harry Truman (D)	52.61%	Thomas Dewey (R)	42.68%
1952	Dwight Eisenhower (R)	54.33%	Adlai Stevenson (D)	44.69%
1956	Dwight Eisenhower (R)	53.91%	Adlai Stevenson (D)	45.44%
1960	Richard Nixon (R)	50.68%	John Kennedy (D)	48.27%
1964	Lyndon Johnson (D)	61.97%	Barry Goldwater (R)	37.37%
1968	Hubert Humphrey (D)	47.23%	Richard Nixon (R)	45.12%
1972	Richard Nixon (R)	56.92%	George McGovern (D)	38.64%
1976	Gerald Ford (R)	50.00%	Jimmy Carter (D)	46.11%
1980	Ronald Reagan (R)	49.66%	Jimmy Carter (D)	37.32%
1984	Ronald Reagan (R)	55.82%	Walter Mondale (D)	42.86%
1988	Michael Dukakis (D)	50.05%	George H.W. Bush (R)	48.46%
1992	Bill Clinton (D)	43.40%	George H.W. Bush (R)	31.96%
1996	Bill Clinton (D)	49.84%	Bob Dole (R)	37.30%
2000	Al Gore (D)	50.16%	George W. Bush (R)	44.58%
2004	John Kerry (D)	52.82%	George W. Bush (R)	45.64%
2008	Barack Obama (D)	57.65%	John McCain (R)	40.48%
2012	Barack Obama (D)	56.16%	Mitt Romney (R)	41.30%
2016	Hillary Clinton (D)	52.54%	Donald Trump (R)	36.83%

Home-state qualified candidacies

Year	Candidate	Party	Position	N	W	CS
1972	Henry Jackson	D	Senator	—	—	15.37
1976	Henry Jackson	D	Senator	—	—	14.30

WEST VIRGINIA

Basics

State winners (all-time) ....D 20, R 19
General match (all-time) 29-10 (74.36%)
State winners (Modern Era) ....D 8, R 7
General match (Modern Era) 10-5 (66.67%)
Home-state candidacies 2
Home-state nominees...1
Home-state winners..0

Statewide results since 1856

Year	Winner	PV%	Second	PV%
1864	Abraham Lincoln (R)	68.24%	George McClellan (D)	31.76%
1868	Ulysses Grant (R)	58.83%	Horatio Seymour (D)	41.17%
1872	Ulysses Grant (R)	51.74%	Horace Greeley (D-LR)	47.28%
1876	Samuel Tilden (D)	56.75%	Rutherford Hayes (R)	42.15%
1880	Winfield Hancock (D)	50.95%	James Garfield (R)	41.05%
1884	Grover Cleveland (D)	50.94%	James Blaine (R)	47.75%
1888	Grover Cleveland (D)	49.35%	Benjamin Harrison (R)	49.03%
1892	Grover Cleveland (D)	49.37%	Benjamin Harrison (R)	46.93%
1896	William McKinley (R)	52.23%	William J. Bryan (D-POP)	46.83%
1900	William McKinley (R)	54.27%	William Jennings Bryan (D)	44.75%
1904	Theodore Roosevelt (R)	55.26%	Alton Parker (D)	42.03%
1908	William Howard Taft (R)	53.42%	William Jennings Bryan (D)	43.17%
1912	Woodrow Wilson (D)	42.09%	Theodore Roosevelt (P)	29.44%
1916	Charles Evans Hughes (R)	49.41%	Woodrow Wilson (D)	48.47%
1920	Warren Harding (R)	55.30%	James Cox (D)	43.30%
1924	Calvin Coolidge (R)	49.45%	John Davis (D)	44.07%
1928	Herbert Hoover (R)	58.43%	Alfred Smith (D)	41.04%
1932	Franklin Roosevelt (D)	54.47%	Herbert Hoover (R)	44.47%
1936	Franklin Roosevelt (D)	60.56%	Alfred Landon (R)	39.20%
1940	Franklin Roosevelt (D)	57.10%	Wendell Willkie (R)	42.90%
1944	Franklin Roosevelt (D)	54.89%	Thomas Dewey (R)	45.11%
1948	Harry Truman (D)	57.32%	Thomas Dewey (R)	42.24%
1952	Adlai Stevenson (D)	51.92%	Dwight Eisenhower (R)	48.08%
1956	Dwight Eisenhower (R)	54.08%	Adlai Stevenson (D)	45.92%
1960	John Kennedy (D)	52.73%	Richard Nixon (R)	47.27%
1964	Lyndon Johnson (D)	67.94%	Barry Goldwater (R)	32.06%
1968	Hubert Humphrey (D)	49.60%	Richard Nixon (R)	40.78%
1972	Richard Nixon (R)	63.61%	George McGovern (D)	36.39%
1976	Jimmy Carter (D)	58.05%	Gerald Ford (R)	41.91%
1980	Jimmy Carter (D)	49.81%	Ronald Reagan (R)	45.30%
1984	Ronald Reagan (R)	55.11%	Walter Mondale (D)	44.60%
1988	Michael Dukakis (D)	52.20%	George H.W. Bush (R)	47.46%
1992	Bill Clinton (D)	48.41%	George H.W. Bush (R)	35.39%
1996	Bill Clinton (D)	51.51%	Bob Dole (R)	36.76%
2000	George W. Bush (R)	51.92%	Al Gore (D)	45.59%

Year	Winner	PV%	Second	PV%
2004	George W. Bush (R)	56.06%	John Kerry (D)	43.20%
2008	John McCain (R)	55.71%	Barack Obama (D)	42.59%
2012	Mitt Romney (R)	62.30%	Barack Obama (D)	35.54%
2016	Donald Trump (R)	68.50%	Hillary Clinton (D)	26.43%

Home-state qualified candidacies

Year	Candidate	Party	Position	N	W	CS
1920	John Davis	D	Ambassador	—	—	12.87
1924	John Davis	D	Former ambassador	X	—	63.46

WISCONSIN

Basics

State winners (all-time) ....D 17, R 25, Other 1
General match (all-time) 33-10 (76.74%)
State winners (Modern Era) ....D 9, R 6
General match (Modern Era) 11-4 (73.33%)
Home-state candidacies 5
Home-state nominees 0
Home-state winners 0

Statewide results since 1856

Year	Winner	PV%	Second	PV%
1856	John Fremont (R)	55.67%	James Buchanan (D)	43.85%
1860	Abraham Lincoln (R)	56.59%	Stephen Douglas (D)	42.73%
1864	Abraham Lincoln (R)	55.88%	George McClellan (D)	44.12%
1868	Ulysses Grant (R)	56.25%	Horatio Seymour (D)	43.75%
1872	Ulysses Grant (R)	54.62%	Horace Greeley (D-LR)	44.94%
1876	Rutherford Hayes (R)	50.69%	Samuel Tilden (D)	48.07%
1880	James Garfield (R)	54.04%	Winfield Hancock (D)	42.91%
1884	James Blaine (R)	50.39%	Grover Cleveland (D)	45.79%
1888	Benjamin Harrison (R)	49.79%	Grover Cleveland (D)	43.78%
1892	Grover Cleveland (D)	47.74%	Benjamin Harrison (R)	46.06%
1896	William McKinley (R)	59.93%	William J. Bryan (D-POP)	37.00%
1900	William McKinley (R)	60.06%	William Jennings Bryan (D)	35.97%
1904	Theodore Roosevelt (R)	63.21%	Alton Parker (D)	28.01%
1908	William Howard Taft (R)	54.52%	William Jennings Bryan (D)	36.67%
1912	Woodrow Wilson (D)	41.06%	William Howard Taft (R)	32.65%
1916	Charles Evans Hughes (R)	49.39%	Woodrow Wilson (D)	42.80%
1920	Warren Harding (R)	71.10%	James Cox (D)	16.17%
1924	Robert La Follette (P)	53.96%	Calvin Coolidge (R)	37.06%
1928	Herbert Hoover (R)	53.52%	Alfred Smith (D)	44.28%
1932	Franklin Roosevelt (D)	63.46%	Herbert Hoover (R)	31.19%
1936	Franklin Roosevelt (D)	63.80%	Alfred Landon (R)	30.26%
1940	Franklin Roosevelt (D)	50.15%	Wendell Willkie (R)	48.32%
1944	Thomas Dewey (R)	50.37%	Franklin Roosevelt (D)	48.57%
1948	Harry Truman (D)	50.70%	Thomas Dewey (R)	46.28%
1952	Dwight Eisenhower (R)	60.95%	Adlai Stevenson (D)	38.71%
1956	Dwight Eisenhower (R)	61.58%	Adlai Stevenson (D)	37.84%
1960	Richard Nixon (R)	51.77%	John Kennedy (D)	48.05%
1964	Lyndon Johnson (D)	62.09%	Barry Goldwater (R)	37.74%
1968	Richard Nixon (R)	47.89%	Hubert Humphrey (D)	44.27%
1972	Richard Nixon (R)	53.40%	George McGovern (D)	43.73%
1976	Jimmy Carter (D)	49.44%	Gerald Ford (R)	47.76%
1980	Ronald Reagan (R)	47.90%	Jimmy Carter (D)	43.18%
1984	Ronald Reagan (R)	54.19%	Walter Mondale (D)	45.02%
1988	Michael Dukakis (D)	51.41%	George H.W. Bush (R)	47.80%
1992	Bill Clinton (D)	41.13%	George H.W. Bush (R)	36.78%
1996	Bill Clinton (D)	48.81%	Bob Dole (R)	38.48%
2000	Al Gore (D)	47.83%	George W. Bush (R)	47.61%

Year	Winner	PV%	Second	PV%
2004	John Kerry (D)	49.70%	George W. Bush (R)	49.32%
2008	Barack Obama (D)	56.22%	John McCain (R)	42.31%
2012	Barack Obama (D)	52.83%	Mitt Romney (R)	45.89%
2016	Donald Trump (R)	47.22%	Hillary Clinton (D)	46.45%

Home-state qualified candidacies

Year	Candidate	Party	Position	N	W	CS
1868	James Doolittle	D	Senator	—	—	13.27
1912	Robert La Follette	R	Senator	—	—	15.18
1916	Robert La Follette	R	Senator	—	—	12.89
1924	Robert La Follette	R/P	Senator	—	—	46.37
1944	Douglas MacArthur	R	General	—	—	15.89

WYOMING

Basics

State winners (all-time) .... D 8, R 24
General match (all-time) 23-9 (71.88%)
State winners (Modern Era) .... D 1, R 14
General match (Modern Era) 9-6 (60.00%)
Home-state candidacies 0
Home-state nominees 0
Home-state winners 0

Statewide results since 1856

Year	Winner	PV%	Second	PV%
1892	Benjamin Harrison (R)	50.61%	James Weaver (POP)	46.23%
1896	William J. Bryan (D-POP)	49.19%	William McKinley (R)	47.75%
1900	William McKinley (R)	58.61%	William Jennings Bryan (D)	41.14%
1904	Theodore Roosevelt (R)	66.93%	Alton Parker (D)	29.17%
1908	William Howard Taft (R)	55.43%	William Jennings Bryan (D)	39.67%
1912	Woodrow Wilson (D)	36.21%	William Howard Taft (R)	34.44%
1916	Woodrow Wilson (D)	54.67%	Charles Evans Hughes (R)	41.80%
1920	Warren Harding (R)	62.38%	James Cox (D)	30.98%
1924	Calvin Coolidge (R)	52.39%	Robert La Follette (P)	31.51%
1928	Herbert Hoover (R)	63.68%	Alfred Smith (D)	35.37%
1932	Franklin Roosevelt (D)	56.07%	Herbert Hoover (R)	40.82%
1936	Franklin Roosevelt (D)	60.58%	Alfred Landon (R)	37.47%
1940	Franklin Roosevelt (D)	52.82%	Wendell Willkie (R)	46.89%
1944	Thomas Dewey (R)	51.23%	Franklin Roosevelt (D)	48.77%
1948	Harry Truman (D)	51.62%	Thomas Dewey (R)	47.27%
1952	Dwight Eisenhower (R)	62.71%	Adlai Stevenson (D)	37.09%
1956	Dwight Eisenhower (R)	60.08%	Adlai Stevenson (D)	39.92%
1960	Richard Nixon (R)	55.02%	John Kennedy (D)	44.99%
1964	Lyndon Johnson (D)	56.56%	Barry Goldwater (R)	43.44%
1968	Richard Nixon (R)	55.76%	Hubert Humphrey (D)	35.51%
1972	Richard Nixon (R)	69.01%	George McGovern (D)	30.47%
1976	Gerald Ford (R)	59.30%	Jimmy Carter (D)	39.81%
1980	Ronald Reagan (R)	62.64%	Jimmy Carter (D)	27.97%
1984	Ronald Reagan (R)	70.51%	Walter Mondale (D)	28.24%
1988	George H.W. Bush (R)	60.53%	Michael Dukakis (D)	38.01%
1992	George H.W. Bush (R)	39.56%	Bill Clinton (D)	33.98%
1996	Bob Dole (R)	49.81%	Bill Clinton (D)	36.84%
2000	George W. Bush (R)	67.76%	Al Gore (D)	27.70%
2004	George W. Bush (R)	68.86%	John Kerry (D)	29.08%
2008	John McCain (R)	64.78%	Barack Obama (D)	32.54%
2012	Mitt Romney (R)	68.64%	Barack Obama (D)	27.82%
2016	Donald Trump (R)	68.17%	Hillary Clinton (D)	21.88%

Home-state qualified candidacies

(None)

4

RECORDS

This chapter is very much in the spirit of a record book for any sport you might choose. Only the sport here is presidential politics.

You'll find 179 lists of extreme accomplishments — the most, the fewest, the largest, the smallest, the oldest, the youngest — all organized under 12 broad subheadings.

The concepts and statistical categories you'll encounter have been thoroughly explained throughout this book. But a few points deserve emphasis or reiteration:

1. Most lists show the top or bottom 10 performances within a given category. The exceptions are career rankings (which extend to 25 places) and a few general lists (which include every candidate who met the designated criteria).

2. All statistics in this chapter are actual numbers unless otherwise noted. The sole exception is career rankings, where both actual and equalized totals have been listed (and are clearly labeled as such).

3. Career totals encompass all elections in which a given candidate received votes, even if he failed to meet qualification standards in one or more of those years.

4. Listings for single-year performances typically begin with a candidate's name, followed in parentheses by his party and the election year. If two parties are linked by a hyphen, the candidate ran simultaneously on both tickets. If they're separated by a slash, the candidate began the year in one party before switching to the second. These are the party abbreviations:

AI: American Independent
AM: Anti-Masonic
AW: American-Whig

CU: Constitutional Union
D: Democratic
DR: Democratic-Republican
F: Federalist
FL: Farmer-Labor
FS: Free Soil
GBK: Greenback
GRN: Green
I: Independent
LIB: Libertarian
LR: Liberal Republican
LTY: Liberty
NR: National Republican
NU: National Unity
P: Progressive
POP: Populist
PRO: Prohibition
R: Republican
REF: Reform
SD: Southern Democratic
SOC: Socialist
SRD: States' Rights Democratic
TC: Taxpayers and Constitution
U: Union
W: Whig

5. Career listings do not include a candidate's parties or the years in which he ran. You can find that information in the election-by-election statistical profiles in Chapter 1 or the candidate summaries in Chapter 2.

6. Additional explanations are required for several rankings. Look for notes at the bottom of those particular lists.

QUALIFIED CANDIDATES

Most candidates to qualify in an election

1. 1880 15
1. 2016 15
3. 1920 14
4. 1796 13
4. 1988 13
6. 1789 12
6. 1916 12
6. 1972 12
6. 1976 12
10. 1860 11
10. 1876 11
10. 1896 11

Fewest candidates to qualify in an election

1. 1804 2
1. 1812 2
1. 1816 2
1. 1820 2
1. 1828 2
1. 1900 2
7. 1808 3
8. 1824 4
8. 1832 4
8. 1840 4
8. 1944 4

Individuals with five qualified candidacies

James Blaine (R-1876, 1880, 1884, 1888, 1892)
Henry Clay (DR-1824; NR-1832; W-1840, 1844, 1848)

Individuals with four qualified candidacies

John Adams (F-1789, 1792, 1796, 1800)
George Clinton (DR-1789, 1792, 1796, 1808)
Eugene Debs (SOC-1904, 1908, 1912, 1920)
Ulysses Grant (R-1864, 1868, 1872, 1880)
Thomas Hendricks (D-1872, 1876, 1880, 1884)
Hubert Humphrey (D-1960, 1968, 1972, 1976)
Thomas Jefferson (DR-1792, 1796, 1800, 1804)
Lyndon Johnson (D-1956, 1960, 1964, 1968)
Richard Nixon (R-1960, 1964, 1968, 1972)
Charles Cotesworth Pinckney (F-1796, 1800, 1804, 1808)
Ronald Reagan (R-1968, 1976, 1980, 1984)
Franklin Roosevelt (D-1932, 1936, 1940, 1944)
Alfred Smith (D-1920, 1924, 1928, 1932)
Martin Van Buren (D-1836, 1840, 1844; FS-1848)
George Wallace (D-1964; D/AI-1968; D-1972, 1976)

Individuals with three qualified candidacies

John Quincy Adams (DR-1820, 1824; NR-1828)
Thomas Bayard (D-1876, 1880, 1884)
Jerry Brown (D-1976, 1980, 1992)
William Jennings Bryan (D-POP-1896; D-1900, 1908)
James Buchanan (D-1848, 1852, 1856)
Aaron Burr (DR-1792, 1796, 1800)
George H.W. Bush (R-1980, 1988, 1992)
Lewis Cass (D-1844, 1848, 1852)
Grover Cleveland (D-1884, 1888, 1892)
Thomas Dewey (R-1940, 1944, 1948)
Stephen Douglas (D-1852, 1856, 1860)
Winfield Hancock (D-1868, 1876, 1880)
Herbert Hoover (R-1920, 1928, 1932)
Andrew Jackson (DR-1824, 1828; D-1832)
John Jay (F-1789, 1796, 1800)
Robert La Follette (R-1912, 1916; R/P-1924)
George McGovern (D-1968, 1972, 1984)
William McKinley (R-1892, 1896, 1900)
Ron Paul (R/TC-2008; R-2012, 2016)
Theodore Roosevelt (R-1904; R/P-1912; R-1916)
Winfield Scott (W-1840, 1848, 1852)
Adlai Stevenson (D-1952, 1956, 1960)
Robert Taft (R-1940, 1948, 1952)
George Washington (F-1789, 1792, 1796)
Daniel Webster (W-1836, 1848, 1852)

Qualified candidacies by home-state candidates

1. New York...75
2. Ohio...34
3. Illinois..29
4. California...24
4. Massachusetts..24
6. Texas...21
6. Virginia..21
8. Indiana...19
8. Pennsylvania...19
10. Tennessee..16
11. New Jersey...13
12. Kentucky..12
13. Georgia..11
14. Missouri...10
15. Michigan..9
15. Minnesota..9
17. Iowa...8
17. Maryland..8
19. Alabama...7
19. Maine...7
19. South Carolina...7
22. Connecticut..6
23. Arizona...5
23. Arkansas...5

23. Delaware 5
23. Nebraska 5
23. New Hampshire 5
23. North Carolina...5
23. Wisconsin 5
30. Kansas 4
30. South Dakota 4
30. Vermont 4
33. Florida 3
33. Oklahoma 3
35. Colorado..2
35. Idaho..2
35. Montana 2
35. New Mexico..2
35. Washington 2
35. West Virginia 2
41. Louisiana 1
41. Mississippi..1
41. North Dakota 1
41. Oregon 1
41. Utah 1

NOTE: A home state is the place where an individual maintains a voting address during his or her presidential candidacy. Individuals with two or more qualified candidacies are counted multiple times above.

States that have never been home to a qualified candidate

Alaska
District of Columbia
Hawaii
Nevada
Rhode Island
Wyoming

Youngest average ages of qualified candidates

1. 1900 (2 candidates)...49.19
2. 1864 (5 candidates)...49.53
3. 1792 (5 candidates)...51.45
4. 1904 (5 candidates)...51.81
5. 1789 (12 candidates) 52.65
5. 1812 (2 candidates)...52.65
7. 1868 (10 candidates) 53.16
7. 1876 (11 candidates) 53.16
9. 1964 (7 candidates)...53.56
10. 1824 (4 candidates) 53.80

NOTE: All ages are as of November 1 of the given year, which also applies to the next three lists.

Oldest average ages of qualified candidates

1. 1848 (8 candidates)...64.13
1. 2016 (15 candidates) 64.13
3. 1808 (3 candidates)...63.19
4. 1928 (10 candidates) 62.11

5. 2008 (10 candidates) 61.54
6. 1828 (2 candidates) 61.47
7. 2012 (8 candidates) 61.22
8. 1840 (4 candidates) 60.89
9. 1804 (2 candidates) 60.12
10. 1816 (2 candidates) 60.06

Youngest qualified candidates

1. William Jennings Bryan (D-POP-1896) 36.62
2. Aaron Burr (DR-1792) 36.73
3. George McClellan (D-1864) 37.91
4. Jerry Brown (D-1976) 38.57
5. Thomas Dewey (R-1940) 38.61
6. Stephen Douglas (D-1852) 39.52
7. John Breckinridge (D/SD-1860) 39.79
8. Al Gore (D-1988) 40.59
9. William Jennings Bryan (D-1900) 40.62
10. Aaron Burr (DR-1796) 40.73

Oldest qualified candidates

1. Ron Paul (R-2016) 81.20
2. Colin Powell (R-2016) 79.57
3. Jacob Coxey (R/FL-1932) 78.54
4. Ron Paul (R-2012) 77.20
5. Bernie Sanders (D-2016) 75.15
6. Alben Barkley (D-1952) 74.94
7. Lyndon LaRouche (D-1996) 74.15
8. Samuel Adams (DR-1796) 74.10
9. Ronald Reagan (R-1984) 73.73
10. Harry Byrd (D-1960) 73.39

NOMINATIONS

Major-party nominations by home-state candidates

1. New York 26
2. Ohio 10
3. Illinois 9
3. Massachusetts 9
3. Virginia 9
6. California 7
7. Tennessee 6
8. Texas 5
9. New Jersey 4
10. Kentucky 3
10. Nebraska 3
12. Arizona 2
12. Arkansas 2
12. Georgia 2
12. Indiana 2
12. Kansas 2
12. Michigan 2
12. Minnesota 2
12. Pennsylvania 2
12. South Carolina 2
21. Louisiana 1
21. Maine 1
21. Missouri 1
21. New Hampshire 1
21. South Dakota 1
21. West Virginia 1

NOTE: A home state is the place where an individual maintains a voting address during his or her presidential candidacy. Individuals with two or more major-party nominations are counted multiple times above.

Nominees from the smallest states (electoral votes)

1. John Fremont (R-1856, California) 4
1. George McGovern (D-1972, South Dakota) 4
3. Lewis Cass (D-1848, Michigan) 5
3. Franklin Pierce (D-1852, New Hampshire) 5
3. Barry Goldwater (R-1964, Arizona) 5
6. Zachary Taylor (W-1848, Louisiana) 6
6. James Blaine (R-1884, Maine) 6
6. Bill Clinton (D-1992, Arkansas) 6
6. Bill Clinton (D-1996, Arkansas) 6
6. Bob Dole (R-1996, Kansas) 6

NOTE: Home states are ranked by the number of electoral votes they cast in a given election, which also applies to the next list.

Nominees from the largest states (electoral votes)

1. Franklin Roosevelt (D-1932, New York)..47
1. Franklin Roosevelt (D-1936, New York)..47
1. Franklin Roosevelt (D-1940, New York)..47
1. Wendell Willkie (R-1940, New York)..47
1. Franklin Roosevelt (D-1944, New York)..47
1. Thomas Dewey (R-1944, New York)..47
1. Thomas Dewey (R-1948, New York)..47
1. Ronald Reagan (R-1984, California)..47
9. Charles Evans Hughes (R-1916, New York) 45
9. Alfred Smith (D-1928, New York) 45
9. Dwight Eisenhower (R-1952, New York)..45
9. Dwight Eisenhower (R-1956, New York)..45
9. Richard Nixon (R-1972, California)..45
9. Ronald Reagan (R-1980, California)...45

Nominees from the smallest states (share of electoral votes)

1. George McGovern (D-1972, South Dakota) 0.74%
2. Barry Goldwater (R-1964, Arizona) 0.93%
3. Bill Clinton (D-1992, Arkansas) 1.12%
3. Bill Clinton (D-1996, Arkansas) 1.12%
3. Bob Dole (R-1996, Kansas)...1.12%
6. John Fremont (R-1856, California)..1.35%
7. James Blaine (R-1884, Maine)..1.50%
8. John Davis (D-1924, West Virginia)...1.51%
9. William Jennings Bryan (D-1908, Nebraska) 1.66%
10. Franklin Pierce (D-1852, New Hampshire) 1.69%

NOTE: Home states are ranked by the share of the nation's electoral votes that they cast in a given election, which also applies to the next list.

Nominees from the largest states (share of electoral votes)

1. George Washington (F-1792, Virginia) 15.91%
2. Thomas Jefferson (DR-1796, Virginia)..................................15.22%
2. Thomas Jefferson (DR-1800, Virginia)..................................15.22%
4. George Washington (F-1789, Virginia) 14.49%
5. Martin Van Buren (D-1836, New York)..................................14.29%
5. Martin Van Buren (D-1840, New York)..................................14.29%
7. James Madison (DR-1808, Virginia).......................................13.71%
8. Thomas Jefferson (DR-1804, Virginia)..................................13.64%
9. DeWitt Clinton (F-DR-1812, New York) 13.36%
9. Rufus King (F-1816, New York) 13.36%

Youngest average ages of major-party nominees

1. 1896..45.19
2. 1960..45.62
3. 1860..46.35
4. 1864..46.82
5. 1900..49.19
6. 1904..49.24

7. 1908..49.87
8. 1884..51.19
9. 1924..51.94
10. 1936..51.95

NOTE: All ages are as of November 1 of the given election year, which also applies to the remaining lists in this section.

Oldest average ages of major-party nominees

1. 2016..69.70
2. 1984..65.28
3. 1848..65.00
4. 1980..62.91
5. 1840..62.82
6. 1820..62.51
7. 1996..61.74
8. 1828..61.47
9. 1956..61.39
10. 1800..61.28

Youngest major-party nominees

1. William Jennings Bryan (D-1896)...............................36.62
2. George McClellan (D-1864)...37.91
3. John Breckinridge (SD-1860)......................................39.79
4. William Jennings Bryan (D-1900)...............................40.62
5. Thomas Dewey (R-1944)..42.61
6. John Kennedy (D-1960)...43.43
7. DeWitt Clinton (F-1812)..43.67
8. John Fremont (R-1856)..43.78
9. Theodore Roosevelt (R-1904).....................................46.01
10. Bill Clinton (D-1992)...46.20

Oldest major-party nominees

1. Ronald Reagan (R-1984)..73.73
2. Bob Dole (R-1996)...73.28
3. John McCain (R-2008)..72.17
4. Donald Trump (R-2016)..70.38
5. Ronald Reagan (R-1980)..69.73
6. Hillary Clinton (D-2016)..69.02
7. George H.W. Bush (R-1992)...68.39
8. William Henry Harrison (W-1840)...............................67.73
9. Henry Clay (W-1844)...67.55
10. Winfield Scott (W-1852)..66.39

Largest age gaps between major-party nominees

1. 2008 (John McCain-Barack Obama)............................24.93
2. 1996 (Bob Dole-Bill Clinton)......................................23.08
3. 1992 (George H.W. Bush-Bill Clinton)........................22.19
4. 1856 (James Buchanan-John Fremont).......................21.75
5. 1944 (Franklin Roosevelt-Thomas Dewey)..................20.15
6. 1844 (Henry Clay-James Polk).....................................18.56

7. 1852 (Winfield Scott-Franklin Pierce) 18.45
8. 1812 (James Madison-DeWitt Clinton) 17.96
9. 1948 (Harry Truman-Thomas Dewey) 17.88
10. 1864 (Abraham Lincoln-George McClellan) 17.81

NOTE: The older nominee is listed first. The age gap is expressed in years. (Ages beyond two decimal points have been used in these calculations, which means a few gaps differ by 0.01 from results that would be obtained by using the published ages for candidates.) This note also applies to the next list.

Smallest age gaps between major-party nominees

1. 1824 (Andrew Jackson-John Quincy Adams) 0.32
1. 1828 (Andrew Jackson-John Quincy Adams) 0.32
3. 1964 (Lyndon Johnson-Barry Goldwater) 0.35
4. 1928 (Alfred Smith-Herbert Hoover) 0.61
5. 1836 (William Henry Harrison-Hugh White) 0.72
5. 1912 (Woodrow Wilson-William Howard Taft) 0.72
7. 1924 (Calvin Coolidge-John Davis) 0.78
8. 2016 (Donald Trump-Hillary Clinton) 1.37
9. 1968 (Hubert Humphrey-Richard Nixon) 1.62
10. 2000 (George W. Bush-Al Gore) 1.73

NOTE: There were three major-party nominees in 1836. The gap between the two oldest nominees is shown.

PRIMARIES

Most primary elections held by one party in a year

1. 2000 Republican 43
2. 1996 Republican 42
3. 2008 Republican 41
4. 1992 Democratic 40
4. 2000 Democratic 40
4. 2008 Democratic 40
7. 2012 Republican 39
7. 2016 Democratic 39
9. 1992 Republican 38
9. 2016 Republican 38

NOTE: Lists in this section encompass Democratic and Republican primaries since 1912 in the 50 states and the District of Columbia, but not in Puerto Rico or other territories.

Most votes cast in one party's primaries in a year

1. 2008 Democratic 36,848,204
2. 2016 Democratic 30,830,749
3. 2016 Republican 30,192,856
4. 1988 Democratic 22,961,936
5. 2008 Republican 20,790,899
6. 2000 Republican 20,624,401
7. 1992 Democratic 20,304,046
8. 2012 Republican 18,770,036
9. 1980 Democratic 18,746,379
10. 1984 Democratic 18,009,192

Most primary wins in a career

1. George H.W. Bush 78
2. Bill Clinton 65
2. Ronald Reagan 65
4. George W. Bush 63
5. Barack Obama 51
6. Hillary Clinton 48
7. Al Gore 44
8. Jimmy Carter 40
8. Bob Dole 40
8. John McCain 40
11. Richard Nixon 38
12. Franklin Roosevelt 35
13. Mitt Romney 34
14. John Kerry 33
14. Donald Trump 33
16. Woodrow Wilson 25
17. Michael Dukakis 22
18. Estes Kefauver 21
19. Dwight Eisenhower 20
20. Gerald Ford 16

Most primary votes (actual) in a career

Most primary votes (equalized) in a career

19. William Gibbs McAdoo 7,292,693
20. Thomas Dewey 7,278,548
21. Calvin Coolidge 6,869,141
22. Harry Truman 6,518,419
23. John Kerry 6,105,491
24. Hiram Johnson 5,889,635
25. Theodore Roosevelt 5,567,036

Most primary wins in a year

1. Bob Dole (R-1996) 39
1. Al Gore (D-2000) 39
3. George H.W. Bush (R-1992) 38
4. George W. Bush (R-2000) 36
5. George H.W. Bush (R-1988) 35
6. Bill Clinton (D-1996) 34
7. John Kerry (D-2004) 33
7. John McCain (R-2008) 33
7. Donald Trump (R-2016) 33
10. Bill Clinton (D-1992) 31
10. Mitt Romney (R-2012) 31

Most primary votes in a year

1. Hillary Clinton (D-2008) 17,714,951
2. Barack Obama (D-2008) 17,423,182
3. Hillary Clinton (D-2016) 17,119,048
4. Donald Trump (R-2016) 13,757,263
5. Bernie Sanders (D-2016) 13,209,430
6. George W. Bush (R-2000) 12,390,575
7. Al Gore (D-2000) 11,081,274
8. Bill Clinton (D-1992) 10,503,503
9. Mitt Romney (R-2012) 9,841,300
10. Michael Dukakis (D-1988) 9,817,185

Largest percentages of primary votes in a year

1. Woodrow Wilson (D-1916) 98.78%
2. Ronald Reagan (R-1984) 98.62%
3. George W. Bush (R-2004) 98.04%
4. Franklin Roosevelt (D-1936) 92.92%
5. Barack Obama (D-2012) 91.40%
6. Richard Nixon (R-1960) 89.85%
7. Bill Clinton (D-1996) 88.57%
8. Richard Nixon (R-1972) 86.92%
9. Dwight Eisenhower (R-1956) 85.93%
10. Al Gore (D-2000) 75.56%

Fewest primary wins by major-party nominees

1. John Davis (D-1924) 0
1. Wendell Willkie (R-1940) 0
1. Adlai Stevenson (D-1952) 0
1. Hubert Humphrey (D-1968) 0
5. William Howard Taft (R-1912) 1
5. Warren Harding (R-1920) 1

5. James Cox (D-1920) 1
8. Charles Evans Hughes (R-1916) 2
8. Herbert Hoover (R-1932)..2
8. Alfred Landon (R-1936) 2
8. Thomas Dewey (R-1948) 2

Smallest percentages of primary votes by major-party nominees

1. John Davis (D-1924)..0.00%
2. Wendell Willkie (R-1940) 0.66%
3. Adlai Stevenson (D-1952)...1.60%
4. Hubert Humphrey (D-1968) 2.21%
5. Charles Evans Hughes (R-1916)..4.20%
6. Warren Harding (R-1920) 4.54%
7. Thomas Dewey (R-1948) 11.47%
8. Thomas Dewey (R-1944) 11.57%
9. James Cox (D-1920) 15.08%
10. Lyndon Johnson (D-1964)... 17.72%

Most primary wins by someone not nominated

1. Hillary Clinton (D-2008)... 19
2. Gary Hart (D-1984) 16
3. Estes Kefauver (D-1952) 12
4. Ronald Reagan (R-1976).. 10
4. Edward Kennedy (D-1980) 10
4. Bernie Sanders (D-2016) 10
7. Theodore Roosevelt (R-1912)..9
7. William Gibbs McAdoo (D-1924)..9
7. Estes Kefauver (D-1956) 9
10. Leonard Wood (R-1920) 8

Largest percentages of primary votes by someone not nominated

1. Estes Kefauver (D-1952) 64.32%
2. William Gibbs McAdoo (D-1924)..59.79%
3. Theodore Roosevelt (R-1912) 51.51%
4. Thomas Dewey (R-1940) 49.75%
5. Joseph France (R-1932) 48.49%
6. Hillary Clinton (D-2008)..48.08%
7. Ronald Reagan (R-1976)..45.87%
8. William Borah (R-1936) 44.41%
9. Bernie Sanders (D-2016) 42.85%
10. Champ Clark (D-1912) 41.60%

CONVENTIONS

Most delegates at a major-party convention

1. 2012 Democratic..5,552
2. 2016 Democratic..4,762
3. 2008 Democratic..4,419
4. 2000 Democratic..4,339
5. 2004 Democratic..4,322
6. 1996 Democratic..4,289
7. 1992 Democratic..4,288
8. 1988 Democratic..4,161
9. 1984 Democratic..3,933
10. 1980 Democratic..3,331

NOTE: Lists in this section encompass conventions since 1832 of the Democratic, National Republican, Republican, and Whig parties, but not of minor parties.

Fewest delegates at a major-party convention

1. 1832 National Republican 168
2. 1864 Democratic...226
3. 1840 Democratic...244
4. 1840 Whig 254
5. 1836 Democratic...265
6. 1844 Democratic...266
7. 1844 Whig 275
8. 1848 Whig 280
9. 1832 Democratic...283
10. 1852 Democratic...288

Most first-ballot convention votes (actual) in a career

1. Barack Obama...8,613
2. Bill Clinton 7,649
3. Ronald Reagan 5,424
4. George W. Bush 4,574
5. George H.W. Bush 4,456
6. Jimmy Carter 4,362
7. Al Gore..4,340
8. John Kerry 4,253
9. Hillary Clinton 3,853
10. Franklin Roosevelt 3,799
11. Richard Nixon 3,360
12. Michael Dukakis 2,876
13. Lyndon Johnson 2,807
14. John McCain 2,341
15. Walter Mondale...2,193
16. Dwight Eisenhower 2,168
17. Mitt Romney 2,063
18. Herbert Hoover 1,986
19. William Jennings Bryan 1,964
20. Bob Dole..1,928

21. Hubert Humphrey 1,903
22. George McGovern... 1,879
23. Bernie Sanders 1,865
24. Thomas Dewey.. 1,850
25. Grover Cleveland.. 1,831

NOTE: Fractional totals have been rounded to the nearest whole number, which also applies to the remaining lists in this section.

Most first-ballot Democratic convention votes (actual) in a career

1. Barack Obama... 8,613
2. Bill Clinton 7,649
3. Jimmy Carter 4,362
4. Al Gore... 4,340
5. John Kerry 4,253
6. Hillary Clinton 3,853
7. Franklin Roosevelt... 3,799
8. Michael Dukakis.. 2,876
9. Lyndon Johnson 2,807
10. Walter Mondale.. 2,193

Most first-ballot Republican convention votes (actual) in a career

1. Ronald Reagan 5,424
2. George W. Bush 4,574
3. George H.W. Bush.. 4,456
4. Richard Nixon.. 3,360
5. John McCain... 2,341
6. Dwight Eisenhower 2,168
7. Mitt Romney... 2,063
8. Herbert Hoover 1,986
9. Bob Dole 1,928
10. Thomas Dewey... 1,850

Most first-ballot convention votes (equalized) in a career

1. Franklin Roosevelt.. 3,360
2. Henry Clay.. 2,746
3. Ronald Reagan 2,582
4. Martin Van Buren... 2,549
5. Richard Nixon.. 2,510
6. Ulysses Grant... 2,444
7. Grover Cleveland... 2,156
8. William Jennings Bryan 2,036
9. George W. Bush 2,000
10. George H.W. Bush.. 1,987
11. William McKinley.. 1,919
12. Bill Clinton... 1,783
13. Herbert Hoover 1,768
14. Thomas Dewey... 1,754
15. Dwight Eisenhower 1,701
16. Barack Obama 1,699
17. James Blaine 1,404
18. Jimmy Carter.. 1,381
19. Lyndon Johnson 1,327

20. Woodrow Wilson 1,296
21. Alfred Smith 1,266
22. William Howard Taft 1,246
23. Abraham Lincoln 1,171
24. Theodore Roosevelt 1,168
25. Lewis Cass 1,163

Most last-ballot convention votes (actual) in a career

1. Thomas Dewey 1,105
2. Woodrow Wilson 990
3. Charles Evans Hughes 950
4. Franklin Roosevelt 945
5. James Blaine 939
6. John Davis 896
7. Winfield Hancock 763
8. James Cox 701
9. Grover Cleveland 683
10. Wendell Willkie 655
11. William Jennings Bryan 652
12. Warren Harding 645
13. Adlai Stevenson 618
14. Benjamin Harrison 544
15. Samuel Tilden 536
16. James Garfield 399
17. Rutherford Hayes 384
18. Abraham Lincoln 340
19. James Buchanan 329
20. Robert Taft 318
21. Horatio Seymour 317
22. Ulysses Grant 306
23. William Gibbs McAdoo 282
24. Franklin Pierce 279
25. Estes Kefauver 276

NOTE: *Last-ballot votes are the votes cast on the deciding ballot of a multi-ballot convention. Single-ballot conventions are not included. This note also applies to the next list.*

Most last-ballot convention votes (equalized) in a career

1. James Blaine 1,186
2. James Buchanan 1,114
3. Winfield Hancock 1,034
4. Thomas Dewey 1,011
5. Horatio Seymour 1,000
6. Franklin Pierce 969
7. Charles Evans Hughes 962
8. Woodrow Wilson 905
9. James Polk 868
10. Grover Cleveland 833
11. Winfield Scott 825
12. Franklin Roosevelt 819
13. John Davis 817
14. Lewis Cass 733

15. Abraham Lincoln...730
16. Samuel Tilden...726
17. William Jennings Bryan...701
18. Warren Harding..655
18. Wendell Willkie..655
20. Benjamin Harrison..654
21. James Cox...640
22. Stephen Douglas..636
23. Zachary Taylor...611
24. William Henry Harrison..583
25. James Garfield...528

Most ballots needed to achieve a nomination

1. John Davis (D-1924)...103
2. Stephen Douglas (D-1860)...59
3. Winfield Scott (W-1852)...53
4. Franklin Pierce (D-1852)..49
5. Woodrow Wilson (D-1912)...46
6. James Cox (D-1920)...44
7. James Garfield (R-1880)...36
8. Horatio Seymour (D-1868)...22
9. James Buchanan (D-1856)...17
10. Warren Harding (R-1920)...10

Unanimous victories at a major-party convention

Andrew Jackson (D-1832)
Martin Van Buren (D-1836)
Martin Van Buren (D-1840)
Henry Clay (W-1844)
*James Buchanan (D-1856)
*Horatio Seymour (D-1868)
Ulysses Grant (R-1868)
Ulysses Grant (R-1872)
Grover Cleveland (D-1888)
William Jennings Bryan (D-1900)
William McKinley (R-1900)
Theodore Roosevelt (R-1904)
Woodrow Wilson (D-1916)
Franklin Roosevelt (D-1936)
*Thomas Dewey (R-1948)
Dwight Eisenhower (R-1956)
Lyndon Johnson (D-1964)
George H.W. Bush (R-1988)
Al Gore (D-2000)
George W. Bush (R-2000)

NOTE: An asterisk indicates a unanimous victory on the last ballot of a multi-ballot convention; all others were on the first ballot.

Smallest margins of victory at a convention

1. Rutherford Hayes-James Blaine (R-1876)..4.37
2. Gerald Ford-Ronald Reagan (R-1976)..5.18
3. James Garfield-Ulysses Grant (R-1880)..12.30
4. Winfield Scott-Millard Fillmore (W-1852)..15.88
5. Hillary Clinton-Bernie Sanders (D-2016)..20.52
6. William Henry Harrison-Henry Clay (W-1840)..............................22.84
7. Walter Mondale-Gary Hart (D-1984)...25.18
8. John Kennedy-Lyndon Johnson (D-1960)..26.10
9. Adlai Stevenson-Estes Kefauver (D-1952)..27.81
10. Jimmy Carter-Edward Kennedy (D-1980).......................................29.20

NOTE: The nominee is listed first. The margin of victory is expressed in percentage points, showing the difference between percentages for the top two candidates on a convention's decisive ballot. (Percentages beyond two decimal points have been used in these calculations, which means a few margins differ by 0.01 from results that would be obtained by using the published percentages for candidates.)

Smallest first-ballot percentages by leading candidates

1. Winfield Hancock (D-1880) 23.17%
2. William Gibbs McAdoo (D-1920).. 24.31%
3. Richard Bland (D-1896).. 25.27%
4. Charles Evans Hughes (R-1916)... 25.68%
5. John Sherman (R-1888)... 27.52%
6. Estes Kefauver (D-1952) 27.64%
7. Leonard Wood (R-1920)... 29.22%
8. George Pendleton (D-1868).. 33.12%
9. Thomas Dewey (R-1940) 36.00%
10. William Seward (R-1860)... 37.23%

NOTE: A leading candidate is the individual who receives the most votes of any candidate on a convention's first ballot.

Smallest first-ballot percentages by multi-ballot nominees

1. James Polk (D-1844) 0.00%
1. Franklin Pierce (D-1852)..0.00%
1. Horatio Seymour (D-1868) 0.00%
1. James Garfield (R-1880) 0.00%
5. John Davis (D-1924)...2.82%
6. Warren Harding (R-1920) 6.66%
7. Rutherford Hayes (R-1876) 8.07%
8. Benjamin Harrison (R-1888)... 10.22%
9. Wendell Willkie (R-1940) 10.50%
10. James Cox (D-1920)... 12.25%

Largest first-ballot percentages by someone not nominated

1. Martin Van Buren (D-1844)... 54.89%
2. Ronald Reagan (R-1976).. 47.37%
3. Millard Fillmore (W-1852)... 44.93%
4. Franklin Pierce (D-1856) 41.39%
5. Henry Clay (W-1840).. 40.55%

6. Lewis Cass (D-1852) 40.28%
7. Champ Clark (D-1912) 40.27%
8. Ulysses Grant (R-1880) 40.21%
9. William Gibbs McAdoo (D-1924) 39.30%
10. Bernie Sanders (D-2016) 39.16%

Largest gains from first ballot to last ballot

1. Horatio Seymour (D-1868, from 0.00% on FB to
   100.00% on LB) 100.00
2. Franklin Pierce (D-1852, from 0.00% on FB to 96.88% on LB) 96.88
3. James Polk (D-1844, from 0.00% on FB to 86.84% on LB) 86.84
4. John Davis (D-1924, from 2.82% on FB to 76.87% on LB) 74.04
5. Winfield Hancock (D-1880, from 23.17% on FB to
   95.53% on LB) 72.36
6. Charles Evans Hughes (R-1916, from 25.68% on FB to
   96.20% on LB) 70.52
7. Woodrow Wilson (D-1912, from 29.62% on FB to
   90.49% on LB) 60.88
8. Thomas Dewey (R-1948, from 39.67% on FB to
   100.00% on LB) 60.33
9. Warren Harding (R-1920, from 6.66% on FB to
   65.52% on LB) 58.86
10. William Jennings Bryan (D-1896, from 14.73% on FB
    to 70.11% on LB) 55.38

*NOTE: Changes are expressed in percentage points. (Percentages beyond
two decimal points have been used in these calculations, which means a
few changes differ by 0.01 from results that would be obtained by using the
published percentages for candidates.) This note also applies to the next list.*

Largest drops from first ballot to last ballot

1. Martin Van Buren (D-1844, from 54.89% on FB to 0.00% on LB) ...-54.89
2. Franklin Pierce (D-1856, from 41.39% on FB to 0.00% on LB) ....-41.39
3. Lewis Cass (D-1852, from 40.28% on FB to 0.69% on LB) ....-39.58
4. William Gibbs McAdoo (D-1924, from 39.30% on FB to
   1.05% on LB) ....-38.25
5. Thomas Dewey (R-1940, from 36.00% on FB to 1.10% on LB) ....-34.90
6. George Pendleton (D-1868, from 33.12% on FB to
   0.00% on LB) ....-33.12
7. Champ Clark (D-1912, from 40.27% on FB to 7.68% on LB) ....-32.59
8. James Buchanan (D-1852, from 32.29% on FB to 0.00% on LB) ....-32.29
9. James Blaine (R-1880, from 37.57% on FB to 5.56% on LB) ....-32.01
10. Richard Bland (D-1896, from 25.27% on FB to 1.18% on LB) ....-24.09

GENERAL ELECTIONS

Largest national voter-turnout rates

1. 1876...81.8%
2. 1860...81.2%
3. 1840...80.2%
4. 1880...79.4%
5. 1888...79.3%
5. 1896...79.3%
7. 1844...78.9%
7. 1856...78.9%
9. 1868...78.1%
10. 1884..77.5%

Smallest national voter-turnout rates

1. 1824...26.9%
2. 1924...48.9%
3. 1996...49.0%
4. 1920...49.2%
5. 1988...50.3%
5. 2000...50.3%
7. 1948...51.1%
8. 1932...52.6%
9. 1980...52.8%
10. 1984..53.3%

Most popular votes cast in a general election

1. 2016..136,669,276
2. 2008..131,313,820
3. 2012..129,085,403
4. 2004..122,295,345
5. 2000..105,405,100
6. 1992..104,425,014
7. 1996..96,277,223
8. 1984..92,652,842
9. 1988..91,594,809
10. 1980...86,513,813

Largest raw gains in popular votes from previous election

1. 2004..16,890,245
2. 1952..12,859,424
3. 1992..12,830,205
4. 2000..9,127,877
5. 2008..9,018,475
6. 1920..8,233,012
7. 1928..7,702,389

8. 2016..7,583,873
9. 1960..6,811,311
10. 1984 6,139,029

NOTE: This list shows the change in total popular votes between the election four years earlier and the given election, which also applies to the next list.

Largest raw drops in popular votes from previous election

1. 1996..-8,147,791
2. 2012..-2,228,417
3. 1944..-1,840,500
4. 1988..-1,058,033
5. 1864..-654,575
6. 1904..-453,486

NOTE: These are the only six elections where the total of popular votes was smaller than in the previous election.

Largest percentage gains in popular votes from previous election

1. 1828..213.81%
2. 1840.. 60.41%
3. 1920.. 44.42%
4. 1868.. 41.96%
5. 1876.. 30.00%
6. 1856.. 28.24%
7. 1928.. 26.47%
8. 1952.. 26.41%
9. 1916.. 23.22%
10. 1836 .... 16.20%

NOTE: This list shows the percentage change in total popular votes between the election four years earlier and the given election, which also applies to the next list.

Largest percentage drops in popular votes from previous election

1. 1864..-13.97%
2. 1996.. -7.80%
3. 1944.. -3.69%
4. 1904.. -3.25%
5. 2012.. -1.70%
6. 1988.. -1.14%

NOTE: These are the only six elections where the total of popular votes was smaller than in the previous election.

General-election victories by a party

1. Republican 24
2. Democratic 21
3. Democratic-Republican 8
4. Federalist 3
5. Whig 2

Longest general-election winning streaks by a party

1. Democratic-Republican (1800-1828) 8
2. Republican (1860-1880) 6
3. Democratic (1932-1948) 5
4. Republican (1896-1908) 4
5. Federalist (1789-1796) 3
5. Republican (1920-1928) 3
5. Republican (1980-1988) 3
8. Democratic (1832-1836) 2
8. Democratic (1852-1856) 2
8. Democratic (1912-1916) 2
8. Republican (1952-1956) 2
8. Democratic (1960-1964) 2
8. Republican (1968-1972) 2
8. Democratic (1992-1996) 2
8. Republican (2000-2004) 2
8. Democratic (2008-2012) 2

Most consecutive elections won by a different party

1. 1836-1852 (D-W-D-W-D) 5
1. 1880-1896 (R-D-R-D-R) 5
3. 1972-1980 (R-D-R) 3

NOTE: These are the only instances with a different party winning three or more consecutive elections.

Most consecutive elections won by a different candidate

1. 1832-1860 (Andrew Jackson-Abraham Lincoln) 8
2. 1872-1896 (Ulysses Grant-William McKinley) 7
3. 1916-1932 (Woodrow Wilson-Franklin Roosevelt) 5
4. 1900-1912 (William McKinley-Woodrow Wilson) 4
4. 1956-1968 (Dwight Eisenhower-Richard Nixon) 4
6. 1792-1800 (George Washington-Thomas Jefferson) 3
6. 1820-1828 (James Monroe-Andrew Jackson) 3
6. 1944-1952 (Franklin Roosevelt-Dwight Eisenhower) 3
6. 1972-1980 (Richard Nixon-Ronald Reagan) 3
6. 1984-1992 (Ronald Reagan-Bill Clinton) 3

NOTE: The first and last presidents in each streak are listed.

Individuals on five major-party tickets

Franklin Roosevelt (PRES: D-1932, 1936, 1940, 1944; VPRES: D-1920)
Richard Nixon (PRES: R-1960, 1968, 1972; VPRES: R-1952, 1956)

NOTE: This list shows candidates who were nominated by a major party for president (PRES) or vice president (VPRES). Vice-presidential nominees under the double-ballot system (1789-1800) are based on the parties' stated intentions, even though all electoral votes counted toward the presidency. This note also applies to the next two lists.

Individuals on four major-party tickets

John Adams (PRES: F-1796, 1800; VPRES: F-1789, 1792)
George H.W. Bush (PRES: R-1988, 1992; VPRES: R-1980, 1984)

Individuals on three major-party tickets

Thomas Jefferson (PRES: DR-1796, 1800, 1804)
Charles Cotesworth Pinckney (PRES: F-1804, 1808; VPRES: F-1800)
Rufus King (PRES: F-1816; VPRES: F-1804, 1808)
Andrew Jackson (PRES: DR-1824, 1828, D-1832)
Martin Van Buren (PRES: D-1836, 1840; VPRES: D-1832)
Grover Cleveland (PRES: D-1884, 1888, 1892)
William Jennings Bryan (PRES: D-1896, 1900, 1908)
Walter Mondale (PRES: D-1984; VPRES: D-1976, 1980)
Al Gore (PRES: D-2000; VPRES: D-1992, 1996)

NOTE: Jefferson ran for president in 1796, but was elected vice president under the double-ballot system.

Major-party nominees who faced each other in two elections

1796 and 1800 (John Adams and Thomas Jefferson with one win apiece)
1824 and 1828 (John Quincy Adams and Andrew Jackson with one win apiece)
1836 and 1840 (Martin Van Buren and William Henry Harrison with one win apiece)
1888 and 1892 (Benjamin Harrison and Grover Cleveland with one win apiece)
1896 and 1900 (William McKinley with two wins over William Jennings Bryan)
1952 and 1956 (Dwight Eisenhower with two wins over Adlai Stevenson)

General-election wins by home-state candidates

1. New York 12
2. Virginia 8
3. Ohio 7
4. Illinois 6
5. California 4
5. Massachusetts 4
5. Texas 4
8. Tennessee 3
9. Arkansas 2
9. New Jersey 2
11. Georgia 1
11. Indiana 1
11. Louisiana 1
11. Missouri 1
11. New Hampshire 1
11. Pennsylvania 1

NOTE: A home state is the place where an individual maintains a voting address during his or her presidential candidacy. Individuals with two or more qualified candidacies are counted multiple times above.

Winners from the smallest states (electoral votes)

1. Franklin Pierce (D-1852, New Hampshire) 5
2. Zachary Taylor (W-1848, Louisiana) 6
2. Bill Clinton (D-1992, Arkansas) 6
2. Bill Clinton (D-1996, Arkansas) 6

5. George Washington (F-1789, Virginia) 10
6. Andrew Jackson (DR-1828, Tennessee) 11
6. Abraham Lincoln (R-1860, Illinois).. 11
8. Jimmy Carter (D-1976, Georgia)... 12
9. James Polk (D-1844, Tennessee) 13
9. Herbert Hoover (R-1928, California) 13

NOTE: Home states are ranked by the number of electoral votes they cast in a given election, which also applies to the next list.

Winners from the largest states (electoral votes)

1. Franklin Roosevelt (D-1932, New York)... 47
1. Franklin Roosevelt (D-1936, New York)... 47
1. Franklin Roosevelt (D-1940, New York)... 47
1. Franklin Roosevelt (D-1944, New York)... 47
1. Ronald Reagan (R-1984, California).. 47
6. Dwight Eisenhower (R-1952, New York).. 45
6. Dwight Eisenhower (R-1956, New York).. 45
6. Richard Nixon (R-1972, California).. 45
6. Ronald Reagan (R-1980, California).. 45
10. Richard Nixon (R-1968, New York)... 43

Winners from the smallest states (share of electoral votes)

1. Bill Clinton (D-1992, Arkansas) 1.12%
1. Bill Clinton (D-1996, Arkansas) 1.12%
3. Franklin Pierce (D-1852, New Hampshire)... 1.69%
4. Zachary Taylor (W-1848, Louisiana) 2.07%
5. Jimmy Carter (D-1976, Georgia)... 2.23%
6. Herbert Hoover (R-1928, California) 2.45%
7. Woodrow Wilson (D-1912, New Jersey)... 2.64%
7. Woodrow Wilson (D-1916, New Jersey)... 2.64%
9. Harry Truman (D-1948, Missouri).. 2.83%
10. John Kennedy (D-1960, Massachusetts).. 2.98%

NOTE: Home states are ranked by the share of the nation's electoral votes that they cast in a given election, which also applies to the next list.

Winners from the largest states (share of electoral votes)

1. George Washington (F-1792, Virginia) 15.91%
2. Thomas Jefferson (DR-1800, Virginia)... 15.22%
3. George Washington (F-1789, Virginia) 14.49%
4. Martin Van Buren (D-1836, New York)... 14.29%
5. James Madison (DR-1808, Virginia)... 13.71%
6. Thomas Jefferson (DR-1804, Virginia)... 13.64%
7. John Adams (F-1796, Massachusetts) 11.59%
8. James Madison (DR-1812, Virginia)... 11.52%
8. James Monroe (DR-1816, Virginia) 11.52%
10. James Monroe (DR-1820, Virginia)... 10.78%

Elections with two major-party nominees from the same state

1860 (Illinois, Abraham Lincoln-Stephen Douglas)
1904 (New York, Theodore Roosevelt-Alton Parker)
1920 (Ohio, Warren Harding-James Cox)
1940 (New York, Franklin Roosevelt-Wendell Willkie)
1944 (New York, Franklin Roosevelt-Thomas Dewey)
2016 (New York, Donald Trump-Hillary Clinton)

NOTE: The national winner is listed first. The first five national winners also carried their home states, but Trump did not.

Youngest general-election winners

1. John Kennedy (D-1960)..43.43
2. Theodore Roosevelt (R-1904)..46.01
3. Bill Clinton (D-1992)..46.20
4. Ulysses Grant (R-1868)...46.51
5. Barack Obama (D-2008)...47.24
6. Grover Cleveland (D-1884)..47.62
7. Franklin Pierce (D-1852)..47.94
8. James Garfield (R-1880)..48.95
9. James Polk (D-1844)...48.99
10. Bill Clinton (D-1996)...50.20

NOTE: All ages are as of November 1 of the given election year, which also applies to the next list.

Oldest general-election winners

1. Ronald Reagan (R-1984)...73.73
2. Donald Trump (R-2016)...70.38
3. Ronald Reagan (R-1980)...69.73
4. William Henry Harrison (W-1840)..67.73
5. Dwight Eisenhower (R-1956)...66.05
6. Andrew Jackson (D-1832)..65.63
7. James Buchanan (D-1856)...65.52
8. Harry Truman (D-1948)...64.48
9. George H.W. Bush (R-1988)...64.39
10. Zachary Taylor (W-1848)...63.94

STATES CARRIED

States carried the most times by Democrats
1. Arkansas...32
2. Georgia...31
3. Missouri..29
3. Virginia...29
5. Alabama..28
5. Louisiana..28
5. Maryland...28
5. North Carolina 28
9. Mississippi 27
10. South Carolina..26
10. Texas 26

NOTE: The District of Columbia is counted as a state. If two or more parties tie for the most electoral votes from a state, no party is given credit for carrying that state. This note applies to all remaining party lists in this section.

States carried the most times by Republicans
1. Vermont 33
2. Indiana...32
2. Kansas..32
4. Maine 31
4. Nebraska..31
6. Iowa 30
7. New Hampshire..29
7. Ohio..29
9. Michigan...28
10. South Dakota..27

States carried the most times by Federalists
1. Connecticut..8
1. Delaware...8
3. Massachusetts 7
4. New Hampshire..6
5. New Jersey 5
5. Rhode Island..5
7. Maryland..3
7. Vermont 3
9. New York..2
9. Pennsylvania 2
9. South Carolina...2

States carried the most times by Democratic-Republicans
1. Georgia...9
1. Kentucky...9
1. North Carolina 9
1. Pennsylvania 9
1. Tennessee...9
1. Virginia...9

7. South Carolina 8
8. New York 7
8. Ohio 7
10. Maryland 6
10. Vermont 6

States carried the most times by Whigs

1. Kentucky 5
1. Massachusetts 5
1. Tennessee 5
1. Vermont 5
5. Delaware 4
5. Maryland 4
5. New Jersey 4
8. Connecticut 3
8. Georgia 3
8. North Carolina 3
8. Ohio 3
8. Rhode Island 3

States carried the most times by minor parties

1. Alabama 3
1. Mississippi 3
3. Louisiana 2
3. South Carolina 2
5. Arkansas 1
5. California 1
5. Colorado 1
5. Georgia 1
5. Idaho 1
5. Kansas 1
5. Kentucky 1
5. Maryland 1
5. Michigan 1
5. Minnesota 1
5. Nevada 1
5. Pennsylvania 1
5. South Dakota 1
5. Tennessee 1
5. Vermont 1
5. Virginia 1
5. Washington 1
5. Wisconsin 1

NOTE: A minor party is any but the seven major parties (Democratic, Republican, Federalist, Democratic-Republican, National Republican, Whig, and Southern Democratic).

States carried the most times by Democrats (Modern Era)

1. District of Columbia 14
1. Minnesota 14
3. Hawaii 13
3. Massachusetts 13

NOTE: *The Modern Era encompasses elections from 1960 through 2016, which also applies to the next two lists.*

States carried the most times by Republicans (Modern Era)

States carried the most times by minor parties (Modern Era)

NOTE: *These are the only states carried by minor parties since 1960. A minor party is any but the seven major parties (Democratic, Republican, Federalist, Democratic-Republican, National Republican, Whig, and Southern Democratic).*

Most states carried in a career

19. Theodore Roosevelt 38
20. Benjamin Harrison 37
20. Warren Harding 37
22. Calvin Coolidge 35
23. Thomas Jefferson 32
24. William Howard Taft 31
24. Jimmy Carter 31

NOTE: The District of Columbia is counted as a state. If two or more candidates tie for the most electoral votes from a state, each candidate is given credit for carrying that state. (This differs from the party rule, which does not give such credit to parties.) This note applies to all remaining candidate lists in this section.

Largest percentages of states carried in a career

1. George Washington (25 of 25) 100.00%
2. James Monroe (40 of 43) 93.02%
3. Ronald Reagan (93 of 102) 91.18%
4. Lyndon Johnson (45 of 51) 88.24%
5. Franklin Pierce (27 of 31) 87.10%
6. Franklin Roosevelt (162 of 192) 84.38%
7. Dwight Eisenhower (80 of 96) 83.33%
8. Ulysses Grant (55 of 69) 79.71%
9. Warren Harding (37 of 48) 77.08%
10. Woodrow Wilson (70 of 96) 72.92%
10. Calvin Coolidge (35 of 48) 72.92%
12. Richard Nixon (107 of 152) 70.39%
13. Abraham Lincoln (40 of 58) 68.97%
14. James Madison (23 of 35) 65.71%
15. Bill Clinton (65 of 102) 63.73%
16. James Buchanan (19 of 31) 61.29%
17. George W. Bush (61 of 102) 59.80%
18. Donald Trump (30 of 51) 58.82%
19. Andrew Jackson (42 of 72) 58.33%
19. Harry Truman (28 of 48) 58.33%
21. James Polk (15 of 26) 57.69%
22. George H.W. Bush (58 of 102) 56.86%
23. William McKinley (51 of 90) 56.67%
24. Rutherford Hayes (21 of 38) 55.26%
25. Barack Obama (56 of 102) 54.90%

NOTE: The number of states carried and the total number of states are listed in parentheses. Percentages are based only on those years in which a candidate met the qualification standards for the general election itself.

Most states carried in an election

1. Richard Nixon (R-1972) 49
1. Ronald Reagan (R-1984) 49
3. Franklin Roosevelt (D-1936) 46
4. Lyndon Johnson (D-1964) 45
5. Ronald Reagan (R-1980) 44
6. Franklin Roosevelt (D-1932) 42

Largest percentages of states carried in an election

General-election winners who carried a minority of states

John Quincy Adams (DR-1824, 7 of 24)
John Kennedy (D-1960, 22 of 50)
Jimmy Carter (D-1976, 24 of 51)

General-election winners who did not carry their home states

James Polk (D-1844, Tennessee)
Woodrow Wilson (D-1916, New Jersey)
Richard Nixon (R-1968, New York)
Donald Trump (R-2016, New York)

NOTE: A home state is the place where an individual maintains a voting address during his or her presidential candidacy. This note also applies to the next list.

General-election losers who did not carry their home states

Charles Cotesworth Pinckney (F-1804, South Carolina)
Charles Cotesworth Pinckney (F-1808, South Carolina)
Rufus King (F-1816, New York)
Martin Van Buren (D-1840, New York)
Winfield Scott (W-1852, New Jersey)
John Fremont (R-1856, California)
Stephen Douglas (D-1860, Illinois)
John Breckinridge (SD-1860, Kentucky)
Horace Greeley (D-1872, New York)
Winfield Hancock (D-1880, Pennsylvania)
Grover Cleveland (D-1888, New York)
Benjamin Harrison (R-1892, Indiana)
William Jennings Bryan (D-1900, Nebraska)
Alton Parker (D-1904, New York)
William Howard Taft (R-1912, Ohio)
James Cox (D-1920, Ohio)
John Davis (D-1924, West Virginia)
Alfred Smith (D-1928, New York)
Herbert Hoover (R-1932, California)
Alfred Landon (R-1936, Kansas)

Wendell Willkie (R-1940, New York)
Thomas Dewey (R-1944, New York)
Adlai Stevenson (D-1952, Illinois)
Adlai Stevenson (D-1956, Illinois)
George McGovern (D-1972, South Dakota)
Al Gore (D-2000, Tennessee)
Mitt Romney (R-2012, Massachusetts)

NOTE: This list is restricted to major-party nominees who failed to win the general election.

Longest streaks of being carried by one party

1. Vermont (Republican, 1856-1960)..27
2. Georgia (Democratic, 1868-1960)..24
3. Arkansas (Democratic, 1876-1964) 23
4. Alabama (Democratic, 1876-1944)..18
4. Mississippi (Democratic, 1876-1944)...18
6. Louisiana (Democratic, 1880-1944) 17
6. South Carolina (Democratic, 1880-1944)...................................17
8. District of Columbia (Democratic, 1964-2016) 14
8. Iowa (Republican, 1856-1908)...14
8. Maine (Republican, 1856-1908) 14
8. Massachusettts (Republican, 1856-1908)..................................14
8. Michigan (Republican, 1856-1908)...14
8. New Hampshire (Republican, 1856-1908)..................................14
8. Ohio (Republican, 1856-1908)...14
8. Rhode Island (Republican, 1856-1908)......................................14
8. Texas (Democratic, 1872-1924)...14

NOTE: A streak is defined as a consecutive string of elections. Any deviation (voting for a different party, having a tie, or skipping an election because of the Civil War or Reconstruction) breaks the streak. The first and last elections of the streak are listed.

States with best records of matching general-election winners

1. New Mexico (24 matches, 3 misses) 88.89%
2. Ohio (45 matches, 9 misses) 83.33%
3. Illinois (41 matches, 9 misses) 82.00%
4. Pennsylvania (47 matches, 11 misses) 81.03%
5. California (34 matches, 8 misses) 80.95%
6. Nevada (31 matches, 8 misses)..79.49%
7. New York (45 matches, 11 misses, 1 tie) 78.95%
8. Arizona (21 matches, 6 misses)..77,78%
9. Wisconsin (33 matches, 10 misses).......................................76.74%
10. Montana (24 matches, 8 misses) 75.00%

NOTE: This list shows how frequently a state has been carried by the national winner (a match) or by one of the losing candidates (a miss). If two candidates from different parties receive the same number of electoral votes (as occasionally happened before 1804), a tie is declared. A tie counts the same as a miss in determining a state's percentage. This note also applies to the next three lists.

States with worst records of matching general-election winners

1. District of Columbia (6 matches, 8 misses)...................................... 42.86%
2. Alabama (25 matches, 24 misses).. 51.02%
3. Mississippi (25 matches, 23 misses).. 52.08%
4. Georgia (32 matches, 24 misses, 1 tie)... 56.14%
5. South Carolina (33 matches, 23 misses, 1 tie) 57.90%
6. Texas (24 matches, 17 misses)... 58.54%
7. Arkansas (26 matches, 18 misses).. 59.09%
8. South Dakota (19 matches, 13 misses) 59.38%
9. Alaska (9 matches, 6 misses).. 60.00%
9. Hawaii (9 matches, 6 misses).. 60.00%

States with best records of matching winners (Modern Era)

1. Ohio (14 matches, 1 miss).. 93.33%
2. Florida (13 matches, 2 misses) 86.67%
2. Missouri (13 matches, 2 misses) 86.67%
2. Nevada (13 matches, 2 misses).. 86.67%
5. Arkansas (12 matches, 3 misses).. 80.00%
5. Delaware (12 matches, 3 misses).. 80.00%
5. Kentucky (12 matches, 3 misses) 80.00%
5. New Mexico (12 matches, 3 misses) 80.00%
5. North Carolina (12 matches, 3 misses).. 80.00%
5. Pennsylvania (12 matches, 3 misses).. 80.00%
5. Tennessee (12 matches, 3 misses) 80.00%

NOTE: The Modern Era encompasses elections from 1960 through 2016, which also applies to the next list.

States with worst records of matching winners (Modern Era)

1. District of Columbia (6 matches, 8 misses)....................................... 42.86%
2. Alabama (8 matches, 7 misses).. 53.33%
2. Minnesota (8 matches, 7 misses) 53.33%
2. Mississippi (8 matches, 7 misses)... 53.33%
2. Washington (8 matches, 7 misses) 53.33%
6. Alaska (9 matches, 6 misses)... 60.00%
6. Arizona (9 matches, 6 misses) 60.00%
6. Georgia (9 matches, 6 misses).. 60.00%
6. Hawaii (9 matches, 6 misses)... 60.00%
6. Idaho (9 matches, 6 misses).. 60.00%
6. Kansas (9 matches, 6 misses)... 60.00%
6. Maine (9 matches, 6 misses)... 60.00%
6. Massachusetts (9 matches, 6 misses) 60.00%
6. Nebraska (9 matches, 6 misses).. 60.00%
6. North Dakota (9 matches, 6 misses) 60.00%
6. Oklahoma (9 matches, 6 misses)... 60.00%
6. Oregon (9 matches, 6 misses) 60.00%
6. Rhode Island (9 matches, 6 misses) 60.00%
6. South Dakota (9 matches, 6 misses) 60.00%
6. Utah (9 matches, 6 misses).. 60.00%
6. Wyoming (9 matches, 6 misses) 60.00%

Longest streaks of matching national winners

1. Nevada (1912-1972) 16
1. New Mexico (1912-1972) 16
3. Idaho (1904-1956) 14
3. Illinois (1920-1972) 14
3. Montana (1904-1956) 14
3. Ohio (1964-2016) 14
3. Pennsylvania (1828-1880) 14
8. Missouri (1904-1952) 13
9. Arizona (1912-1956) 12
9. Delaware (1952-1996) 12
9. Minnesota (1920-1964) 12
9. Missouri (1960-2004) 12
9. Ohio (1896-1940) 12

NOTE: A streak is defined as a consecutive string of elections. Any deviation (voting for a national loser, having a tie, or skipping an election because of the Civil War or Reconstruction) breaks the streak. The first and last elections of the streak are listed.

POPULAR VOTES

Popular votes (actual) by all of a party's qualified candidates

1. Republican 1,000,415,198
2. Democratic 992,337,949
3. Independent (Perot) 19,741,657
4. American Independent 9,906,473
5. Reform 8,085,402
6. Whig 6,061,853
7. National Unity 5,720,060
8. Progressive (La Follette) 4,827,184
9. Libertarian 4,493,014
10. Progressive (Roosevelt) 4,120,207
11. Socialist 4,113,562
12. Green 2,882,955
13. States' Rights Democratic 1,169,156
14. Progressive (Wallace) 1,157,172
15. Populist 1,029,357
16. Democratic-Republican 995,333
17. National Republican 985,102
18. Union 892,361
19. American-Whig 873,053
20. Southern Democratic 848,019
21. Constitutional Union 590,901
22. Prohibition 520,892
23. Free Soil 446,711
24. Greenback 306,921
25. Anti-Masonic 100,715
26. Liberty 62,103

NOTE: This list is confined to a party's qualified candidates. A party may have received votes in other elections without reaching qualification levels. If a candidate ran on two tickets (such as William Jennings Bryan in 1896), all popular votes have been awarded to the major party. This note also applies to the next list.

Popular votes (equalized) by all of a party's qualified candidates

1. Democratic 2,186,624,138
2. Republican 1,967,256,176
3. Whig 241,205,968
4. Democratic-Republican 152,402,616
5. National Republican 81,051,482
6. Progressive (Roosevelt) 27,389,475
7. American-Whig 21,532,158
8. Socialist 20,616,565
9. Independent (Perot) 18,905,104
10. Southern Democratic 18,098,559
11. Progressive (La Follette) 16,588,762
12. Free Soil 15,033,297
13. American Independent 13,531,238
14. Constitutional Union 12,611,105

15. Populist...8,527,133
16. Reform...8,398,042
17. Anti-Masonic...7,783,393
18. National Unity...6,611,730
19. Prohibition...4,437,820
20. Greenback...3,328,790
21. Libertarian...3,289,547
22. Green...2,735,119
23. States' Rights Democratic................................2,401,150
24. Progressive (Wallace).....................................2,376,538
25. Liberty...2,296,998
26. Union...1,954,917

Most popular votes (actual) in a career

1. Barack Obama...135,414,312
2. Richard Nixon...113,063,548
3. George W. Bush...112,496,612
4. Franklin Roosevelt.......................................103,425,434
5. Ronald Reagan..98,359,228
6. Bill Clinton..92,311,683
7. George H.W. Bush..87,989,988
8. Jimmy Carter...76,314,646
9. Dwight Eisenhower..69,368,417
10. Hillary Clinton...65,853,514
11. Donald Trump..62,984,828
12. Mitt Romney..60,933,500
13. John McCain...59,948,323
14. John Kerry..59,028,439
15. Adlai Stevenson..53,337,744
16. Al Gore...50,999,897
17. Thomas Dewey..43,984,224
18. Lyndon Johnson...43,129,566
19. Michael Dukakis...41,809,065
20. Bob Dole..39,198,755
21. Gerald Ford..39,147,793
22. Walter Mondale..37,577,185
23. Herbert Hoover..37,193,248
24. John Kennedy...34,226,731
25. Hubert Humphrey...31,275,166

Most popular votes (equalized) in a career

1. Franklin Roosevelt.......................................226,275,350
2. Richard Nixon...153,657,272
3. Andrew Jackson...151,554,896
4. Grover Cleveland...143,491,778
5. William Jennings Bryan.................................134,364,271
6. Dwight Eisenhower.......................................112,257,137
7. Ronald Reagan...109,521,380
8. Ulysses Grant..108,275,674
9. Martin Van Buren...107,755,054
10. Barack Obama...103,989,225
11. William McKinley..102,764,828

12. George W. Bush 98,598,801
13. Henry Clay 98,498,789
14. Herbert Hoover 97,890,056
15. Abraham Lincoln 94,916,847
16. Bill Clinton 92,241,569
17. Jimmy Carter 91,080,044
18. Woodrow Wilson 91,077,886
19. Thomas Dewey 91,006,105
20. George H.W. Bush 90,818,989
21. Benjamin Harrison 90,790,591
22. William Henry Harrison 89,515,830
23. Adlai Stevenson 86,331,852
24. Theodore Roosevelt 83,795,844
25. William Howard Taft 74,751,639

Most popular votes in an election

1. Barack Obama (D-2008) 69,498,516
2. Barack Obama (D-2012) 65,915,796
3. Hillary Clinton (D-2016) 65,853,514
4. Donald Trump (R-2016) 62,984,828
5. George W. Bush (R-2004) 62,040,610
6. Mitt Romney (R-2012) 60,933,500
7. John McCain (R-2008) 59,948,323
8. John Kerry (D-2004) 59,028,439
9. Ronald Reagan (R-1984) 54,455,075
10. Al Gore (D-2000) 50,999,897
11. George W. Bush (R-2000) 50,456,002
12. George H.W. Bush (R-1988) 48,886,106
13. Bill Clinton (D-1996) 47,402,357
14. Richard Nixon (R-1972) 47,169,911
15. Bill Clinton (D-1992) 44,909,326
16. Ronald Reagan (R-1980) 43,904,153
17. Lyndon Johnson (D-1964) 43,129,566
18. Michael Dukakis (D-1988) 41,809,065
19. Jimmy Carter (D-1976) 40,830,763
20. Bob Dole (R-1996) 39,198,755
21. Gerald Ford (R-1976) 39,147,793
22. George H.W. Bush (R-1992) 39,103,882
23. Walter Mondale (D-1984) 37,577,185
24. Dwight Eisenhower (R-1956) 35,590,472
25. Jimmy Carter (D-1980) 35,483,883

Largest popular-vote percentages in an election

1. Lyndon Johnson (D-1964) 61.05%
2. Franklin Roosevelt (D-1936) 60.80%
3. Richard Nixon (R-1972) 60.69%
4. Warren Harding (R-1920) 60.34%
5. Ronald Reagan (R-1984) 58.77%
6. Herbert Hoover (R-1928) 58.24%
7. Franklin Roosevelt (D-1932) 57.41%
8. Dwight Eisenhower (R-1956) 57.38%
9. Theodore Roosevelt (R-1904) 56.41%

10. Andrew Jackson (DR-1828)..55.97%
11. Ulysses Grant (R-1872)...55.61%
12. Abraham Lincoln (R-1864)..55.09%
13. Dwight Eisenhower (R-1952)...54.88%
14. Franklin Roosevelt (D-1940)..54.69%
15. Andrew Jackson (D-1832)..54.24%
16. Calvin Coolidge (R-1924)...54.04%
17. Franklin Roosevelt (D-1944)..53.39%
18. George H.W. Bush (R-1988)...53.37%
19. Barack Obama (D-2008)...52.93%
20. William Henry Harrison (W-1840)..52.88%
21. Ulysses Grant (R-1868)...52.66%
22. William McKinley (R-1900)..51.67%
23. William Howard Taft (R-1908)...51.58%
24. William McKinley (R-1896)..51.10%
25. Barack Obama (D-2012)...51.06%

Smallest popular-vote percentages by election winners

1. John Quincy Adams (DR-1824)..30.92%
2. Abraham Lincoln (R-1860)..39.82%
3. Woodrow Wilson (D-1912)..41.84%
4. Bill Clinton (D-1992)...43.01%
5. Richard Nixon (R-1968)..43.42%
6. James Buchanan (D-1856)..45.28%
7. Grover Cleveland (D-1892)...46.01%
8. Donald Trump (R-2016)..46.09%
9. Zachary Taylor (W-1848)..47.28%
10. Benjamin Harrison (R-1888)..47.82%

Smallest popular-vote percentages by major-party nominees

1. Hugh White (W-1836)..9.72%
2. John Breckinridge (SD-1860)..18.10%
3. William Howard Taft (R-1912)...23.18%
4. John Davis (D-1924)..28.82%
5. Stephen Douglas (D-1860)..29.46%
6. John Quincy Adams (DR-1824)..30.92%
7. John Fremont (R-1856)...33.11%
8. James Cox (D-1920)...34.12%
9. Alfred Landon (R-1936)..36.54%
10. William Henry Harrison (W-1836)..36.64%

Largest popular-vote percentages by election losers

1. Samuel Tilden (D-1876)..50.98%
2. Richard Nixon (R-1960)..49.55%
3. Grover Cleveland (D-1888)...48.61%
4. Al Gore (D-2000)..48.39%
5. John Kerry (D-2004)...48.27%
6. James Blaine (R-1884)..48.25%
7. Winfield Hancock (D-1880)...48.21%
8. Hillary Clinton (D-2016)..48.19%
9. Henry Clay (W-1844)...48.08%
10. Gerald Ford (R-1976)..48.00%

Most popular votes by minor-party candidates

1. Ross Perot (I-1992)...19,741,657
2. George Wallace (AI-1968) 9,906,473
3. Ross Perot (REF-1996) 8,085,402
4. John Anderson (NU-1980)..5,720,060
5. Robert La Follette (P-1924)..4,827,184
6. Gary Johnson (LIB-2016)..4,489,341
7. Theodore Roosevelt (P-1912)..4,120,207
8. Ralph Nader (GRN-2000)..2,882,955
9. Strom Thurmond (SRD-1948)..1,169,156
10. Henry Wallace (P-1948) 1,157,172

NOTE: A minor party is any but the seven major parties (Democratic, Republican, Federalist, Democratic-Republican, National Republican, Whig, and Southern Democratic). This note also applies to the next list.

Largest popular-vote percentages by minor-party candidates

1. Theodore Roosevelt (P-1912)...27.39%
2. Millard Fillmore (AW-1856)..21.53%
3. Ross Perot (I-1992)..18.91%
4. Robert La Follette (P-1924)..16.59%
5. George Wallace (AI-1968) 13.53%
6. John Bell (CU-1860)...12.61%
7. Martin Van Buren (FS-1848) 10.12%
8. James Weaver (POP-1892)..8.53%
9. Ross Perot (REF-1996) 8.40%
10. William Wirt (AM-1832)...7.78%

Largest margins in popular votes

1. 1972 (Richard Nixon-George McGovern)....................................17,999,528
2. 1984 (Ronald Reagan-Walter Mondale) 16,877,890
3. 1964 (Lyndon Johnson-Barry Goldwater)..................................15,951,378
4. 1936 (Franklin Roosevelt-Alfred Landon) 11,071,183
5. 1956 (Dwight Eisenhower-Adlai Stevenson).............................9,567,720
6. 2008 (Barack Obama-John McCain)..9,550,193
7. 1980 (Ronald Reagan-Jimmy Carter)..8,420,270
8. 1996 (Bill Clinton-Bob Dole) 8,203,602
9. 1924 (Calvin Coolidge-John Davis) 7,337,778
10. 1988 (George H.W. Bush-Michael Dukakis)...............................7,077,041

NOTE: The top two candidates are listed in parentheses, with the popular-vote leader coming first. The margin is the difference between the candidates' vote totals. This note also applies to the next two lists.

Smallest margins in popular votes

1. 1880 (James Garfield-Winfield Hancock)..8,355
2. 1824 (Andrew Jackson-John Quincy Adams)....................................38,149
3. 1844 (James Polk-Henry Clay)..39,490
4. 1884 (Grover Cleveland-James Blaine) 62,670
5. 1888 (Grover Cleveland-Benjamin Harrison)....................................89,293
6. 1960 (John Kennedy-Richard Nixon)...118,574

7. 1848 (Zachary Taylor-Lewis Cass) 137,933
8. 1828 (Andrew Jackson-John Quincy Adams)................................... 141,656
9. 1840 (William Henry Harrison-Martin Van Buren) 146,536
10. 1836 (Martin Van Buren-William Henry Harrison) 213,360

Smallest margins in popular votes (since 1900)

1. 1960 (John Kennedy-Richard Nixon)... 118,574
2. 1968 (Richard Nixon-Hubert Humphrey)... 510,314
3. 2000 (Al Gore-George W. Bush) 543,895
4. 1916 (Woodrow Wilson-Charles Evans Hughes) 579,033
5. 1900 (William McKinley-William Jennings Bryan)........................... 861,495
6. 1908 (William Howard Taft-William Jennings Bryan)................. 1,269,724
7. 1976 (Jimmy Carter-Gerald Ford) 1,682,970
8. 1948 (Harry Truman-Thomas Dewey)... 2,135,746
9. 1912 (Woodrow Wilson-Theodore Roosevelt) 2,174,120
10. 1904 (Theodore Roosevelt-Alton Parker) 2,542,098

Largest margins in popular-vote percentages

1. 1920 (Warren Harding-James Cox).. 26.22
2. 1924 (Calvin Coolidge-John Davis) 25.22
3. 1936 (Franklin Roosevelt-Alfred Landon) 24.25
4. 1972 (Richard Nixon-George McGovern).. 23.16
5. 1964 (Lyndon Johnson-Barry Goldwater)... 22.58
6. 1904 (Theodore Roosevelt-Alton Parker)... 18.80
7. 1984 (Ronald Reagan-Walter Mondale) 18.22
8. 1932 (Franklin Roosevelt-Herbert Hoover) 17.76
9. 1928 (Herbert Hoover-Alfred Smith) 17.47
10. 1832 (Andrew Jackson-Henry Clay)... 16.82

NOTE: The top two candidates are listed in parentheses, with the popular-vote leader coming first. The margin is expressed in percentage points, showing the difference between the candidates' percentages. (Percentages beyond two decimal points have been used in these calculations, which means a few margins differ by 0.01 from results that would be obtained by using the published percentages for candidates.) This note also applies to the next list.

Smallest margins in popular-vote percentages

1. 1880 (James Garfield-Winfield Hancock)... 0.09
2. 1960 (John Kennedy-Richard Nixon)... 0.17
3. 2000 (Al Gore-George W. Bush) 0.52
4. 1884 (Grover Cleveland-James Blaine) 0.62
5. 1968 (Richard Nixon-Hubert Humphrey)... 0.70
6. 1888 (Grover Cleveland-Benjamin Harrison) 0.78
7. 1844 (James Polk-Henry Clay).. 1.46
8. 1976 (Jimmy Carter-Gerald Ford) 2.06
9. 2016 (Hillary Clinton-Donald Trump) 2.10
10. 2004 (George W. Bush-John Kerry) 2.46

ELECTORAL VOTES

Electoral votes (actual) by all of a party's candidates

1. Republican 10,358
2. Democratic 10,077
3. Democratic-Republican 1,599
4. Federalist 811
5. Whig 668
6. National Republican 132
7. Progressive (Roosevelt) 88
8. Southern Democratic 72
9. American Independent 46
10. Constitutional Union 39
10. States' Rights Democratic 39
12. Populist 22
13. Progressive (La Follette) 13
14. American-Whig 8
15. Anti-Masonic 7
16. Libertarian 1

NOTE: If a candidate ran on two tickets (such as William Jennings Bryan in 1896), all electoral votes have been awarded to the major party. This note also applies to the next list.

Electoral votes (equalized) by all of a party's candidates

1. Republican 11,790
2. Democratic 11,727
3. Democratic-Republican 4,402
4. Federalist 3,498
5. Whig 1,239
6. National Republican 263
7. Southern Democratic 128
8. Progressive (Roosevelt) 89
9. Constitutional Union 69
10. American Independent 46
11. States' Rights Democratic 40
12. Populist 27
13. American-Whig 15
14. Anti-Masonic 13
14. Progressive (La Follette) 13
16. Libertarian 1

Most electoral votes (actual) in a career

1. Franklin Roosevelt 1,876
2. Richard Nixon 1,040
3. Ronald Reagan 1,015
4. Dwight Eisenhower 899
5. Bill Clinton 749
6. Woodrow Wilson 712
7. Barack Obama 697
8. Grover Cleveland 664

9. George H.W. Bush 594
10. William McKinley 563
11. George W. Bush 557
12. Herbert Hoover 503
13. Ulysses Grant 500
14. Andrew Jackson 496
15. William Jennings Bryan 493
16. Lyndon Johnson 486
17. Theodore Roosevelt 424
18. James Monroe 414
19. Warren Harding 404
20. Abraham Lincoln 392
21. Calvin Coolidge 382
22. Benjamin Harrison 378
23. Jimmy Carter 346
24. William Howard Taft 329
25. William Henry Harrison 307
25. Thomas Jefferson 307

Most electoral votes (equalized) in a career

1. Franklin Roosevelt 1,901
2. John Adams 1,109
3. George Washington 1,084
4. Thomas Jefferson 1,061
5. Richard Nixon 1,040
6. Ronald Reagan 1,015
7. James Monroe 990
8. Andrew Jackson 983
9. Dwight Eisenhower 911
10. Grover Cleveland 855
11. Ulysses Grant 833
12. Abraham Lincoln 810
13. Bill Clinton 749
14. Woodrow Wilson 722
15. Barack Obama 697
16. James Madison 692
17. William McKinley 677
18. George H.W. Bush 594
19. William Jennings Bryan 579
20. William Henry Harrison 562
21. George W. Bush 558
22. Herbert Hoover 510
23. Benjamin Harrison 489
24. Lyndon Johnson 486
25. Theodore Roosevelt 469

Most electoral votes in an election

1. Ronald Reagan (R-1984) 525
2. Franklin Roosevelt (D-1936) 523
3. Richard Nixon (R-1972) 520
4. Ronald Reagan (R-1980) 489
5. Lyndon Johnson (D-1964) 486

6. Franklin Roosevelt (D-1932) 472
7. Dwight Eisenhower (R-1956)..457
8. Franklin Roosevelt (D-1940) 449
9. Herbert Hoover (R-1928)..444
10. Dwight Eisenhower (R-1952)..442
11. Woodrow Wilson (D-1912)..435
12. Franklin Roosevelt (D-1944) 432
13. George H.W. Bush (R-1988) 426
14. Warren Harding (R-1920)..404
15. Calvin Coolidge (R-1924) 382
16. Bill Clinton (D-1996) 379
17. Bill Clinton (D-1992) 370
18. Barack Obama (D-2008)..365
19. Theodore Roosevelt (R-1904) 336
20. Barack Obama (D-2012)..332
21. William Howard Taft (R-1908)..321
22. Donald Trump (R-2016)..304
23. Harry Truman (D-1948) 303
23. John Kennedy (D-1960) 303
25. Richard Nixon (R-1968) 301

Largest electoral-vote percentages in an election

1. George Washington (F-1789) 100.00%
1. George Washington (F-1792) 100.00%
3. James Monroe (DR-1820) 99.57%
4. Franklin Roosevelt (D-1936) 98.49%
5. Ronald Reagan (R-1984)...97.58%
6. Richard Nixon (R-1972)...96.65%
7. Thomas Jefferson (DR-1804).....................................92.05%
8. Abraham Lincoln (R-1864)...90.99%
9. Ronald Reagan (R-1980)...90.89%
10. Lyndon Johnson (D-1964)...90.34%
11. Franklin Roosevelt (D-1932) 88.89%
12. Dwight Eisenhower (R-1956) 86.06%
13. Franklin Pierce (D-1852)...85.81%
14. Franklin Roosevelt (D-1940) 84.56%
15. James Monroe (DR-1816) 84.33%
16. Herbert Hoover (R-1928)...83.62%
17. Dwight Eisenhower (R-1952) 83.24%
18. Ulysses Grant (R-1872)...81.95%
19. Woodrow Wilson (D-1912)...81.92%
20. Franklin Roosevelt (D-1944) 81.36%
21. William Henry Harrison (W-1840).............................79.59%
22. George H.W. Bush (R-1988).......................................79.18%
23. Andrew Jackson (D-1832)...76.57%
24. Warren Harding (R-1920)..76.08%
25. Ulysses Grant (R-1868)...72.79%

Smallest electoral-vote percentages by election winners

1. John Quincy Adams (DR-1824)...................................32.18%
2. Rutherford Hayes (R-1876) 50.14%
3. George W. Bush (R-2000) 50.47%

4. John Adams (F-1796) 51.45%
5. Woodrow Wilson (D-1916) 52.17%
6. Thomas Jefferson (DR-1800) 52.90%
7. George W. Bush (R-2004) 53.16%
8. Grover Cleveland (D-1884) 54.61%
9. Jimmy Carter (D-1976) 55.20%
10. Richard Nixon (R-1968) 55.95%

Smallest electoral-vote percentages by major-party nominees

1. William Howard Taft (R-1912) 1.51%
1. Alfred Landon (R-1936) 1.51%
3. Walter Mondale (D-1984) 2.42%
4. George McGovern (D-1972) 3.16%
5. Stephen Douglas (D-1860) 3.96%
6. Charles Cotesworth Pinckney (F-1804) 7.96%
7. Hugh White (W-1836) 8.84%
8. George McClellan (D-1864) 9.01%
9. Jimmy Carter (D-1980) 9.11%
10. Barry Goldwater (R-1964) 9.67%

NOTE: *This list does not include Horace Greeley, who died between the general election and the day the Electoral College cast its votes in 1872.*

Largest electoral-vote percentages by election losers

1. John Adams (F-1792) 58.33%
2. Aaron Burr (DR-1800) 52.90%
3. Samuel Tilden (D-1876) 49.86%
4. Al Gore (D-2000) 49.53%
5. John Adams (F-1789) 49.28%
5. Thomas Jefferson (DR-1796) 49.28%
7. Charles Evans Hughes (R-1916) 47.83%
8. John Adams (F-1800) 47.10%
9. John Kerry (D-2004) 46.65%
10. Charles Cotesworth Pinckney (F-1800) 46.38%

NOTE: *John Adams (1789 and 1792), Thomas Jefferson (1796), and Aaron Burr (1800), who are all on this list, were elected vice president under the double-ballot system.*

Largest electoral-vote percentages by losers (after 1800)

1. Samuel Tilden (D-1876) 49.86%
2. Al Gore (D-2000) 49.53%
3. Charles Evans Hughes (R-1916) 47.83%
4. John Kerry (D-2004) 46.65%
5. James Blaine (R-1884) 45.39%
6. Gerald Ford (R-1976) 44.61%
7. Lewis Cass (D-1848) 43.79%
8. Hillary Clinton (D-2016) 42.19%
9. Winfield Hancock (D-1880) 42.01%
10. Grover Cleveland (D-1888) 41.90%

NOTE: *This list removes all candidates who ran under the double-ballot system.*

Most electoral votes by minor-party candidates

1. Theodore Roosevelt (P-1912) 88
2. George Wallace (AI-1968) 46
3. John Bell (CU-1860) 39
3. Strom Thurmond (SRD-1948) 39
5. James Weaver (POP-1892) 22
6. Robert La Follette (P-1924) 13
7. Millard Fillmore (AW-1856) 8
8. William Wirt (AM-1832) 7
9. John Hospers (LIB-1972) 1

NOTE: These are the only nine candidates who qualified for this list. A minor party is any but the seven major parties (Democratic, Republican, Federalist, Democratic-Republican, National Republican, Whig, and Southern Democratic). This list does not include individuals who received electoral votes as independent candidates even though they hadn't formally entered the race, such as Walter Jones in 1956 and Harry Byrd in 1960. This note also applies to the next list.

Largest electoral-vote percentages by minor-party candidates

1. Theodore Roosevelt (P-1912) 16.57%
2. John Bell (CU-1860) 12.87%
3. George Wallace (AI-1968) 8.55%
4. Strom Thurmond (SRD-1948) 7.35%
5. James Weaver (POP-1892) 4.96%
6. Millard Fillmore (AW-1856) 2.70%
7. William Wirt (AM-1832) 2.45%
7. Robert La Follette (P-1924) 2.45%
9. John Hospers (LIB-1972) 0.19%

Largest margins in electoral votes

1. 1936 (Franklin Roosevelt-Alfred Landon) 515
2. 1984 (Ronald Reagan-Walter Mondale) 512
3. 1972 (Richard Nixon-George McGovern) 503
4. 1980 (Ronald Reagan-Jimmy Carter) 440
5. 1964 (Lyndon Johnson-Barry Goldwater) 434
6. 1932 (Franklin Roosevelt-Herbert Hoover) 413
7. 1956 (Dwight Eisenhower-Adlai Stevenson) 384
8. 1940 (Franklin Roosevelt-Wendell Willkie) 367
9. 1928 (Herbert Hoover-Alfred Smith) 357
10. 1952 (Dwight Eisenhower-Adlai Stevenson) 353

NOTE: The top two candidates are listed in parentheses, with the electoral-vote leader coming first. The margin is the difference between the candidates' vote totals. This note also applies to the next list.

Smallest margins in electoral votes

1. 1800 (Thomas Jefferson-Aaron Burr) 0
2. 1876 (Rutherford Hayes-Samuel Tilden) 1
3. 1796 (John Adams-Thomas Jefferson) 3
4. 2000 (George W. Bush-Al Gore) 5
5. 1824 (Andrew Jackson-John Quincy Adams) 15
6. 1916 (Woodrow Wilson-Charles Evans Hughes) 23

7. 1789 (George Washington-John Adams) 35
7. 2004 (George W. Bush-John Kerry) 35
9. 1848 (Zachary Taylor-Lewis Cass) 36
10. 1884 (Grover Cleveland-James Blaine) 37

Largest margins in electoral-vote percentages

1. 1820 (James Monroe-John Quincy Adams) 99.14
2. 1936 (Franklin Roosevelt-Alfred Landon) 96.99
3. 1984 (Ronald Reagan-Walter Mondale) 95.17
4. 1972 (Richard Nixon-George McGovern) 93.49
5. 1804 (Thomas Jefferson-Charles Cotesworth Pinckney) 84.09
6. 1864 (Abraham Lincoln-George McClellan) 81.97
7. 1980 (Ronald Reagan-Jimmy Carter) 81.78
8. 1964 (Lyndon Johnson-Barry Goldwater) 80.67
9. 1932 (Franklin Roosevelt-Herbert Hoover) 77.78
10. 1956 (Dwight Eisenhower-Adlai Stevenson) 72.32

NOTE: The top two candidates are listed in parentheses, with the electoral-vote leader first. The margin is expressed in percentage points, showing the difference between the candidates' percentages. (Percentages beyond two decimal points have been used in these calculations, which means a few margins differ by 0.01 from results that would be obtained by using the published percentages for candidates.) This note also applies to the next list.

Smallest margins in electoral-vote percentages

1. 1800 (Thomas Jefferson-Aaron Burr) 0.00
2. 1876 (Rutherford Hayes-Samuel Tilden) 0.27
3. 2000 (George W. Bush-Al Gore) 0.93
4. 1796 (John Adams-Thomas Jefferson) 2.17
5. 1916 (Woodrow Wilson-Charles Evans Hughes) 4.33
6. 1824 (Andrew Jackson-John Quincy Adams) 5.75
7. 2004 (George W. Bush-John Kerry) 6.51
8. 1884 (Grover Cleveland-James Blaine) 9.23
9. 1976 (Jimmy Carter-Gerald Ford) 10.59
10. 1848 (Zachary Taylor-Lewis Cass) 12.41

Largest rises between a candidate's EV and PV percentages

1. Ronald Reagan (R-1980, 90.89% for EV, 50.75% for PV) 40.14
2. Woodrow Wilson (D-1912, 81.92% for EV, 41.84% for PV) 40.08
3. Ronald Reagan (R-1984, 97.58% for EV, 58.77% for PV) 38.81
4. Franklin Roosevelt (D-1936, 98.49% for EV, 60.80% for PV) 37.70
5. Richard Nixon (R-1972, 96.65% for EV, 60.69% for PV) 35.96
6. Abraham Lincoln (R-1864, 90.99% for EV, 55.09% for PV) 35.89
7. Franklin Pierce (D-1852, 85.81% for EV, 50.84% for PV) 34.97
8. Franklin Roosevelt (D-1932, 88.89% for EV, 57.41% for PV) 31.48
9. Franklin Roosevelt (D-1940, 84.56% for EV, 54.69% for PV) 29.87
10. Lyndon Johnson (D-1964, 90.34% for EV, 61.05% for PV) 29.28

NOTE: This list covers all elections since 1828. The difference between a candidate's electoral-vote percentage and popular-vote percentage is expressed in percentage points. (Percentages beyond two decimal points have been used in these calculations, which means a few margins differ by 0.01 from results that would be obtained by using the published percentages for candidates.) This note also applies to the next list.

Largest drops between a candidate's EV and PV percentages

1. Walter Mondale (D-1984, 2.42% for EV, 40.56% for PV)....................-38.14
2. George McClellan (D-1864, 9.01% for EV, 44.89% for PV)...............-35.88
3. Alfred Landon (R-1936, 1.51% for EV, 36.54% for PV).......................-35.03
4. George McGovern (D-1972, 3.16% for EV, 37.53% for PV)..............-34.37
5. Jimmy Carter (D-1980, 9.11% for EV, 41.02% for PV).....................-31.91
6. Winfield Scott (W-1852, 14.19% for EV, 43.87% for PV)..................-29.68
7. Wendell Willkie (R-1940, 15.44% for EV, 44.83% for PV).................-29.39
8. Barry Goldwater (R-1964, 9.67% for EV, 38.47% for PV)..................-28.81
9. Herbert Hoover (R-1932, 11.11% for EV, 39.65% for PV).................-28.54
10. Adlai Stevenson (D-1956, 13.75% for EV, 41.95% for PV)..............-28.21

Electoral votes by home-state candidates

1. New York...6,359
2. California..2,372
3. Ohio...2,130
4. Illinois..1,764
5. Massachusetts..1,702
6. Texas...1,639
7. Virginia..1,200
8. Tennessee...997
9. New Jersey..775
10. Arkansas...749
11. Nebraska..493
12. Indiana...420
13. Georgia..393
14. Michigan..367
15. Pennsylvania..329
16. Missouri...321
17. Kentucky..263
18. New Hampshire..254
19. South Carolina..230
20. Arizona...225
21. Minnesota..204
22. Maine...182
23. Kansas..167
24. Louisiana..163
25. West Virginia..136
26. Alabama...47
27. Iowa...22
28. South Dakota..18
29. North Carolina..17
30. Maryland..15
31. Connecticut..13
31. Wisconsin...13
33. Vermont...1

NOTE: A home state is the place where an individual maintains a voting address during his or her presidential candidacy. This note also applies to the next list.

Home-state electoral votes per 100 EV cast by same state

1. New York (6,359 received, 2,096 cast) 303.39
2. Arkansas (749 received, 295 cast)..253.90
3. California (2,372 received, 1,071 cast)...221.48
4. Nebraska (493 received, 223 cast) 221.08
5. Texas (1,639 received, 860 cast)..190.58
6. Ohio (2,130 received, 1,143 cast) 186.35
7. Massachusetts (1,702 received, 915 cast) 186.01
8. Illinois (1,764 received, 1,035 cast) 170.43
9. Tennessee (997 received, 605 cast) 164.79
10. Arizona (225 received, 152 cast) 148.03
11. Virginia (1,200 received, 908 cast) 132.16
12. New Jersey (775 received, 700 cast)..110.71
13. New Hampshire (254 received, 309 cast) 82.20
14. Indiana (420 received, 633 cast) 66.35
15. Georgia (393 received, 650 cast)...60.46
16. Maine (182 received, 302 cast) 60.26
17. Kansas (167 received, 297 cast)..56.23
18. Michigan (367 received, 674 cast)...54.45
19. Minnesota (204 received, 378 cast) 53.97
19. West Virginia (136 received, 252 cast)..53.97
21. Missouri (321 received, 609 cast)..52.71
22. South Carolina (230 received, 525 cast)...43.81
23. Kentucky (263 received, 626 cast)..42.01
24. Louisiana (163 received, 406 cast) 40.15
25. Pennsylvania (329 received, 1,670 cast)..19.70
26. South Dakota (18 received, 124 cast)..14.52
27. Alabama (47 received, 468 cast) 10.04
28. Iowa (22 received, 409 cast) 5.38
29. Wisconsin (13 received, 462 cast)...2.81
30. Connecticut (13 received, 464 cast) 2.80
31. Maryland (15 received, 551 cast)..2.72
32. North Carolina (17 received, 752 cast)..2.26
33. Vermont (1 received, 259 cast) 0.39
34. Alaska (0 received, 45 cast)..0.00
34. Colorado (0 received, 221 cast)...0.00
34. Delaware (0 received, 188 cast)..0.00
34. District of Columbia (0 received, 41 cast)..0.00
34. Florida (0 received, 462 cast)...0.00
34. Hawaii (0 received, 59 cast) 0.00
34. Idaho (0 received, 123 cast)...0.00
34. Mississippi (0 received, 355 cast)...0.00
34. Montana (0 received, 116 cast) 0.00
34. Nevada (0 received, 131 cast) 0.00
34. New Mexico (0 received, 109 cast)..0.00
34. North Dakota (0 received, 118 cast) 0.00
34. Oklahoma (0 received, 242 cast)...0.00
34. Oregon (0 received, 207 cast) 0.00
34. Rhode Island (0 received, 245 cast) 0.00
34. Utah (0 received, 131 cast)...0.00

34. Washington (0 received, 268 cast) 0.00
34. Wyoming (0 received, 96 cast) 0.00

NOTE: This list compares the number of electoral votes received by home-state candidates with the number of electoral votes cast by the same state in all general elections. The rate is the number of electoral votes received per 100 electoral votes cast.

Electoral votes (equalized) in a career prior to 40th birthday

1. William Jennings Bryan 212
2. John Breckinridge 128
3. George McClellan 48
4. Aaron Burr...4

NOTE: All ages are as of November 1 of any given year, which applies to all remaining lists in this section. These are the only four candidates to receive electoral votes before turning 40.

Electoral votes (equalized) in a career prior to 45th birthday

1. Aaron Burr...406
2. William Jennings Bryan 399
3. John Kennedy 304
4. DeWitt Clinton 221
5. John Fremont..207
6. John Breckinridge 128
7. Thomas Dewey..100
8. John Jay..70
9. George McClellan 48
10. Robert Harrison 47

Electoral votes (equalized) in a career prior to 50th birthday

1. William Jennings Bryan 579
2. Franklin Pierce 462
3. Aaron Burr..406
4. Ulysses Grant...392
5. Theodore Roosevelt..380
6. Bill Clinton...370
7. Barack Obama..365
8. James Polk..333
9. James Garfield 312
10. John Kennedy...304

Electoral votes (equalized) in a career prior to 55th birthday

1. Franklin Roosevelt...1,008
2. Ulysses Grant...833
3. Bill Clinton...749
4. Barack Obama..697
5. William Jennings Bryan 579
6. Grover Cleveland 519
7. Theodore Roosevelt..469
8. Franklin Pierce 462
9. Herbert Hoover 450
10. Warren Harding..409

Electoral votes (equalized) in a career prior to 60th birthday

1. Franklin Roosevelt...1,463
2. Richard Nixon...1,040
3. Grover Cleveland...855
4. Ulysses Grant..833
5. Abraham Lincoln...810
6. Bill Clinton..749
7. Woodrow Wilson...722
8. Barack Obama...697
9. William McKinley...677
10. John Adams..579
10. William Jennings Bryan..579

Electoral votes (equalized) in a career prior to 65th birthday

1. Franklin Roosevelt...1,901
2. George Washington..1,084
3. Thomas Jefferson...1,061
4. Richard Nixon...1,040
5. James Monroe..990
6. John Adams..856
7. Grover Cleveland...855
8. Ulysses Grant..833
9. Abraham Lincoln...810
10. Bill Clinton..749

Electoral votes (equalized) in a career prior to 70th birthday

1. Franklin Roosevelt...1,901
2. John Adams...1,109
3. George Washington..1,084
4. Thomas Jefferson...1,061
5. Richard Nixon...1,040
6. James Monroe..990
7. Andrew Jackson...983
8. Dwight Eisenhower..911
9. Grover Cleveland...855
10. Ulysses Grant..833

Electoral votes (equalized) in a career prior to 75th birthday

1. Franklin Roosevelt...1,901
2. John Adams...1,109
3. George Washington..1,084
4. Thomas Jefferson...1,061
5. Richard Nixon...1,040
6. Ronald Reagan..1,015
7. James Monroe..990
8. Andrew Jackson...983
9. Dwight Eisenhower..911
10. Grover Cleveland...855

ELECTION FLIPS

Elections that could have been reversed by one flip

1844 (Henry Clay over James Polk by flipping New York)

1848 (Lewis Cass over Zachary Taylor by flipping Pennsylvania)

1876 (Samuel Tilden over Rutherford Hayes by flipping any of 20 states, with South Carolina having the smallest margin)

1880 (Winfield Hancock over James Garfield by flipping New York)

1884 (James Blaine over Grover Cleveland by flipping New York)

1888 (Grover Cleveland over Benjamin Harrison by flipping New York)

1916 (Charles Evans Hughes over Woodrow Wilson by flipping any of 9 states, with California having the smallest margin)

1976 (Gerald Ford over Jimmy Carter by flipping New York)

2000 (Al Gore over George W. Bush by flipping any of 30 states, with Florida having the smallest margin)

2004 (John Kerry over George W. Bush by flipping any of 3 states, with Ohio having the smallest margin)

NOTE: The candidate listed first would have been the national winner if the flip had occurred. A flip is the hypothetical reversal of a state's popular-vote results, achieved by switching a sufficient number of votes from the candidate who carried the state to the runnerup. (The size of a state's flip is the next whole number larger than one-half of its popular-vote margin.) A flip alters the distribution of electoral votes and potentially the outcome of the election. This note applies to all lists in this section.

Elections that could have been reversed by two flips

1828 (John Quincy Adams over Andrew Jackson by flipping Pennsylvania and Virginia)

1856 (John Fremont over James Buchanan by flipping Pennsylvania and either Illinois or Indiana)

1896 (William Jennings Bryan over William McKinley by flipping New York and any of 8 states, with Indiana having the smallest margin, or by flipping Pennsylvania and either Illinois or Ohio)

1960 (Richard Nixon over John Kennedy by flipping New York and any of 16 states, with Illinois having the smallest margin, or by flipping Pennsylvania and any of 3 states, with Illinois again having the smallest margin, or by flipping Illinois and Texas)

2012 (Mitt Romney over Barack Obama by flipping California and any of 14 states, with Florida having the smallest margin)

2016 (Hillary Clinton over Donald Trump by flipping Florida and Texas)

Smallest flips to reverse an election (popular votes)

1. 2000 (Al Gore-George W. Bush)..269
2. 1876 (Samuel Tilden-Rutherford Hayes)......................................445
3. 1884 (James Blaine-Grover Cleveland)..524
4. 1916 (Charles Evans Hughes-Woodrow Wilson).................... 1,711
5. 1844 (Henry Clay-James Polk).. 2,554
6. 1848 (Lewis Cass-Zachary Taylor) 3,706

7. 1888 (Grover Cleveland-Benjamin Harrison) 7,187
8. 1840 (Martin Van Buren-William Henry Harrison) 8,182
9. 1880 (Winfield Hancock-James Garfield) 8,420
10. 1976 (Gerald Ford-Jimmy Carter) 15,629

NOTE: These hypothetical flips are based on a specific number of popular votes being switched in specific states to change the national winner in electoral votes. The minimum switch of popular votes necessary to effect a flip is shown above. The candidate listed first would have been the national winner if the flip had occurred. This note also applies to the next three lists.

Smallest flips to reverse an election (share of popular votes)

1. 2000 (Al Gore-George W. Bush) 0.0003%
2. 1884 (James Blaine-Grover Cleveland) 0.0052%
3. 1876 (Samuel Tilden-Rutherford Hayes) 0.0053%
4. 1916 (Charles Evans Hughes-Woodrow Wilson) 0.0092%
5. 1976 (Gerald Ford-Jimmy Carter) 0.0192%
6. 1960 (Richard Nixon-John Kennedy) 0.0265%
7. 2016 (Hillary Clinton-Donald Trump) 0.0284%
8. 2004 (John Kerry-George W. Bush) 0.0480%
9. 1948 (Thomas Dewey-Harry Truman) 0.0602%
10. 1888 (Grover Cleveland-Benjamin Harrison) 0.0631%

NOTE: This list expresses in a different way the minimum number of popular votes to be flipped, presenting it as a percentage of all votes cast nationally.

Largest flips to reverse an election (popular votes)

1. 1972 (George McGovern-Richard Nixon) 3,454,319
2. 1984 (Walter Mondale-Ronald Reagan) 2,973,774
3. 1964 (Barry Goldwater-Lyndon Johnson) 2,325,630
4. 1936 (Alfred Landon-Franklin Roosevelt) 2,261,822
5. 1956 (Adlai Stevenson-Dwight Eisenhower) 1,229,767
6. 1932 (Herbert Hoover-Franklin Roosevelt) 1,001,890
7. 1952 (Adlai Stevenson-Dwight Eisenhower) 948,205
8. 1980 (Jimmy Carter-Ronald Reagan) 801,579
9. 1924 (John Davis-Calvin Coolidge) 727,135
10. 1996 (Bob Dole-Bill Clinton) 694,191

NOTE: This list shows the minimum switch of popular votes necessary to effect a flip, which also applies to the next list.

Largest flips to reverse an election (share of popular votes)

1. 1936 (Alfred Landon-Franklin Roosevelt) 4.9550%
2. 1972 (George McGovern-Richard Nixon) 4.4447%
3. 1860 (Stephen Douglas-Abraham Lincoln) 3.7311%
4. 1964 (Barry Goldwater-Lyndon Johnson) 3.2920%
5. 1984 (Walter Mondale-Ronald Reagan) 3.2096%
6. 1932 (Herbert Hoover-Franklin Roosevelt) 2.5206%
7. 1924 (John Davis-Calvin Coolidge) 2.4988%
8. 1920 (James Cox-Warren Harding) 2.4955%
9. 1912 (Theodore Roosevelt-Woodrow Wilson) 2.1654%
10. 1956 (Adlai Stevenson-Dwight Eisenhower) 1.9826%

NOTE: This list expresses in a different way the minimum number of popular votes to be flipped, presenting it as a percentage of all votes cast nationally.

CAMPAIGN SCORES

Largest cumulative campaign scores in a career

1. Franklin Roosevelt.....................366.37
2. John Adams................................281.71
3. Thomas Jefferson.......................271.57
4. Ronald Reagan............................262.11
5. Henry Clay...................................260.55
6. Richard Nixon..............................256.38
7. Andrew Jackson..........................241.67
8. Martin Van Buren........................237.77
9. Grover Cleveland........................231.78
10. Ulysses Grant............................230.60
11. George Washington...................213.78
12. William Jennings Bryan.............209.28
13. Charles Cotesworth Pinckney....207.40
14. James Blaine..............................199.73
15. William McKinley.......................190.58
16. James Monroe...........................186.14
17. Dwight Eisenhower....................180.63
18. George H.W. Bush......................178.87
19. Thomas Dewey..........................175.94
20. Abraham Lincoln.......................170.55
21. Theodore Roosevelt..................167.11
22. Bill Clinton.................................166.23
23. Barack Obama............................165.62
24. Herbert Hoover..........................165.32
25. James Madison...........................164.53

Largest cumulative campaign scores by someone not elected

1. Henry Clay...................................260.55
2. William Jennings Bryan...............209.28
3. Charles Cotesworth Pinckney......207.40
4. James Blaine................................199.73
5. Thomas Dewey............................175.94
6. George Clinton............................152.62
7. Lewis Cass...................................150.11
8. Adlai Stevenson..........................139.28
9. Aaron Burr..................................138.62
10. Alfred Smith..............................125.83

NOTE: This list is confined to candidates who never won a general election.

Largest cumulative campaign scores by someone not nominated

1. George Clinton............................152.62
2. Aaron Burr..................................138.62
3. George Wallace...........................103.10
4. Thomas Hendricks.........................99.17
5. John Jay.......................................98.79

6. Millard Fillmore 91.00
7. Eugene Debs 88.81
8. Robert Taft 87.14
9. Ross Perot 80.65
10. Robert La Follette 77.96
NOTE: This list is confined to candidates who never won a major-party nomination.

Largest campaign scores in a year

1. George Washington (F-1789) 96.18
1. George Washington (F-1792) 96.18
3. James Monroe (DR-1820) 96.04
4. Franklin Roosevelt (D-1936) 95.88
5. Richard Nixon (R-1972) 95.25
6. Ronald Reagan (R-1984) 95.13
7. Lyndon Johnson (D-1964) 93.24
8. Thomas Jefferson (DR-1804) 93.05
9. Abraham Lincoln (R-1864) 92.17
10. Franklin Roosevelt (D-1932) 91.94

Smallest campaign scores by qualified candidates in a year

1. Carly Fiorina (R-2016) 10.07
2. Michele Bachmann (R-2012) 10.11
2. Chris Christie (R-2016) 10.11
4. Rand Paul (R-2016) 10.13
5. Rick Perry (R-2012) 10.14
6. Alan Cranston (D-1984) 10.17
6. Bill Richardson (D-2008) 10.17
8. Gary Bauer (R-2000) 10.19
9. Bruce Babbitt (D-1988) 10.20
10. Richard Gephardt (D-2004) 10.23

Smallest campaign scores by general-election winners

1. John Quincy Adams (DR-1824) 67.41
2. Rutherford Hayes (R-1876) 77.12
3. George W. Bush (R-2000) 77.21
4. John Adams (F-1796) 77.27
5. Thomas Jefferson (DR-1800) 77.84
6. Richard Nixon (R-1968) 78.01
7. Woodrow Wilson (D-1916) 78.07
8. Abraham Lincoln (R-1860) 78.38
9. George W. Bush (R-2004) 78.71
10. Grover Cleveland (D-1884) 78.78

Smallest campaign scores by major-party nominees

1. Hugh White (W-1836) 54.62
2. William Howard Taft (R-1912) 55.09
3. Stephen Douglas (D-1860) 57.06
4. Alfred Landon (R-1936) 57.76
5. George McGovern (D-1972) 58.46
6. Horace Greeley (D-LR-1872) 58.76
7. Walter Mondale (D-1984) 58.83

8. Charles Cotesworth Pinckney (F-1804).............................59.38
9. Barry Goldwater (R-1964) 60.59
10. John Breckinridge (SD-1860) 60.76

Largest campaign scores by election losers

1. Samuel Tilden (D-1876) 75.14
2. Al Gore (D-2000) 74.51
3. Thomas Jefferson (DR-1796)..74.00
4. John Kerry (D-2004)..73.65
5. Charles Evans Hughes (R-1916)...................................73.55
6. James Blaine (R-1884) 73.26
7. John Adams (F-1800) 73.21
8. Gerald Ford (R-1976) 72.98
9. Hillary Clinton (D-2016)...72.30
10. Grover Cleveland (D-1888) 72.27

Largest margins in campaign scores

1. 1820 (James Monroe-John Quincy Adams)....................78.08
2. 1936 (Franklin Roosevelt-Alfred Landon) 38.12
3. 1972 (Richard Nixon-George McGovern)......................36.79
4. 1984 (Ronald Reagan-Walter Mondale) 36.30
5. 1804 (Thomas Jefferson-Charles Cotesworth Pinckney) 33.67
6. 1964 (Lyndon Johnson-Barry Goldwater).....................32.65
7. 1789 (George Washington-John Adams).......................32.18
8. 1932 (Franklin Roosevelt-Herbert Hoover) 30.66
9. 1872 (Ulysses Grant-Horace Greeley)..........................30.52
10. 1864 (Abraham Lincoln-George McClellan)..................30.51

NOTE: The top two candidates are listed in parentheses, with the campaign-score leader coming first. The margin is the difference between the candidates' campaign scores. This note also applies to the next list.

Smallest margins in campaign scores

1. 1876 (Rutherford Hayes-Samuel Tilden) 1.98
2. 1824 (Andrew Jackson-John Quincy Adams)...................2.24
3. 2000 (George W. Bush-Al Gore) 2.70
4. 1796 (John Adams-Thomas Jefferson)...........................3.27
5. 1916 (Woodrow Wilson-Charles Evans Hughes) 4.52
6. 1800 (Thomas Jefferson-John Adams) 4.63
7. 2004 (George W. Bush-John Kerry).................................5.06
8. 1884 (Grover Cleveland-James Blaine) 5.52
9. 1976 (Jimmy Carter-Gerald Ford) 6.25
10. 2016 (Donald Trump-Hillary Clinton)............................6.49

Largest campaign scores by incumbent presidents

1. George Washington (F-1792) 96.18
2. James Monroe (DR-1820) 96.04
3. Franklin Roosevelt (D-1936) 95.88
4. Richard Nixon (R-1972)...95.25
5. Ronald Reagan (R-1984)..95.13

6. Lyndon Johnson (D-1964) 93.24
7. Thomas Jefferson (DR-1804) 93.05
8. Abraham Lincoln (R-1864) 92.17
9. Dwight Eisenhower (R-1956) 91.03
10. Franklin Roosevelt (D-1940) 89.94

NOTE: This list shows the campaign scores for incumbent presidents who ran for another term. This note also applies to the next list.

Smallest campaign scores by incumbent presidents

1. Theodore Roosevelt (R-1908) 0.24
2. Harry Truman (D-1952) 0.63
3. Calvin Coolidge (R-1928) 1.02
4. Lyndon Johnson (D-1968) 11.53
5. George Washington (F-1796) 21.42
6. Andrew Johnson (D-1868) 26.37
7. Chester Arthur (R-1884) 37.07
8. Franklin Pierce (D-1856) 43.05
9. Millard Fillmore (W-1852) 45.85
10. William Howard Taft (R-1912) 55.09

NOTE: The first five presidents on this list either did not run for reelection or dropped out in the early stages of the race. They still received some support in primaries, at the convention, and/or in the general election, which yielded the campaign scores shown above.

Largest gains in campaign scores by incumbent presidents

1. Richard Nixon (78.01 in 1968, 95.25 in 1972) 17.24
2. Thomas Jefferson (77.84 in 1800, 93.05 in 1804) 15.21
3. Abraham Lincoln (78.38 in 1860, 92.17 in 1864) 13.79
4. James Monroe (90.10 in 1816, 96.04 in 1820) 5.94
5. Ronald Reagan (91.16 in 1980, 95.13 in 1984) 3.97
6. Franklin Roosevelt (91.94 in 1932, 95.88 in 1936) 3.94
7. Ulysses Grant (85.63 in 1868, 89.28 in 1872) 3.65
8. Andrew Jackson (84.82 in 1828, 87.20 in 1832) 2.38
9. Bill Clinton (82.15 in 1992, 84.08 in 1996) 1.93
10. William McKinley (81.24 in 1896, 82.89 in 1900) 1.65

NOTE: This list is confined to candidates who won the presidency and then sought reelection four years later, showing the difference between their two campaign scores. This note also applies to the next list.

Largest drops in campaign scores by incumbent presidents

1. Franklin Pierce (89.52 in 1852, 43.05 in 1856) ....-46.47
2. Herbert Hoover (90.41 in 1928, 61.28 in 1932) ....-29.13
3. William Howard Taft (83.31 in 1908, 55.09 in 1912) ....-28.22
4. George H.W. Bush (87.86 in 1988, 66.86 in 1992) ....-21.00
5. Jimmy Carter (79.23 in 1976, 60.93 in 1980) ....-18.30
6. Martin Van Buren (80.26 in 1836, 65.49 in 1840) ....-14.77
7. Benjamin Harrison (79.71 in 1888, 68.40 in 1892) ....-11.31
8. Woodrow Wilson (86.26 in 1912, 78.07 in 1916) ....-8.19
9. Grover Cleveland (78.78 in 1884, 72.27 in 1888) ....-6.51
10. Franklin Roosevelt (95.88 in 1936, 89.94 in 1940) ....-5.94

Largest campaign scores by former presidents

1. Grover Cleveland (D-1892)..80.73
2. Theodore Roosevelt (R/P-1912)...66.37
3. Martin Van Buren (D-1844)...50.00
4. Millard Fillmore (AW-1856)...45.15
5. Ulysses Grant (R-1880)..42.34
6. Martin Van Buren (FS-1848)..42.02
7. Theodore Roosevelt (R-1916)...14.78
8. Herbert Hoover (R-1940)..1.03
9. William Howard Taft (R-1916)...0.84
10. Calvin Coolidge (R-1932)..0.24

NOTE: This list is confined to former presidents who sought another term after leaving office. The final four individuals on the list were not formal candidates, yet still received some support in primaries or at the convention, which yielded the campaign scores shown above.

Largest campaign scores by sitting vice presidents

1. George H.W. Bush (R-1988)..87.86
2. Martin Van Buren (D-1836)...80.26
3. Thomas Jefferson (DR-1800)...77.84
4. John Adams (F-1796)...77.27
5. Al Gore (D-2000)..74.51
6. Richard Nixon (R-1960)...72.12
7. Hubert Humphrey (D-1968)...69.19
8. John Adams (F-1792)...67.23
9. John Breckinridge (D/SD-1860)..60.76
10. George Clinton (DR-1808)...28.01

NOTE: The term "sitting" means the individual was serving as vice president while running for president. The same concept applies to the next four lists. The first four individuals on this list are the only incumbent vice presidents to be directly elected to the presidency.

Largest campaign scores by sitting Cabinet members

1. Herbert Hoover (R-1928)..90.41
2. James Monroe (DR-1816)..90.10
3. James Madison (DR-1808)...84.36
4. William Howard Taft (R-1908)..83.31
5. John Quincy Adams (DR-1824)..67.41
6. John Jay (F-1789)...51.15
7. William Crawford (DR-1824)..46.97
8. Mitchell Palmer (D-1920)..27.09
9. Thomas Jefferson (DR-1792)...26.68
10. James Buchanan (D-1848)..25.17

Largest campaign scores by sitting governors

1. Franklin Roosevelt (D-1932)..91.94
2. Woodrow Wilson (D-1912)..86.26
3. Bill Clinton (D-1992)..82.15
4. Grover Cleveland (D-1884)...78.78
5. George W. Bush (R-2000)..77.21
6. Rutherford Hayes (R-1876)..77.12

7. Samuel Tilden (D-1876) 75.14
8. Thomas Dewey (R-1948) 69.67
9. Michael Dukakis (D-1988) 65.32
10. Thomas Dewey (R-1944) 64.76

Largest campaign scores by sitting senators

1. Warren Harding (R-1920) 88.37
2. Barack Obama (D-2008) 84.03
3. John Kennedy (D-1960) 79.58
4. John Kerry (D-2004) 73.65
5. Lewis Cass (D-1848) 71.66
6. Andrew Jackson (DR-1824) 69.65
7. John McCain (R-2008) 68.78
8. Bob Dole (R-1996) 67.01
9. Henry Clay (NR-1832) 62.61
10. Rufus King (F-1816) 62.07

Largest campaign scores by sitting representatives

1. James Garfield (R-1880) 79.77
2. James Blaine (R-1876) 47.05
3. Henry Clay (DR-1824) 46.84
4. Champ Clark (D-1912) 42.45
5. John Anderson (R/NU-1980) 38.97
6. William Randolph Hearst (D-1904) 24.45
7. James Weaver (GBK-1880) 20.66
8. Morris Udall (D-1976) 18.22
9. Ron Paul (R-2012) 18.11
10. Samuel Randall (D-1884) 17.58

POTENTIAL INDEXES

Largest potential indexes by qualified candidates

1. Theodore Roosevelt (R/P-1912)..10.0
1. Franklin Roosevelt (D-1936) 10.0
3. George Washington (F-1792) 9.7
4. Theodore Roosevelt (R-1916) 9.6
4. Franklin Roosevelt (D-1940) 9.6
6. Franklin Roosevelt (D-1944) 9.4
7. Lyndon Johnson (D-1964) 9.3
7. George W. Bush (R-2004) 9.3
9. Thomas Jefferson (DR-1804)...9.2
9. Grover Cleveland (D-1888)..9.2

Smallest potential indexes by qualified candidates

1. Eugene Debs (SOC-1920) 0.1
2. John Bidwell (PRO-1892) 0.4
3. Ralph Nader (GRN-2000)..1.3
4. Eugene Debs (SOC-1912) 1.5
5. William Lemke (U-1936) 1.8
6. Walter Jones (D-1956) 1.9
7. Robert La Follette (R/P-1924) 2.2
7. Strom Thurmond (SRD-1948)..2.2
9. Robert Harrison (F-1789) 2.3
9. Stephen Field (D-1880)..2.3
9. Faith Spotted Eagle (D-2016) 2.3

Largest potential indexes by general-election winners

1. Franklin Roosevelt (D-1936) 10.0
2. George Washington (F-1792) 9.7
3. Franklin Roosevelt (D-1940) 9.6
4. Franklin Roosevelt (D-1944) 9.4
5. Lyndon Johnson (D-1964) 9.3
5. George W. Bush (R-2004) 9.3
7. Thomas Jefferson (DR-1804)...9.2
8. Grover Cleveland (D-1892)...9.1
8. Calvin Coolidge (R-1924) 9.1
10. Ulysses Grant (R-1872)..9.0

Smallest potential indexes by general-election winners

1. Donald Trump (R-2016) 3.1
2. Herbert Hoover (R-1928)...4.0
3. Zachary Taylor (W-1848) 4.1
4. James Buchanan (D-1856)...5.1
5. George Washington (F-1789) 5.6
5. John Quincy Adams (DR-1824)..5.6
5. Dwight Eisenhower (R-1952)...5.6

8. John Adams (F-1796) 5.7
8. Ronald Reagan (R-1980) 5.7
10. William Howard Taft (R-1908) 6.0
10. Warren Harding (R-1920) 6.0

Largest potential indexes by general-election losers

1. Grover Cleveland (D-1888) 9.2
2. Martin Van Buren (D-1840) 9.1
3. Jimmy Carter (D-1980) 9.0
4. Al Gore (D-2000) 8.8
5. Benjamin Harrison (R-1892) 8.5
6. William Howard Taft (R-1912) 8.2
6. George H.W. Bush (R-1992) 8.2
8. Charles Evans Hughes (R-1916) 8.0
8. Richard Nixon (R-1960) 8.0
10. Hubert Humphrey (D-1968) 7.8
10. Walter Mondale (D-1984) 7.8

NOTE: This list is confined to major-party nominees who lost general elections.

Smallest potential indexes by major-party nominees

1. Donald Trump (R-2016) 3.1
2. DeWitt Clinton (F-DR-1812) 3.7
3. Charles Cotesworth Pinckney (F-1808) 3.9
4. Winfield Scott (W-1852) 4.2
5. John Davis (D-1924) 4.4
6. William Jennings Bryan (D-POP-1896) 4.6
7. John Breckinridge (SD-1860) 4.7
7. George McClellan (D-1864) 4.7
7. Wendell Willkie (R-1940) 4.7
10. Horace Greeley (D-LR-1872) 4.8
10. Alfred Landon (R-1936) 4.8

Largest margins in potential indexes

1. 1936 (Franklin Roosevelt-Alfred Landon) 5.2
2. 1812 (James Madison-DeWitt Clinton) 5.0
3. 1940 (Franklin Roosevelt-Wendell Willkie) 4.9
4. 1924 (Calvin Coolidge-John Davis) 4.7
5. 1864 (Abraham Lincoln-George McClellan) 4.2
5. 1872 (Ulysses Grant-Horace Greeley) 4.2
7. 1804 (Thomas Jefferson-Charles Cotesworth Pinckney) 4.1
8. 1904 (Theodore Roosevelt-Alton Parker) 3.9
9. 1820 (James Monroe-John Quincy Adams) 3.7
10. 1896 (William McKinley-William Jennings Bryan) 3.6

NOTE: The margin is the difference between the potential indexes for the two candidates with the largest campaign scores. The candidate with the larger potential index is listed first. This note also applies to the next list.

Smallest margins in potential indexes

1. 1920 (Warren Harding-James Cox)..0.1
2. 1816 (James Monroe-Rufus King)..0.2
2. 1856 (John Fremont-James Buchanan) 0.2
2. 1988 (Michael Dukakis-George H.W. Bush)..0.2
5. 1824 (Andrew Jackson-John Quincy Adams)..0.3
5. 1984 (Ronald Reagan-Walter Mondale) 0.3
7. 1800 (Thomas Jefferson-John Adams) 0.4
7. 1840 (Martin Van Buren-William Henry Harrison)......................................0.4
9. 1892 (Grover Cleveland-Benjamin Harrison)..0.6
9. 1916 (Woodrow Wilson-Charles Evans Hughes) 0.6

RETURNS ON POTENTIAL

Largest returns on potential by qualified candidates

1. Eugene Debs (SOC-1920) 2,094
2. John Bidwell (PRO-1892) 430
3. Donald Trump (R-2016) 254
4. Herbert Hoover (R-1928) 226
5. Robert La Follette (R/P-1924) 211
6. Robert Harrison (F-1789) 199
7. Eugene Debs (SOC-1912) 194
8. Zachary Taylor (W-1848) 193
9. DeWitt Clinton (F-DR-1812) 192
10. George Clinton (DR-1792) 187

Smallest returns on potential by qualified candidates

1. Phil Gramm (R-1996) 12
2. Lyndon Johnson (D-1968) 13
2. John Edwards (D-2008) 13
2. Rand Paul (R-2016) 13
5. Howard Baker (R-1980) 14
5. John Connally (R-1980) 14
5. Lloyd Bentsen (D-1988) 14
5. Rick Perry (R-2012) 14
9. Charles Fairbanks (R-1908) 15
9. Theodore Roosevelt (R-1916) 15
9. Birch Bayh (D-1976) 15
9. Alan Cranston (D-1984) 15
9. Lamar Alexander (R-1996) 15
9. Joseph Lieberman (D-2004) 15
9. Fred Thompson (R-2008) 15
9. Jon Huntsman (R-2012) 15
9. Jeb Bush (R-2016) 15
9. Chris Christie (R-2016) 15

Largest returns on potential by general-election winners

1. Donald Trump (R-2016) 254
2. Herbert Hoover (R-1928) 226
3. Zachary Taylor (W-1848) 193
4. George Washington (F-1789) 172
5. Dwight Eisenhower (R-1952) 160
5. Ronald Reagan (R-1980) 160
7. James Buchanan (D-1856) 156
8. Warren Harding (R-1920) 147
9. William Howard Taft (R-1908) 139
10. John Adams (F-1796) 136
10. Ulysses Grant (R-1868) 136

Smallest returns on potential by general-election winners

1. George W. Bush (R-2004) 85
2. Grover Cleveland (D-1892)... 89
3. Woodrow Wilson (D-1916) 91
4. James Madison (DR-1812).. 92
5. Rutherford Hayes (R-1876) 93
5. William McKinley (R-1900)... 93
7. Calvin Coolidge (R-1924) 94
7. Franklin Roosevelt (D-1940) 94
7. Franklin Roosevelt (D-1944) 94
10. Franklin Roosevelt (D-1936)... 96

Largest returns on potential by general-election losers

1. DeWitt Clinton (F-DR-1812) 192
2. Charles Cotesworth Pinckney (F-1808)............................169
3. William Jennings Bryan (D-POP-1896) 154
4. Winfield Scott (W-1852) 150
5. John Davis (D-1924)..144
6. Alton Parker (D-1904)..135
6. Wendell Willkie (R-1940) 135
8. William Henry Harrison (W-1836).................................132
8. William Jennings Bryan (D-1908)..................................132
10. George McClellan (D-1864) 131

NOTE: This list is confined to major-party nominees who lost general elections.

Smallest returns on potential by major-party nominees

1. William Howard Taft (R-1912) 67
2. Jimmy Carter (D-1980)...68
3. Martin Van Buren (D-1840)...72
4. Walter Mondale (D-1984)...75
5. Grover Cleveland (D-1888)...79
6. Benjamin Harrison (R-1892)...80
7. Stephen Douglas (D-1860)...82
7. Adlai Stevenson (D-1956)...82
7. George H.W. Bush (R-1992)...82
10. Herbert Hoover (R-1932)..84

5

ELECTION 2020

The ideal way to conclude a book about the past is to look toward the future. This chapter contains statistical profiles for 31 actual or potential candidates for president in the 2020 election.

The entries on the following pages are published alphabetically. But there is a second way to approach these 31 contenders, and that's to rank them by potential index (PI).

The incumbent is first in the PI standings, to no one's surprise, followed by a raft of Democratic challengers. The order may surprise you, but keep in mind that we're ranking by *potential* — and not by actual performance. Some candidates will fail to fulfill their promise, while others will exceed expectations:

1. Donald Trump (R)..8.2
2. Kamala Harris (D) 8.0
3. Kirsten Gillibrand (D)...7.8
4. Cory Booker (D)..7.0
5. Michael Bennet (D) 6.9
6. Amy Klobuchar (D)..6.4
6. Deval Patrick (D)..6.4
8. Steve Bullock (D)..6.1
8. Jay Inslee (D)...6.1
8. Elizabeth Warren (D)...6.1
11. William Weld (R)..6.0
12. Beto O'Rourke (D) 5.5
13. John Hickenlooper (D) 5.4
14. Bernie Sanders (D) 5.2
15. Julian Castro (D)..4.8
16. Mark Sanford (R)...4.7
17. Joe Walsh (R)..4.6
18. Joseph Biden (D)...4.4
19. Wayne Messam (D) 4.3
20. John Delaney (D)...4.2
20. Tim Ryan (D)...4.2
22. Eric Swalwell (D) 4.1
23. Tom Steyer (D) 3.9

24. Bill De Blasio (D)... 3.8
25. Joe Sestak (D) 3.7
25. Marianne Williamson (D) 3.7
27. Andrew Yang (D)... 3.5
28. Seth Moulton (D)... 3.4
29. Michael Bloomberg (D)... 2.8
30. Tulsi Gabbard (D)... 2.7
31. Pete Buttigieg (D)... 2.5

It's important to remember that the potential index takes trends from the past and projects them into the future. It's based on nine quantifiable factors that have an impact on a presidential hopeful's chances for success. The PI does a good job of determining the likelihood of a particular candidate reaching the White House, but it cannot measure spirit, intensity, and other intangible qualities.

Millions of words have already been written about the 2020 field in newspapers and on the internet — and there are millions more to come. The profiles in this book are different. They're statistically based, of course, and they offer four different perspectives on each candidate. Here's what they'll tell you:

Basics

Potential index: Rating of candidate's potential on a 10-point scale. See pages 20-21 for details.

Party: Political party.

Age: Age as of November 1, 2020, rounded to two decimal places.

Birthday: Date of birth.

State: State in which the candidate maintains a voting address.

Position: Position by which the candidate is best known, typically his or her current or most recent position (as of November 1, 2019).

Prior candidacies: Previous campaigns (both qualified and nonqualified) for the presidency.

Prior major tickets: Previous appearances on a major-party ticket as a presidential or vice presidential nominee.

Modern Era candidates with comparable PIs

Candidate: Any qualified candidate in the Modern Era (1960-2016) who had a PI within one-tenth of a point of the 2020 candidate in question. Entries are ranked by campaign scores.

Year: Election.

Party: Political party. See pages 18-20 for abbreviations.

PI: Potential index.

N: Major-party nominees are designated by an X.

W: General-election winners are designated by an X.

CS: Campaign score.

Modern Era candidates from home state

Candidate: Any qualified candidate in the Modern Era (1960-2016) who came from the same state as the 2020 candidate in question. They are ranked by campaign scores.

Other columns: Same as for the chart of Modern Era candidates with comparable PIs.

All-time leaders (1789-2016) in similarity scores

Candidate: The 25 presidential candidates in American history who were most similar to the 2020 candidate in question. They are ranked by similarity scores, which are based on comparisons of 15 factors, including potential index, age, political party, home state, position, and prior experience (if any) as a presidential candidate. Each current candidate was matched against all 459 qualified candidacies from 1789 to 2016, with the 25 closest matches displayed here. (There is one exception to this rule. If a current candidate also ran in a previous election, he or she was not compared to any prior personal candidacy.)

Other columns: Same as for the chart of Modern Era candidates with comparable PIs.

MICHAEL BENNET

Basics

Potential index 6.9
Party .... Democratic
Age (as of November 1, 2020)...55.93
Birthday.. November 28, 1964
State .... Colorado
Position (as of November 1, 2019)... Senator
Prior candidacies .... None
Prior major tickets .... None

Modern Era (1960-2016) candidates with comparable PIs

Candidate	Year	Party	PI	N	W	CS
Barack Obama	2008	D	6.8	X	X	84.03
Bob Dole	1996	R	6.8	X	—	67.01
Hillary Clinton	2008	D	7.0	—	—	43.42
Edward Kennedy	1980	D	6.8	—	—	39.18
Eugene McCarthy	1968	D	6.9	—	—	33.16
Jerry Brown	1992	D	6.8	—	—	24.83
Paul Tsongas	1992	D	7.0	—	—	21.82
Bob Dole	1988	R	7.0	—	—	21.51
William Scranton	1964	R	6.9	—	—	19.42
Harry Byrd	1960	D	6.9	—	—	19.25
Al Gore	1988	D	6.8	—	—	18.19
Stuart Symington	1960	D	6.9	—	—	13.00
John Glenn	1984	D	6.8	—	—	12.08
Fred Harris	1976	D	6.9	—	—	10.94
Tom Harkin	1992	D	6.9	—	—	10.83
Birch Bayh	1976	D	6.9	—	—	10.32
Alan Cranston	1984	D	7.0	—	—	10.17

Modern Era candidates from Colorado

Candidate	Year	Party	PI	N	W	CS
Gary Hart	1984	D	6.3	—	—	37.76
Gary Hart	1988	D	6.7	—	—	11.02

All-time leaders (1789-2016) in similarity scores

Candidate	Year	Party	PI	N	W	CS
1. Gary Hart	1984	D	6.3	—	—	37.76
2. Henry Jackson	1972	D	6.3	—	—	15.37
3. Gary Hart	1988	D	6.7	—	—	11.02
4. Frank Church	1976	D	6.5	—	—	13.23
5. Henry Jackson	1976	D	6.2	—	—	14.30
6. Eugene McCarthy	1968	D	6.9	—	—	33.16
7. Tom Harkin	1992	D	6.9	—	—	10.83
8. Arthur Gorman	1892	D	7.4	—	—	13.19
9. Stuart Symington	1960	D	6.9	—	—	13.00
10. Andrew Johnson	1860	D	6.9	—	—	13.19
11. John Kerry	2004	D	6.6	X	—	73.65

Candidate	Year	Party	PI	N	W	CS
12. Hubert Humphrey	1960	D	7.1	—	—	14.46
13. James Doolittle	1868	D	7.9	—	—	13.27
14. Joseph Blackburn	1896	D	6.2	—	—	17.03
15. Birch Bayh	1976	D	6.9	—	—	10.32
16. Edward Kennedy	1980	D	6.8	—	—	39.18
17. Andrew Jackson	1824	DR	5.9	X	—	69.65
18. Bob Kerrey	1992	D	6.4	—	—	10.95
19. Robert Hunter	1860	D	7.0	—	—	21.10
20. Thomas Bayard	1880	D	7.1	—	—	26.61
21. Thomas Bayard	1876	D	7.1	—	—	13.59
22. Harry Byrd	1944	D	5.1	—	—	14.55
23. John Edwards	2004	D	7.8	—	—	22.22
24. Thomas Walsh	1924	D	4.0	—	—	13.17
25. Lewis Cass	1848	D	6.9	X	—	71.66

JOSEPH BIDEN

Basics

Potential index 4.4
Party .... Democratic
Age (as of November 1, 2020)...77.95
Birthday.. November 20, 1942
State ....Delaware
Position (as of November 1, 2019)...Former vice president
Prior candidacies ....Nonqualified (1988, 2008)
Prior major tickets ....Vice presidential nominee (2008, 2012)

Modern Era (1960-2016) candidates with comparable PIs

Candidate	Year	Party	PI	N	W	CS
Newt Gingrich	2012	R	4.3	—	—	18.59
Morris Udall	1976	D	4.3	—	—	18.22
Pat Robertson	1988	R	4.5	—	—	15.41
Shirley Chisholm	1972	D	4.5	—	—	12.62
Ben Carson	2016	R	4.3	—	—	11.69
Wilbur Mills	1972	D	4.3	—	—	10.36
Sam Yorty	1972	D	4.3	—	—	10.30
Michele Bachmann	2012	R	4.3	—	—	10.11

Modern Era candidates from Delaware

Candidate	Year	Party	PI	N	W	CS
Pete du Pont	1988	R	6.6	—	—	10.25

All-time leaders (1789-2016) in similarity scores

Candidate	Year	Party	PI	N	W	CS
1. George Gray	1908	D	6.3	—	—	14.71
2. Alben Barkley	1952	D	4.2	—	—	12.74
3. Bernie Sanders	2016	D	5.5	—	—	44.15
4. George Clinton	1808	DR	4.0	—	—	28.01
5. Richard Johnson	1844	D	5.6	—	—	17.19
6. Joseph Lieberman	2004	D	7.2	—	—	11.04
7. Edmund Muskie	1972	D	7.2	—	—	17.06
8. Thomas Bayard	1884	D	6.2	—	—	26.53
9. Charles Fairbanks	1916	R	4.7	—	—	16.32
10. Walter Mondale	1984	D	7.8	X	—	58.83
11. Samuel Adams	1796	DR	3.7	—	—	50.36
12. Thomas Walsh	1924	D	4.0	—	—	13.17
13. Thomas Bayard	1880	D	7.1	—	—	26.61
14. Thomas Bayard	1876	D	7.1	—	—	13.59
15. Thomas Walsh	1928	D	3.5	—	—	10.95
16. Lewis Cass	1852	D	6.9	—	—	42.18
17. Sargent Shriver	1976	D	4.2	—	—	11.14
18. Franklin Pierce	1856	D	8.1	—	—	43.05
19. John Kerry	2004	D	6.6	X	—	73.65
20. Woodrow Wilson	1916	D	8.6	X	X	78.07
21. Harry Truman	1948	D	7.6	X	X	79.72

Candidate	Year	Party	PI	N	W	CS
22. Thomas Seymour	1864	D	6.8	—	—	23.41
23. James Reed	1928	D	4.8	—	—	16.09
24. William Murray	1932	D	5.1	—	—	12.73
25. Lewis Cass	1844	D	5.1	—	—	34.91

MICHAEL BLOOMBERG

Basics

Potential index 2.8
Party .... Democratic
Age (as of November 1, 2020)..78.71
Birthday..February 14, 1942
State ....New York
Position (as of November 1, 2019).. Former mayor
Prior candidacies ....None
Prior major tickets ....None

Modern Era (1960-2016) candidates with comparable PIs

Candidate	Year	Party	PI	N	W	CS
Ross Perot	1992	I	2.9	—	—	43.78

Modern Era candidates from New York

Candidate	Year	Party	PI	N	W	CS
Donald Trump	2016	R	3.1	X	X	78.79
Richard Nixon	1968	R	6.2	X	X	78.01
Hillary Clinton	2016	D	6.6	X	—	72.30
Hillary Clinton	2008	D	7.0	—	—	43.42
Nelson Rockefeller	1968	R	7.1	—	—	21.48
Nelson Rockefeller	1964	R	7.6	—	—	20.93
Robert Kennedy	1968	D	6.6	—	—	19.18
Shirley Chisholm	1972	D	4.5	—	—	12.62
Colin Powell	2016	R	3.2	—	—	11.84
Rudy Giuliani	2008	R	3.9	—	—	11.71
Jack Kemp	1988	R	5.2	—	—	11.63
Richard Nixon	1964	R	6.7	—	—	11.00

All-time leaders (1789-2016) in similarity scores

Candidate	Year	Party	PI	N	W	CS
1. Rudy Giuliani	2008	R	3.9	—	—	11.71
2. Donald Trump	2016	R	3.1	X	X	78.79
3. Sanford Church	1868	D	5.0	—	—	18.54
4. Alton Parker	1904	D	4.9	X	—	66.33
5. Lyndon LaRouche	1996	D	3.6	—	—	13.27
6. Horace Greeley	1872	D-LR	4.8	X	—	58.76
7. Jacob Coxey	1932	R/FL	1.0	—	—	10.92
8. Colin Powell	2016	R	3.2	—	—	11.84
9. Allan Benson	1916	SOC	2.7	—	—	20.19
10. Norman Thomas	1932	SOC	3.0	—	—	17.13
11. Walter Jones	1956	D	1.9	—	—	10.62
12. Faith Spotted Eagle	2016	D	2.3	—	—	10.62
13. Ross Perot	1992	I	2.9	—	—	43.78
14. Sam Yorty	1972	D	4.3	—	—	10.30
15. Ross Perot	1996	REF	2.6	—	—	36.87
16. Jesse Jackson	1984	D	3.3	—	—	23.30
17. Ralph Nader	2000	GRN	1.3	—	—	18.76

Candidate	Year	Party	PI	N	W	CS
18. George Clinton	1796	DR	3.0	—	—	33.54
19. Shirley Chisholm	1972	D	4.5	—	—	12.62
20. George Clinton	1792	DR	3.2	—	—	59.98
21. Averell Harriman	1952	D	5.8	—	—	15.10
22. John Nance Garner	1932	D	3.3	—	—	16.36
23. Jesse Jackson	1988	D	3.6	—	—	33.32
24. DeWitt Clinton	1812	F-DR	3.7	X	—	71.10
25. Chauncey Depew	1888	R	4.9	—	—	19.50

CORY BOOKER

Basics

Potential index 7.0
Party .... Democratic
Age (as of November 1, 2020)...51.51
Birthday.. April 27, 1969
State .... New Jersey
Position (as of November 1, 2019)..................................Senator
Prior candidacies ....None
Prior major tickets ....None

Modern Era (1960-2016) candidates with comparable PIs

Candidate	Year	Party	PI	N	W	CS
Hillary Clinton	2008	D	7.0	—	—	43.42
Eugene McCarthy	1968	D	6.9	—	—	33.16
Bill Bradley	2000	D	7.1	—	—	22.10
Paul Tsongas	1992	D	7.0	—	—	21.82
Bob Dole	1988	R	7.0	—	—	21.51
Nelson Rockefeller	1968	R	7.1	—	—	21.48
William Scranton	1964	R	6.9	—	—	19.42
Harry Byrd	1960	D	6.9	—	—	19.25
Hubert Humphrey	1960	D	7.1	—	—	14.46
Stuart Symington	1960	D	6.9	—	—	13.00
Paul Simon	1988	D	7.1	—	—	12.66
Fred Harris	1976	D	6.9	—	—	10.94
Tom Harkin	1992	D	6.9	—	—	10.83
Jeb Bush	2016	R	7.1	—	—	10.58
Birch Bayh	1976	D	6.9	—	—	10.32
Alan Cranston	1984	D	7.0	—	—	10.17

Modern Era candidates from New Jersey

Candidate	Year	Party	PI	N	W	CS
Bill Bradley	2000	D	7.1	—	—	22.10
Steve Forbes	1996	R	3.6	—	—	16.96
Steve Forbes	2000	R	4.0	—	—	10.52
Chris Christie	2016	R	6.7	—	—	10.11

All-time leaders (1789-2016) in similarity scores

Candidate	Year	Party	PI	N	W	CS
1. Edward Kennedy	1980	D	6.8	—	—	39.18
2. Bill Bradley	2000	D	7.1	—	—	22.10
3. Arthur Gorman	1892	D	7.4	—	—	13.19
4. Thomas Bayard	1876	D	7.1	—	—	13.59
5. Thomas Bayard	1880	D	7.1	—	—	26.61
6. John Kerry	2004	D	6.6	X	—	73.65
7. John Kennedy	1960	D	6.2	X	X	79.58
8. Paul Tsongas	1992	D	7.0	—	—	21.82
9. Andrew Johnson	1860	D	6.9	—	—	13.19
10. Robert Hunter	1860	D	7.0	—	—	21.10

Candidate	Year	Party	PI	N	W	CS
11. Birch Bayh	1976	D	6.9	—	—	10.32
12. Eugene McCarthy	1968	D	6.9	—	—	33.16
13. Hubert Humphrey	1960	D	7.1	—	—	14.46
14. John Edwards	2004	D	7.8	—	—	22.22
15. Tom Harkin	1992	D	6.9	—	—	10.83
16. Hillary Clinton	2008	D	7.0	—	—	43.42
17. Stuart Symington	1960	D	6.9	—	—	13.00
18. Franklin Pierce	1852	D	7.0	X	X	89.52
19. Thomas Bayard	1884	D	6.2	—	—	26.53
20. James Doolittle	1868	D	7.9	—	—	13.27
21. Barack Obama	2008	D	6.8	X	X	84.03
22. Frank Church	1976	D	6.5	—	—	13.23
23. Joseph Blackburn	1896	D	6.2	—	—	17.03
24. Gary Hart	1984	D	6.3	—	—	37.76
25. Bob Kerrey	1992	D	6.4	—	—	10.95

STEVE BULLOCK

Basics

Potential index 6.1
Party .... Democratic
Age (as of November 1, 2020)..54.56
Birthday... April 11, 1966
State .... Montana
Position (as of November 1, 2019)..Governor
Prior candidacies ....None
Prior major tickets ....None

Modern Era (1960-2016) candidates with comparable PIs

Candidate	Year	Party	PI	N	W	CS
John Kennedy	1960	D	6.2	X	X	79.58
Richard Nixon	1968	R	6.2	X	X	78.01
John McCain	2000	R	6.2	—	—	29.92
Mitt Romney	2008	R	6.1	—	—	23.13
Jerry Brown	1976	D	6.2	—	—	21.16
Henry Jackson	1976	D	6.2	—	—	14.30
Howard Dean	2004	D	6.0	—	—	13.32
George McGovern	1968	D	6.0	—	—	12.79
George McGovern	1984	D	6.2	—	—	11.14
Bruce Babbitt	1988	D	6.2	—	—	10.20

Modern Era candidates from Montana

(None)

All-time leaders (1789-2016) in similarity scores

Candidate	Year	Party	PI	N	W	CS
1. Bruce Babbitt	1988	D	6.2	—	—	10.20
2. Bill Richardson	2008	D	5.9	—	—	10.17
3. Michael Dukakis	1988	D	6.7	X	—	65.32
4. Woodrow Wilson	1912	D	6.6	X	X	86.26
5. Bill Clinton	1992	D	6.5	X	X	82.15
6. Edward Edwards	1920	D	6.6	—	—	13.28
7. George Wallace	1972	D	6.5	—	—	26.62
8. George Wallace	1964	D	6.4	—	—	13.23
9. Howard Dean	2004	D	6.0	—	—	13.32
10. John Johnson	1908	D	6.8	—	—	13.67
11. Horace Boies	1892	D	6.3	—	—	19.02
12. Claude Matthews	1896	D	7.3	—	—	13.19
13. George Wallace	1976	D	5.6	—	—	17.84
14. Joel Parker	1868	D	6.7	—	—	13.27
15. Frank Lausche	1956	D	5.7	—	—	11.62
16. James English	1868	D	7.0	—	—	13.99
17. George Clinton	1789	DR	2.6	—	—	31.09
18. Jerry Brown	1976	D	6.2	—	—	21.16
19. Jerry Brown	1980	D	6.4	—	—	11.84
20. Jimmy Carter	1976	D	7.4	X	X	79.23

Candidate	Year	Party	PI	N	W	CS
21. Frank Church	1976	D	6.5	—	—	13.23
22. William Murray	1932	D	5.1	—	—	12.73
23. James Cox	1920	D	5.9	X	—	64.01
24. Alfred Smith	1920	D	6.5	—	—	15.99
25. Earl Warren	1948	R	5.7	—	—	19.04

PETE BUTTIGIEG

Basics

Potential index 2.5
Party .... Democratic
Age (as of November 1, 2020)...38.78
Birthday..January 19, 1982
State ....Indiana
Position (as of November 1, 2019)...Mayor
Prior candidacies ....None
Prior major tickets ....None

Modern Era (1960-2016) candidates with comparable PIs

Candidate	Year	Party	PI	N	W	CS
Ross Perot	1996	REF	2.6	—	—	36.87

Modern Era candidates from Indiana

Candidate	Year	Party	PI	N	W	CS
Richard Lugar	1996	R	6.5	—	—	10.51
Birch Bayh	1976	D	6.9	—	—	10.32

All-time leaders (1789-2016) in similarity scores

Candidate	Year	Party	PI	N	W	CS
1. Eugene Debs	1904	SOC	2.9	—	—	19.53
2. Jesse Jackson	1984	D	3.3	—	—	23.30
3. Eugene Debs	1908	SOC	2.9	—	—	19.04
4. Jesse Jackson	1988	D	3.6	—	—	33.32
5. James Birney	1844	LTY	2.6	—	—	17.35
6. Eugene Debs	1912	SOC	1.5	—	—	29.16
7. John R. McLean	1896	D	5.0	—	—	14.63
8. Faith Spotted Eagle	2016	D	2.3	—	—	10.62
9. William Jennings Bryan	1896	D-POP	4.6	X	—	70.98
10. Richard Gephardt	1988	D	4.0	—	—	13.63
11. Jacob Coxey	1932	R/FL	1.0	—	—	10.92
12. Walter Jones	1956	D	1.9	—	—	10.62
13. Oscar Underwood	1912	D	3.0	—	—	16.41
14. Lyndon LaRouche	1996	D	3.6	—	—	13.27
15. Claude Matthews	1896	D	7.3	—	—	13.19
16. George McClellan	1864	D	4.7	X	—	61.66
17. Eugene Debs	1920	SOC	0.1	—	—	20.94
18. James Weaver	1880	GBK	4.2	—	—	20.66
19. Henry Ford	1916	R	3.8	—	—	13.29
20. John Davis	1920	D	3.7	—	—	12.87
21. Champ Clark	1912	D	3.7	—	—	42.45
22. Sam Yorty	1972	D	4.3	—	—	10.30
23. Richard Gephardt	2004	D	3.9	—	—	10.23
24. John Johnson	1908	D	6.8	—	—	13.67
25. George Clinton	1789	DR	2.6	—	—	31.09

JULIAN CASTRO

Basics

Potential index 4.8
Party ....Democratic
Age (as of November 1, 2020)...46.13
Birthday.. September 16, 1974
State ....Texas
Position (as of November 1, 2019)..........................Former Cabinet member
Prior candidacies ....None
Prior major tickets ....None

Modern Era (1960-2016) candidates with comparable PIs

Candidate	Year	Party	PI	N	W	CS
John Anderson	1980	R/NU	4.7	—	—	38.97
Ron Paul	2008	R/TC	4.8	—	—	13.62
Henry Cabot Lodge	1964	R	4.8	—	—	12.05
Paul McCloskey	1972	R	4.7	—	—	11.31
Phil Crane	1980	R	4.7	—	—	10.46

Modern Era candidates from Texas

Candidate	Year	Party	PI	N	W	CS
Lyndon Johnson	1964	D	9.3	X	X	93.24
George H.W. Bush	1988	R	6.5	X	X	87.86
George W. Bush	2004	R	9.3	X	X	78.71
George W. Bush	2000	R	7.9	X	X	77.21
George H.W. Bush	1992	R	8.2	X	—	66.86
Ross Perot	1992	I	2.9	—	—	43.78
Ross Perot	1996	REF	2.6	—	—	36.87
Ted Cruz	2016	R	7.9	—	—	28.72
George H.W. Bush	1980	R	5.2	—	—	24.15
Lyndon Johnson	1960	D	8.1	—	—	23.50
Ron Paul	2012	R	4.6	—	—	18.11
Ron Paul	2008	R/TC	4.8	—	—	13.62
Lyndon Johnson	1968	D	8.7	—	—	11.53
Ron Paul	2016	R	3.8	—	—	10.62
Lloyd Bentsen	1988	D	7.6	—	—	10.62
John Connally	1980	R	7.4	—	—	10.38
Phil Gramm	1996	R	8.4	—	—	10.30
Rick Perry	2012	R	7.5	—	—	10.14

All-time leaders (1789-2016) in similarity scores

Candidate	Year	Party	PI	N	W	CS
1. Mitchell Palmer	1920	D	4.9	—	—	27.09
2. William Gibbs McAdoo	1920	D	6.3	—	—	27.41
3. Averell Harriman	1952	D	5.8	—	—	15.10
4. James Guthrie	1860	D	3.9	—	—	19.34
5. Lyndon Johnson	1956	D	4.5	—	—	12.89
6. James Farley	1940	D	6.3	—	—	13.95
7. Shirley Chisholm	1972	D	4.5	—	—	12.62

Candidate	Year	Party	PI	N	W	CS
8. James Madison	1808	DR	6.8	X	X	84.36
9. John Nance Garner	1932	D	3.3	—	—	16.36
10. Thomas Jefferson	1796	DR	6.9	X	—	74.00
11. William Crawford	1824	DR	5.4	—	—	46.97
12. William Gibbs McAdoo	1924	D	3.6	—	—	43.53
13. Winfield Hancock	1868	D	6.0	—	—	18.46
14. John Floyd	1832	D	4.2	—	—	22.71
15. William Marcy	1852	D	5.9	—	—	17.50
16. John Quincy Adams	1820	DR	5.0	—	—	17.96
17. Thomas Jefferson	1792	DR	6.7	—	—	26.68
18. George H.W. Bush	1980	R	5.2	—	—	24.15
19. James Buchanan	1856	D	5.1	X	X	79.35
20. Oscar Underwood	1912	D	3.0	—	—	16.41
21. Henry Clay	1824	DR	3.7	—	—	46.84
22. Cordell Hull	1928	D	3.7	—	—	12.75
23. Benjamin Bristow	1876	R	4.0	—	—	21.90
24. James Monroe	1816	DR	7.3	X	X	90.10
25. Lewis Cass	1844	D	5.1	—	—	34.91

BILL DE BLASIO

Basics

Potential index 3.8
Party .... Democratic
Age (as of November 1, 2020)...59.48
Birthday..May 8, 1961
State ....New York
Position (as of November 1, 2019)..Mayor
Prior candidacies ....None
Prior major tickets ....None

Modern Era (1960-2016) candidates with comparable PIs

Candidate	Year	Party	PI	N	W	CS
Gary Johnson	2016	LIB	3.9	—	—	20.52
Alan Keyes	2000	R	3.7	—	—	13.04
Rudy Giuliani	2008	R	3.9	—	—	11.71
Ron Paul	2016	R	3.8	—	—	10.62
Richard Gephardt	2004	D	3.9	—	—	10.23
Carly Fiorina	2016	R	3.9	—	—	10.07

Modern Era candidates from New York

Candidate	Year	Party	PI	N	W	CS
Donald Trump	2016	R	3.1	X	X	78.79
Richard Nixon	1968	R	6.2	X	X	78.01
Hillary Clinton	2016	D	6.6	X	—	72.30
Hillary Clinton	2008	D	7.0	—	—	43.42
Nelson Rockefeller	1968	R	7.1	—	—	21.48
Nelson Rockefeller	1964	R	7.6	—	—	20.93
Robert Kennedy	1968	D	6.6	—	—	19.18
Shirley Chisholm	1972	D	4.5	—	—	12.62
Colin Powell	2016	R	3.2	—	—	11.84
Rudy Giuliani	2008	R	3.9	—	—	11.71
Jack Kemp	1988	R	5.2	—	—	11.63
Richard Nixon	1964	R	6.7	—	—	11.00

All-time leaders (1789-2016) in similarity scores

Candidate	Year	Party	PI	N	W	CS
1. Sanford Church	1868	D	5.0	—	—	18.54
2. Alton Parker	1904	D	4.9	X	—	66.33
3. Sam Yorty	1972	D	4.3	—	—	10.30
4. Horace Greeley	1872	D-LR	4.8	X	—	58.76
5. Rudy Giuliani	2008	R	3.9	—	—	11.71
6. DeWitt Clinton	1812	F-DR	3.7	X	—	71.10
7. Donald Trump	2016	R	3.1	X	X	78.79
8. Shirley Chisholm	1972	D	4.5	—	—	12.62
9. Norman Thomas	1932	SOC	3.0	—	—	17.13
10. Averell Harriman	1952	D	5.8	—	—	15.10
11. Allan Benson	1916	SOC	2.7	—	—	20.19
12. Chauncey Depew	1888	R	4.9	—	—	19.50

Candidate	Year	Party	PI	N	W	CS
13. Jesse Jackson	1988	D	3.6	—	—	33.32
14. John R. McLean	1896	D	5.0	—	—	14.63
15. William Gibbs McAdoo	1920	D	6.3	—	—	27.41
16. George Clinton	1792	DR	3.2	—	—	59.98
17. George Clinton	1796	DR	3.0	—	—	33.54
18. Jesse Jackson	1984	D	3.3	—	—	23.30
19. Ross Perot	1992	I	2.9	—	—	43.78
20. Samuel Randall	1884	D	6.3	—	—	17.58
21. Samuel Tilden	1876	D	7.2	X	—	75.14
22. Asa Packer	1868	D	6.0	—	—	16.55
23. Lyndon LaRouche	1996	D	3.6	—	—	13.27
24. James Farley	1940	D	6.3	—	—	13.95
25. Wendell Willkie	1940	R	4.7	X	—	63.60

JOHN DELANEY

Basics

Potential index 4.2
Party .... Democratic
Age (as of November 1, 2020)...57.54
Birthday...April 16, 1963
State ....Maryland
Position (as of November 1, 2019).. Former representative
Prior candidacies ....None
Prior major tickets ....None

Modern Era (1960-2016) candidates with comparable PIs

Candidate	Year	Party	PI	N	W	CS
Newt Gingrich	2012	R	4.3	—	—	18.59
Morris Udall	1976	D	4.3	—	—	18.22
John Ashbrook	1972	R	4.2	—	—	13.02
Wesley Clark	2004	D	4.2	—	—	12.00
Ben Carson	2016	R	4.3	—	—	11.69
Sargent Shriver	1976	D	4.2	—	—	11.14
Wilbur Mills	1972	D	4.3	—	—	10.36
Sam Yorty	1972	D	4.3	—	—	10.30
Michele Bachmann	2012	R	4.3	—	—	10.11

Modern Era candidates from Maryland

Candidate	Year	Party	PI	N	W	CS
Alan Keyes	2000	R	3.7	—	—	13.04
Alan Keyes	1996	R	3.2	—	—	11.81
Sargent Shriver	1976	D	4.2	—	—	11.14

All-time leaders (1789-2016) in similarity scores

Candidate	Year	Party	PI	N	W	CS
1. Richard Bland	1896	D	5.5	—	—	30.20
2. Asa Packer	1868	D	6.0	—	—	16.55
3. Cordell Hull	1928	D	3.7	—	—	12.75
4. Morris Udall	1976	D	4.3	—	—	18.22
5. William Wirt	1832	AM	3.9	—	—	35.63
6. James Weaver	1892	POP	4.1	—	—	38.80
7. William Jennings Bryan	1896	D-POP	4.6	X	—	70.98
8. Wilbur Mills	1972	D	4.3	—	—	10.36
9. Richard Gephardt	1988	D	4.0	—	—	13.63
10. Richard Gephardt	2004	D	3.9	—	—	10.23
11. Champ Clark	1912	D	3.7	—	—	42.45
12. John Davis	1924	D	4.4	X	—	63.46
13. Oscar Underwood	1912	D	3.0	—	—	16.41
14. John Davis	1920	D	3.7	—	—	12.87
15. Samuel Randall	1884	D	6.3	—	—	17.58
16. Henry Payne	1880	D	5.6	—	—	18.78
17. Shirley Chisholm	1972	D	4.5	—	—	12.62
18. John Nance Garner	1932	D	3.3	—	—	16.36

Candidate	Year	Party	PI	N	W	CS
19. Wesley Clark	2004	D	4.2	—	—	12.00
20. Clinton Fisk	1888	PRO	3.8	—	—	17.02
21. Thomas Reed	1896	R	5.2	—	—	17.27
22. Sargent Shriver	1976	D	4.2	—	—	11.14
23. William Morrison	1880	D	6.5	—	—	16.71
24. James Weaver	1880	GBK	4.2	—	—	20.66
25. Joseph Martin	1940	R	5.1	—	—	12.63

TULSI GABBARD

Basics

Potential index 2.7
Party ....Democratic
Age (as of November 1, 2020)...39.55
Birthday...April 12, 1981
State ....Hawaii
Position (as of November 1, 2019)...Representative
Prior candidacies ....None
Prior major tickets ....None

Modern Era (1960-2016) candidates with comparable PIs

Candidate	Year	Party	PI	N	W	CS
Ross Perot	1996	REF	2.6	—	—	36.87

Modern Era candidates from Hawaii

(None)

All-time leaders (1789-2016) in similarity scores

Candidate	Year	Party	PI	N	W	CS
1. Morris Udall	1976	D	4.3	—	—	18.22
2. Oscar Underwood	1912	D	3.0	—	—	16.41
3. Richard Gephardt	1988	D	4.0	—	—	13.63
4. Cordell Hull	1928	D	3.7	—	—	12.75
5. William Jennings Bryan	1896	D-POP	4.6	X	—	70.98
6. Wilbur Mills	1972	D	4.3	—	—	10.36
7. James Weaver	1880	GBK	4.2	—	—	20.66
8. William Lemke	1936	U	1.8	—	—	16.26
9. Champ Clark	1912	D	3.7	—	—	42.45
10. Richard Gephardt	2004	D	3.9	—	—	10.23
11. Henry Clay	1824	DR	3.7	—	—	46.84
12. John Nance Garner	1932	D	3.3	—	—	16.36
13. Shirley Chisholm	1972	D	4.5	—	—	12.62
14. Stephen Field	1880	D	2.3	—	—	17.03
15. Joseph Lane	1852	D	3.1	—	—	13.59
16. John Davis	1920	D	3.7	—	—	12.87
17. George McClellan	1864	D	4.7	X	—	61.66
18. John Anderson	1980	R/NU	3.2	—	—	38.97
19. James Blaine	1876	R	5.1	—	—	47.05
20. William Gibbs McAdoo	1924	D	3.6	—	—	43.53
21. William Morrison	1880	D	6.5	—	—	16.71
22. Paul McCloskey	1972	R	4.7	—	—	11.31
23. John Ashbrook	1972	R	4.2	—	—	13.02
24. Samuel Randall	1884	D	6.3	—	—	17.58
25. Michele Bachmann	2012	R	4.3	—	—	10.11

KIRSTEN GILLIBRAND

Basics

Potential index 7.8
Party .... Democratic
Age (as of November 1, 2020)...53.90
Birthday.. December 9, 1966
State ....New York
Position (as of November 1, 2019)...Senator
Prior candidacies ....None
Prior major tickets ....None

Modern Era (1960-2016) candidates with comparable PIs

Candidate	Year	Party	PI	N	W	CS
George W. Bush	2000	R	7.9	X	X	77.21
Hubert Humphrey	1968	D	7.8	X	—	69.19
Walter Mondale	1984	D	7.8	X	—	58.83
Ted Cruz	2016	R	7.9	—	—	28.72
John Edwards	2004	D	7.8	—	—	22.22
Marco Rubio	2016	R	7.7	—	—	17.61
Lamar Alexander	1996	R	7.8	—	—	11.97
Howard Baker	1980	R	7.7	—	—	10.51
Rand Paul	2016	R	7.8	—	—	10.13

Modern Era candidates from New York

Candidate	Year	Party	PI	N	W	CS
Donald Trump	2016	R	3.1	X	X	78.79
Richard Nixon	1968	R	6.2	X	X	78.01
Hillary Clinton	2016	D	6.6	X	—	72.30
Hillary Clinton	2008	D	7.0	—	—	43.42
Nelson Rockefeller	1968	R	7.1	—	—	21.48
Nelson Rockefeller	1964	R	7.6	—	—	20.93
Robert Kennedy	1968	D	6.6	—	—	19.18
Shirley Chisholm	1972	D	4.5	—	—	12.62
Colin Powell	2016	R	3.2	—	—	11.84
Rudy Giuliani	2008	R	3.9	—	—	11.71
Jack Kemp	1988	R	5.2	—	—	11.63
Richard Nixon	1964	R	6.7	—	—	11.00

All-time leaders (1789-2016) in similarity scores

Candidate	Year	Party	PI	N	W	CS
1. Hillary Clinton	2008	D	7.0	—	—	43.42
2. David Hill	1892	D	8.5	—	—	19.98
3. Robert Kennedy	1968	D	6.6	—	—	19.18
4. Arthur Gorman	1892	D	7.4	—	—	13.19
5. Edward Kennedy	1980	D	6.8	—	—	39.18
6. Lyndon Johnson	1960	D	8.1	—	—	23.50
7. John Kerry	2004	D	6.6	X	—	73.65
8. John Edwards	2004	D	7.8	—	—	22.22
9. Paul Simon	1988	D	7.1	—	—	12.66

Candidate	Year	Party	PI	N	W	CS
10. Thomas Bayard	1880	D	7.1	—	—	26.61
11. Robert Hunter	1860	D	7.0	—	—	21.10
12. Thomas Bayard	1876	D	7.1	—	—	13.59
13. Lloyd Bentsen	1988	D	7.6	—	—	10.62
14. James Doolittle	1868	D	7.9	—	—	13.27
15. John Kennedy	1960	D	6.2	X	X	79.58
16. Allen Thurman	1880	D	7.7	—	—	17.43
17. Andrew Johnson	1860	D	6.9	—	—	13.19
18. Roscoe Conkling	1876	R	8.2	—	—	20.46
19. Bill Bradley	2000	D	7.1	—	—	22.10
20. Barack Obama	2008	D	6.8	X	X	84.03
21. Aaron Burr	1796	DR	4.7	—	—	54.24
22. Aaron Burr	1792	DR	4.7	—	—	19.07
23. John Glenn	1984	D	6.8	—	—	12.08
24. William Seward	1860	R	8.2	—	—	39.70
25. Paul Tsongas	1992	D	7.0	—	—	21.82

KAMALA HARRIS

Basics

Potential index 8.0
Party .... Democratic
Age (as of November 1, 2020)..56.03
Birthday.. October 20, 1964
State .... California
Position (as of November 1, 2019)..Senator
Prior candidacies ....None
Prior major tickets ....None

Modern Era (1960-2016) candidates with comparable PIs

Candidate	Year	Party	PI	N	W	CS
Ronald Reagan	1984	R	8.1	X	X	95.13
George W. Bush	2000	R	7.9	X	X	77.21
Richard Nixon	1960	R	8.0	X	—	72.12
Ted Cruz	2016	R	7.9	—	—	28.72
Lyndon Johnson	1960	D	8.1	—	—	23.50

Modern Era candidates from California

Candidate	Year	Party	PI	N	W	CS
Richard Nixon	1972	R	8.8	X	X	95.25
Ronald Reagan	1984	R	8.1	X	X	95.13
Ronald Reagan	1980	R	5.7	X	X	91.16
Richard Nixon	1960	R	8.0	X	—	72.12
Ronald Reagan	1976	R	6.7	—	—	47.60
Ronald Reagan	1968	R	7.3	—	—	28.22
Jerry Brown	1992	D	6.8	—	—	24.83
Jerry Brown	1976	D	6.2	—	—	21.16
Jerry Brown	1980	D	6.4	—	—	11.84
Paul McCloskey	1972	R	4.7	—	—	11.31
John Hospers	1972	LIB	3.3	—	—	10.62
Sam Yorty	1972	D	4.3	—	—	10.30
Alan Cranston	1984	D	7.0	—	—	10.17

All-time leaders (1789-2016) in similarity scores

Candidate	Year	Party	PI	N	W	CS
1. Alan Cranston	1984	D	7.0	—	—	10.17
2. David Hill	1892	D	8.5	—	—	19.98
3. Frank Church	1976	D	6.5	—	—	13.23
4. Henry Jackson	1972	D	6.3	—	—	15.37
5. James Doolittle	1868	D	7.9	—	—	13.27
6. Hillary Clinton	2008	D	7.0	—	—	43.42
7. Robert Kennedy	1968	D	6.6	—	—	19.18
8. Gary Hart	1984	D	6.3	—	—	37.76
9. Lyndon Johnson	1960	D	8.1	—	—	23.50
10. Jerry Brown	1992	D	6.8	—	—	24.83
11. John Edwards	2004	D	7.8	—	—	22.22
12. Paul Simon	1988	D	7.1	—	—	12.66

Candidate	Year	Party	PI	N	W	CS
13. Robert Hunter	1860	D	7.0	—	—	21.10
14. Arthur Gorman	1892	D	7.4	—	—	13.19
15. Allen Thurman	1880	D	7.7	—	—	17.43
16. Lloyd Bentsen	1988	D	7.6	—	—	10.62
17. Andrew Johnson	1860	D	6.9	—	—	13.19
18. Henry Jackson	1976	D	6.2	—	—	14.30
19. Stuart Symington	1960	D	6.9	—	—	13.00
20. Eugene McCarthy	1968	D	6.9	—	—	33.16
21. Tom Harkin	1992	D	6.9	—	—	10.83
22. Andrew Jackson	1824	DR	5.9	X	—	69.65
23. John Glenn	1984	D	6.8	—	—	12.08
24. Joseph Blackburn	1896	D	6.2	—	—	17.03
25. Hubert Humphrey	1960	D	7.1	—	—	14.46

JOHN HICKENLOOPER

Basics

Potential index 5.4
Party .... Democratic
Age (as of November 1, 2020)...68.73
Birthday.. February 7, 1952
State ....Colorado
Position (as of November 1, 2019)................................Former governor
Prior candidacies ....None
Prior major tickets ....None

Modern Era (1960-2016) candidates with comparable PIs

Candidate	Year	Party	PI	N	W	CS
George Wallace	1968	D/AI	5.4	—	—	45.41
Bernie Sanders	2016	D	5.5	—	—	44.15
Hubert Humphrey	1976	D	5.5	—	—	10.29

Modern Era candidates from Colorado

Candidate	Year	Party	PI	N	W	CS
Gary Hart	1984	D	6.3	—	—	37.76
Gary Hart	1988	D	6.7	—	—	11.02

All-time leaders (1789-2016) in similarity scores

Candidate	Year	Party	PI	N	W	CS
1. Charles Jenkins	1872	D	5.1	—	—	11.89
2. Bruce Babbitt	1988	D	6.2	—	—	10.20
3. Horace Boies	1896	D	6.3	—	—	15.75
4. Gary Johnson	2016	LIB	3.9	—	—	20.52
5. Howard Dean	2004	D	6.0	—	—	13.32
6. Joel Parker	1868	D	6.7	—	—	13.27
7. Horace Boies	1892	D	6.3	—	—	19.02
8. Bill Richardson	2008	D	5.9	—	—	10.17
9. Jimmy Carter	1976	D	7.4	X	X	79.23
10. Frank Lausche	1956	D	5.7	—	—	11.62
11. Thomas Seymour	1864	D	6.8	—	—	23.41
12. Edward Edwards	1920	D	6.6	—	—	13.28
13. George Wallace	1976	D	5.6	—	—	17.84
14. Woodrow Wilson	1912	D	6.6	X	X	86.26
15. George Wallace	1968	D/AI	5.4	—	—	45.41
16. William Murray	1932	D	5.1	—	—	12.73
17. Michael Dukakis	1988	D	6.7	X	—	65.32
18. William Allen	1876	D	6.9	—	—	15.83
19. Mitt Romney	2012	R	5.9	X	—	70.93
20. Gary Hart	1984	D	6.3	—	—	37.76
21. Jerry Brown	1992	D	6.8	—	—	24.83
22. Henry Jackson	1976	D	6.2	—	—	14.30
23. Mitt Romney	2008	R	6.1	—	—	23.13
24. Edward Telfair	1789	DR	4.8	—	—	21.42
25. Henry Jackson	1972	D	6.3	—	—	15.37

JAY INSLEE

Basics

Potential index 6.1
Party .... Democratic
Age (as of November 1, 2020)..69.73
Birthday... February 9, 1951
State .... Washington
Position (as of November 1, 2019)...Governor
Prior candidacies ....None
Prior major tickets ....None

Modern Era (1960-2016) candidates with comparable PIs

Candidate	Year	Party	PI	N	W	CS
John Kennedy	1960	D	6.2	X	X	79.58
Richard Nixon	1968	R	6.2	X	X	78.01
John McCain	2000	R	6.2	—	—	29.92
Mitt Romney	2008	R	6.1	—	—	23.13
Jerry Brown	1976	D	6.2	—	—	21.16
Henry Jackson	1976	D	6.2	—	—	14.30
Howard Dean	2004	D	6.0	—	—	13.32
George McGovern	1968	D	6.0	—	—	12.79
George McGovern	1984	D	6.2	—	—	11.14
Bruce Babbitt	1988	D	6.2	—	—	10.20

Modern Era candidates from Washington

Candidate	Year	Party	PI	N	W	CS
Henry Jackson	1972	D	6.3	—	—	15.37
Henry Jackson	1976	D	6.2	—	—	14.30

All-time leaders (1789-2016) in similarity scores

Candidate	Year	Party	PI	N	W	CS
1. Bill Richardson	2008	D	5.9	—	—	10.17
2. Henry Jackson	1976	D	6.2	—	—	14.30
3. Henry Jackson	1972	D	6.3	—	—	15.37
4. William Murray	1932	D	5.1	—	—	12.73
5. Judson Harmon	1912	D	5.6	—	—	20.47
6. George White	1932	D	6.1	—	—	12.70
7. James English	1868	D	7.0	—	—	13.99
8. Horace Boies	1892	D	6.3	—	—	19.02
9. James Cox	1920	D	5.9	X	—	64.01
10. Adlai Stevenson	1952	D	6.7	X	—	63.90
11. Edward Edwards	1920	D	6.6	—	—	13.28
12. Woodrow Wilson	1912	D	6.6	X	X	86.26
13. William Allen	1876	D	6.9	—	—	15.83
14. Michael Dukakis	1988	D	6.7	X	—	65.32
15. Samuel Adams	1796	DR	3.7	—	—	50.36
16. Thomas Seymour	1864	D	6.8	—	—	23.41
17. Frank Lausche	1956	D	5.7	—	—	11.62
18. Horace Boies	1896	D	6.3	—	—	15.75

Candidate	Year	Party	PI	N	W	CS
19. Thomas Walsh	1924	D	4.0	—	—	13.17
20. Bruce Babbitt	1988	D	6.2	—	—	10.20
21. George Gray	1908	D	6.3	—	—	14.71
22. Charles Jenkins	1872	D	5.1	—	—	11.89
23. Averell Harriman	1956	D	7.4	—	—	17.64
24. Thomas Walsh	1928	D	3.5	—	—	10.95
25. Francis Cockrell	1904	D	7.0	—	—	13.35

AMY KLOBUCHAR

Basics

Potential index 6.4
Party .... Democratic
Age (as of November 1, 2020) 60.44
Birthday .... May 25, 1960
State .... Minnesota
Position (as of November 1, 2019) .... Senator
Prior candidacies ....None
Prior major tickets ....None

Modern Era (1960-2016) candidates with comparable PIs

Candidate	Year	Party	PI	N	W	CS
George H.W. Bush	1988	R	6.5	X	X	87.86
Bill Clinton	1992	D	6.5	X	X	82.15
George McGovern	1972	D	6.4	X	—	58.46
Gary Hart	1984	D	6.3	—	—	37.76
George Wallace	1972	D	6.5	—	—	26.62
Hubert Humphrey	1972	D	6.5	—	—	25.90
Henry Jackson	1972	D	6.3	—	—	15.37
Frank Church	1976	D	6.5	—	—	13.23
George Wallace	1964	D	6.4	—	—	13.23
Jerry Brown	1980	D	6.4	—	—	11.84
Bob Kerrey	1992	D	6.4	—	—	10.95
Richard Lugar	1996	R	6.5	—	—	10.51

Modern Era candidates from Minnesota

Candidate	Year	Party	PI	N	W	CS
Hubert Humphrey	1968	D	7.8	X	—	69.19
Walter Mondale	1984	D	7.8	X	—	58.83
Eugene McCarthy	1968	D	6.9	—	—	33.16
Hubert Humphrey	1972	D	6.5	—	—	25.90
Hubert Humphrey	1960	D	7.1	—	—	14.46
Hubert Humphrey	1976	D	5.5	—	—	10.29
Michele Bachmann	2012	R	4.3	—	—	10.11

All-time leaders (1789-2016) in similarity scores

Candidate	Year	Party	PI	N	W	CS
1. Eugene McCarthy	1968	D	6.9	—	—	33.16
2. Hubert Humphrey	1960	D	7.1	—	—	14.46
3. Stuart Symington	1960	D	6.9	—	—	13.00
4. Tom Harkin	1992	D	6.9	—	—	10.83
5. Lewis Cass	1848	D	6.9	X	—	71.66
6. Bob Kerrey	1992	D	6.4	—	—	10.95
7. John Glenn	1984	D	6.8	—	—	12.08
8. Paul Simon	1988	D	7.1	—	—	12.66
9. Henry Jackson	1972	D	6.3	—	—	15.37
10. Birch Bayh	1976	D	6.9	—	—	10.32
11. James Doolittle	1868	D	7.9	—	—	13.27

Candidate	Year	Party	PI	N	W	CS
12. John Kerry	2004	D	6.6	X	—	73.65
13. George McGovern	1972	D	6.4	X	—	58.46
14. Francis Cockrell	1904	D	7.0	—	—	13.35
15. George McGovern	1968	D	6.0	—	—	12.79
16. Joseph Blackburn	1896	D	6.2	—	—	17.03
17. James Reed	1928	D	4.8	—	—	16.09
18. Barack Obama	2008	D	6.8	X	X	84.03
19. Henry Jackson	1976	D	6.2	—	—	14.30
20. Andrew Jackson	1824	DR	5.9	X	—	69.65
21. Allen Thurman	1880	D	7.7	—	—	17.43
22. Harry Byrd	1944	D	5.1	—	—	14.55
23. Stephen Douglas	1860	D	7.0	X	—	57.06
24. Stephen Douglas	1852	D	6.9	—	—	15.51
25. Stephen Douglas	1856	D	7.1	—	—	18.86

WAYNE MESSAM

Basics

Potential index 4.3
Party .... Democratic
Age (as of November 1, 2020) 46.40
Birthday .... June 7, 1974
State .... Florida
Position (as of November 1, 2019) .... Mayor
Prior candidacies .... None
Prior major tickets .... None

Modern Era (1960-2016) candidates with comparable PIs

Candidate	Year	Party	PI	N	W	CS
Newt Gingrich	2012	R	4.3	—	—	18.59
Morris Udall	1976	D	4.3	—	—	18.22
John Ashbrook	1972	R	4.2	—	—	13.02
Wesley Clark	2004	D	4.2	—	—	12.00
Ben Carson	2016	R	4.3	—	—	11.69
Sargent Shriver	1976	D	4.2	—	—	11.14
Wilbur Mills	1972	D	4.3	—	—	10.36
Sam Yorty	1972	D	4.3	—	—	10.30
Michele Bachmann	2012	R	4.3	—	—	10.11

Modern Era candidates from Florida

Candidate	Year	Party	PI	N	W	CS
Marco Rubio	2016	R	7.7	—	—	17.61
Ben Carson	2016	R	4.3	—	—	11.69
Jeb Bush	2016	R	7.1	—	—	10.58

All-time leaders (1789-2016) in similarity scores

Candidate	Year	Party	PI	N	W	CS
1. John R. McLean	1896	D	5.0	—	—	14.63
2. Sam Yorty	1972	D	4.3	—	—	10.30
3. Jesse Jackson	1988	D	3.6	—	—	33.32
4. Jesse Jackson	1984	D	3.3	—	—	23.30
5. Ben Carson	2016	R	4.3	—	—	11.69
6. Sanford Church	1868	D	5.0	—	—	18.54
7. Alton Parker	1904	D	4.9	X	—	66.33
8. Ross Perot	1992	I	2.9	—	—	43.78
9. Lyndon LaRouche	1996	D	3.6	—	—	13.27
10. Oscar Underwood	1912	D	3.0	—	—	16.41
11. DeWitt Clinton	1812	F-DR	3.7	X	—	71.10
12. Lyndon Johnson	1956	D	4.5	—	—	12.89
13. Shirley Chisholm	1972	D	4.5	—	—	12.62
14. Henry Clay	1824	DR	3.7	—	—	46.84
15. Cordell Hull	1928	D	3.7	—	—	12.75
16. John Nance Garner	1932	D	3.3	—	—	16.36
17. Mitchell Palmer	1920	D	4.9	—	—	27.09
18. John Floyd	1832	D	4.2	—	—	22.71

Candidate	Year	Party	PI	N	W	CS
19. Ross Perot	1996	REF	2.6	—	—	36.87
20. Eugene Debs	1904	SOC	2.9	—	—	19.53
21. John Milton	1789	F	3.1	—	—	26.29
22. Richard Gephardt	1988	D	4.0	—	—	13.63
23. Walter Jones	1956	D	1.9	—	—	10.62
24. David Davis	1872	D	5.1	—	—	10.97
25. Norman Thomas	1932	SOC	3.0	—	—	17.13

SETH MOULTON

Basics

Potential index 3.4
Party ....Democratic
Age (as of November 1, 2020)..42.02
Birthday..October 24, 1978
State ....Massachusetts
Position (as of November 1, 2019)..Representative
Prior candidacies ....None
Prior major tickets ....None

Modern Era (1960-2016) candidates with comparable PIs

Candidate	Year	Party	PI	N	W	CS
Jesse Jackson	1984	D	3.3	—	—	23.30
John Hospers	1972	LIB	3.3	—	—	10.62

Modern Era candidates from Massachusetts

Candidate	Year	Party	PI	N	W	CS
John Kennedy	1960	D	6.2	X	X	79.58
John Kerry	2004	D	6.6	X	—	73.65
Mitt Romney	2012	R	5.9	X	—	70.93
Michael Dukakis	1988	D	6.7	X	—	65.32
Edward Kennedy	1980	D	6.8	—	—	39.18
Mitt Romney	2008	R	6.1	—	—	23.13
Paul Tsongas	1992	D	7.0	—	—	21.82
Henry Cabot Lodge	1964	R	4.8	—	—	12.05

All-time leaders (1789-2016) in similarity scores

Candidate	Year	Party	PI	N	W	CS
1. Richard Gephardt	1988	D	4.0	—	—	13.63
2. Oscar Underwood	1912	D	3.0	—	—	16.41
3. Cordell Hull	1928	D	3.7	—	—	12.75
4. Shirley Chisholm	1972	D	4.5	—	—	12.62
5. Morris Udall	1976	D	4.3	—	—	18.22
6. James Weaver	1880	GBK	4.2	—	—	20.66
7. John Davis	1920	D	3.7	—	—	12.87
8. Champ Clark	1912	D	3.7	—	—	42.45
9. Richard Gephardt	2004	D	3.9	—	—	10.23
10. Henry Clay	1824	DR	3.7	—	—	46.84
11. Joseph Martin	1940	R	5.1	—	—	12.63
12. William Jennings Bryan	1896	D-POP	4.6	X	—	70.98
13. Wilbur Mills	1972	D	4.3	—	—	10.36
14. John Nance Garner	1932	D	3.3	—	—	16.36
15. James Blaine	1876	R	5.1	—	—	47.05
16. George McClellan	1864	D	4.7	X	—	61.66
17. Samuel Randall	1884	D	6.3	—	—	17.58
18. John Davis	1924	D	4.4	X	—	63.46
19. John Kennedy	1960	D	6.2	X	X	79.58
20. William Morrison	1880	D	6.5	—	—	16.71

Candidate	Year	Party	PI	N	W	CS
21. Thomas Reed	1896	R	5.2	—	—	17.27
22. John Anderson	1980	R/NU	3.2	—	—	38.97
23. William Lemke	1936	U	1.8	—	—	16.26
24. John Quincy Adams	1820	DR	5.0	—	—	17.96
25. John Ashbrook	1972	R	4.2	—	—	13.02

BETO O'ROURKE

Basics

Potential index 5.5
Party ....Democratic
Age (as of November 1, 2020)..48.10
Birthday...September 26, 1972
State ....Texas
Position (as of November 1, 2019)...Former representative
Prior candidacies ....None
Prior major tickets ....None

Modern Era (1960-2016) candidates with comparable PIs

Candidate	Year	Party	PI	N	W	CS
George Wallace	1968	D/AI	5.4	—	—	45.41
Bernie Sanders	2016	D	5.5	—	—	44.15
George Wallace	1976	D	5.6	—	—	17.84
Hubert Humphrey	1976	D	5.5	—	—	10.29

Modern Era candidates from Texas

Candidate	Year	Party	PI	N	W	CS
Lyndon Johnson	1964	D	9.3	X	X	93.24
George H.W. Bush	1988	R	6.5	X	X	87.86
George W. Bush	2004	R	9.3	X	X	78.71
George W. Bush	2000	R	7.9	X	X	77.21
George H.W. Bush	1992	R	8.2	X	—	66.86
Ross Perot	1992	I	2.9	—	—	43.78
Ross Perot	1996	REF	2.6	—	—	36.87
Ted Cruz	2016	R	7.9	—	—	28.72
George H.W. Bush	1980	R	5.2	—	—	24.15
Lyndon Johnson	1960	D	8.1	—	—	23.50
Ron Paul	2012	R	4.6	—	—	18.11
Ron Paul	2008	R/TC	4.8	—	—	13.62
Lyndon Johnson	1968	D	8.7	—	—	11.53
Ron Paul	2016	R	3.8	—	—	10.62
Lloyd Bentsen	1988	D	7.6	—	—	10.62
John Connally	1980	R	7.4	—	—	10.38
Phil Gramm	1996	R	8.4	—	—	10.30
Rick Perry	2012	R	7.5	—	—	10.14

All-time leaders (1789-2016) in similarity scores

Candidate	Year	Party	PI	N	W	CS
1. Shirley Chisholm	1972	D	4.5	—	—	12.62
2. John Nance Garner	1932	D	3.3	—	—	16.36
3. Asa Packer	1868	D	6.0	—	—	16.55
4. Richard Bland	1896	D	5.5	—	—	30.20
5. Henry Payne	1880	D	5.6	—	—	18.78
6. Samuel Randall	1884	D	6.3	—	—	17.58
7. George Pendleton	1868	D	6.7	—	—	36.43
8. Mitchell Palmer	1920	D	4.9	—	—	27.09

Candidate	Year	Party	PI	N	W	CS
9. Lyndon Johnson	1956	D	4.5	—	—	12.89
10. Oscar Underwood	1912	D	3.0	—	—	16.41
11. William Morrison	1880	D	6.5	—	—	16.71
12. William Jennings Bryan	1896	D-POP	4.6	X	—	70.98
13. Cordell Hull	1928	D	3.7	—	—	12.75
14. Henry Clay	1824	DR	3.7	—	—	46.84
15. Richard Gephardt	1988	D	4.0	—	—	13.63
16. Wilbur Mills	1972	D	4.3	—	—	10.36
17. Winfield Hancock	1868	D	6.0	—	—	18.46
18. Ron Paul	2016	R	3.8	—	—	10.62
19. James Farley	1940	D	6.3	—	—	13.95
20. James Madison	1808	DR	6.8	X	X	84.36
21. William Gibbs McAdoo	1920	D	6.3	—	—	27.41
22. George H.W. Bush	1980	R	5.2	—	—	24.15
23. Morris Udall	1976	D	4.3	—	—	18.22
24. Winfield Hancock	1876	D	6.5	—	—	18.14
25. Averell Harriman	1952	D	5.8	—	—	15.10

DEVAL PATRICK

Basics

Potential index 6.4
Party .... Democratic
Age (as of November 1, 2020)...64.25
Birthday...July 31, 1956
State .... Massachusetts
Position (as of November 1, 2019)..Former governor
Prior candidacies ....None
Prior major tickets ....None

Modern Era (1960-2016) candidates with comparable PIs

Candidate	Year	Party	PI	N	W	CS
George H.W. Bush	1988	R	6.5	X	X	87.86
Bill Clinton	1992	D	6.5	X	X	82.15
George McGovern	1972	D	6.4	X	—	58.46
Gary Hart	1984	D	6.3	—	—	37.76
George Wallace	1972	D	6.5	—	—	26.62
Hubert Humphrey	1972	D	6.5	—	—	25.90
Henry Jackson	1972	D	6.3	—	—	15.37
Frank Church	1976	D	6.5	—	—	13.23
George Wallace	1964	D	6.4	—	—	13.23
Jerry Brown	1980	D	6.4	—	—	11.84
Bob Kerrey	1992	D	6.4	—	—	10.95
Richard Lugar	1996	R	6.5	—	—	10.51

Modern Era candidates from Massachusetts

Candidate	Year	Party	PI	N	W	CS
John Kennedy	1960	D	6.2	X	X	79.58
John Kerry	2004	D	6.6	X	—	73.65
Mitt Romney	2012	R	5.9	X	—	70.93
Michael Dukakis	1988	D	6.7	X	—	65.32
Edward Kennedy	1980	D	6.8	—	—	39.18
Mitt Romney	2008	R	6.1	—	—	23.13
Paul Tsongas	1992	D	7.0	—	—	21.82
Henry Cabot Lodge	1964	R	4.8	—	—	12.05

All-time leaders (1789-2016) in similarity scores

Candidate	Year	Party	PI	N	W	CS
1. Thomas Seymour	1864	D	6.8	—	—	23.41
2. John Kerry	2004	D	6.6	X	—	73.65
3. Michael Dukakis	1988	D	6.7	X	—	65.32
4. James English	1868	D	7.0	—	—	13.99
5. Joel Parker	1868	D	6.7	—	—	13.27
6. Paul Tsongas	1992	D	7.0	—	—	21.82
7. Howard Dean	2004	D	6.0	—	—	13.32
8. Mitt Romney	2008	R	6.1	—	—	23.13
9. Edward Kennedy	1980	D	6.8	—	—	39.18
10. James Polk	1844	D	6.7	X	X	81.33

Candidate	Year	Party	PI	N	W	CS
11. William Allen	1876	D	6.9	—	—	15.83
12. Mitt Romney	2012	R	5.9	X	—	70.93
13. William Murray	1932	D	5.1	—	—	12.73
14. John Quincy Adams	1824	DR	5.6	X	X	67.41
15. Edward Edwards	1920	D	6.6	—	—	13.28
16. John Kennedy	1960	D	6.2	X	X	79.58
17. Bill Richardson	2008	D	5.9	—	—	10.17
18. George Gray	1908	D	6.3	—	—	14.71
19. Horace Boies	1896	D	6.3	—	—	15.75
20. Woodrow Wilson	1912	D	6.6	X	X	86.26
21. Samuel Adams	1796	DR	3.7	—	—	50.36
22. Charles Jenkins	1872	D	5.1	—	—	11.89
23. Bill Bradley	2000	D	7.1	—	—	22.10
24. John Quincy Adams	1820	DR	5.0	—	—	17.96
25. Edward Telfair	1789	DR	4.8	—	—	21.42

TIM RYAN

Basics

Potential index 4.2
Party .... Democratic
Age (as of November 1, 2020)..47.30
Birthday...July 16, 1973
State ....Ohio
Position (as of November 1, 2019)..Representative
Prior candidacies ....None
Prior major tickets ....None

Modern Era (1960-2016) candidates with comparable PIs

Candidate	Year	Party	PI	N	W	CS
Newt Gingrich	2012	R	4.3	—	—	18.59
Morris Udall	1976	D	4.3	—	—	18.22
John Ashbrook	1972	R	4.2	—	—	13.02
Wesley Clark	2004	D	4.2	—	—	12.00
Ben Carson	2016	R	4.3	—	—	11.69
Sargent Shriver	1976	D	4.2	—	—	11.14
Wilbur Mills	1972	D	4.3	—	—	10.36
Sam Yorty	1972	D	4.3	—	—	10.30
Michele Bachmann	2012	R	4.3	—	—	10.11

Modern Era candidates from Ohio

Candidate	Year	Party	PI	N	W	CS
John Kasich	2016	R	6.6	—	—	19.98
James Rhodes	1968	R	6.6	—	—	16.17
John Ashbrook	1972	R	4.2	—	—	13.02
John Glenn	1984	D	6.8	—	—	12.08

All-time leaders (1789-2016) in similarity scores

Candidate	Year	Party	PI	N	W	CS
1. Richard Gephardt	1988	D	4.0	—	—	13.63
2. Champ Clark	1912	D	3.7	—	—	42.45
3. James Weaver	1880	GBK	4.2	—	—	20.66
4. John Ashbrook	1972	R	4.2	—	—	13.02
5. Richard Gephardt	2004	D	3.9	—	—	10.23
6. William Morrison	1880	D	6.5	—	—	16.71
7. Oscar Underwood	1912	D	3.0	—	—	16.41
8. Morris Udall	1976	D	4.3	—	—	18.22
9. Cordell Hull	1928	D	3.7	—	—	12.75
10. Shirley Chisholm	1972	D	4.5	—	—	12.62
11. William Jennings Bryan	1896	D-POP	4.6	X	—	70.98
12. Henry Payne	1880	D	5.6	—	—	18.78
13. James Garfield	1880	R	6.6	X	X	79.77
14. Richard Bland	1896	D	5.5	—	—	30.20
15. Henry Clay	1824	DR	3.7	—	—	46.84
16. John Anderson	1980	R/NU	3.2	—	—	38.97
17. John Nance Garner	1932	D	3.3	—	—	16.36

Candidate	Year	Party	PI	N	W	CS
18. Wilbur Mills	1972	D	4.3	—	—	10.36
19. George Pendleton	1868	D	6.7	—	—	36.43
20. Phil Crane	1980	R	4.7	—	—	10.46
21. John R. McLean	1896	D	5.0	—	—	14.63
22. Michele Bachmann	2012	R	4.3	—	—	10.11
23. Samuel Randall	1884	D	6.3	—	—	17.58
24. James Weaver	1892	POP	4.1	—	—	38.80
25. William Lemke	1936	U	1.8	—	—	16.26

BERNIE SANDERS

Basics

Potential index 5.2
Party .... Democratic
Age (as of November 1, 2020) 79.15
Birthday ....September 8, 1941
State ....Vermont
Position (as of November 1, 2019) .... Senator
Prior candidacies ....Qualified (2016)
Prior major tickets ....None

Modern Era (1960-2016) candidates with comparable PIs

Candidate	Year	Party	PI	N	W	CS
George H.W. Bush	1980	R	5.2	—	—	24.15
Pat Buchanan	1992	R	5.2	—	—	23.85
Jack Kemp	1988	R	5.2	—	—	11.63
Gary Bauer	2000	R	5.1	—	—	10.19

Modern Era candidates from Vermont

Candidate	Year	Party	PI	N	W	CS
Bernie Sanders	2016	D	5.5	—	—	44.15
Howard Dean	2004	D	6.0	—	—	13.32

All-time leaders (1789-2016) in similarity scores

Candidate	Year	Party	PI	N	W	CS
1. Thomas Bayard	1884	D	6.2	—	—	26.53
2. Thomas Walsh	1928	D	3.5	—	—	10.95
3. George Gray	1908	D	6.3	—	—	14.71
4. John Kerry	2004	D	6.6	X	—	73.65
5. Harry Byrd	1960	D	6.9	—	—	19.25
6. Thomas Bayard	1880	D	7.1	—	—	26.61
7. Henry Jackson	1976	D	6.2	—	—	14.30
8. Thomas Walsh	1924	D	4.0	—	—	13.17
9. Lewis Cass	1848	D	6.9	X	—	71.66
10. Oscar Underwood	1924	D	4.5	—	—	15.57
11. James Reed	1928	D	4.8	—	—	16.09
12. Thomas Bayard	1876	D	7.1	—	—	13.59
13. Richard Russell	1952	D	5.1	—	—	23.13
14. Arthur Gorman	1892	D	7.4	—	—	13.19
15. Harry Byrd	1944	D	5.1	—	—	14.55
16. Estes Kefauver	1956	D	5.1	—	—	21.72
17. Henry Jackson	1972	D	6.3	—	—	15.37
18. George Edmunds	1884	R	7.0	—	—	19.02
19. Aaron Burr	1796	DR	4.7	—	—	54.24
20. John Kennedy	1960	D	6.2	X	X	79.58
21. John Henry	1796	DR	4.7	—	—	21.42

Candidate	Year	Party	PI	N	W	CS
22. Joseph Lieberman	2004	D	7.2	—	—	11.04
23. Francis Cockrell	1904	D	7.0	—	—	13.35
24. George McGovern	1972	D	6.4	X	—	58.46
25. Edward Kennedy	1980	D	6.8	—	—	39.18

MARK SANFORD

Basics

Potential index 4.7
Party ....Republican
Age (as of November 1, 2020)...60.43
Birthday.. May 28, 1960
State .... South Carolina
Position (as of November 1, 2019)............................. Former representative
Prior candidacies ....None
Prior major tickets ....None

Modern Era (1960-2016) candidates with comparable PIs

Candidate	Year	Party	PI	N	W	CS
John Anderson	1980	R/NU	4.7	—	—	38.97
Ron Paul	2012	R	4.6	—	—	18.11
Ron Paul	2008	R/TC	4.8	—	—	13.62
Henry Cabot Lodge	1964	R	4.8	—	—	12.05
Paul McCloskey	1972	R	4.7	—	—	11.31
Phil Crane	1980	R	4.7	—	—	10.46

Modern Era candidates from South Carolina

(None)

All-time leaders (1789-2016) in similarity scores

Candidate	Year	Party	PI	N	W	CS
1. Newt Gingrich	2012	R	4.3	—	—	18.59
2. Edward Bates	1860	R	5.2	—	—	18.22
3. John Rutledge	1789	F	4.5	—	—	45.73
4. Charles Cotesworth Pinckney	1800	F	4.4	—	—	63.01
5. Abraham Lincoln	1860	R	6.2	X	X	78.38
6. Michele Bachmann	2012	R	4.3	—	—	10.11
7. Thomas Reed	1896	R	5.2	—	—	17.27
8. Charles Cotesworth Pinckney	1796	F	3.9	—	—	18.98
9. Hugh White	1836	W	6.3	X	—	54.62
10. Zachary Taylor	1848	W	4.1	X	X	78.93
11. Thomas Pinckney	1796	F	4.1	—	—	61.70
12. James Weaver	1892	POP	4.1	—	—	38.80
13. Fred Thompson	2008	R	7.2	—	—	10.81
14. Joseph France	1932	R	5.6	—	—	19.88
15. Joseph Martin	1940	R	5.1	—	—	12.63
16. Howard Baker	1980	R	7.7	—	—	10.51
17. Lamar Alexander	1996	R	7.8	—	—	11.97
18. John Bell	1860	CU	4.6	—	—	46.37
19. George Norris	1928	R	4.3	—	—	12.58
20. Samuel Johnston	1796	F	6.5	—	—	21.42
21. James Watson	1928	R	5.1	—	—	13.57
22. Robert La Follette	1916	R	5.2	—	—	12.89
23. Rand Paul	2016	R	7.8	—	—	10.13
24. Pat Buchanan	1996	R	5.0	—	—	23.11
25. Gary Bauer	2000	R	5.1	—	—	10.19

JOE SESTAK

Basics

Potential index 3.7
Party .... Democratic
Age (as of November 1, 2020)...68.89
Birthday...December 12, 1951
State .... Pennsylvania
Position (as of November 1, 2019)..................................Former representative
Prior candidacies ....None
Prior major tickets ....None

Modern Era (1960-2016) candidates with comparable PIs

Candidate	Year	Party	PI	N	W	CS
Jesse Jackson	1988	D	3.6	—	—	33.32
Steve Forbes	1996	R	3.6	—	—	16.96
Lyndon LaRouche	1996	D	3.6	—	—	13.27
Alan Keyes	2000	R	3.7	—	—	13.04
Ron Paul	2016	R	3.8	—	—	10.62

Modern Era candidates from Pennsylvania

Candidate	Year	Party	PI	N	W	CS
Rick Santorum	2012	R	7.3	—	—	22.25
William Scranton	1964	R	6.9	—	—	19.42

All-time leaders (1789-2016) in similarity scores

Candidate	Year	Party	PI	N	W	CS
1. Asa Packer	1868	D	6.0	—	—	16.55
2. Henry Payne	1880	D	5.6	—	—	18.78
3. Richard Bland	1896	D	5.5	—	—	30.20
4. Champ Clark	1912	D	3.7	—	—	42.45
5. Samuel Randall	1884	D	6.3	—	—	17.58
6. John Nance Garner	1932	D	3.3	—	—	16.36
7. Richard Gephardt	2004	D	3.9	—	—	10.23
8. Cordell Hull	1928	D	3.7	—	—	12.75
9. Wilbur Mills	1972	D	4.3	—	—	10.36
10. James Weaver	1892	POP	4.1	—	—	38.80
11. Newt Gingrich	2012	R	4.3	—	—	18.59
12. James Guthrie	1860	D	3.9	—	—	19.34
13. Shirley Chisholm	1972	D	4.5	—	—	12.62
14. Oscar Underwood	1912	D	3.0	—	—	16.41
15. Morris Udall	1976	D	4.3	—	—	18.22
16. Mitchell Palmer	1920	D	4.9	—	—	27.09
17. Winfield Hancock	1880	D	5.6	X	—	72.24
18. William Jennings Bryan	1896	D-POP	4.6	X	—	70.98
19. Richard Gephardt	1988	D	4.0	—	—	13.63
20. Edward Bates	1860	R	5.2	—	—	18.22
21. John Anderson	1980	R/NU	3.2	—	—	38.97

Candidate	Year	Party	PI	N	W	CS
22. William Morrison	1880	D	6.5	—	—	16.71
23. John Davis	1920	D	3.7	—	—	12.87
24. James Buchanan	1856	D	5.1	X	X	79.35
25. Clinton Fisk	1888	PRO	3.8	—	—	17.02

TOM STEYER

Basics

Potential index 3.9
Party .... Democratic
Age (as of November 1, 2020)...63.35
Birthday... June 27, 1957
State .... California
Position (as of November 1, 2019)... Business executive
Prior candidacies .... None
Prior major tickets .... None

Modern Era (1960-2016) candidates with comparable PIs

Candidate	Year	Party	PI	N	W	CS
Gary Johnson	2016	LIB	3.9	—	—	20.52
Richard Gephardt	1988	D	4.0	—	—	13.63
Rudy Giuliani	2008	R	3.9	—	—	11.71
Ron Paul	2016	R	3.8	—	—	10.62
Steve Forbes	2000	R	4.0	—	—	10.52
Richard Gephardt	2004	D	3.9	—	—	10.23
Carly Fiorina	2016	R	3.9	—	—	10.07

Modern Era candidates from California

Candidate	Year	Party	PI	N	W	CS
Richard Nixon	1972	R	8.8	X	X	95.25
Ronald Reagan	1984	R	8.1	X	X	95.13
Ronald Reagan	1980	R	5.7	X	X	91.16
Richard Nixon	1960	R	8.0	X	—	72.12
Ronald Reagan	1976	R	6.7	—	—	47.60
Ronald Reagan	1968	R	7.3	—	—	28.22
Jerry Brown	1992	D	6.8	—	—	24.83
Jerry Brown	1976	D	6.2	—	—	21.16
Jerry Brown	1980	D	6.4	—	—	11.84
Paul McCloskey	1972	R	4.7	—	—	11.31
John Hospers	1972	LIB	3.3	—	—	10.62
Sam Yorty	1972	D	4.3	—	—	10.30
Alan Cranston	1984	D	7.0	—	—	10.17

All-time leaders (1789-2016) in similarity scores

Candidate	Year	Party	PI	N	W	CS
1. Sam Yorty	1972	D	4.3	—	—	10.30
2. John Hospers	1972	LIB	3.3	—	—	10.62
3. Ross Perot	1992	I	2.9	—	—	43.78
4. Ross Perot	1996	REF	2.6	—	—	36.87
5. Wendell Willkie	1940	R	4.7	X	—	63.60
6. Stephen Field	1880	D	2.3	—	—	17.03
7. Chauncey Depew	1888	R	4.9	—	—	19.50
8. William Gibbs McAdoo	1924	D	3.6	—	—	43.53
9. Carly Fiorina	2016	R	3.9	—	—	10.07
10. Jerry Brown	1992	D	6.8	—	—	24.83

Candidate	Year	Party	PI	N	W	CS
11. Alton Parker	1904	D	4.9	X	—	66.33
12. Sanford Church	1868	D	5.0	—	—	18.54
13. Donald Trump	2016	R	3.1	X	X	78.79
14. Horace Greeley	1872	D-LR	4.8	X	—	58.76
15. Herbert Hoover	1920	R	2.6	—	—	12.56
16. Henry Ford	1916	R	3.8	—	—	13.29
17. Lyndon LaRouche	1996	D	3.6	—	—	13.27
18. Jerry Brown	1976	D	6.2	—	—	21.16
19. Alan Cranston	1984	D	7.0	—	—	10.17
20. Norman Thomas	1932	SOC	3.0	—	—	17.13
21. Jerry Brown	1980	D	6.4	—	—	11.84
22. Faith Spotted Eagle	2016	D	2.3	—	—	10.62
23. Averell Harriman	1952	D	5.8	—	—	15.10
24. John R. McLean	1896	D	5.0	—	—	14.63
25. Morris Udall	1976	D	4.3	—	—	18.22

ERIC SWALWELL

Basics

Potential index 4.1
Party .... Democratic
Age (as of November 1, 2020) 39.96
Birthday .... November 16, 1980
State .... California
Position (as of November 1, 2019) ....Representative
Prior candidacies ....None
Prior major tickets ....None

Modern Era (1960-2016) candidates with comparable PIs

Candidate	Year	Party	PI	N	W	CS
Richard Gephardt	1988	D	4.0	—	—	13.63
John Ashbrook	1972	R	4.2	—	—	13.02
Wesley Clark	2004	D	4.2	—	—	12.00
Sargent Shriver	1976	D	4.2	—	—	11.14
Steve Forbes	2000	R	4.0	—	—	10.52

Modern Era candidates from California

Candidate	Year	Party	PI	N	W	CS
Richard Nixon	1972	R	8.8	X	X	95.25
Ronald Reagan	1984	R	8.1	X	X	95.13
Ronald Reagan	1980	R	5.7	X	X	91.16
Richard Nixon	1960	R	8.0	X	—	72.12
Ronald Reagan	1976	R	6.7	—	—	47.60
Ronald Reagan	1968	R	7.3	—	—	28.22
Jerry Brown	1992	D	6.8	—	—	24.83
Jerry Brown	1976	D	6.2	—	—	21.16
Jerry Brown	1980	D	6.4	—	—	11.84
Paul McCloskey	1972	R	4.7	—	—	11.31
John Hospers	1972	LIB	3.3	—	—	10.62
Sam Yorty	1972	D	4.3	—	—	10.30
Alan Cranston	1984	D	7.0	—	—	10.17

All-time leaders (1789-2016) in similarity scores

Candidate	Year	Party	PI	N	W	CS
1. Paul McCloskey	1972	R	4.7	—	—	11.31
2. Shirley Chisholm	1972	D	4.5	—	—	12.62
3. Morris Udall	1976	D	4.3	—	—	18.22
4. Richard Gephardt	1988	D	4.0	—	—	13.63
5. Sam Yorty	1972	D	4.3	—	—	10.30
6. Oscar Underwood	1912	D	3.0	—	—	16.41
7. Samuel Randall	1884	D	6.3	—	—	17.58
8. Cordell Hull	1928	D	3.7	—	—	12.75
9. Henry Clay	1824	DR	3.7	—	—	46.84
10. James Weaver	1880	GBK	4.2	—	—	20.66
11. William Jennings Bryan	1896	D-POP	4.6	X	—	70.98
12. Champ Clark	1912	D	3.7	—	—	42.45

Candidate	Year	Party	PI	N	W	CS
13. William Morrison	1880	D	6.5	—	—	16.71
14. John Nance Garner	1932	D	3.3	—	—	16.36
15. Wilbur Mills	1972	D	4.3	—	—	10.36
16. Richard Gephardt	2004	D	3.9	—	—	10.23
17. Jerry Brown	1976	D	6.2	—	—	21.16
18. William Gibbs McAdoo	1924	D	3.6	—	—	43.53
19. John Ashbrook	1972	R	4.2	—	—	13.02
20. Mitchell Palmer	1920	D	4.9	—	—	27.09
21. John Anderson	1980	R/NU	3.2	—	—	38.97
22. John Hospers	1972	LIB	3.3	—	—	10.62
23. Jerry Brown	1980	D	6.4	—	—	11.84
24. George McClellan	1864	D	4.7	X	—	61.66
25. James Farley	1940	D	6.3	—	—	13.95

DONALD TRUMP

Basics

Potential index 8.2
Party ....Republican
Age (as of November 1, 2020)...74.38
Birthday...June 14, 1946
State ....Florida
Position (as of November 1, 2019)..President
Prior candidacies ....Qualified (2016)
Prior major tickets .... Presidential nominee (2016)

Modern Era (1960-2016) candidates with comparable PIs

Candidate	Year	Party	PI	N	W	CS
Ronald Reagan	1984	R	8.1	X	X	95.13
Barack Obama	2012	D	8.3	X	X	81.59
George H.W. Bush	1992	R	8.2	X	—	66.86
Lyndon Johnson	1960	D	8.1	—	—	23.50

Modern Era candidates from Florida

Candidate	Year	Party	PI	N	W	CS
Marco Rubio	2016	R	7.7	—	—	17.61
Ben Carson	2016	R	4.3	—	—	11.69
Jeb Bush	2016	R	7.1	—	—	10.58

All-time leaders (1789-2016) in similarity scores

Candidate	Year	Party	PI	N	W	CS
1. George H.W. Bush	1992	R	8.2	X	—	66.86
2. George Washington	1796	F	9.1	—	—	21.42
3. William Howard Taft	1912	R	8.2	X	—	55.09
4. Dwight Eisenhower	1956	R	8.7	X	X	91.03
5. George W. Bush	2004	R	9.3	X	X	78.71
6. George Washington	1792	F	9.7	X	X	96.18
7. Herbert Hoover	1932	R	7.3	X	—	61.28
8. Abraham Lincoln	1864	R	8.9	X	X	92.17
9. George H.W. Bush	1988	R	6.5	X	X	87.86
10. Chester Arthur	1884	R	8.8	—	—	37.07
11. Ulysses Grant	1872	R	9.0	X	X	89.28
12. Ronald Reagan	1984	R	8.1	X	X	95.13
13. John Adams	1800	F	7.2	X	—	73.21
14. James Madison	1812	DR	8.7	X	X	80.17
15. John Quincy Adams	1828	NR	7.7	X	—	68.27
16. William McKinley	1900	R	8.9	X	X	82.89
17. Millard Fillmore	1852	W	9.1	—	—	45.85
18. Ulysses Grant	1880	R	8.5	—	—	42.34
19. Gerald Ford	1976	R	6.6	X	—	72.98
20. Andrew Jackson	1832	D	7.8	X	X	87.20
21. Richard Nixon	1972	R	8.8	X	X	95.25

Candidate	Year	Party	PI	N	W	CS
22. Calvin Coolidge	1924	R	9.1	X	X	85.63
23. James Monroe	1820	DR	8.7	X	X	96.04
24. Benjamin Harrison	1892	R	8.5	X	—	68.40
25. Lyndon Johnson	1968	D	8.7	—	—	11.53

JOE WALSH

Basics

Potential index 4.6
Party ....Republican
Age (as of November 1, 2020)...58.85
Birthday...December 27, 1961
State ....Illinois
Position (as of November 1, 2019)... Former representative
Prior candidacies ....None
Prior major tickets ....None

Modern Era (1960-2016) candidates with comparable PIs

Candidate	Year	Party	PI	N	W	CS
John Anderson	1980	R/NU	4.7	—	—	38.97
Ron Paul	2012	R	4.6	—	—	18.11
Pat Robertson	1988	R	4.5	—	—	15.41
Shirley Chisholm	1972	D	4.5	—	—	12.62
Paul McCloskey	1972	R	4.7	—	—	11.31
Phil Crane	1980	R	4.7	—	—	10.46

Modern Era candidates from Illinois

Candidate	Year	Party	PI	N	W	CS
Barack Obama	2008	D	6.8	X	X	84.03
Barack Obama	2012	D	8.3	X	X	81.59
John Anderson	1980	R/NU	4.7	—	—	38.97
Jesse Jackson	1988	D	3.6	—	—	33.32
Jesse Jackson	1984	D	3.3	—	—	23.30
Adlai Stevenson	1960	D	7.2	—	—	12.86
Paul Simon	1988	D	7.1	—	—	12.66
Phil Crane	1980	R	4.7	—	—	10.46

All-time leaders (1789-2016) in similarity scores

Candidate	Year	Party	PI	N	W	CS
1. Abraham Lincoln	1860	R	6.2	X	X	78.38
2. Phil Crane	1980	R	4.7	—	—	10.46
3. Edward Bates	1860	R	5.2	—	—	18.22
4. Joseph Cannon	1908	R	5.3	—	—	14.71
5. Michele Bachmann	2012	R	4.3	—	—	10.11
6. James Weaver	1892	POP	4.1	—	—	38.80
7. Elihu Washburne	1880	R	4.4	—	—	13.19
8. John Anderson	1980	R/NU	3.2	—	—	38.97
9. Newt Gingrich	2012	R	4.3	—	—	18.59
10. John Ashbrook	1972	R	4.2	—	—	13.02
11. Joseph Martin	1940	R	5.1	—	—	12.63
12. Richard Bland	1896	D	5.5	—	—	30.20
13. James Garfield	1880	R	6.6	X	X	79.77
14. Thomas Reed	1896	R	5.2	—	—	17.27
15. Ulysses Grant	1864	R	5.6	—	—	13.35
16. William Morrison	1880	D	6.5	—	—	16.71

Candidate	Year	Party	PI	N	W	CS
17. Ulysses Grant	1868	R	6.3	X	X	85.63
18. Douglas MacArthur	1944	R	3.9	—	—	15.89
19. James Weaver	1880	GBK	4.2	—	—	20.66
20. Henry Payne	1880	D	5.6	—	—	18.78
21. Jack Kemp	1988	R	5.2	—	—	11.63
22. William Howard Taft	1908	R	6.0	X	X	83.31
23. Lawrence Sherman	1916	R	6.1	—	—	15.63
24. Frank Knox	1936	R	3.5	—	—	12.97
25. Frank Lowden	1920	R	6.3	—	—	25.31

ELIZABETH WARREN

Basics

Potential index 6.1
Party .... Democratic
Age (as of November 1, 2020)...71.36
Birthday...June 22, 1949
State ....Massachusetts
Position (as of November 1, 2019)...Senator
Prior candidacies ....None
Prior major tickets ....None

Modern Era (1960-2016) candidates with comparable PIs

Candidate	Year	Party	PI	N	W	CS
John Kennedy	1960	D	6.2	X	X	79.58
Richard Nixon	1968	R	6.2	X	X	78.01
John McCain	2000	R	6.2	—	—	29.92
Mitt Romney	2008	R	6.1	—	—	23.13
Jerry Brown	1976	D	6.2	—	—	21.16
Henry Jackson	1976	D	6.2	—	—	14.30
Howard Dean	2004	D	6.0	—	—	13.32
George McGovern	1968	D	6.0	—	—	12.79
George McGovern	1984	D	6.2	—	—	11.14
Bruce Babbitt	1988	D	6.2	—	—	10.20

Modern Era candidates from Massachusetts

Candidate	Year	Party	PI	N	W	CS
John Kennedy	1960	D	6.2	X	X	79.58
John Kerry	2004	D	6.6	X	—	73.65
Mitt Romney	2012	R	5.9	X	—	70.93
Michael Dukakis	1988	D	6.7	X	—	65.32
Edward Kennedy	1980	D	6.8	—	—	39.18
Mitt Romney	2008	R	6.1	—	—	23.13
Paul Tsongas	1992	D	7.0	—	—	21.82
Henry Cabot Lodge	1964	R	4.8	—	—	12.05

All-time leaders (1789-2016) in similarity scores

Candidate	Year	Party	PI	N	W	CS
1. John Kerry	2004	D	6.6	X	—	73.65
2. Bernie Sanders	2016	D	5.5	—	—	44.15
3. Edward Kennedy	1980	D	6.8	—	—	39.18
4. John Kennedy	1960	D	6.2	X	X	79.58
5. George Gray	1908	D	6.3	—	—	14.71
6. Paul Tsongas	1992	D	7.0	—	—	21.82
7. Harry Byrd	1960	D	6.9	—	—	19.25
8. Arthur Gorman	1892	D	7.4	—	—	13.19
9. Francis Cockrell	1904	D	7.0	—	—	13.35
10. Henry Jackson	1976	D	6.2	—	—	14.30
11. Henry Jackson	1972	D	6.3	—	—	15.37
12. Thomas Bayard	1884	D	6.2	—	—	26.53

Candidate	Year	Party	PI	N	W	CS
13. Joseph Blackburn	1896	D	6.2	—	—	17.03
14. Hillary Clinton	2008	D	7.0	—	—	43.42
15. Lewis Cass	1848	D	6.9	X	—	71.66
16. Daniel Webster	1848	W	7.0	—	—	16.31
17. James Reed	1928	D	4.8	—	—	16.09
18. Andrew Jackson	1824	DR	5.9	X	—	69.65
19. Stuart Symington	1960	D	6.9	—	—	13.00
20. Joseph Lieberman	2004	D	7.2	—	—	11.04
21. Thomas Bayard	1880	D	7.1	—	—	26.61
22. Harry Byrd	1944	D	5.1	—	—	14.55
23. Thomas Bayard	1876	D	7.1	—	—	13.59
24. John Glenn	1984	D	6.8	—	—	12.08
25. John Weeks	1916	R	6.5	—	—	16.35

WILLIAM WELD

Basics

Potential index 6.0
Party ....Republican
Age (as of November 1, 2020)...75.25
Birthday...July 31, 1945
State ....Massachusetts
Position (as of November 1, 2019)...Former governor
Prior candidacies ....None
Prior major tickets ....None

Modern Era (1960-2016) candidates with comparable PIs

Candidate	Year	Party	PI	N	W	CS
Mitt Romney	2012	R	5.9	X	—	70.93
John McCain	2008	R	5.9	X	—	68.78
Mitt Romney	2008	R	6.1	—	—	23.13
Howard Dean	2004	D	6.0	—	—	13.32
George McGovern	1968	D	6.0	—	—	12.79
Bill Richardson	2008	D	5.9	—	—	10.17

Modern Era candidates from Massachusetts

Candidate	Year	Party	PI	N	W	CS
John Kennedy	1960	D	6.2	X	X	79.58
John Kerry	2004	D	6.6	X	—	73.65
Mitt Romney	2012	R	5.9	X	—	70.93
Michael Dukakis	1988	D	6.7	X	—	65.32
Edward Kennedy	1980	D	6.8	—	—	39.18
Mitt Romney	2008	R	6.1	—	—	23.13
Paul Tsongas	1992	D	7.0	—	—	21.82
Henry Cabot Lodge	1964	R	4.8	—	—	12.05

All-time leaders (1789-2016) in similarity scores

Candidate	Year	Party	PI	N	W	CS
1. Mitt Romney	2012	R	5.9	X	—	70.93
2. Mitt Romney	2008	R	6.1	—	—	23.13
3. Pete du Pont	1988	R	6.6	—	—	10.25
4. Daniel Webster	1848	W	7.0	—	—	16.31
5. Frank Lowden	1928	R	5.7	—	—	20.32
6. John Weeks	1916	R	6.5	—	—	16.35
7. Lamar Alexander	1996	R	7.8	—	—	11.97
8. Jon Huntsman	2012	R	6.7	—	—	10.27
9. John Connally	1980	R	7.4	—	—	10.38
10. Daniel Webster	1836	W	5.0	—	—	26.29
11. John Hancock	1789	F	4.3	—	—	35.97
12. Daniel Webster	1852	W	6.0	—	—	18.52
13. John Kasich	2016	R	6.6	—	—	19.98
14. Joseph France	1932	R	5.6	—	—	19.88
15. Russell Alger	1888	R	7.8	—	—	19.58
16. John McCain	2008	R	5.9	X	—	68.78

Candidate	Year	Party	PI	N	W	CS
17. Samuel Huntington	1789	F	4.7	—	—	26.29
18. Thomas Seymour	1864	D	6.8	—	—	23.41
19. Chris Christie	2016	R	6.7	—	—	10.11
20. Elihu Root	1916	R	6.0	—	—	16.23
21. Richard Lugar	1996	R	6.5	—	—	10.51
22. John McCain	2000	R	6.2	—	—	29.92
23. Fred Thompson	2008	R	7.2	—	—	10.81
24. Frank Lowden	1920	R	6.3	—	—	25.31
25. Samuel Adams	1796	DR	3.7	—	—	50.36

MARIANNE WILLIAMSON

Basics

Potential index 3.7
Party .... Democratic
Age (as of November 1, 2020)...68.32
Birthday.. July 8, 1952
State .... California
Position (as of November 1, 2019)..Author
Prior candidacies ....None
Prior major tickets ....None

Modern Era (1960-2016) candidates with comparable PIs

Candidate	Year	Party	PI	N	W	CS
Jesse Jackson	1988	D	3.6	—	—	33.32
Steve Forbes	1996	R	3.6	—	—	16.96
Lyndon LaRouche	1996	D	3.6	—	—	13.27
Alan Keyes	2000	R	3.7	—	—	13.04
Ron Paul	2016	R	3.8	—	—	10.62

Modern Era candidates from California

Candidate	Year	Party	PI	N	W	CS
Richard Nixon	1972	R	8.8	X	X	95.25
Ronald Reagan	1984	R	8.1	X	X	95.13
Ronald Reagan	1980	R	5.7	X	X	91.16
Richard Nixon	1960	R	8.0	X	—	72.12
Ronald Reagan	1976	R	6.7	—	—	47.60
Ronald Reagan	1968	R	7.3	—	—	28.22
Jerry Brown	1992	D	6.8	—	—	24.83
Jerry Brown	1976	D	6.2	—	—	21.16
Jerry Brown	1980	D	6.4	—	—	11.84
Paul McCloskey	1972	R	4.7	—	—	11.31
John Hospers	1972	LIB	3.3	—	—	10.62
Sam Yorty	1972	D	4.3	—	—	10.30
Alan Cranston	1984	D	7.0	—	—	10.17

All-time leaders (1789-2016) in similarity scores

Candidate	Year	Party	PI	N	W	CS
1. Sam Yorty	1972	D	4.3	—	—	10.30
2. John Hospers	1972	LIB	3.3	—	—	10.62
3. Stephen Field	1880	D	2.3	—	—	17.03
4. William Gibbs McAdoo	1924	D	3.6	—	—	43.53
5. Lyndon LaRouche	1996	D	3.6	—	—	13.27
6. Jerry Brown	1992	D	6.8	—	—	24.83
7. Alton Parker	1904	D	4.9	X	—	66.33
8. Sanford Church	1868	D	5.0	—	—	18.54
9. Alan Cranston	1984	D	7.0	—	—	10.17
10. Faith Spotted Eagle	2016	D	2.3	—	—	10.62
11. Horace Greeley	1872	D-LR	4.8	X	—	58.76
12. Walter Jones	1956	D	1.9	—	—	10.62

Candidate	Year	Party	PI	N	W	CS
13. Ross Perot	1992	I	2.9	—	—	43.78
14. Ross Perot	1996	REF	2.6	—	—	36.87
15. Norman Thomas	1932	SOC	3.0	—	—	17.13
16. Jerry Brown	1976	D	6.2	—	—	21.16
17. Jerry Brown	1980	D	6.4	—	—	11.84
18. James Guthrie	1860	D	3.9	—	—	19.34
19. Jesse Jackson	1988	D	3.6	—	—	33.32
20. Averell Harriman	1952	D	5.8	—	—	15.10
21. John McLean	1896	D	5.0	—	—	14.63
22. John Nance Garner	1932	D	3.3	—	—	16.36
23. Champ Clark	1912	D	3.7	—	—	42.45
24. Morris Udall	1976	D	4.3	—	—	18.22
25. Jesse Jackson	1984	D	3.3	—	—	23.30

ANDREW YANG

Basics

Potential index 3.5
Party .... Democratic
Age (as of November 1, 2020)...45.80
Birthday...January 13, 1975
State ....New York
Job (as of November 1, 2019).. Business executive
Prior candidacies ....None
Prior major tickets ....None

Modern Era (1960-2016) candidates with comparable PIs

Candidate	Year	Party	PI	N	W	CS
Jesse Jackson	1988	D	3.6	—	—	33.32
Steve Forbes	1996	R	3.6	—	—	16.96
Lyndon LaRouche	1996	D	3.6	—	—	13.27

Modern Era candidates from New York

Candidate	Year	Party	PI	N	W	CS
Donald Trump	2016	R	3.1	X	X	78.79
Richard Nixon	1968	R	6.2	X	X	78.01
Hillary Clinton	2016	D	6.6	X	—	72.30
Hillary Clinton	2008	D	7.0	—	—	43.42
Nelson Rockefeller	1968	R	7.1	—	—	21.48
Nelson Rockefeller	1964	R	7.6	—	—	20.93
Robert Kennedy	1968	D	6.6	—	—	19.18
Shirley Chisholm	1972	D	4.5	—	—	12.62
Colin Powell	2016	R	3.2	—	—	11.84
Rudy Giuliani	2008	R	3.9	—	—	11.71
Jack Kemp	1988	R	5.2	—	—	11.63
Richard Nixon	1964	R	6.7	—	—	11.00

All-time leaders (1789-2016) in similarity scores

Candidate	Year	Party	PI	N	W	CS
1. Wendell Willkie	1940	R	4.7	X	—	63.60
2. Chauncey Depew	1888	R	4.9	—	—	19.50
3. Alton Parker	1904	D	4.9	X	—	66.33
4. Donald Trump	2016	R	3.1	X	X	78.79
5. Sanford Church	1868	D	5.0	—	—	18.54
6. Allan Benson	1916	SOC	2.7	—	—	20.19
7. Norman Thomas	1932	SOC	3.0	—	—	17.13
8. Shirley Chisholm	1972	D	4.5	—	—	12.62
9. Ross Perot	1992	I	2.9	—	—	43.78
10. Jesse Jackson	1984	D	3.3	—	—	23.30
11. Jesse Jackson	1988	D	3.6	—	—	33.32
12. John McLean	1896	D	5.0	—	—	14.63
13. Ross Perot	1996	REF	2.6	—	—	36.87
14. Horace Greeley	1872	D-LR	4.8	X	—	58.76
15. Henry Ford	1916	R	3.8	—	—	13.29

Candidate	Year	Party	PI	N	W	CS
16. George Clinton	1792	DR	3.2	—	—	59.98
17. William Randolph Hearst	1904	D	5.5	—	—	24.45
18. Mitchell Palmer	1920	D	4.9	—	—	27.09
19. Alfred Smith	1920	D	6.5	—	—	15.99
20. John Davis	1920	D	3.7	—	—	12.87
21. Thomas Dewey	1940	R	4.0	—	—	41.51
22. George Clinton	1789	DR	2.6	—	—	31.09
23. Grover Cleveland	1884	D	7.5	X	X	78.78
24. Steve Forbes	1996	R	3.6	—	—	16.96
25. James Farley	1940	D	6.3	—	—	13.95

KEY SOURCES

Popular- and electoral-vote counts for presidential elections from 1789 to 2016 were obtained from the following sources.

Bain, Richard, and Judith Parris. *Convention Decisions and Voting Records.* Washington: Brookings Institution, 1973.

Burnham, W. Dean. *Presidential Ballots, 1836-1892.* Baltimore: Johns Hopkins University Press, 1955.

Clerk of the House of Representatives. *Statistics of the Presidential and Congressional Election.* Washington: United States House of Representatives, 1920-2016, quadrennial.

Cook, Rhodes. *United States Presidential Primary Elections, 1968-1996.* Washington: CQ Press, 2000.

Dubin, Michael. *United States Presidential Elections, 1788-1860.* Jefferson, North Carolina: McFarland & Co., 2002.

Federal Election Commission. *Federal Elections: Election Results for the U.S. President, the U.S. Senate, and the U.S. House of Representatives.* Washington: Federal Election Commission, 1985-2017, quadrennial.

Guide to U.S. Elections. Washington: CQ Press, 2005.

McGillivray, Alice, and Richard Scammon. *America at the Polls, 1920-1956.* Washington: Congressional Quarterly, 1994.

McGillivray, Alice, Richard Scammon, and Rhodes Cook. *America at the Polls, 1960-2004.* Washington: CQ Press, 2005.

Petersen, Svend. *A Statistical History of the American Presidential Elections.* New York: Frederick Ungar, 1963.

Presidential Elections, 1789-2008. Washington: CQ Press, 2010.

Robinson, Edgar Eugene. *The Presidential Vote, 1896-1932.* New York: Octagon, 1970.

Runyon, John, Jennefer Verdini, and Sally Runyon. *Source Book of American Presidential Campaign and Election Statistics, 1948-1968*. New York: Frederick Ungar, 1971.

Scammon, Richard. *America at the Polls, 1920-1964*. Pittsburgh: University of Pittsburgh Press, 1965.

Thomas, G. Scott. *Counting the Votes*. Santa Barbara: Praeger, 2015.

Thomas, G. Scott. *The Pursuit of the White House*. New York: Greenwood, 1987.

United States Census Bureau. *Historical Statistics of the United States, Colonial Times to 1970*. Washington: United States Government Printing Office, 1975.

United States Census Bureau. *Statistical Abstract of the United States, 2012*. Washington: United States Government Printing Office, 2011.